(using nearest convenient equivalents, acceptable in cooking—see
pages immediately preceding index for more detailed conversions)

LIQUIDS

fluid ounces	*British measures*	*U.S. measures*	*nearest metric equivalent (dl = deciliter)*
1	2 tablespoons	2 tablespoons	¼ dl
2	4 tablespoons	¼ cup	½ dl
4		½ cup	1 dl
5	¼ pint or 1 gill	⅔ cup	1½ dl
6		¾ cup	1¾ dl
8		1 cup or ½ pint	2¼ dl
10	½ pint	1¼ cups	2¾ dl
16		2 cups or 1 pint	4½ dl
20	1 pint	2½ cups	5½ dl
32		4 cups or 1 quart	9 dl
36	1⅓ pints plus 1 ounce	4½ cups	1 liter

INFORMAL BRITISH MEASURES USED

dessertspoon = 2 teaspoons
liqueur glass = about 1½ ounces
glass (wine) = about 4 ounces
coffeecup = about 4-5 ounces
teacup = about 6 ounces
tumbler = about 6 ounces (like an old-fashioned glass)
breakfastcup = almost 8 ounces
gill = ⅔ cup

ELIZABETH DAVID CLASSICS

ELIZABETH DAVID CLASSICS

Mediterranean Food

French Country Cooking

Summer Cooking

 ALFRED A. KNOPF NEW YORK 1980

Copyright © 1950, 1951, 1955, 1958, 1965, 1980
by Elizabeth David
Preface Copyright © 1980 by James Beard

All rights reserved under International and Pan-American
Copyright Conventions. Published in the United States by
Alfred A. Knopf, Inc., New York. Distributed by Random
House, Inc., New York. Originally published in Great Britain
by Jill Norman Ltd., London.

Mediterranean Food first published by John Lehmann in 1950;
revised edition published by Macdonald & Co. in 1958. *French
Country Cooking* first published by John Lehmann in 1951;
revised edition published by Macdonald & Co. in 1965. *Summer
Cooking* first published by Museum Press in 1955.

LIBRARY OF CONGRESS CATALOGING IN PUBLICATION DATA
David, Elizabeth, [date]
Elizabeth David classics.
Previously published as three separate works: A book of Medi-
terranean food, French country cooking, and Summer cooking.
Includes index.
1. Cookery, Mediterranean. 2. Cookery, French. 3. Cookery,
English. I. David, Elizabeth, [date] Book of Mediterranean
food. II. David, Elizabeth, [date] French country cooking. III.
David, Elizabeth, [date] Summer cooking. IV. Title.
TX725.M35D38   641.59′1182′2   80−7648
ISBN 0−394−49153−X

Manufactured in the United States of America

First American Edition

FOREWORD

WHAT A JOY it is to have three of Elizabeth David's early books, *Mediterranean Food, French Country Cooking* and *Summer Cooking*, in one volume. When *Mediterranean Food* came out in 1950, I was living in Paris and making fairly frequent trips to London. Britain was still in the grip of post-war austerity and hardly the most exciting of places, gastronomically speaking. At that time I had not met Mrs. David. I was attracted by the book jacket and title, bought the book and found it a delight. Here was someone with great understanding and appreciation of the simple, earthy cooking of the Mediterranean basin and the ability to write about it brilliantly.

The book must have been a revelation to the British, starved for color, flavor and imaginative, mouth-watering food far removed from the monotony of their limited diet — exotic things like tarama, mousaka, gazpacho, aioli and the many glorious dishes based on common elements of garlic, olive oil, lemons, tomatoes, aromatic herbs and spices. With this book, followed a year later by *French Country Cooking*, Elizabeth David shook her readers out of their culinary rut, challenging them to explore a different world of food and to seek out and use unfamiliar ingredients and flavorings. She was a leader, ahead of her time, and it is largely due to her influence that the current generation of British cooks is more adventurous and the stores carry foods and cooking utensils that were not around before.

Her writing evokes the sensuous satisfactions of marketing, cooking and eating in places where, as she says, "the Latin genius flashes from the kitchen pans." She has the rare

gift of stimulating the imagination in both mind and mouth
and making you want to head straight for the kitchen.
While she has a strong penchant for the cooking of the Mediterranean and regional France, she also has great respect for
the traditional cooking of her own country and has done
more than anyone to research and revive old recipes and
lore. In *Summer Cooking,* a particular favorite of mine, there
are lovely recipes for summer pudding and gooseberry fool,
Eliza Acton's lobster salad and cold spiced salted beef along-
side the French, Italian and Middle Eastern.

I have been a friend of Elizabeth David's for a number of
years, and have enjoyed her expertise in the kitchen, her
thoughts about food and her extensive knowledge of its his-
tory and background. She is to me probably the greatest
food writer we have, a purist and perfectionist, intolerant of
mediocrity and totally honest, yet not above breaking with
tradition to get at what she feels is the essential nature of a
dish. While many others have written since about French,
Italian, Mediterranean and British food, her books are classics and her recipes some of the best you can find. She may
throw you a bit at first because she does not write a recipe in
the detailed, spelled-out style to which we are accustomed.
Instead she gives her readers just as much guidance as she
feels is necessary, regarding them not as children to be led by
the hand but intelligent cooks capable of figuring things out
for themselves. She is adamant about refusing to alter British weights and measures to American cups, which is one
reason her books have never been as popular here as in Britain, although there has long been an underground cult of
food lovers who have picked up her books in the Penguin
editions, reveled in them and cooked from them devotedly.

While it has taken some time, I feel we in America are
now ready for Elizabeth David. We have come of age in the

culinary sense and acquired the skills and confidence to accept her on her own terms. I am sure that this collection of three of her early gems will introduce her to the wider public she deserves and bring her many new admirers and disciples.

JAMES A. BEARD

A Book of
MEDITERRANEAN FOOD

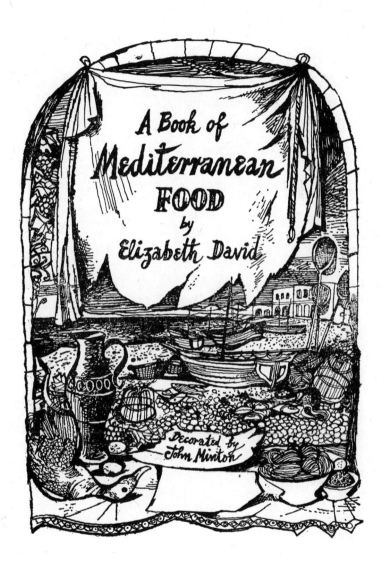

A Book of
Mediterranean
FOOD
by
Elizabeth David

Decorated by
John Minton

To
Veronica Nicholson

INTRODUCTION

THE COOKING of the Mediterranean shores, endowed with all the natural resources, the colour and flavour of the South, is a blend of tradition and brilliant improvisation. The Latin genius flashes from the kitchen pans.

It is honest cooking, too; none of the sham Grande Cuisine of the International Palace Hotel.

"It is not really an exaggeration," wrote Marcel Boulestin, "to say that peace and happiness begin, geographically, where garlic is used in cooking." From Gibraltar to the Bosphorus, down the Rhone Valley, through the great sea-ports of Marseilles, Barcelona and Genoa, across to Tunis and Alexandria, embracing all the Mediterranean islands, Corsica, Sicily, Sardinia, Crete, the Cyclades, Cyprus (where the Byzantine influence begins to be felt), to the mainland of Greece and the much-disputed territories of Syria, the Lebanon, Constantinople and Smyrna, stretches the influence of Mediterranean cooking, conditioned naturally by variations in climate and soil and the relative industry or indolence of the inhabitants.

The ever-recurring elements in the food throughout these countries are the oil, the saffron, the garlic, the pungent local wines; the aromatic perfume of rosemary, wild marjoram and basil drying in the kitchens; the brilliance of the market stalls piled high with pimentos, aubergines, tomatoes, olives, melons, figs and limes; the great heaps of shiny fish, silver, vermilion or tiger-striped, and those long needle fish whose bones so mysteriously turn out to be green. There are, too, all manner of unfamiliar cheeses made from sheep or goat's milk; the butchers' stalls are festooned with every imaginable portion of the inside of every edible animal (anyone who has lived for long in Greece will be familiar with the sound of air gruesomely whistling through sheep's lungs frying in oil).

There are endless varieties of currants and raisins, figs from Smyrna on long strings, dates, almonds, pistachios and pine kernel nuts, dried melon seeds and sheets of apricot paste which is dissolved in water to make a cooling drink.

All these ingredients make rich and colourful dishes. Over-picturesque, perhaps, for every day; but then who wants to eat the same food every day? I have, therefore, varied this collection with some classic dishes and recipes from regions of France other than those bordering the Mediterranean. I have also devoted a special chapter to dishes which constitute a meal in themselves, such as Paëlla, Cassoulets and Pilaffs, and another chapter to cold food, fine dishes which are parti-cularly suitable to our servantless lives; prepared in advance and either preceded or followed by a spicy, aromatic southern dish, what more could one want?

With this selection (it does not claim to be more) of Mediter-ranean dishes, I hope to give some idea of the lovely cookery of those regions to people who do not already know them, and to stir the memories of those who have eaten this food on its native shores, and who would like sometimes to bring a flavour of those blessed lands of sun and sea and olive trees into their English kitchens.

E. D.

ACKNOWLEDGMENTS

MY THANKS are due to *Mr. Norman Douglas* and to his publishers Messrs. CHAPMAN & HALL and Messrs. SECKER & WARBURG for permission to include the recipe from "Birds and Beasts of the Greek Anthology" and the extracts from "South Wind" respectively; also to Messrs. FABER & FABER for two extracts from "Prospero's Cell" by *Lawrence Durrell*; to JOHN LANE (THE BODLEY HEAD) for a quotation from "The Autobiography of Alice B. Toklas" by *Gertrude Stein*; to Messrs. HUTCHINSON & CO. for permission to reproduce a passage from "Cross Channel" by *Alan Houghton Brodrick*; to Messrs. WILLIAM HEINEMANN and *Mrs. Frieda Lawrence* for the extract from *D. H. Lawrence's* "Sea and Sardinia", and also to Messrs. MACMILLAN for the passage from *Sir Osbert Sitwell's* "Great Morning"; to Messrs. CASSELL & CO. for permission to quote from *Mr. Compton Mackenzie's* "First Athenian Memories"; to Messrs. EDWARD ARNOLD for permission to reproduce a recipe from *Colonel Kenney-Herbert's* "Fifty Luncheons"; to the owner of the copyright of "Things that have Interested Me" by *Arnold Bennett*; to *Mr. Innes Rose* of JOHN FARQUHARSON LTD. for his permission to include an extract from *Henry James's* "A Little Tour in France"; to ALFRED KNOPF INC. of New York for permission to give the passage from *Theophile Gauthier's* book "Un Voyage en Espagne", translated into English by Catherine Alison Phillips under the title "A Romantic in Spain"; and to LES EDITIONS DENOEL and Messrs. IVOR NICHOLSON & WATSON for the passage from "The Happy Glutton" by *Alin Laubreaux*.

My acknowledgments are also due to the editor and publishers of HARPER'S BAZAAR, in which magazine many of the following recipes first appeared.

I should also like to take this opportunity of thanking a number of friends who have most kindly helped me with recipes and with advice, and especially *The Hon. Edward Gathorne-Hardy* of the British Embassy in Cairo, *Mrs. Esmat Hammuda* of Cairo, and *Mr. Robin Chancellor* for his generous and practical assistance.

Above all I have a debt of gratitude to *Mr. Norman Douglas*, whose great knowledge and enchanting talk taught me so much about the Mediterranean.

E. D.

PREFACE
TO THE SECOND EDITION (REVISED)

THIS book first appeared in 1950, when almost every essential ingredient of good cooking was either rationed or unobtainable. To produce the simplest meal consisting of even two or three genuine dishes required the utmost ingenuity and devotion. But even if people could not very often make the dishes here described, it was stimulating to think about them; to escape from the deadly boredom of queueing and the frustration of buying the weekly rations; to read about real food cooked with wine and olive oil, eggs and butter and cream, and dishes richly flavoured with onions, garlic, herbs, and brightly coloured Southern vegetables.

In revising the recipes for the present edition I have had little to alter as far as the ingredients were concerned, but here and there I have increased the number of eggs or added a little more stock or bacon or meat to a recipe; I have taken out one or two dishes which were substitute cooking in that, although no false ingredients were used, a good deal of extra seasoning, in the form of tomato purée or wine and vegetables, was added to make up for lack of flavour which should have been supplied by meat or stock or butter.

Because in those days poor quality and lack of ingredients necessitated the use of devious means to achieve the right results, and also because during the last few years I have had opportunities of learning a good deal more than I knew at the time about different methods of cooking, I have been able to simplify the instructions for making some of the dishes. A few recipes which had nothing to do with Mediterranean cooking and which I included perhaps out of over-enthusiasm, I have

9

replaced with Mediterranean recipes which I have since collected. Some of these are for Eastern Mediterranean dishes, from Greece, Syria, Turkey, and the Middle East, others from Italy, Spain, and Provence.

So startlingly different is the food situation now as compared with only two years ago that I think there is scarcely a single ingredient, however exotic, mentioned in this book which cannot be obtained somewhere in this country, even if it is only in one or two shops. Those who make an occasional marketing expedition to Soho or to the region of Tottenham Court Road can buy Greek cheese and Calamata olives, Tahina paste from the Middle East, little birds preserved in oil from Cyprus, stuffed vine leaves from Turkey, Spanish sausages, Egyptian brown beans, chick peas, Armenian ham, Spanish, Italian, and Cypriot olive oil, Italian salame and rice, even occasionally Neapolitan Mozzarella cheese, and honey from Mount Hymettus. These are the details which complete the flavour of a Mediterranean meal, but the ingredients which make this cookery so essentially different from our own are available to all; they are the olive oil, wine, lemons, garlic, onions, tomatoes, and the aromatic herbs and spices which go to make up what is so often lacking in English cooking: variety of flavour and colour, and the warm, rich, stimulating smells of genuine food.

E. D.

CONTENTS

Soups

*Le plus entendu de touts n'eust pas quitté son écuelle de
soupe pour recouvrir la liberté de la respublique de Platon.*

La Boètie

Soupe au Pistou

The origin of *Pistou* is Genoese, but it has become naturalised
in Nice and the surrounding country.

Into 3 pints of boiling water put 1 lb. of french beans cut
in inch lengths, 4 medium-sized potatoes, chopped finely, and
3 chopped, peeled tomatoes. Season with salt and pepper and
let them boil fairly quickly. When the vegetables are almost
cooked, throw in ¼ lb. of vermicelli and finish cooking gently.

Have ready the following preparation, known as an *aïllade*.
In a mortar pound 3 cloves of garlic, a handful of sweet basil
and a grilled tomato without the skin and pips. When this
paste is thoroughly smooth, add 3 tablespoons of the liquid
from the *Pistou*. Pour the *Pistou* into a tureen, stir in the
aïllade and some grated Gruyère cheese.

Soupe Basque

Brown ¼ lb. of chopped onions in lard; add ½ lb. of pumpkin
cut in pieces; add the cut-up leaves of a white cabbage, ½ lb.
previously soaked dried haricot beans, 2 cloves of garlic, salt
and pepper and 2 quarts of stock or water. Cook 3 hours in
a covered pan.

Avgolémono

The best known of all Greek soups.

To 2 pints of strained chicken broth, add 2 ozs. rice and boil
in the broth until well cooked. In a basin beat up 2 eggs and
the juice of a lemon. Add a little boiling broth to the eggs

in the basin, spoon by spoon, stirring all the time. Add this
mixture to the rest of the broth and stir for a few minutes
over a very slow fire.

SOUPE CATALANE

3 large onions, 2 ozs. chopped ham or bacon, 1 glass white wine,
1 small stick celery, 3 tomatoes, 2 potatoes, 2 egg yolks, 3 pints
stock or water, thyme, parsley, a pinch of nutmeg.

Slice the onions thinly and brown them in the pan in which
you are going to cook the soup, in olive oil or bacon fat.
Stir frequently to prevent them catching. When they start to
brown, add the diced ham or bacon, the tomatoes cut in
quarters and the chopped celery. Continue stirring for a few
minutes, then pour in the glass of wine; let it reduce and then
add the stock or water, the potatoes cut in small pieces and
the seasoning.

Cook the soup for about 30 minutes. When ready to serve,
beat the yolks of eggs with a few spoons of the soup, then
pour over the rest of the very hot soup and stir well. Add a
good handful of chopped parsley.

The same soup can be made without the egg yolks by adding
some vermicelli as soon as the soup has come to the boil, or
make it without any thickening and serve with grated cheese.

PURÉE LÉONTINE

2 lbs. leeks, 1 cup each of spinach, green peas and shredded
lettuce, 1 tablespoon each of chopped parsley, mint, celery,
½ tumbler olive oil, lemon juice, salt and pepper.

Clean and cut the leeks into chunks. Into a thick marmite
put the olive oil and when it is warm put in the leeks, seasoned
with salt, pepper and the lemon juice. Simmer slowly for
about 20 minutes. Now add the spinach, the peas and the
lettuce, stir a minute or two, and add a quart of water. Cook

until all the vegetables are soft—about 10 minutes, then press the whole mixture through a sieve. If the purée is too thick add a little milk, and before serving stir in the chopped parsley, mint and celery.

This soup turns out an appetising pale green. Enough for six people.

Soup of Haricot Beans

With the remains of a Cassoulet (p. 107) a most delicious soup can be made.

Heat up the beans which are left over in a little extra water, and pound them through a sieve. Reheat the purée, adding sufficient milk to thin down the soup, and put in some pieces of sausage cut in dice.

Soup with Risotto

For using left-over Risotto (p. 98).

Make the rice into little balls the size of a nut. Egg and breadcrumb them and fry them in butter, and when they are dry add them to any kind of hot soup—chicken broth, for instance, or a simple vegetable soup.

Potage de Topinambours à la Provençale

Cook 2 lbs. of Jerusalem artichokes in 3 pints of salted water. Sieve, and heat up, adding gradually ½ pint of milk.

In a small frying-pan heat 2 tablespoons of olive oil and in this fry two chopped tomatoes, a clove of garlic, a small piece of chopped celery, a little parsley, and 2 tablespoons of chopped ham or bacon. Let this mixture cook only a minute or two, then pour it, with the oil, into the soup. Heat, and serve quickly.

Hot Cucumber Soup

1 lb. potatoes, 2 large onions, 2 whole cucumbers, milk, parsley, chives, 1 pickled cucumber, leek tops, mint, salt and pepper.

Boil the potatoes and 1 onion in water. When they are soft pass through a sieve and proceed as for potato soup, making a thin smooth purée with the milk. Grate into this soup 2 whole unpeeled cucumbers, 1 raw onion, add the pickled cucumber cut into small pieces and all the other ingredients chopped fine, and reheat cautiously, so that the vinegar in the pickled cucumber does not curdle the milk.

Zuppa di Pesce

There are many versions of fish soup in Italy, and most of them are, like the Bouillabaisse, more of a stew than a soup. The varieties of bony and spiny fish used in the Genoese *Burrida*, the Livornese *Cacciucco*, and the Neapolitan Zuppa di Pesce are much the same as in a Bouillabaisse (see p. 60), but with the addition of squid cut in rings, small clams called *vongole*, sometimes small red mullet, prawns, mussels, small lobsters or *langouste*.

The basis of Italian fish soups is usually a broth made with oil and tomato, flavoured with garlic, onion, and herbs, sometimes dried mushrooms, sometimes white wine or a little vinegar. In this broth the fish are cooked and served, accompanied by slices of French bread baked in the oven.

A very simple version of an Italian fish soup can be made with mussels, and prawns. To make the broth, put 2 or 3 tablespoons of olive oil in a wide, heavy pan. When it has warmed put in a small chopped onion; let it melt a little, add a tablespoon each of chopped celery leaves and parsley and a clove or two of garlic. Cook a minute, then add 1 lb. of chopped and skinned tomatoes. Simmer until the tomatoes are reduced to a sauce. Add a small glass of white wine and the same amount of water. Season rather highly with pepper, and if you like a little cayenne, and a very little salt. If the broth is too thick add a little more water. In this preparation cook 4 pints of cleaned mussels and 1 pint of large prawns (these *should* be in their shells and uncooked, although personally I do not care for the very strong flavour which the prawn shells give to the soup, and I usually buy cooked prawns and shell them before adding them).[1] If you are using Dublin Bay prawns, use the tails only and slit the shells down the centre before putting them into the pan, to facilitate shelling when they are served. (Dublin Bay prawn shells have nothing like the strong flavour of those of ordinary prawns.)

As soon as the mussels have all opened sprinkle a little chopped parsley and if you like a little lemon juice or chopped lemon peel over the top, and serve at once in very hot soup plates, with slices of bread baked in the oven. For those who like it, rub the slices of baked bread with a cut clove of garlic before serving.

Another way of making a simplified Zuppa di Pesce is to cook slices of any fish such as red or grey mullet, mackerel, brill, whiting, haddock, or gurnard in the prepared tomato broth, then add the mussels and prawns, but in half the quantities given. Those who don't like fishing bones out of the soup can use filleted fish.

A MEDITERRANEAN FISH SOUP

A cod's head, a cooked crawfish, 2 pints cockles or mussels, 1 pint prawns, 1 pimento, 1½ lbs. tomatoes, a lemon, a few celery leaves, a carrot, 2 onions, 6 cloves of garlic, 3 tablespoons rice, coarse salt, ground black pepper, thyme, marjoram, basil, fennel, parsley, a piece of orange peel, ½ pint white wine, 4 pints water, saffron, parsley.

Make a stock with the cod's head, the shells of the crawfish and the prawns, the celery, onions, carrot, a slice each of lemon and orange peel, marjoram, thyme, white wine and water, and a teaspoonful of saffron. Simmer this stock for an hour.

---

[1] In this case use half the quantity.

In the meantime chop the tomatoes and put them to cook in a thick pan with the pimento and a clove of garlic, and a very little olive oil, simmering them until reduced to a purée.

Clean the mussels or cockles and open them in a very little water over a quick fire; take them out of their shells and strain the liquid through a muslin.

When the stock has cooked, strain it, return it to the pan; bring it to the boil, put in the rice and simmer it for 15 minutes; now add the tomatoes, sieved, the crawfish cut into small pieces, the whole prawns, and stock from the mussels or cockles. Let all this heat together for 5 minutes; by this time the soup should be of a fairly thick and creamy consistency. As the soup bubbles and is ready to serve stir in a handful of fresh parsley, basil, or fennel, the mussels or cockles, a dessertspoon of grated lemon peel and a small clove of garlic crushed in a mortar. Another minute and the soup is ready. The addition of the herbs, the lemon and the garlic at the last moment gives the soup its fresh flavour.

White Fish Soup

2 lbs. any firm white fish, 1 cod's head, 1 onion, 1 leek, celery, garlic, parsley, 3 tablespoons tomato purée, a glass white wine, 1 cup milk, a few sprigs of fennel, lemon peel, flour.

Put the fish and vegetables into a pan and cover with water. When the fish is cooked, remove it carefully, taking out any bones, cut in large pieces, and keep it aside. Continue cooking the rest of the stock for 20 minutes. Then strain it through a sieve and return to the pan. Add the white wine, the tomato purée; thicken with 2 tablespoons of flour stirred in a cup of milk and poured into the soup through a strainer when it is off the boil.

When the soup is smooth (it should not be very thick) put in the pieces of cooked fish, add a large handful of coarsely chopped parsley, the chopped fennel, and chopped lemon peel. There should be at least one large piece of fish for each plate of soup. Serve with slices of toasted French bread.

Soupe aux Moules

2 pints mussels, 1 small onion, 1 stick celery, 1 clove of garlic, 1 glass white wine, parsley, lemon, 2 eggs.

Cook the mussels as for *Moules Marinière* (p. 51). When they have opened, take them out of their shells and keep them aside. Strain the liquid in which they have cooked through muslin (there is always a little sand or grit deposited from the mussels, however carefully they have been cleaned).

Heat up this stock, put back the shelled mussels and a handful of chopped parsley and cook 2 minutes more. The less the mussels are re-cooked, once they have been shelled, the better they will be. Beat up the eggs in a bowl with a little lemon juice, pour some of the stock into it, stir well, return the mixture to the pan, and continue stirring until the soup is hot, but it must not boil.

Tomato and Shell-fish Soup

This is typical of the way many soups are made in Mediterranean countries. Sometimes French beans are added or potatoes cut in dice.

1 lb. onions, 2 lbs. tomatoes, 1 glass olive oil, herbs and seasoning, garlic, 1 breakfast cup any cooked shell fish (mussels, prawns, clams or *scampi*), 1 oz. vermicelli, parsley.

Heat the olive oil in a thick pan and put in the sliced onions and let them cook slowly until they are melted and golden. Now add the tomatoes, chopped roughly, salt and pepper and a clove or two of garlic, and let the whole mixture simmer until the tomatoes are soft.

Now add 1½ pints of water or stock from the shell fish. Cook slowly for 20 to 30 minutes. Put the soup through a sieve.

Return it to the pan, bring it to the boil and throw in the vermicelli in very small pieces and whatever shell fish you are using. In 5 minutes it will be ready.

MELOKHIA

Melokhia is a glutinous soup much beloved by the Arabs, particularly in Egypt. *Melokhia* is a kind of mallow (Greek *malakhe*, Latin *malva*).

> 1 lb. green *melokhia*, 3 glasses rabbit stock, several cloves of garlic, a small cup dried coriander, salt, and *shatta* (ground dried chillies) or cayenne pepper.

Wash the *melokhia* well and drain it until dry. Take the green leaves only and chop them finely—this is done with the two-handled chopper called a *makhrata*.[1] Put the stock into a pan and heat it. When it is boiling add half the coriander and garlic pounded together into the stock. Add the chopped *melokhia* and stir it well for a minute or two, and remove the pan from the fire. Fry the rest of the pounded coriander and garlic in hot fat and add it to the *melokhia*, with the *shatta* or cayenne. Leave the casserole uncovered on a low flame for a few minutes. This is served in a soup plate, accompanied by another plate of boiled rice with rabbit or chicken.

ICED CUCUMBER JELLY SOUP

Grate 2 large cucumbers with the peel. Add half a small onion grated, lemon juice, salt, pepper and some very finely chopped mint. Stir in some melted aspic jelly (see p. 147) and leave to set. Garnish each cup of soup with a few prawns.

---

[1] *Hâchoir* in French, *Mezzaluna* in Italian. These instruments can now be bought at a few good kitchen stores (William Page, Shaftesbury Avenue, Staines of Victoria Street, Cadec, 27 Greek Street, Soho, etc.). Once you have used one, it is unthinkable to be without it.

GASPACHO

Gaspacho, the popular iced Spanish soup, was described,
somewhat disparagingly, by Théophile Gautier after a journey
to Spain in 1840; like all good Frenchmen he was apt to be
suspicious of foreign food.

"Our supper was of the simplest kind; all the serving men
and maids of the hostelry had gone to the dance, and we had
to be content with a mere gaspacho. This gaspacho is worthy
of a special description, and we shall here give the recipe,
which would have made the hair of the late Brillat-Savarin
stand on end. You pour some water into a soup tureen, and
to this water you add a dash of vinegar, some cloves of garlic,
some onions cut into quarters, some slices of cucumber, a few
pieces of pimiento, a pinch of salt; then one cuts some bread
and sets it to soak in this pleasing mixture, serving it cold.
At home, a dog of any breeding would refuse to sully its
nose with such a compromising mixture. It is the favourite
dish of the Andalusians, and the prettiest women do not shrink
from swallowing bowlfuls of this hell-broth of an evening.
Gaspacho is considered highly refreshing, an opinion which
strikes me as rather rash, but, strange as it may seem the first
time one tastes it, one ends by getting used to it and even
liking it. As a most providential compensation we had a
decanter of an excellent dry white Malaga wine to wash down
this meagre repast, and drained it conscientiously to the last
drop, thus restoring our strength, exhausted by a nine hours'
spell upon indescribable roads at a temperature like that of a
kiln."[1]

Here is another rather more sophisticated version of Gaspacho. Make a fairly thick tomato soup with $\frac{1}{2}$ lb. of onions
and 2 lbs. of fresh tomatoes or 1 large can of tomatoes, salt,

[1] *Un Voyage en Espagne*, translated by Catherine Alison Phillips, and published by
Alfred A. Knopf under the title of *A Romantic in Spain*.

pepper, a little sugar and half a glass of red wine. Put them through a sieve.

In a mortar pound 3 cloves of garlic, add salt, pepper and a tablespoon of paprika powder and then 2 or 3 tablespoons of olive oil, drop by drop. When this mixture has the consistency of mayonnaise stir in gradually the cold tomato soup. Put in a cucumber cut in small cubes and a dozen stoned black olives. Stand in the refrigerator, and before serving put a cube of ice and a handful of chopped parsley into each plate.

Iced Chicken and Tomato Consommé

For 1 pint of chicken stock take ¼ pint of fresh (or canned) tomato juice and cook for 5 minutes with a clove of garlic, 2 lumps of sugar, salt, pepper and basil. Strain and add the chicken consommé and a glass of white wine. Heat again and then chill in the ice box.

Iced Beetroot Soup

Cook 4 large beetroots in the oven, exactly as for potatoes baked in their jackets—they will take 2 or 3 hours, and the resulting delicious flavour happily bears no resemblance to the bloodless things sold ready cooked by the greengrocers. Peel them and grate them into 2 pints of aspic jelly (p. 147), add a little vinegar and seasoning and heat this mixture gently for 10 minutes, then pour it through a sieve. The liquid should be a strong clear red. Put it into a bowl to set. To serve, put a cold poached egg into the bottom of each shallow soup bowl and pile the jellied beetroot on top in spoonfuls. Iced soup ought not to be served in a set piece or it looks like a nursery jelly.

Okrochka

There are many variations of *Okrochka*, and it can be made with different kinds of fish, fish and meat mixed, or simply with pieces of cold cooked chicken. The essential ingredients are the fresh and pickled cucumbers and the fennel which gives it its characteristic flavour.

The *Okrochka* which I enjoyed many times at the Russian Club in Athens was made with *Kwass*[1] and Yoghourt was served separately. Here is a recipe which can quite easily be made in England. It is a filling soup and should be served in small quantities, when it makes a cool first dish on a hot evening.

> 1 cup diced fresh cucumber, ¾ cup diced frankfurter sausage or cold chicken, 1 cup cooked shrimps or lobster, ¼ cup chopped onion tops or leeks, ¼ cup chopped fennel, ¼ cup diced pickled cucumbers, ½ cup chopped parsley, 2 hard-boiled eggs, ¼ pint Yoghourt, 1 cup milk, salt and freshly ground black pepper.

Mix the milk into the Yoghourt to thin it down, then add all the other ingredients except the hard-boiled eggs. Leave on the ice at least 2 hours, and before serving put a cube or two of ice into each cup, a piece of chopped hard-boiled egg, and sprinkle over some more parsley.

Iced Pimento Soup

From a small tin of red spanish pimentos (preferably the roasted kind) mash half into a purée and cook a few minutes with twice the quantity of tomato juice. Add the rest of the pimentos cut in strips, and ice. If fresh pimentos are used, grill, skin, seed, and pound them before mixing with the tomato. Very fine slices of raw pimento can be used for garnishing.

[1] A Russian fermented liquor.

Eggs and
Luncheon Dishes

"THE WELL-FED Bressois are surely a good-natured people. I call them well-fed both on general and on particular grounds. Their province has the most savoury aroma, and I found an opportunity to test its reputation. I walked back into the town from the church (there was really nothing to be seen by the way), and as the hour of the midday breakfast had struck, directed my steps to the inn. The table d'hôte was going on, and a gracious, bustling, talkative landlady welcomed me. I had an excellent repast—the best repast possible—which consisted simply of boiled eggs and bread and butter. It was the quality of these simple ingredients that made the occasion memorable. The eggs were so good that I am ashamed to say how many of them I consumed. 'La plus belle fille du monde,' as the French proverb says, 'ne peut donner que ce qu'elle a'; and it might seem that an egg which has succeeded in being fresh has done all that can reasonably be expected of it. But there was a bloom of punctuality, so to speak, about these eggs of Bourg, as if it had been the intention of the very hens themselves that they should be promptly served. 'Nous sommes en Bresse, et le beurre n'est pas mauvais,' the landlady said with a sort of dry coquetry, as she placed this article before me. It was the poetry of butter, and I ate a pound or two of it; after which I came away with a strange mixture of impressions of late gothic sculpture and thick *tartines*."

A Little Tour in France,
by Henry James

The Savoury Omelette

Egg dishes and omelettes are the perfect dishes for small luncheons. Everyone has favourite recipes for these, so I have only included a very few.

As far as omelettes are concerned I cannot do better than to quote "Wyvern's" wholly admirable views on the subject:

"The recipe for this *omelette* differs somewhat from those usually propounded, being that of the *cuisinière bourgeoise* rather than that of the *Chef.* The latter looks very nice, and is often finished tastefully with a pattern skilfully wrought with glaze, *cordons* of *purées* and other decoration. To my mind the *omelette* suffers in being made so pretty, and is not as good a thing to eat as that of roadside inn or *cabaret.*

"An *omelette* ought never to be stiff enough to retain a very neatly rolled up appearance. If cooked with proper rapidity it should be too light to present a fixed form, and on reaching the hot dish should spread itself, rather, on account of the delicacy of its substance. Books that counsel you to *turn* an *omelette*, to fold it, to let it brown on one side, to let it fry for about five minutes, etc., are not to be trusted. If you follow such advice you will only produce, at best, a neat-looking egg pudding.

"Timed by the seconds hand of a watch, an *omelette* of six eggs, cooked according to my method 'by the first intention', takes forty-five seconds from the moment of being poured into the pan to that of being turned into the dish.

"Though cream is considered by some to be an improvement, I do not recommend it. Milk is certainly a mistake, for it makes the *omelette* leathery. I confess that I like a very little minced chives in all savoury omelettes; but this is a matter of taste. Finely chopped parsley should be added with a seasoning of salt and pepper. The general rules to be observed in omelette-making, according to my process, then, may be thus summed up:

"1. Mix thoroughly but do not *beat* the eggs, and never use more than six for one *omelette*, omitting two of the whites.

"2. It is better to make two of six than one of twelve eggs. Success is *impossible* if the vessel be too full. If using four eggs omit one white.

"3. Three eggs mixed whole make a nice-sized *omelette,* quite the best for the beginner to commence with.

"4. Use a proper utensil, rather shallow, with narrow, well-sloping sides; a twelve-inch fireproof china pan will be found excellent; see that it is clean and quite dry.

"5. Do not overdo the amount of butter that you use for the frying—enough to lubricate the pan evenly to the extent of a quarter of an inch is sufficient.[1]

"6. Be sure that your pan is *ready* to receive your mixture. If not hot enough your *omelette* will be leathery, or you will have to mix it in the pan like scrambled eggs (*œufs brouillés*).

"7. The moment the butter ceases to fizz and turns brownish, the moisture having been expelled, the pan is ready.

"8. Pour the mixture into the pan so that it may spread well over the lubricated surface, then instantly lift up the part of the *omelette* that sets at the moment of contact, and let the unformed portion run under it; repeat this two or three times if the pan be at all full, keep the left hand at work with a gentle see-saw motion to encourage rapidity in setting, give a finishing shake, and turn the *omelette* into the hot dish *before* the whole of the mixture on the surface has quite set.

"9. The *omelette*, slightly assisted by the spoon, will roll over almost of its own accord if the sides of the pan be sloped as I have described, burying within it the slightly unformed

---

[1] I'm not quite sure what this means. A film of butter covering the pan is really enough.—E.D.

juicy part of the mixture which remained on the surface; it will not require folding.

"10. Three-quarters of a minute is ample time for the whole operation, if the pan be properly hot when the mixture is poured into it, and the heat evenly maintained.

"11. Have the hot dish close by the fire, so that you can turn the *omelette* into it *instanter*. A little melted butter, with some chopped parsley and chives, may, with advantage, be put into the dish.

"12. It is above all things necessary to have a brisk fire under the pan while the *omelette* is being cooked. A fair-sized gas boiler serves the purpose. The small three-egg *omelette* can be made successfully over a powerful methylated spirit lamp. The ordinary kitchen fire is unsuited for this work unless it can be brought up level with the hot plate, with a clear live coal surface.

"As it lies in the dish this *omelette* will not look like a bolster —it will take a natural, rather flat, irregular oval shape, golden yellow in colour, and flecked with green, with the juicy part escaping from beneath its folds."[1]

Colonel Kenney-Herbert's "twelve-inch fireproof china pan" would be difficult to come by nowadays, but there are plenty of substitutes, and even heavy iron omelette pans *can*, with trouble, be found in England.

ETIQUETTE

Regarding the world of subtlety which can be infused into the serving of a dish of eggs, I cannot resist quoting here the lucid opinion of a French cook, as related by Gertrude Stein.

The dinner was cooked by Hélène. I must tell a little about Hélène.

Hélène had already been three years with Gertrude Stein and

[1] *Fifty Luncheons*, by A. Kenney-Herbert.

her brother. She was one of those admirable bonnes, in other words excellent maids of all work, good cooks thoroughly occupied with the welfare of their employers and of themselves, firmly convinced that everything purchasable was far too dear. "Oh, but it is dear!" was her answer to any question. She wasted nothing and carried on the household at the regular rate of 8 francs a day. She even wanted to include guests at that price, it was her pride, but of course that was difficult since she for the honour of her house as well as to satisfy her employers always had to give everyone enough to eat. She was a most excellent cook and she made a very good soufflé. In those days most of the guests were living more or less precariously; no one starved, someone always helped, but still most of them did not live in abundance. It was Braque who said about four years later when they were all beginning to be known, with a sigh and a smile, "How life has changed! We all now have cooks who can make a soufflé."

Hélène had her opinions; she did not, for instance, like Matisse. She said a Frenchman should not stay unexpectedly to a meal, particularly if he asked the servant beforehand what there was for dinner. She said foreigners had a perfect right to do these things but not a Frenchman, and Matisse had once done it. So when Miss Stein said to her, "Monsieur Matisse is staying for dinner this evening," she would say, "In that case I will not make an omelette but fry the eggs. It takes the same number of eggs and the same amount of butter but it shows less respect, and he will understand."[1]

TARTE À L'OIGNON ET AUX ŒUFS

7 ozs. flour, 2 ozs. butter, 1½ ozs. lard, ¼ glass water, salt.

Make a paste with all the ingredients and spread it in a buttered flan dish.

[1] *The Autobiography of Alice B. Toklas*, by Gertrude Stein

Have ready the following preparation.

Put 1½ lbs. of onions into boiling salted water and cook them until they are reduced to a purée. Mix this purée with a large cup of rather thick *béchamel*.

Spread the mixture on the uncooked pastry. Arrange more strips of pastry criss-cross over the onions and bake about 45 minutes.

Serve with poached eggs on top.

RATATOUILLE AUX ŒUFS (Courgettes)

1 lb. potatoes, ¾ lb. onions, 2 cloves of garlic, 3 small marrows, 3 tomatoes, 3 green pimentos, eggs.

Clean all the vegetables and cut them into rounds. Into a heavy frying pan put half a glass of oil and 2 tablespoons of lard; put in the vegetables, season with salt and pepper, and simmer with the pan covered for 45 minutes, and another 30 minutes without the lid.

Turn into a serving dish and place on top a fried egg for each person.

ŒUFS EN MATELOTE

Cook ½ pint of red wine with herbs, onion, garlic, salt and pepper. Boil for 3 minutes and take out the herbs. In the wine poach 6 eggs, put them on slices of fried bread. Quickly reduce the sauce and thicken it with butter worked with flour and pour over the eggs.

CHATCHOUKA

A Tunisian dish.

6 small green pimentos, 8 tomatoes, 4 eggs, butter or olive oil.

Remove the cores and seeds from the pimentos, and cut them in strips. Heat a little oil or butter in a shallow earthenware dish. In this stew the pimentos, and add the tomatoes, whole, when the pimentos are half cooked. Season with salt and pepper. When the tomatoes are soft, break in the eggs, whole, and cover the pan until they are cooked. Serve in the dish in which they have cooked. Sometimes a little chopped or minced chicken or meat is cooked with the pimentos, sometimes onions, and sometimes the Chatchouka is cooked in individual earthenware egg dishes.

HUEVOS AL PLATO À LA BARCINO

A Spanish dish.

6 eggs, ¼ lb. of leg of pork, 2 ozs. ham, 2 ozs. butter, ½ lb. tomatoes, 1 oz. flour, an onion, a little stock.

Slice the onion, the ham and the pork into small strips; let them melt in the butter; when they have turned golden stir in the flour, add the chopped tomatoes and about ¼ pint of meat stock. Simmer this sauce gently for 20 minutes or so, until it is very thick, and season with pepper and salt. Turn it into a fireproof egg dish, break in the eggs, and cook in the oven until the whites have set.

OMELETTE AU BROCCIU

Brocciu is the Corsican cheese made of ewe-milk which gives a characteristic salty tang to many Corsican dishes.

The eggs and cheese are beaten up together, with the addition of chopped wild mint, and made into a flat round omelette.

OMELETTE AUX MOULES

Prepare a mixture of onion lightly browned in olive oil, flavoured with garlic, parsley, and a little white wine.

Add the cooked shelled mussels to this, and at the appropriate moment add them to your omelette, which is served with a little tomato sauce in addition.

MOUSAKÁ

A dish well known all over the Balkans, Turkey, and the Middle East. This is the Greek version.

First prepare a thick batter by cooking together 2 beaten egg yolks and ½ pint of milk, seasoned with salt and pepper, until it is like a very solid custard. Leave to cool.

Mince 1 lb. of cooked beef or lamb very fine. Fry 3 large sliced onions in oil till brown. Cut 3 or 4 unpeeled aubergines into large slices and fry in hot oil.

Put some more oil into a deep square or oblong cake tin[1] and cover the bottom with aubergines; cover the aubergines with the minced meat, and this with the fried onions. Repeat till all the ingredients are in the dish. Then put in ½ cup each of meat stock and fresh tomato sauce, cover with the prepared batter mixture and put the dish in a moderate oven (gas no. 4) for about an hour. The batter should form a kind of crust on the top of the Mousaká, and should be golden brown. Usually served hot, but also very good cold. Can also be reheated very successfully.

TARTE AUX TOMATES

Line a shallow tin with pastry, and pour into it a thick *béchamel* sauce (p. 186) into which you have incorporated a tablespoon of concentrated tomato purée. On top of this put some stoned black olives and some chicken livers which have been chopped and sautéd in butter for 2 or 3 minutes. Cover with a layer of tomatoes cut in half and grilled for a couple of minutes. Bake in a moderate oven until the pastry is cooked.

SCALOPPINE OF CALF'S LIVER WITH PIMENTOS

1 lb. calf's liver cut in thin slices, 4 sweet red pimentos, a small wineglass white wine, lemon juice, salt, pepper, a little flour, olive oil.

[1] The quantities given fill a cake tin 6½ inches square and 2 inches deep.

Prepare the pimentos by putting them under the grill and turning them round until their skins have blackened. When they have cooled, rub off the skins, remove the core and seeds, wash them in cold water, and cut into strips.

Season the slices of liver with salt, pepper, and lemon juice. Dust them lightly with flour. Put them into a frying pan in which you have heated half a coffee-cupful of olive oil, and sauté them quickly on both sides; pour over the white wine (keep out of the way of the sizzling oil), let it bubble, add the pimentos, and cook gently another 5 minutes.

Rognons Braisés au Porto

The beauty of this dish depends on the aroma of the truffle permeating the wine and the kidneys, and the pan must be kept carefully covered during the cooking.

Cut 1 lb. veal kidneys in slices. Put in a shallow sauté pan with 1 onion cut up, salt, pepper, a piece of lemon peel, bay leaf and a sliced truffle. Cover with half water and half port. Cover the pan and stew very slowly for about 1½ hours. Add some mushrooms already sautéd in butter, thicken the sauce with a little flour or cream, and cook another 10 minutes.

Langue de Bœuf en Paupiettes

Remove the horny part from an ox-tongue; blanch it in boiling water for 15 minutes and then cook in a casserole until the skin can be removed. When cold cut in thin slices and cover each piece with a layer of meat stuffing; paint over with a knife dipped in beaten egg to unify the stuffing, roll the slices, put a small piece of bacon on each and tie up or pierce with a skewer. These should be roasted in front of the fire but can be cooked in the oven in a casserole. When they are almost cooked sprinkle breadcrumbs over the paupiettes, and when they are a golden brown serve with a sauce *piquante* (p. 192).

PISSALADINA *or* PISSALADIÈRE

This dish is one of the delights of Marseilles, Toulon and the Var country, where it is sold in the market places and the bakeries in the early morning and can be bought, piping hot, by the slice, off big iron trays.

Get from the baker a piece of uncooked bread, pull it out and spread a baking sheet with it. Cover the bottom of a saucepan with olive oil. Add 2 lbs. of sliced onions; do not brown them but let them slowly melt almost to a purée, which will take about 40 minutes. Pour the purée on to the dough, put stoned black olives on the top and decorate it with criss-cross fillets of anchovy. Cook in the oven.

If bread dough is unobtainable, an excellent dish can be made by spreading the onion purée into a tin lined with the same pastry as for the *tarte à l'oignon* (p. 33) or thick slices of bread cut lengthways from a sandwich loaf. Fry one side lightly in olive oil, spread this side with the purée and put in a tin in the oven with a little more oil and cook about 10 minutes.

The flavour of the olive oil is essential to this dish.

Further along the coast, across the Italian border, these dishes baked on bread dough are called *pizza*, which simply means a pie, and there are many variations of them, the best known being the Neapolitan *pizza* which consists of tomatoes, anchovies and mozzarella cheese (a white buffalo-milk cheese). The local *pizza* of San Remo is very like the Provençal *pissaladière*, but garnished with salted sardines instead of anchovies; it is known locally as *Sardenara*.

If you can get yeast from a local bakery which makes its own bread, the dough for a *pizza* or a *pissaladière* can be made as follows: dissolve a little under ¼ oz. of yeast in a little tepid water; pour ¼ lb. of plain flour in a mound on a pastry board; make a well in the centre, put in the yeast and a teaspoonful of salt. Fold the flour over the yeast, and blend all together. Add about $\frac{1}{8}$ pint of water and knead to a stiff dough. Press the dough out and away from you with the palm of the hand, holding the dough with the other hand. When the dough begins to feel light and springy roll it into a ball, put it on a floured plate, cover with a floured cloth, and leave in a warm place for 2 to 3 hours, by which time it should have risen, and doubled in volume.

To make the *pissaladière* roll out the dough into a large disc or square (about $\frac{1}{4}$ inch thick) and garnish it with the onions, black olives and anchovies, prepared as already explained, and bake in a fairly hot oven for 20 to 30 minutes.

Anchoïade

There are several versions of this Provençal dish.

The one I know (and like best) is made in much the same way as Pissaladina, but instead of the onion mixture the uncooked dough is spread with a mixture of anchovies, tomatoes half cooked in olive oil and highly flavoured with garlic, and basil, and then baked in the oven.

Here is Reboul's recipe for Anchoïade. "Soak some fillets of anchovies in water for a few minutes to remove the salt. Place them in a dish with some olive oil, a pinch of pepper and 2 or 3 cloves of garlic cut up. You can also add a drop of vinegar. Cut the crust lengthways off a whole long loaf, about an inch thick, and cut this in pieces so that there is one for each guest; on each put some fillets of anchovy, and put each slice on a plate.

"Cut some more slices of bread in squares. Each person soaks his slice alternately in the prepared oil and anchovy mixture in the dish and then crushes it down on the anchovies and bread in his own plate. When all is finished, anchovies and sauce, the pieces of bread which remain are toasted before the fire. There results a characteristic aroma which rejoices every *amateur* of Provençal cooking, and is the delight of many gastronomes."

Another way of serving Anchoïade is to spread the prepared mixture of olive oil, garlic and anchovies on pieces of toast and heat them in the oven.

ANCHOÏADE CROZE[1]

Rolls cut in two and filled with a purée made of brined anchovies, almonds or walnuts, figs, onions, garlic, savoury herbs, tarragon, fennel seed, red pimento, olive oil, lemon, and orange-blossom water; baked and served with black olives.

ÉPINARDS EN BOUILLABAISSE

Cook 2 lbs. of cleaned spinach in water for 5 minutes. Drain it and press out all the water, and chop it.

Into a large shallow pan put 3 or 4 dessertspoons of oil and a chopped onion. After a minute or two add the spinach and stir over a slow fire for 5 minutes, then add 5 or 6 raw potatoes cut in thin slices; the waxy kind are best for this dish as they are less likely to disintegrate.

Season with salt, pepper and a pinch of saffron; pour over about 1½ pints of boiling water, add 2 cloves of garlic chopped, a branch of fennel, and simmer with the lid on until the potatoes are cooked. At this moment break into the pan 1 egg for each person and cook gently.

Into each guest's plate put a slice of bread and with a ladle carefully take out an egg (they should be *poached*) and a portion of the vegetables, and place it on the slice of bread, with some of the *bouillon*.

From Reboul's *La Cuisinière Provençale*

BUREK

Burek are little pastries filled either with a mixture of spinach

---

[1] Austin de Croze.

or fresh cream cheese flavoured with mint. They are of Turkish origin. The pastry used is called 'Fila', which is something like flaky pastry, rolled out very thinly. In Greece, Turkey, and Egypt it can be bought ready-made and looks like sheets of paper. In London fila pastry can be bought from John & Pascalis, 35 Grafton Way, Tottenham Court Road, and from the Oriental Provision Stores, 25 Charlotte Street.

For Burek cut the pastry into 2-inch squares, put a spoonful of spinach purée, or fresh cream cheese beaten with an egg and a little chopped mint in the centre of each one and fold the pastry over so that it is triangular shaped. Fry them in plenty of hot oil or dripping.

Spanakopittá

This is a Greek (and also Turkish) dish made with the same fila pastry as the Burek.

3 ozs. fila pastry leaves, 2 lbs. spinach, 3 ozs. butter, ¼ lb. Gruyère cheese.

Clean and cook the spinach in the usual way, and squeeze it very dry. Chop it not too finely, and heat it in a pan with an ounce of butter. Season well. Butter a square cake tin, not too deep. In the bottom put 6 leaves of fila pastry cut to the shape of the tin and a fraction larger, brushing the top of each leaf with melted butter before covering it with the next leaf.

Over the 6 layers of pastry spread the prepared spinach, then a layer of the grated Gruyère. Cover with 6 more layers of pastry, again buttering between each layer, and buttering also the top. See that the edges of the pastry are also well buttered, and cook in a moderate oven for 30 to 40 minutes. Leave to cool for a few minutes, turn upside down on to a baking dish, and return to the oven for 10 minutes or so for the underside to get crisp and golden.

Similar dishes are made using for a filling chicken in a béchamel sauce (Kotópittá) or cheese (Tirópittá).

GRENOUILLES PROVENÇALE

2 lbs. frogs' legs (medium size), ½ lb. butter, 1 tablespoon olive oil, 1 tablespoon chopped parsley, 2 cloves of garlic (finely chopped), ½ cup milk, ½ cup flour, salt and ground pepper, juice of ½ lemon, 1 teaspoon chopped chives.

Dip the frogs' legs in milk seasoned with salt and pepper and roll in flour. Heat 2 tablespoons of butter and 1 tablespoon of oil. Add frogs' legs. Cook until browned, about 12 minutes. Add to them the lemon juice, parsley, chives and pepper. Keep them warm over a low flame. Now brown the remaining butter until it is the colour of a hazel nut (beurre noisette). Add the garlic to the butter and quickly pour it over the frogs' legs. Serve garnished with lemon slices.

BOUDIN PURÉE DE POIS

Take 1½ lbs. of *boudin* (blood sausage, which in the south of France is always highly seasoned with onions), prick the skin, cut in several pieces and grill them.

For the purée cook ½ lb. of dried split peas in water with an onion, a bay leaf, salt and pepper, for 2½ to 3 hours. Put them through a sieve, and if necessary add a little milk and an ounce of butter. Serve piping hot.

TIRI TIGANISMÉNO (Fried Cheese)

Kasséri (hard, salt goat cheese) is simply cut in squares and fried in very hot oil without benefit of batter or bread-crumbs.

This simple dish can be very good indeed, but it depends very much upon the quality of the cheese. This question of quality applies in a certain degree to all Greek food. Greek gourmets know exactly where the best cheese, olives, oil, oranges, figs, melons, wine, and even water (in a country where water is often scarce, this is not really so surprising) are to be found, and go to immense trouble to procure them.

They are also exceedingly generous and hospitable, and when they see that a foreigner is appreciative, take great pride in seeing that he is entertained to the very best which Greece can offer.

SNAILS

"I was once present at a learned discussion between two stubborn gentlemen, who were arguing as to the respective merits of the snails of Bourgogne and of those of Provence. They were not speaking of the manner of preparing the snails, but of their natural flavour. One declared that the Bourguignons were more delicate, since they fed on vine-leaves, and the other that those of Provence were more delicious, owing to their diet of thyme and fennel.

"All that is simply absurd. Whatever the snail's food may be, it is improbable, to say the least of it, that any flavour is left after the animal has been starved for thirty or forty days, cleaned in vinegar and salt, rinsed in ten lots of water, and then boiled for several hours. . . .

"Those who succumb (and with reason) to the winey taste of the Bourgogne snails, and those who are enchanted (and one cannot too highly appreciate their attitude) by the thyme and fennel-scented blanquettes of Provence, forget one thing. They forget that the Bourguignon snails have been cooked for an hour in a litre of Chablis, while the Provençals have under-

gone the same process in salt water, together with a large
bunch of thyme and a still larger quantity of fennel. At that
rate one might impart the taste of wine or fennel to chewing-
gum.

"It is therefore in the manner of preparing them that personal preferences are suited. The choice of snails is of secondary
gastronomic importance. For instance, in the case of a dainty
dish, the big Bourguignon is preferable to the little grey kind
because the shell is thicker and may be left to simmer in its
sauce for a long time without danger of cracking.

"Apart from this, it is all a question of personal taste. Both
methods of cooking are delicious. These, however, are not
the only ways of preparing snails, which you must remember
are essential to *aïoli* (garlic and oil sauce).

"It is in the south of France that one finds the most varied
snail-recipes; there, for instance, they serve them with *sauce
piquante*, tomato sauce and with *sauce verte froide*. At Mont-
pellier, nuts and pounded cracknels are added, together with
a great variety of vegetables and herbs chopped fine, such as
lettuce, chicory, chervil, celery, marjoram and basil; elsewhere just a plain vinegar sauce is preferred. In Languedoc,
where goose-fat is widely used, snails are prepared with the
following sauce:

"You take a fair amount of goose-fat, a large slice of fresh
ham cut in dice—the Languedoc housewives affirm that each
snail must have its bit of ham—an onion chopped small, and
some garlic and parsley also chopped. When this mixture has
been browned you add three or four tablespoons of flour and
stir briskly until it has turned a golden colour. Sprinkle salt
and pepper sparingly before adding the remaining ingredients,
which consist of four or five cloves, a little grated nutmeg,
some juniper leaves, two sliced lemons, and a generous pinch
of saffron. Leave the whole to boil for some minutes.

"Delectable as snails are, people who are lucky enough to live in the country find that the pleasure of eating them is only complete when they have gathered the snails themselves. Few rural delights can compete with that of running through the wet grass, after spring showers, or in the summer after a thunderstorm, in quest of the plump snails. They make their way through shivering grass-blades, or string out across the soft clay like fishing boats leaving port, followed by a silvery wake.

"In catching snails which one will cook oneself, one experiences the joy of the hunter who stalks his prey, anticipating stew, and that of the fisherman casting his line, with *matelote* before his mind's eye."[1]

GARLIC BUTTER FOR SNAILS (for 50 snails)

7 ozs. butter, 1 or 2 cloves of garlic, handful of very fresh parsley, salt, pepper, pinch nutmeg.

Chop the parsley very finely indeed. Pound the garlic in a mortar, removing any shreds and leaving only the oil of the garlic. Put the butter into the mortar and work it so that the garlic impregnates it completely, and then add the parsley, which should also be thoroughly worked in and evenly distributed, then add a very little salt, pepper and nutmeg.

Sometimes a shallot and a few mushrooms, cooked a minute in butter and chopped with the parsley, are added.

The snails which can be bought in tins, with shells in a separate packet, are quite good. It is really the garlic butter which counts. (Always use this butter when it is absolutely freshly made. The garlic very quickly turns the butter rancid, which is the reason that snails bought ready filled at *charcuteries* are not always satisfactory.)

[1] *The Happy Glutton*, by Alin Laubreaux, translated by Naomi Walford.

To prepare the snails, put one into each shell, and fill it up completely with the prepared butter. The snails are then heated in the oven for a few minutes. On no account must the shells turn over during the cooking or all the butter will run out. The French use special dishes with a little compartment for each snail. Failing these, use little metal or china egg dishes filled with mashed potato in which the shells can be embedded.

The special dishes, the tongs to hold the snails with and the little forks for extracting them can be bought from Madame Cadec, 27 Greek Street, Soho, W.1.

Fish

A Venetian Breakfast

"BEGIN WITH a Vermouth Amaro in lieu of a cocktail. For hors d'oeuvres have some small crabs cold, mashed up with sauce tartare and a slice or two of *prosciutto crudo* (raw ham), cut as thin as cigarette paper. After this a steaming risotto with *scampi* (somewhat resembling gigantic prawns), some cutlets done in the Bologna style, a thin slice of ham on top and hot parmesan and grated white truffles and *fegato alla veneziana* complete the repast except for a slice of *strachino* cheese. A bottle of Val Policella is exactly suited to this kind of repast and a glass of fine Champagne and of ruby-coloured Alkermes for the lady, if your wife accompanies you, make a good ending.

"The Maître d'Hôtel will be interested in you directly he finds that you know how a man should breakfast."

The Gourmet's Guide to Europe,
by Lt.-Col. Newnham-Davis and Algernon Bastard.
1903.

FRIED SCAMPI

Make a frying batter of 4 ozs. flour, 3 tablespoons of oil or melted butter, three-quarters of a tumbler of tepid water, a pinch of salt, and the beaten white of an egg. Mix the flour and the butter or oil, adding the water gradually, and keeping the batter smooth and liquid. Make it some time before it is needed, and add the white of egg at the last moment.

Dip the *scampi*, or Dublin Bay prawns, into the batter and fry them in boiling-hot oil. Nothing else will produce such a crisp and light crust.

Pile the *scampi* up on a dish garnished with parsley and lemon, and, if you like, serve a sauce *tartare* separately, but they are really best quite plain. Whenever possible, make this dish with *scampi* which have not been previously cooked. Simply cut off the head of the fish, take the tails out of the shells and dip them raw into the batter.

SCALLOPS or COQUILLES SAINT JACQUES

In spite of the instructions given in nearly every cookery book, my own belief is that scallops should not be served in their shells; they tend to dry up when baked in the oven, and however well cooked are inevitably reminiscent of the unpleasant imitations served in bad restaurants—usually flaked cod with a crust of heavy mashed potato.

COQUILLES SAINT JACQUES À LA CRÈME (sufficient for 2 people)

4 scallops, $\frac{1}{4}$ lb. mushrooms, 1 teaspoon tomato purée, 2 egg yolks, 2 tablespoons sherry, 1 large cup cream, 2 ozs. butter, salt, pepper, lemon juice, parsley.

Cut each cleaned scallop in two. Reserve the red part of the fish and put remainder in a small pan with the butter, salt and pepper. Cook gently for 5 minutes.

At the same time sauté the mushrooms in butter in another pan. Add the sherry, the tomato purée and the cooked mushrooms to the scallops, then stir in the cream and egg yolks, taking care not to let the mixture boil. Put in the red pieces of the scallops, which will be cooked in 2 minutes, the finely chopped garlic, the parsley and a little lemon juice.

Serve with triangles of fried bread.

Fried Scallops à la Provençale

Cut the white part of each scallop into two rounds, season with salt, pepper, and lemon juice, dust with flour, and fry them in butter for a few minutes, put in the coral and a little chopped garlic and parsley, and serve with the butter poured over them.

Moules Marinière

There are several versions of moules marinière. Here are three of them.

3 quarts mussels, 1 small onion, 1 clove of garlic, 1 small glass white wine, a small piece celery, parsley.

Put the chopped onion, garlic, and celery into a large pan with the white wine and about 1 pint of water. Add pepper but not salt. Put in the well-cleaned mussels, cover the pan and cook until the shells open. Take out the mussels, keep them hot, and thicken the liquid in which they have cooked with 1 oz. of butter worked with $\frac{1}{2}$ oz. of flour. Pour the sauce over the mussels in a large tureen and sprinkle with parsley. Serve very hot.

To be eaten out of soup plates, with a fork and a soup spoon.

Another way is to prepare the sauce first; make a little white *roux* in the pan with butter, flour, chopped onion, celery, etc., and the white wine, add the water, and put the mussels in when the liquid has the consistency of a thin soup. The mussels can then be served directly they are opened, a great advantage, as they then do not lose their freshness and savour, which they are apt to do if they are reheated. On no account must the sauce be over-thickened, or you will simply have mussels in a white sauce.

Perhaps the most usual way of cooking moules marinière is simply to put the mussels into the pan with the white wine but no water, throw chopped parsley and onion or garlic over them as they are opening and serve as soon as they are all open.

Always serve plenty of French bread with moules marinière.

STUFFED MUSSELS

This recipe was given me by a fisherman in Marseilles, who made them for me on his boat—and most delicious they were.

For the stuffing: 1 large lettuce, 1 onion, garlic, parsley, 3 ozs. cooked liver or chopped salami sausage.

Boil the lettuce for 10 minutes, drain well and chop finely with the onion, garlic, parsley and meat. Open the mussels, which should be the large ones, without separating the two shells. Stuff with a teaspoon of the mixture and tie up each mussel immediately with string. Cook them slowly for 20 minutes in a tomato sauce to which a glass of white wine has been added. Remove the string and serve hot in the sauce.

The above quantity of stuffing is sufficient for 18 large mussels.

MOULES AU CITRON

    2 ozs. carrots, 2 ozs. butter, ½ oz. shallot, 1 tablespoon flour,
4 pints mussels, 2 lemons, bouquet garni, salt and pepper.

    Clean the mussels. Chop the carrot and shallot and cook
them in a little of the butter, adding salt, pepper and the herbs.
Add the juice of the lemons, then put in the mussels. Cook
them rapidly, shaking the pan. As soon as they open, they
are cooked. Keep them hot. In another pan put the flour and
½ oz. of butter, and when the flour is beginning to turn golden
pour on the stock from the mussels, through a fine sieve.
Cook another minute or two, finish the sauce with the rest
of the butter.

    Serve the mussels on the half shells heaped up in a dish,
and the sauce separately.

CRAYFISH[1] WITH SAUCE PROVENÇALE

    Make a parsley butter with 2 cloves of garlic pounded, to
which you add a ¼ lb. of butter and a handful of chopped
parsley.

    Take 1 lb. of crayfish tails out of their shells and put them
in a fireproof dish with salt and pepper. Cover them with
the parsley butter and place in a hot oven for 10 minutes.

SPAGHETTI WITH MUSSELS

    Cook mussels and *clovisses* (small clams)[2] as for *Moules
Marinière*. Shell them. Add the stock to the water boiling for
spaghetti. Add stoned black olives. When the spaghetti is
cooked, drain it, heat the mussels 1 minute in the liquid which
has come out of their shells, pour on to the spaghetti, sprinkle
with chopped parsley and serve with grated Parmesan cheese.

    [1] By crayfish I mean not river crayfish which are almost unobtainable in England,
but sea crayfish, also called crawfish, or in French *langouste*.
    [2] In England cockles could be used instead.

Lobster à l'Enfant Prodigue[1]

"Get a couple of lobsters and cut them down the back, leaving the shell of the heads intact; remove the non-edible portions and break the claws. Put the whole into a stewpan with a bottle of champagne (sweet champagne will do), 4 spoonfuls fine salad oil, 3 cloves of garlic, a sprig of basil and a lemon sliced and freed from peel and pips, salt, pepper, chervil, parsley, a few mushrooms and 2 lbs. truffles (whole).

When done, take out the sweet herbs, cut off the heads of the lobsters, place them erect in the middle of the dish and dispose the other pieces round. Impale the truffles on the antennæ of the lobsters, pour the sauce over, and, above all, serve Clos de Vougeot, Chambertin or Côte Rôtie with this dish."

Lobster Romesco

Prepare the following sauce: grill or roast in the oven 2 tomatoes, a fresh red chilli, several unpeeled cloves of garlic, up to as much as a whole head. Skin the tomatoes and garlic which should be fairly soft by the time it has been roasted a few minutes but must not be charred, and also discard the skin and seeds of the chilli. Pound all ingredients together in a mortar. Add salt and 1 level dessertspoon of paprika (this is a Spanish recipe, and in Spain they use pimentòn, which is the Spanish version of paprika). The sauce should be quite thick. Now add 4 or 5 tablespoons olive oil and a little vinegar. Press the sauce through a fine sieve. It should be bright red and quite smooth.

Serve it in a bowl with hot or cold boiled lobster, or with any other fish you please.

[1] This recipe is from *Spons Household Manual*, published in the 'eighties.

RAGOÛT OF SHELL FISH

12 cooked *scampi* or Dublin Bay prawns, 2 quarts mussels, 6 scallops, ¼ lb. mushrooms, ½ pint white wine, 1 tablespoon concentrated tomato purée, 1 tablespoon flour, 1 onion, 4 cloves of garlic, seasoning, herbs, 1 dessertspoon sugar, 1 oz. butter, parsley.

First of all split the *scampi* tails in half, retaining 6 halves in their shells for the garnish. From the remaining shells remove the flesh and cut it into fairly large pieces.

In a fairly deep pan sauté a sliced onion in butter, when golden add the tomato purée, the chopped garlic, salt, pepper, and the sugar and herbs. Simmer 5 minutes. Stir in the flour. When thick pour over the heated wine, and cook this sauce for 15 to 20 minutes. Add the flesh of the *scampi*, the sliced mushrooms, the scallops cut into two rounds each, and the mussels, which should have been very carefully cleaned. Turn up the flame and cook until the mussels have opened. At the last minute add the reserved *scampi* in their shells. Turn into a tureen or deep dish, squeeze over a little lemon, sprinkle with parsley, and serve very hot, in soup plates.

The black shells of the mussels and the pink of the prawns make a very decorative dish. The tails of large crawfish (*langouste*) can be used instead of the Dublin Bay prawns or *scampi*, but of course fewer will be needed, and they can be cut into four or six pieces each.

Enough for 4 to 6 people as a first course.

SEA AND FRESHWATER FISH

The Fish of the Côte Niçoise

"NICE IS NOT without variety of fish; though they are not counted so good in their kinds as those of the ocean. Soals, and flat-fish in general, are scarce. Here are some mullets, both grey and red. We sometimes see the dory, which is called *St. Pierre*; with rock-fish, bonita, and mackerel. The gurnard appears pretty often; and there is plenty of a kind of large whiting, which eats pretty well, but has not the delicacy of that which is caught on our coast. One of the best fish of this country is called *Le Loup*, about two or three pounds in weight; white, firm, and well-flavoured. Another, no-way inferior to it, is the *Moustel*, about the same size; of a dark-grey colour, and short blunt snout; growing thinner and flatter from the shoulders downwards, so as to resemble an eel at the tail. This cannot be the *mustela* of the antients, which is supposed to be the sea lamprey. Here too are found the *vyvre*, or, as we call it, weaver; remarkable for its long, sharp spines, so dangerous to the fingers of the fisherman. We have abundance of the *sæpia*, or cuttle-fish, of which the people in this country make a delicate ragoût; as also of the *polype de mer*, which is an ugly animal, with long feelers, like tails, which they often wind about the legs of the fishermen. They are stewed with onions, and eat something like cow-heel. The market sometimes affords the *écrevisse de mer*, which is a lobster without claws, of a sweetish taste; and there are a few rock oysters, very small and very rank. Sometimes the fishermen find under water, pieces of a very hard cement, like plaister of Paris, which contain a kind of muscle, called *la datte*, from its resemblance to a date. These petrifications are commonly of a triangular form, and may weigh about twelve or fifteen pounds each; and one of them may contain a dozen of these muscles, which have nothing extraordinary in the taste or flavour, though extremely curious, as found alive and juicy in the heart of a rock, almost as hard as marble, without any visible communication with the air or water. I take it for granted, however, that the inclosing cement is porous, and admits the finer parts of the surrounding fluid. In order to reach the muscles, this cement must be broke with large hammers, and it may be truly said, the kernal is not worth the trouble of cracking the shell.[1] Among the fish of this country there is a very ugly animal of the eel species, which might pass for a serpent; it is of a dusky, black colour, marked with spots of yellow, about eighteen inches, or two feet long. The Italians call it *murena*; but whether it is the fish which had the same name among the antient Romans, I cannot pretend to determine. The antient murena was counted a great delicacy, and was kept in ponds for extraordinary occasions. Julius Caesar borrowed six thousand for one entertainment;

[1] These are found in great plenty at *Ancona* and other parts of the *Adriatic*, where they go by the name of Bollani, as we are informed by *Keysler*.

but I imagined this was the river lamprey. The murena of this
country is in no esteem, and only eaten by the poor people.
Craw-fish and trout are rarely found in the rivers among the
mountains. The sword-fish is much esteemed in Nice, and
called *l'empereur*, about six or seven feet long; but I have
never seen it.[1] They are very scarce; and when taken, are
generally concealed, because the head belongs to the com-
mandant, who has likewise the privilege of buying the best
fish at a very low price. For which reason, the choice pieces
are concealed by the fishermen, and sent privately to Piedmont
or Genoa. But, the chief fisheries on this coast are of the
sardines, anchovies, and tunny. These are taken in small
quantities all the year; but spring and summer is the season
when they mostly abound. In June and July a fleet of about
fifty fishing-boats puts to sea every evening about eight o'clock,
and catches anchovies in immense quantities. One small boat
sometimes takes in one night twenty-five rup, amounting to
six hundred weight; but it must be observed, that the pound
here, as well as in other parts of Italy, consists but of twelve
ounces. Anchovies, besides their making a considerable article
in the commerce of Nice, are a great resource in all families.
The noblesse and burgeois sup on sallad and anchovies, which
are eaten on all their meagre days. The fishermen and mariners
all along this coast have scarce any other food but dry bread,
with a few pickled anchovies; and when the fish is eaten, they
rub their crusts with the brine. Nothing can be more delicious
than fresh anchovies fried in oil; I prefer them to the smelts
of the Thames. I need not mention that the sardines and
anchovies are caught in nets; salted, barrelled and exported
into all the different kingdoms and states of Europe. The

---

[1] Since I wrote the above letter, I have eaten several times of this fish, which is as
white as the finest veal, and extremely delicate. The emperor associates with the tunny
fish and is always taken in their company.

sardines, however, are largest and fittest in the month of September. A company of adventurers have farmed the tunny-fishery of the king, for six years; a monopoly, for which they pay about three thousand pounds sterling. They are at a very considerable expense for nets, boats, and attendance. Their nets are disposed in a very curious manner across the small bay of St. Hospice, in this neighbourhood, where the fish chiefly resort. They are never removed, except in the winter, and when they want repair; but there are avenues for the fish to enter, and pass, from one inclosure to another. There is a man in a boat, who constantly keeps watch. When he perceives they are fairly entered, he has a method of shutting all the passes, and confining the fish to one apartment of the net, which is lifted up into the boat until the prisoners are taken and secured. The tunny-fish generally runs from fifty to one hundred weight; but some of them are much larger. They are immediately gutted, boiled, and cut in slices. The guts and head afford oil; the slices are partly dried, to be eaten occasionally with oil and vinegar, or barrelled up in oil, to be exported. It is counted a delicacy in Italy and Piedmont, and tastes not unlike sturgeon. The famous pickle of the ancients, called *garum*, was made of the gills and blood of the tunny or thynnus. There is a much more considerable fishery of it in Sardinia, where it is said to employ four hundred persons; but this belongs to the duc de St. Pierre. In the neighbourhood of Villa Franca, there are people always employed in fishing for coral and sponge, which grow adhering to the rocks under water. Their methods do not savour much of ingenuity. For the coral, they lower down a swab, composed of what is called spunyarn on board our ships of war, hanging in distinct threads, and sunk by means of a great weight, which, striking against the coral in its descent, disengages it from the rocks; and some of the pieces being intangled among the threads of the swab, are brought up with it above water. The sponge is got by means of a cross-stick, fitted with hooks, which being lowered down, fastens upon it, and tears it from the rocks. In some parts of the Adriatic and Archipelago, these substances are gathered by divers, who can remain five minutes below water. But I will not detain you one minute longer; though I must observe, that there is plenty of fine samphire growing along all these rocks, neglected and unknown."

Travels Through France and Italy,
by Tobias Smollett

BOUILLABAISSE

The recipe for Bouillabaisse is already widely known, but as this is a book of Mediterranean cookery it must be included here, and I give the one from M. Reboul's *La Cuisinière Provençale:*

"The serving of Bouillabaisse as it is done at Marseille, under perfect conditions, requires at least seven or eight guests. The reason is this: as the preparation requires a large variety of so-called rock fish, it is as well to make it as lavishly as possible in order to use as many different kinds as are available. Several of these fish have a characteristic taste, a unique perfume. It is upon the combination of all these different tastes that the success of the operation depends. One can, it is true, make a passable Bouillabaisse with three or four kinds of fish, but the truth of the foregoing observation will be generally agreed upon.

"To return to the operation. Having obtained the required fish such as crawfish, *rascasse* (this is a red spiny fish found only in the Mediterranean, it has no English equivalent), gurnet, weever, *roucaou*, John Dory, monk or angler fish,

conger eel, whiting, bass, crab, etc., clean and scale them.
Cut them in thick slices and put them on two different dishes;
one for the firm fish—crawfish, *rascasse*, weever, gurnet,
angler fish, crab; the other for the soft fish—bass, *roucaou*,
John Dory, whiting.

"Into a saucepan put three sliced onions, four crushed cloves
of garlic, two peeled tomatoes, a branch of thyme, of fennel,
and of parsley, a bay leaf and a piece of orange peel; arrange
on the top the firm fish, pour over them half a glass of oil and
well cover it all with boiling water. Season with salt, pepper,
and saffron, and put on to a very rapid fire. The saucepan
should be half in the fire—that is to say it should be half surrounded by the flames. When it has been boiling five minutes
add the soft fish. Continue boiling rapidly for another five
minutes, making ten minutes from the time it first came to
the boil. Remove from the fire, pour the liquid on slices of
bread half an inch thick arranged on a deep dish. On another
platter arrange the fish. Sprinkle with chopped parsley and
serve both together.

"It should be noted that the cooking is done very quickly,
it is one of the essential factors; in this way the oil amalgamates
with the *bouillon* and produces a sauce which is perfectly
amalgamated, otherwise it would separate from the liquid and
swim on the surface, which is not very appetising.

"We have rather prolonged this article but this demonstra-
tion was necessary; out of ten cookery books nine will give
it incorrectly; when for example you are told to put all the
fish into the pan together and cook rapidly for 15 minutes, it
is impossible that a piece of John Dory or a slice of whiting
which have been boiling rapidly for a quarter of an hour will
still be presentable. Inevitably, they will be reduced to pulp,
this fish being very delicate.

"To make a rich Bouillabaisse one can first prepare a fish

bouillon with the heads of the fish which are to go into the
Bouillabaisse, a few small rock fish, two tomatoes, two leeks,
and two cloves of garlic. Strain the *bouillon* and use it for
the Bouillabaisse in place of the water.

"Quite a passable Bouillabaisse can be made with fresh-
water fish, such as eels, large perch, medium-sized pike, gray-
ling or trout, and eel-pout; a dozen prawns can take the
place of crawfish. This will not of course be comparable with
the authentic Bouillabaisse of the Mediterranean, but at least
it will conjure up memories . . ."

Fish Plakí

This is a typical Greek way of cooking fish and appears
over and over again in different forms.

Wash a large fish, such as bream, chicken turbot, or John
Dory. Sprinkle with pepper and salt and lemon juice, and put
in a baking dish. Fry some onions, garlic and plenty of parsley
in olive oil; when the onions are soft add some peeled tomatoes.
Fry gently for a few minutes, add a little water, simmer for
a few minutes longer, cover the fish with this mixture, add a
glass of white wine, some more sliced tomatoes and thinly
sliced lemon. Put in a moderate oven and cook about
45 minutes or longer if the fish is large.

Red Mullet, Grilled

Grill the cleaned mullets (do not remove the liver) with
a little olive oil and serve them with butter into which you
have mixed some chopped fennel and a drop of lemon juice.

Cold Red Mullet Niçoise

Brown the fish in olive oil; season with salt and pepper
and put them in a fireproof dish. Arrange round them some

roughly chopped tomatoes, a little minced onion, half a dozen stoned black olives and a chopped clove of garlic. Pour over half a glass of white wine. Cover the dish and cook in a moderate oven. When they are cold, sprinkle over some parsley and arrange a few slices of oranges along the fish.

Mulet au Vin Blanc

The grey mullet (carefully cleaned) is stuffed with a mixture of fennel, parsley, chopped garlic and breadcrumbs.

Place it on a bed of sliced onions already melted in olive oil, add a glass of white wine, and cover with breadcrumbs. Cook in the oven.

Beignets de Sardines

Bone some fresh sardines, flatten them out and dip them in frying batter in which you have crushed a small piece of garlic.

Fry in hot oil.

Maquereaux aux Petits Pois

3 or 4 mackerel, 1 onion, 1 tablespoon olive oil, 1 tablespoon tomato purée, 2 cloves of garlic, bay leaf, fennel, thyme, parsley, 2½ lbs. of fresh peas.

Chop the onion finely and sauté it in a braising pan with the olive oil. As soon as it turns golden, add the tomato purée, give it a stir, and put in the garlic and the herbs. Pour over 2½ pints of boiling water, season with salt, pepper, and a pinch of saffron, and put in the peas.

When they are half cooked, add 3 or 4 mackerel cut in pieces, 2 or 3 according to their size. Bring them to the boil, and when the peas and the mackerel are cooked, take out the mackerel and put them on the serving dish.

In another dish arrange some slices of bread, pour over them the peas and the sauce, and serve them all together.

Anguilla in Tiella al Piselli

This is an Italian dish of eel cooked in a frying pan with green peas. Cut the eel into thick slices, and put it into the pan with about ¼ lb. of bacon cut into squares, and cook until the eel is lightly browned; then add 1½ lbs. of shelled green peas, raw, just cover with a thin tomato sauce, season with salt, pepper and sugar, and simmer until the peas are done.

Truite Sauce aux Noix

Put ½ lb. of peeled walnuts through a mincing machine, then pound them in the mortar with a little salt, adding gradually a cup of water and a little vinegar, stirring all the time as for a mayonnaise.

Serve the sauce with a cold trout which has been simply poached in a *court-bouillon*.

Brandade de Morue

Another triumph of Provençal cooking, designed to abate the rigours of the Friday fast.

Take some good salt cod, about 3 lbs. for 6 people, which has been soaked in cold water for 12 hours. Clean it well and put it into a pan of cold water; cover, and as soon as it comes to the boil remove from the fire. Carefully remove all the bones, and put the pieces into a pan in which you have already crushed up a clove of garlic and placed over a very low flame. In 2 other small saucepans have some milk and some olive oil, both keeping warm, but not hot. You now add the oil and the milk alternately to the fish, spoon by spoon, stirring hard the whole time, with a wooden spoon, and crushing the cod against the sides of the pan. (Hence the name Brandade

—*branler*—to crush or break.) When the whole mixture has attained the appearance of a thick cream the operation is finished; it should be observed however that all three ingredients must be kept merely tepid, or the oil will disintegrate and ruin the whole preparation. Also the stirring and breaking of the cod must be done with considerable energy: some people prefer to pound the cod in a mortar previous to adding the oil and the milk.

Brandade can be served hot or cold, if hot in a *vol au vent* or little pâtés, garnished with a few slices of truffle or simply with triangles of fried bread.

Raïto

Raïto is one of the traditional dishes of Christmas Eve in Provence.

It is a ragoût made of onions, tomatoes, garlic, pounded walnuts, thyme, rosemary, fennel, parsley, bay leaves, red wine, capers and black olives, all simmered in olive oil.

In this sauce either dried salt cod or eels are cooked.

Grillade au Fenouil

This famous Provençal dish is usually made with a *loup de mer*, a kind of sea bass, one of the best fishes of the Mediterranean. A red mullet can be cooked in the same way. The cleaned fish is scored across twice on each side and coated with olive oil or melted butter. Lay a bed of dried fennel stalks in the grilling pan, put the fish on the grid, and grill it, turning it over two or three times. When it is cooked put the fennel underneath the fish in a fireproof serving dish; warm some Armagnac or brandy in a ladle, set light to it, and pour it over the fish. The fennel will catch fire, and give off a fine aromatic scent which flavours the fish.

Tunny Fish

The consistency of fresh tunny fish is not unlike that of veal. It does not often appear in England, although I have seen it in the shops once or twice. In the south of France it is plentiful and very cheap.

The best way to cook it is to cut it into thick slices, like a salmon steak, and sauté it in oil or butter, adding half-way through the cooking 2 or 3 tomatoes, chopped, a handful of cut parsley, and a small glass of wine, either red or white.

Serve plainly cooked potatoes with it.

Bourride

For anyone who likes garlic this is perhaps the best fish dish of Provence, to my taste much superior to the Bouillabaisse or any of the Italian *Zuppe di Pesce*.

Bourride is usually made with a variety of large Mediterranean fish, such as *loup de mer* (bass), *daurade* (sea bream), *baudroie* (angler or frog fish), *mulet* (grey mullet), but is successful with almost any white fish, and one variety alone will do. Grey mullet, a despised fish, but very good when properly treated, is excellent for a bourride, or whiting, rock salmon, gurnard, John Dory, even fresh sardines will do.

Whatever fish is used is poached in a *court bouillon* previously prepared from an onion, bayleaf, lemon peel, fennel, the heads of the fish, salt and pepper all simmered together in water, with the addition of a little white wine or vinegar, for about 15 minutes. Leave this to cool, and strain before putting in the fish and bringing them very gently to the boil, and then just simmering until they are done.

Have ready an aïoli (p. 193) made from at least 2 yolks of eggs and about ½ pint of olive oil. Have also ready at least two slices of French bread for each person, either toasted or baked in the oven (the second method is easier to manage, with two or three other operations going on at the same time). When the fish is all but ready put half the prepared aïoli into the top half of a double pan; stir into it the beaten yolks of 4 eggs, then a ladleful of the strained *court bouillon* in which the fish are cooking. Cook over very gentle heat, whisking all the time until the sauce is thick and frothy. Pour this sauce over the prepared toast in the heated serving dish, arrange the strained fish on the top, and serve quickly, with the reserved half of the aïoli separately.

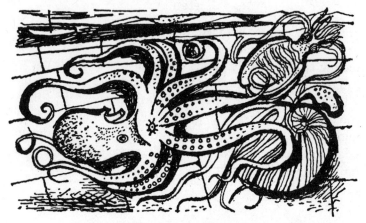

OCTOPUS AND CUTTLEFISH

A Greek Feast

"... WE LEARNT what is meant by a 'Feast of the Church'.

"The tables were disposed up, across, and down, in the form of a rectangle missing one end. At them sat a company of 60 or 70. In the middle, at the top, presided the bishop who had conducted last night's ceremony, spare and dignified, whose diocese in Asia Minor had been annihilated in the war. By his side was Evlogios, handsomest monk on the Mountain, with his flowing iron beard and broadly chiselled aquiline features. The news had reached us at Vatopedi that he had just been appointed to the archbishopric of Tirana, and would thereby become Primate of Albania, an important post for a man of 47. But he was not certain, he said, whether he wished to exchange the idyll of Athonite existency for the turmoil of that uncouth political fiction.

"The courses began with soup, and continued, four in succession, with octopus. There was octopus cooked amid segments of the garlic bulb, and octopus, more subtly delicate perhaps, alone. There was octopus with beans; and there was octopus again alone but for a hot gravy. Then followed roes, hard and round, an inch in diameter and three long. These were garnished with a yellow mayonnaise of beaten caviare. Their advent was pregnant with event; for, unaware of their resilience, I plunged my knife upon one, to see it fly over my elbow on to the spotless sheen of the father next me. He was ruffled. But, drying the spots with my napkin till they were invisible, I bathed him with such tears of remorse that he was restored to calm. The waiting, directed by Boniface, was faultless. And of the plenty of wine it is unnecessary to speak.

"The climax was reached with snails. These, nine to a dozen on each plate, were served with the tops knocked off. They had to be wheedled therefore, not, as in the West, from the snail's own door, but by an adroit twist of the fork from above. Boniface, all those around us, and even Evlogios from his vantage-point, were so concerned lest we should fail fully to appreciate them, that we were at pains to acquire the proper motion. Delicious they were. Meanwhile we drank as though it were ten at night instead of in the morning. All did the same. The conviviality grew. We laughed and shouted and toasted one another across the tables. Then, headed by Evlogios and the bishop, the assembled company took each an empty shell between thumb and forefinger and blew a blast of whistles, as though ten thousand milk-boys were competing for a prize.

"Dessert of apples and grapes was succeeded by coffee and the lighter wine. The sun was in the top of the heavens when, having bidden regretful farewell to Boniface, the fierce Epitropos, and all the others, we started out for Caries."

The Station,
by Robert Byron

Octopus

The octopus sounds alarming to those who have not travelled in the Mediterranean; it is in fact an excellent dish when properly prepared, rich and with a reminiscence of lobster.

In Greece and Cyprus the large octopuses are dried in the sun; the tentacles are cut into small pieces, grilled over a charcoal fire and served with your apéritif.

To cook them fresh the large ones must be carefully cleaned, the ink-bag removed (unless they are to be cooked in their own ink, which makes a rich black sauce, with a very strong flavour), and left in running water for some minutes, then beaten like a steak (in fact I have seen the Greeks bashing them against a rock), for they can be very tough. Then cut off the tentacles and cut the body into strips about the same size. Blanch them in boiling water, drain them and peel off the skin. The pieces are then put in an earthenware casserole with 2 or 3 large onions cut up, garlic, a branch of thyme, salt and pepper, and 2 or 3 tablespoons of tomato pulp, and covered with red wine. Simmer very slowly for 4 or 5 hours.

There are two London fishmongers, Richards and Hitchcock's, both in Brewer Street, Soho, who sell fresh squid, but although octopus are found in great quantities in northern waters I have never seen them for sale in England, so this recipe can be used equally well for squid or ink fish.

Grilled Calamári (cuttlefish, inkfish, squid)

Turn the pocket-like part of the fish inside out, clean under a running tap, remove the ink-bag. Season the fish with salt, pepper, lemon juice and marjoram, sprinkle with oil and put them under the grill for about 10 or 15 minutes. Served cold and cut into strips crossways these creatures make a good hors d'œuvre.

They can also be stuffed, with spinach or with savoury rice, and cooked *en ragoût*, with a wine or tomato sauce. Cut into fairly large pieces, they are often added to a *paëlla* or *risotto aux fruits de mer*.

Very small inkfish, in France *Suppions*, in Italy *Calamaretti*, in Greece *Calamaraka*, are a great delicacy. They are usually dipped in batter, fried crisp in oil and served with lemon.

CIVET OF INKFISH

3 lbs. inkfish, 3 lbs. onions, red wine, pine-nuts or almonds.

Clean the inkfish, keep the ink and mix it with a glass of dry red wine. Cut the inkfish small, and let them soak overnight in red wine. Next day cut the onions in slices and melt them in a mixture of oil and butter. Take them out, and put in the inkfish and let them take colour. Replace the onions, and a handful of pine-nut kernels or of blanched and split almonds. Add the ink with the wine, and the wine of the marinade. Add water if required. Stew till soft.

Meat

See also chapter on Cold Food

"VAOUR IS a village I don't know how many miles off Fenay-rols. I only know that we went there, and it lies eleven kilo-metres from a railway station. The Hôtel du Nord at Vaour is illustrious throughout the region for its cookery. People travel vast distances uphill in order to enjoy it. We did. We arrived at eleven o'clock and lunch was just ending. The land-lord and landlady in the kitchen said that we were unfortun-ately too late for a proper meal, but they would see what they could do for us. Here is what they did for us:

> Soupe
> Jambon du pays
> Confit d'oie
> Omelette nature
> Civet de lièvre
> Ris de veau blanquette
> Perdreau rôti
> Fromage Roquefort
> Fromage Cantal
> Confiture de cerise
> Poires
> Figues.

"We ate everything; every dish was really distinguished. I rank this meal with a meal that I once ate at the Etoile restaurant at Brussels, once, if not still, the finest restaurant in the world—and about the size of, say, Gow's in the Strand.

"In addition, there were three wines, a *vin blanc ordinaire,* a *vin rouge ordinaire*, and a fine wine to finish with. The fine wine was fine.

"The total bill, for two persons, was seven francs."

Things that Have Interested Me,
by Arnold Bennett

VEAL

PAUPIETTES DE VEAU CLÉMENTINE

1 lb. lean veal, capers, juice and peel of half a lemon, ¼ lb. smoked bacon, flour, white wine, herbs, 1 onion, butter.

Have the veal cut in very thin slices. On each small slice of veal squeeze lemon juice and sprinkle pepper and salt. Lay on top of each slice a small piece of smoked bacon. Roll and tie with thread. Roll the paupiettes in flour and fry in butter with the sliced onion, until brown. Add water, a glass of white wine, the lemon peel, capers and herbs, cover the casserole and cook slowly for 45 minutes. Before serving remove the thread from the paupiettes and strain the sauce.

BOCCONCINE

Thin slices of veal (as for escalopes), raw ham or prosciutto, fried bread, Gruyère cheese, egg and breadcrumbs.

The veal must be cut in very thin, fairly small slices. On each piece of seasoned veal put a piece of raw ham and then a piece of Gruyère cheese. Roll and tie with string. Roll in egg and breadcrumbs, fry in butter until golden. When cooked, the Gruyère cheese should be just melting. Remove the string and serve each one on a slice of fried bread.

NORMAN'S RECIPE

Thin escalopes of veal, raw ham or *prosciutto*, fresh sage leaves, fresh tomato sauce, flour, butter.

On each piece of seasoned veal place a slice of raw ham the same size, and then 1 leaf of sage. Roll and tie with thread. Roll in flour and fry them in butter. Finish cooking them in a well seasoned tomato sauce (about 15 minutes).

OSSO BUCO

Saw shin of veal into about 6 thick pieces, leaving the marrow bone in the centre of the veal. Fry some onions in a wide, shallow braising pan. Pepper and salt the veal, roll in flour and brown in the same pan. Add a carrot, bay leaf, celery, garlic, thyme, basil and a piece of lemon peel, and white wine, a little stock, and enough tomato purée to come to the top of the pieces of meat but not to cover them. Cook very slowly for about 4 hours, until the meat is almost coming off the bones. Ten minutes before serving, sprinkle the osso buco with finely chopped celery and lemon peel. Be sure to keep the pieces of meat upright during the cooking, or the marrow in the bones will fall out. Serve a plain risotto as an accompaniment.

CÔTES DE VEAU FOYOT

For 4 good cutlets of veal put about 4 ozs. of chopped onions into a pan with a little butter and let them cook slowly until they are golden, then add a wineglass of white wine and the same amount of brown stock. Season the cutlets with salt and pepper, roll them in grated Parmesan or Gruyère cheese and then in breadcrumbs. Now butter a fireproof dish, put in a layer of breadcrumbs, then the cutlets, then the onion mixture. Cook uncovered in a very slow oven for about 1½ hours, adding a little stock from time to time. Serve with a dish of fresh green peas.

LAMB AND MUTTON

The Ideal Cuisine

" 'YOU ARE quite right,' the Count was saying to Mr. Heard.
'The ideal cuisine should display an individual character; it
should offer a menu judiciously chosen from the kitchen-
workshops of the most diverse lands and peoples—a menu
reflecting the master's alert and fastidious taste. Is there anything better, for instance, than a genuine Turkish pilaff? The
Poles and Spaniards, too, have some notable culinary creations.
And if I were able to carry out my ideas on this point I would
certainly add to my list of dishes a few of those strange Oriental
confections which Mr. Keith has successfully taught his Italian
chef. There is suggestion about them; they conjure up visions
of that rich and glowing East which I would give many years
of my remaining life to see.' "

South Wind,
by Norman Douglas

Gigot à la Provençale

A recipe from an old French cookery book which I have left in its original French; as the author rather severely remarks, this dish is supportable only to those who are accustomed to the cooking of the *Midi*.

"On insère symétriquement dans la partie charnue d'un gigot de moyenne grosseur douze gousses d'ail, et deux fois autant de filets d'anchois bien lavés et employés en guise de lardons. Le gigot ainsi préparé est graissé d'huile et cuit à la broche. Tandis que le gigot est à la broche on épluche d'autre part plein un litre de gousses d'ail qu'on fait blanchir dans l'eau bouillante.

"Elles doivent y être plongées à trois reprises différentes, en changeant l'eau a chaque fois, après quoi, on les laisse refroidir dans l'eau froide, et l'on achève leur cuisson dans une tasse de bouillon. Le gigot étant rôti à point, on dégraisse avec soin le jus qu'il a rendu, on en assaisonne les gousses d'ail, et l'on sert le gigot sur cette garniture.

"Ce mets n'est supportable que pour ceux qui sont habitués à la cuisine du Midi, dans laquelle l'ail fait partie obligée de presque tous les mets."

Arni Souvlákia (lamb on skewers)

Cut a piece of lamb from the leg into inch cubes. Season with salt, pepper, lemon juice and marjoram.[1] Thread the meat onto skewers and grill them. Serve them on a thick bed of parsley, on the skewers, with quarters of lemon.

Eaten on the terrace of a primitive Cretan taverna, flavoured with wood smoke and the mountain herbs, accompanied by the strong red wine of Crete, these kebabs can be the most poetic of foods. Exquisitely simple, they are in fact of Turkish

---

[1] In Greece wild marjoram is used; it is called *rígani* and has a much stronger perfume than our marjoram. *Origanum* means in Greek "the joy of the mountains".

origin, like many Greek dishes, although the Greeks do not always care to admit it.

Mutton or Lamb Kebabs

The unique flavour of these kebabs demands no adornment. They *can* be served on a mound of fried rice, but are best left on the skewers and laid on a thick bed of parsley or watercress.

The lamb or mutton is cut up and seasoned as in the preceding recipe.[1] Put half a tomato on to each skewer, cut side facing the point. Then thread on alternately the squares of meat with pieces of bacon, mushrooms if you like, and thick slices of onion. Sprinkle with salt, pepper, marjoram, and lemon juice, and grill them.

For 6 people allow about 3 lbs. of leg of lamb or mutton, which should provide 2 full skewers for each person.

Lamb on the Bone

In the country districts of Greece, and the islands, the household cooking arrangements are fairly primitive and dishes such as this one are prepared early and sent to the village oven; they emerge deliciously cooked, better than they could ever be in a gas oven, but this method by no means ensures that the food will be served hot. The Greeks in fact prefer their food tepid, and it is useless to argue with them.

Saw a leg of lamb into 4 or 5 pieces, leaving the meat on the bone. Insert a clove of garlic into each piece of meat, season well and sprinkle with rosemary.

Cook in a shallow pan in the oven or over a slow fire, with oil or dripping. About 30 minutes before the meat is done add sliced potatoes and tomatoes. Instead of potatoes, partly

[1] One often sees instructions in cookery books to marinate the meat in wine or vinegar. This is never done in Greece, and would completely ruin the natural beauty of the dish if it were.

cooked rice can be added. In this case, drain off the fat and add plenty of thin tomato purée, which will be absorbed by the rice.

The meat must be very well cooked and almost falling off the bone. Sometimes aubergines cut in half lengthways with the skins left on are added with the potatoes and tomatoes.

Tranche de Mouton à la Catalane

Take a thick slice from a gigot of mutton, put it into a braising pan with a good tablespoon of fat, and fry gently on each side; season with salt and pepper, and place round the meat 20 cloves of garlic[1] and cook for a few more minutes, sprinkle with flour and pour in a cupful of stock or water and a tablespoon of tomato purée.

Simmer until the meat is cooked, adding more stock if it is getting dry. Serve the meat surrounded by the garlic and the sauce poured over.

Kokkorétsi

The insides of a sheep—heart, liver, lungs, kidneys, brains, sweetbreads, everything—are cut into small pieces, heavily seasoned with mountain herbs and lemon and threaded on to skewers.

The intestines of the animal are cleaned and wound round and round the skewers, which are then grilled very slowly on a spit. They are, in fact, a sort of primitive sausage, the intestine on the outside acting as a sausage skin.

Turkish Stuffing for a Whole Roast Sheep

2 cups partly cooked rice, 1 dozen cooked chestnuts, 1 cup currants, 1 cup shelled pistachio nuts, salt, cayenne pepper, 1 teaspoon ground cinnamon, ¼ lb. butter.

[1] The cloves of garlic can be left unpeeled—the skin will come off when they are cooked.

Chop the chestnuts and the pistachio nuts finely, mix with the other ingredients. Melt the butter and cook the stuffing in it gently, stirring until all the ingredients are well amalgamated.

This stuffing can also be used for chicken and turkey.

Gigot de Mouton en Chevreuil (leg of mutton to taste like venison)

A medium leg of mutton, choose it short, not freshly killed and with the fibres close together, and make sure it has no smell of grease. Chop finely a small carrot, a large onion, half a head of celery. Heat in a casserole a wine glass of oil; when it is hot put in the vegetables and brown them lightly. Add ¼ pint of white wine and 2 glasses of wine vinegar. Add 4 or 5 stalks of parsley, 4 large shallots, 2 cloves of garlic, thyme, bay leaf, a good pinch of rosemary, 6 peppercorns, 8 crushed juniper berries, salt. Boil and cook slowly for 30 minutes. Leave to get cold. Remove the skin from the leg of mutton, taking care not to damage the flesh. Lard the surface with 5 or 6 rows of little pieces of bacon, close to each other. Put the leg of mutton into a terrine and pour over the cold marinade. Leave the meat 2 or 3 days in summer, 4 or 5 days in winter. Turn it over with a fork (do not touch with the fingers). Remove any pieces which may be sticking to the meat and wipe thoroughly (important). Put into a roasting dish with melted butter or lard. Start to cook over a very hot fire; this is important, as in a medium oven the meat will boil and not get brown. After it has browned, leave it for 40 or 50 minutes in a good even medium heat and baste frequently.

Serve in a hot dish, surrounded by galettes of pastry and accompanied by a sauce *chevreuil* (see p. 191) and a compote of apples.

FILETS DE MOUTON EN CHEVREUIL (fillets of mutton to taste
like venison)

Take 12 small fillets or *noisettes* of mutton, insert small pieces
of bacon into each and marinade (see Gigot de Mouton en
Chevreuil) for 3 days. To cook them, put them in a casserole
with butter. When they are cooked, serve with a sauce *poivrade*
or any highly seasoned sauce.

Sauce Poivrade

Add to the butter in which the fillets have cooked a good
pinch of ground black pepper, a small glass of wine vinegar
and 2 shallots shredded; reduce this by rapid boiling, and add
2 tablespoons of meat glaze or, failing that, of brown stock,
and half a glass of red wine and reduce again.

BEEF

"Any of us would kill a cow rather than not have beef."
                                        Dr. Johnson

Stiphádo (a Greek ragoût)

Cut 2 lbs. of steak into large pieces. Brown them in oil
with 3 lbs. of small onions and several cloves of garlic. Into
the same pan put ½ pint of thick and highly seasoned tomato
purée and a glass of red wine. Simmer slowly for 4 or 5 hours,
until the meat is very tender and the sauce is reduced almost
to the consistency of jam.

Bœuf à la Mode Italienne

Lard a 3 lb. or 4 lb. piece of beef with cloves of garlic.
Season with salt and pepper, rub with thyme and rosemary
and tie up with pieces of fat bacon. Braise in its own fat in
a deep braising pan or earthenware dish. Add 2 sliced onions,
about ¾ pint of tomato purée, either freshly made, or from 2
tablespoons of concentrated tomato paste thinned with water
or stock, 4 whole carrots, 2 whole turnips, a large piece of

orange peel, a piece of lemon peel and a glass of Burgundy. Cover the pan and simmer very slowly indeed for about 8 hours.

The sauce will have the consistency almost of jam, and the meat should be so soft it will fall apart at a touch.

To serve, cut the carrots and turnips into big strips, sprinkle with fresh parsley and chopped lemon peel and reheat slowly.

To serve cold remove all fat from the sauce, reheat and then leave to cool again.

Bœuf en Daube à la Niçoise

3 lbs. round of beef, 3 cloves of garlic, ½ lb. gammon or bacon, ½ lb. carrots, ½ lb. stoned black olives, 3 tomatoes, herbs. For the marinade: ¼ pint of red wine a coffeecup of olive oil, a small piece of celery, a carrot, 4 shallots, an onion, 3 cloves of garlic, peppercorns, herbs, salt.

Heat the oil in a small pan, put in the sliced onion, shallots, celery, and carrot. Let them simmer a minute or two, add the red wine, peppercorns, garlic, and fresh or dried herbs (bay leaf, thyme, marjoram, or rosemary), and a stalk or two of parsley. Season with a little salt, and simmer the marinade gently for 15–20 minutes. Let it cool before pouring over the meat, which should be left to marinate for at least 12 hours, and should be turned over once or twice.

In an earthenware or other fireproof casserole, into which it will just about fit, put the meat. Arrange the carrots round it, put in fresh herbs and the garlic, put the bacon in one piece on top, and pour over the strained marinade. Cover the pot with greaseproof paper and the lid, and cook in a slow oven (Regulo 3) for 2½ hours. At this stage add the stoned olives and the skinned and chopped tomatoes. Cook another half-hour, and before serving cut the bacon into squares and the meat into good thick slices.

This dish has a really beautiful Southern smell and appearance. Serve with it boiled haricot or flageolet beans, or pasta, or the aïgroissade Toulonnaise (p. 138), and a red Rhône wine.

PEBRONATA DE BŒUF (a Corsican ragoût)

The beef is cut into dice and browned in olive oil. Add white wine, all kinds of herbs and seasoning, and simmer very slowly.

When it is nearly cooked add the following pebronata sauce: a thick tomato purée to which you have added pimentos, onions, garlic, thyme, parsley, pounded juniper berries and red wine.

FILET DE BŒUF FLAMBÉ À L'AVIGNONNAISE

A small thick fillet for each person, a slice of bread for each fillet, butter, brandy, coarsely ground black pepper, garlic, salt.

Rub the fillets over with garlic and roll them in salt and the black pepper. Put a little butter into a thick pan, make it very hot and put in the fillets and let them sizzle until the outsides are very brown. Add a little more butter, and as soon as it has melted drench the steaks in brandy, set it alight and cook another half-minute after the flames have died down.

In the meantime have ready the slices of bread fried in butter. Slip each one under a fillet, and *serve immediately* with the sauce poured over. The whole process takes about 3 minutes.

CULOTTE DE BŒUF AU FOUR

Cover a 2 lb. piece of topside beef with thick pieces of fat bacon, season with salt and herbs and put in a casserole with a glass of white wine. Cover hermetically, seal the lid with paste and cook in the oven 4 or 5 hours. Serve with the sauce.

Filet de Bœuf à l'Amiral

Slice 5 or 6 onions and fry them in dripping; take them out of the pan and add to them 4 or 5 fillets of anchovies chopped, 2 tablespoons of chopped bacon, pepper, thyme, marjoram, parsley and 2 yolks of eggs.

Cut a fillet of beef into slices, but not right through, and between each slice put some of the prepared stuffing. Tie the fillet up and put it in a covered pan with dripping, and bake it slowly in the oven.

PORK

"Cochon.—C'est le roi des animaux immondes; c'est celui dont l'empire est le plus universel, et les qualités les moins contestées: sans lui point de lard, et par conséquent, point de cuisine, sans lui, point de jambons, point de saucissons, point d'andouilles, point de boudins noirs, et par conséquent point de charcutiers.—Ingrats médecins! vous condamnez le cochon; il est, sous le rapport des indigestions, l'un des plus beaux fleurons de votre couronne.—La cochonnaille est beaucoup meilleure à Lyon et à Troyes que partout ailleurs.—Les cuisses et les épaules de cochon ont fait la fortune de deux villes, Mayence et Bayonne. Tout est bon en lui.—Par quel oubli coupable a-t-on pu faire de son nom une injure grossière!"

Calendrier Gastronomique,
by Grimod de la Reynière

Rôti de Porc à la Purée de Pommes

In France a loin or leg of pork is usually sold by the butcher with the rind and some of the fat removed (the French do not set such store by the crackling as we do in England, and the rind is sold separately to enrich stews and soups). This method makes the pork less fat, and also easier to cook. A clove or two of garlic is stuck into the meat, it is seasoned with herbs (marjoram, thyme, or rosemary), and roasted in a rather slow oven. Serve it with a very creamy purée of potatoes, to which should be added, before serving, some of the juice and fat from the roast.

Pork Chops Marinated and Grilled

Strew plenty of fresh herbs, such as fennel, parsley, and marjoram or thyme, chopped with a little garlic, over the pork chops. Season with salt and ground black pepper, and pour over them a little olive oil and lemon juice. Leave them to marinate in this mixture for an hour or two. Grill them and serve with a green salad upon which, instead of dressing, you pour the juices and herbs which have fallen from the meat into the grilling pan.

Filet de Porc aux Pois Nouveaux

For this dish you need a fillet of pork from a young and tender animal. Braise it in a covered pan in bacon fat with onions and a bouquet garni. When it is almost ready, take it out and cut it in slices. Put between each slice a layer of a purée made of fresh green peas which have been cooked with onions and a lettuce heart. Reshape the piece of meat and cover with a well-seasoned béchamel. When ready to serve put a beaten white of egg over the whole and sprinkle with breadcrumbs. Place in the oven until it has risen like a soufflé and is golden brown. (Translated from *Plats Nouveaux*, by Paul Reboux.)

FILET DE PORC EN SANGLIER (pork to taste like wild boar)

3½ lbs. fillet[1] of pork. Soak it for 8 days in a marinade of wine vinegar seasoned with salt, pepper, coriander seeds, juniper berries, 2 cloves of garlic, a branch of thyme, a bay leaf, cloves, a branch of basil, a branch of sage, mint and parsley. Turn the meat each day. Take it out and wipe it. Put it in a very hot oven for the first 15 minutes and leave it to cook 2 hours in a moderate oven. Serve it in a dish surrounded by a purée of chestnuts and accompanied by a sauce *chasseur*.

Strictly a winter dish.

Sauce Chasseur

Reduce the marinade to one-third of its quantity. Make a brown roux with 2 ozs. of butter, 2 ozs. of flour and a glass of stock. Add the marinade and finally the gravy from the roast and if possible 2 soupspoons of fresh cream. Serve very hot.

---

[1] In this, as in the preceding recipe, the fillet means boned loin rather than those little strips of lean meat which are known in England as pork fillets or tenderloins.

THE MEAT of young kid is much appreciated all over the Mediterranean, especially in the more primitive parts such as Corsica and the Greek islands. It is hard to say why there is such a prejudice against this animal in England, and it is only the gastronomically ignorant who, the moment they go abroad, suppose that whatever meat they are eating is disguised horse or goat. The textures of these meats are quite unlike those of veal, beef, or mutton, and there is besides no call for a French or Italian cook to pretend that he is serving mutton when it is in fact goat.

In the same way, foreigners in the Middle East are often heard to complain that they are being served with camel instead of beef. If they had ever eaten camel meat they would soon know the difference.

Young kid is at its best when roasted on a spit over a wood fire, and is also cooked *en ragoût* with red wine, tomatoes, and garlic, or threaded on skewers as for the Greek kebabs, and grilled.

A Corsican way of cooking kid is to stuff a shoulder with a mixture of chopped veal and pork, the liver of the kid, and spinach bound with yolk of egg. The shoulder is roasted and served with *Polenta di Castagne*, a purée of chestnut flour. This chestnut flour is used in all kinds of ways in Corsica, for cakes, pancakes, soups, fritters and sauces.

STRICTLY speaking of course boar counts as game, but as it is rare in England I have included it in the meat section, hoping that the recipe might be tried, as Mr. Norman Douglas suggests, with a saddle of mutton, with venison perhaps, or even with a leg of pork.

SADDLE OF BOAR

"Trim a saddle of boar and give it a good shape; salt and pepper it, and steep it for 12 to 14 hours in one litre of dry white wine, together with the following seasoning:

> 100 grammes chopped onions
> 100 grammes chopped carrots
> 2 heads of garlic
> 1 head of celery cut in slices
> 1 bay leaf
> 2 cloves
> 10 grammes black pepper
> a pinch of parsley and thyme.

"The saddle should be turned at frequent intervals to absorb the ingredients.

"Now braise it in a stewpan over a slow fire together with the above vegetable seasoning, adding 100 grammes of butter. Baste the saddle with the liquor in which it was lying, and, when this is at an end, with *jus de viande*. The operation should take about two hours, according to the size of the saddle. Then remove from the fire and strain through a sieve the liquor in which it was lying.

"The following hot and thick sauce must meanwhile be held in readiness:

"Put 30 grammes of sugar into a saucepan and melt brown over the fire; then add a claret-glass of wine-vinegar and bring to the boil. Now add the above strained liquor, together with 25 grammes of roasted pine nuts, 20 grammes each of dried raisins, candied citron peel cut into small squares, and currants (the latter having previously been soaked in water), and 100 grammes of best powdered chocolate. Stir well over the fire. If not sufficiently thick, a little potato flour should be added.

"Serve both as hot as may be. The saddle must be cut in slices immediately, and the sauce poured over the whole. A single non-assertive vegetable, such as purée of chestnuts or lentils—not mashed potatoes: they have no *cachet*—should be served with this, and a rough red wine will be found to marry well with the rather cloying sauce.

" 'Not a dish for every day,' someone may remark. Assuredly not. The longer one lives, the more one realises that nothing is a dish for every day. And if anybody will take the trouble to dress a saddle of mutton in the same manner, he will be pleasantly surprised at the result. But I fear we shall go on roasting the beast to the end of time."[1]

For the benefit of the adventurous who attempt Mr. Norman Douglas's splendid recipe, his measures can be translated approximately as follows:

1¾ pints wine, 3 ozs. each chopped onion and carrots, ⅓ oz. black pepper, 3 ozs. butter, 1 oz. sugar, just under 1 oz. roasted pine nuts, ⅔ oz. each candied citron peel and currants, 3 ozs. chocolate.

[1] *Birds and Beasts of the Greek Anthology*, by Norman Douglas.

Substantial Dishes

A Portuguese Supper Party

"THE PLAY ended, we hastened back to the palace, and traversing a number of dark vestibules and guard-chambers (all of a snore with jaded equeries) were almost blinded with a blaze of light from the room in which supper was served up. There we found in addition to all the Marialvas, the old marquis only excepted, the Camareira-mor, and five or six other hags of supreme quality, feeding like cormorants upon a variety of high-coloured and high-seasoned dishes. I suppose the keen air from the Tagus, which blows right into the palace-windows, operates as a powerful whet, for I never beheld eaters or eateresses, no, not even our old acquaintance Madame la Presidente at Paris, lay about them with greater intrepidity. To be sure, it was a splendid repast, quite a banquet. We had manjar branco and manjar real, and among other good things a certain preparation of rice and chicken which suited me exactly, and no wonder, for this excellent mess had been just tossed up by Donna Isabel de Castro with her own illustrious hands, in a nice little kitchen adjoining the queen's apartment, in which all the utensils are of solid silver."

The Travel-Diaries of William Beckford of Fonthill,
edited by Guy Chapman

RISOTTO WITH MUSHROOMS

This is a very simple form of risotto and, needless to say, all sorts of things can be added—slices of chicken, sautéd chicken livers, beef marrow. It should also be noted that risotto is made with *Italian* rice, which is a round, absorbent variety; no other will serve the purpose so well, the long Patna type of rice being wasted on this dish, for it is not sufficiently absorbent and makes your risotto tough and brittle, whereas a poor quality or small-grained rice will turn into a pudding.

Take 2 cups of Italian rice, 2 pints of chicken stock, 1 medium onion chopped fine, 2 cloves of garlic, 1 wineglass of oil, $\frac{1}{4}$ lb. of white mushrooms cut into slices. Into a heavy sauté pan put the oil, and as soon as it is warm put in the onion, the garlic and the mushrooms. As soon as the onion begins to brown, add the rice and stir until it takes on a transparent look. This is the moment to start adding the stock, which should be kept just on the boil by the side of the fire. Pour in about 2 cups at a time, and go on stirring, and adding stock each time it has been absorbed. The whole process is done over a low flame, and in about 45 to 50 minutes, the risotto should be ready. It should be creamy, homogeneous, but on no account reduced to porridge. One must be able to *taste* each grain of rice although it is not separated as in a pilaff. Grated Parmesan cheese is served with it, and sometimes stirred in before bringing the risotto to the table. In any case a risotto must be eaten immediately it is ready, and cannot be kept warm in the oven, steamed over a pan of boiling water, or otherwise kept waiting.

RISOTTO AUX FRUITS DE MER

For 4 people you need:

4 or 5 pints mussels, 1 pint prawns, $\frac{1}{2}$ lb. rice, a glass of white wine, 2 shallots or small onions, a clove of garlic, grated cheese, olive oil, black pepper, 2 or 3 tomatoes, and a green or red pimento.

Clean the mussels and put them to cook with 2 pints of water and the white wine, a chopped clove of garlic and shallot, and ground black pepper. When they are open, strain the stock into a basin and leave it while you shell the mussels, and the prawns. Now strain the stock through a muslin, and put it into a pan to heat up. In a heavy pan heat a little olive oil, enough to cover the bottom of the pan, and in it sauté a chopped shallot or onion; add the uncooked rice and stir it round in the oil until it is shiny all over, taking care not to let it stick to the pan; now add a large cupful of the mussel stock, which should be kept simmering on the stove; when the first cupful of stock has been absorbed, add some more; it is not necessary to stir continually, but the pan should be kept on a low flame, and stirred every time more stock is added; as the rice begins to swell and cook, larger quantities of stock can be added and care must be taken that the rice does not stick to the sides of the pan.

In the meantime sauté the tomatoes and the pimento in a little more olive oil, and when the rice is soft add the mussels and the prawns and let them get hot; add this mixture to the risotto only at the last minute, stirring it lightly round. Serve the grated cheese separately, and if you like garnish the dish with a few mussels which have been left in their shells; they make a good decoration.

PAËLLA

Spanish paëlla takes its name from the dish in which it is cooked, and its great characteristic is the diversity of ingredients used and the mixture of all kinds of fish with chicken, or chicken livers. As with a pilaff there is no hard and fast rule for making paëlla; it depends upon what ingredients one has to hand. This recipe and the next are only two of many variations.

2 onions, 4 cloves of garlic, 3 tomatoes, 2 red or green pimentos, 12 black olives, 2 pints of mussels, 1 cup cooked lobster, 1 cup of

any other shell fish available, such as prawns, shrimps, crawfish tails, oysters, or tinned Spanish clams (almejas), or a mixture of two or three of these, 3 teacups (12 ozs.) round-grained rice, a few chicken livers, saffron, olive oil. Cooked octopus or cuttlefish (see p. 70) can also be added. Tinned calamari (inkfish) is quite good for this purpose.

First cook the cleaned mussels in a little olive oil until they open, shell them and strain their liquid. Fry the sliced onions, pimentos, garlic, tomatoes, stoned olives, and chicken livers in oil, then add the lobster, prawns, etc., and keep them warm.

In a large pan heat a coffee-cupful of olive oil, put in the rice and stir it until all the oil is absorbed. Pour over 2 pints of boiling water, add salt and a good pinch of powdered saffron. Cook fairly fast, stirring occasionally, for 12 minutes. Add the liquid from the mussels and cook another 4 minutes or so. It should by now be tender, and have absorbed all the liquid. Add the shell fish, tomatoes, etc., then the mussels, and serve quickly, preferably in the pan in which it has cooked. Enough for 6.

PAËLLA VALENCIANA

Chicken, lean bacon, oil, garlic, tomato, ground paprika, vegetables, snails, eels, rice, saffron, and crayfish.

Method: First select a medium-sized chicken, cut into 14 or 16 pieces, and salt. Put a decilitre (2½ oz.) of good oil into a medium-sized casserole and, when very hot, put the chicken into it and fry lightly, with some pieces of the lean bacon, for five minutes. Then add a small tomato, peeled and cut into pieces, a clove of chopped garlic, French beans, and a couple of leaf artichokes (when beans or artichokes cannot be obtained, green peas can be substituted). Then add a teaspoonful of ground red paprika and 400 grammes (about 13 oz.) of rice, all well fried, and a litre (all but 2 pints) of hot water. When the water is boiling, add a little saffron, eight small pieces of eel and a dozen snails, and salt to taste.

When the rice is half cooked, add two crayfish per person. The rice should be cooked on a medium fire. After two or three minutes, cook on a slow heat for another ten or twelve minutes, which is all that is required to have the rice perfect. If you have an oven, it can be put in the oven to dry, but it is more typical to put the casserole on a small fire for a couple of minutes.

If chicken is unobtainable any kind of game or domestic poultry should be used. But if the flesh is not tender, the paëlla can be cooked as above, except that the rice, previously fried, will not be added until the meat has been cooked for about an hour.

For 4 people.

This recipe came from the Martinez Restaurant in Swallow Street, London, and is reprinted by kind permission of the Wine and Food Society, who originally published it. But I only cut my chicken into 6 or 8 pieces.

Arroz a la Catalana

½ lb. rice, 2–3 ozs. Spanish sausage,[1] 2 ozs. fresh pork, 2 ozs. pork fat, 2 large tomatoes, ½ lb. fresh peas, 2 artichokes, 2 sweet red peppers, a squid, a dozen mussels, a few almonds and pine nuts, 2 cloves of garlic, an onion, saffron, parsley.

Heat the pork fat in a large casserole, and put in the pork and the sausage cut in small pieces, together with the sliced onion. Let them fry a minute or two and add the pimentos, tomatoes, and the squid, all cleaned and cut in slices. Simmer for 15 minutes, add the rice, the peas, the cooked and shelled mussels, the hearts of the artichokes each cut into quarters, the garlic, the almonds and pine nuts, and saffron. Pour over 2 pints of

[1] Chorizos. These can be bought at Gomez Ortega, 74 Old Compton Street, W.1, at E. Parmigiani, opposite, and at delicatessen shops.

boiling water. Let the whole mixture bubble for a few minutes, then lower the heat and cook gently until the rice is tender. Serve in the pan in which it was cooked, garnished with parsley.

GENOESE RICE

½ lb. rice, an onion, olive oil or butter, 1 lb. of fresh green peas, a few dried mushrooms, ½ lb. of coarse country sausage, 2 pints of meat or chicken broth, grated Parmesan cheese.

Chop the onion and put it into a thick pan in which 3 tablespoons of olive oil or 1 oz. butter has been heated. When the onion is just slightly golden add the sausage cut into dice, 3 or 4 dried mushrooms, previously soaked ten minutes in warm water, and the shelled peas. Add the heated broth and leave to cook gently while the rice is cooked for 5 minutes in plentiful boiling salted water. Strain the rice, add it to the first mixture, and simmer until most of the liquid is absorbed, but the rice must not be quite dry. Stir in a handful of grated Parmesan, turn the whole mixture into a fairly deep fireproof dish, sprinkle with more cheese and put into a moderate oven for about 20 minutes, until a golden crust has formed on top of the rice.

SULIMAN'S PILAFF (one of the most comforting dishes imaginable)

Into a thick pan put 3 or 4 tablespoons of good dripping or oil, and when it is warm put in 2 cupfuls of rice and stir for a few minutes until the rice takes on a transparent look. Then pour over about 4 pints of boiling water and cook very fast for about 12 minutes. The time of cooking varies according to the rice, but it should be rather under than overdone.

In the meantime, have ready a savoury preparation of small pieces of cooked mutton, fried onions, raisins, currants, garlic, tomatoes and pine nuts, if you can get them, or roasted almonds, all sautéd in dripping with plenty of seasoning.

Put your strained rice into a thick pan and stir in the meat and onion mixture, add a little more dripping if necessary, and stir for a few minutes over a low flame before serving.

Hand with the pilaff a bowl of sour cream or Yoghourt.

To Boil Rice

There are a number of ways of boiling rice and many people have their own pet method. However, for the benefit of people who have had no experience of cooking it I give here the method I always use and which I have found entirely successful and exceedingly simple.

First: Allow 2 ozs. of rice per person. Do not wash it.

Second: Have ready a very large saucepan (not less than 6-pint capacity for 8 ozs. of rice) full of fast-boiling salted water.

Third: Put in the rice, bring the water to the boil again, and let it boil fast for about 15 minutes. The exact time varies with the quality of the rice, the heat of the fire, and so on, and the only way you can be sure it is cooked is to taste it. Strain the rice through a colander, shaking it so that all the water drains out.

Fourth: While the rice is boiling make your oven hot, and have ready a hot dish (preferably a large shallow fireproof platter on which you can serve the rice). When the rice is drained put it on to the hot dish, turn off the oven and put the rice in it to dry for 3 or 4 minutes. Do not leave the oven on, or the heat will make the grains hard and brittle.

When the rice is to be served plain, a half lemon boiled in the water with it is an improvement.

POLENTA

Polenta is finely ground Indian corn meal; it makes a filling but excellent dish and this is the recipe as it is cooked by the Italian country people with large families to feed.

1 lb. of polenta will feed 6 hungry people. First prepare a very large heavy pan full of boiling salted water; when the water boils pour in the polenta, little by little, stirring all the time to eliminate lumps and adding more salt and pepper. It will take about 30 minutes to cook, and when ready is the consistency of a thick purée (rather like a purée of dried peas) and is poured out on to a very large wooden board, where it should form a layer about a quarter of an inch thick. Over it is poured a hot and rich tomato or meat sauce (see sauce *Bolognese* for spaghetti), which is topped with grated Parmesan cheese. The board is placed in the centre of the table and everybody helps himself. Whatever is left over is trimmed into squares about the size of a piece of toast, and grilled over a very slow charcoal fire; the top crust of sauce and cheese remains undisturbed and the under side, being nearest the heat, is deliciously browned.

To Cook Spaghetti

Buy imported Italian spaghetti.[1]

Do not break it up unless you want it to turn to a pudding. Allow approximately 3 ozs. of spaghetti per person; use a very large saucepan, at least 8 pints capacity for a half pound. Have the water well salted and boiling rapidly. The time of cooking varies between 10 and 20 minutes according to the quality of the spaghetti. Have a heated dish, preferably one which will bear a flame underneath, to receive the cooked *pasta*, with a coating of good olive oil on the bottom.

Put the drained spaghetti into this receptacle and stir it round, much as you would toss a salad, for a minute or two, so that the whole mass receives a coating of oil and assumes

[1] Since this was written the production of spaghetti in England has made great progress, and there is now good English-manufactured spaghetti on the market.

an attractive shiny appearance instead of the porridgy mass too often seen.

Lastly, if you are serving the classic spaghetti *Bolognese*, that is, with a thick tomato and mushroom sauce (see p. 189), see that it is highly flavoured, of a suitable thickness, and *plentiful*, accompanied by a generous dish of grated cheese.

Neapolitan Spaghetti

Neapolitans often like to eat their spaghetti simply with olive oil and garlic; no sauce or cheese.

When the spaghetti is almost ready put several cloves of coarsely chopped garlic with a cupful of the best olive oil into a small pan, and as soon as it is warm pour it over the drained spaghetti in the serving dish and mix it well.

Neapolitan Spaghetti with Fresh Tomato Sauce

This is another favourite Neapolitan way of serving spaghetti. Heat a little olive oil in a frying-pan and put in a pound of very red and ripe peeled tomatoes (or the contents of a tin of Italian peeled tomatoes, which make a good stubstitute). Let them cook a few minutes only, until they are soft but not mushy, add a little chopped garlic, salt and pepper and a handful of coarsely chopped fresh sweet basil or parsley. Pour the sauce over the spaghetti as soon as it is ready.

Spaghetti à la Sicilienne

Cook about ¾ lb. of spaghetti in the usual way. Meanwhile make ready the following preparation: 4 rashers of bacon cut in large pieces, ¼ lb. mushrooms, ½ lb. chopped onions, 2 chopped cloves of garlic, a handful of stoned black olives, and 4 anchovy fillets. First fry the onions crisp in fat, add all the other ingredients to the pan, with a handful of coarsely chopped parsley, and cook together for a few minutes. Have ready a hot serving dish into which you put a tablespoon of olive oil, and when the spaghetti is cooked and drained put into the dish, stir round with the oil, pile the onion mixture on to the top in a thick layer and serve very hot, with grated Parmesan handed separately.

NOODLES IN CHICKEN BROTH

Cook the noodles about 8 minutes in the usual way. Drain them well.

Have ready in another pan about 1½ pints of good chicken broth. When it is boiling, put in the noodles and simmer until they are cooked. Stir in then the same mixture as for Spaghetti à la Sicilienne (p. 105) with the oil in which it has been fried.

Serve in soup plates with plenty of broth to each helping, and grated cheese.

FOIE DE VEAU AUX CAROTTES

1½ lbs. calf's liver, 2 onions, 3 lbs. carrots, a piece of pig's caul.

Soak the piece of caul in warm salted water for 5 minutes. Slice the liver, season and tie up in the caul. Fry in butter with the chopped onions. When golden remove from the pan and, with the juice that has come from the liver as a basis, make an Espagnole sauce (p. 186) but cook only for 20 minutes. Slice the carrots in rounds. Place the Espagnole sauce in the bottom of a thick pan, put in the carrots and then the liver, still wrapped up in the caul. Cover the pan and cook as slowly as possible for 2½ hours. Before serving unwrap the liver.

Liver cooked in this way also makes an excellent stuffing for tomatoes, aubergines, etc.

Cassoulet Toulousain

Of all the great dishes which French regional cookery has produced the cassoulet is perhaps the most typical of true country food, the genuine, abundant, earthy, richly flavoured and patiently simmered dish of the ideal farmhouse kitchen. Hidden beneath a layer of creamy, golden-crusted haricot beans in a deep, wide, earthen pot, the cassoulet contains garlicky pork sausages, smoked bacon, salt pork, a wing or leg of preserved goose, perhaps a piece of mutton, or a couple of pig's feet, or half a duck, and some chunks of pork rind. The beans are tender, juicy, moist but not mushy, aromatic smells of garlic and herbs escape from the pot as the cassoulet is brought smoking hot from the oven to the table. French novelists, gourmets, and cooks have devoted pages to praise of the cassoulet, and its fame spread from south-western France, where it originated, first to Paris restaurants, then all over France; recently it has achieved some popularity in this country, no doubt because it seems an attractive solution to the entertaining of a fairly large number of people with little fuss or expense.

A genuine cassoulet is not, however, a cheap dish. Neither are the materials always easy to find. When you consider that in the rich agricultural country of the Languedoc every farmer's wife has the ingredients of the dish within arm's length, festoons of sausages and hams hanging in her kitchen, jars of goose and pork preserved in their own fat on her larder shelves, you understand how the cassoulet came into being; it was evolved to make the best use of the local materials; when you have to go out and buy these things the cost is high (this is just as much the case in France as in England) and although quite a good dish can be made at moderate cost it should be remembered that tinned beans and sausages served in an earthenware casserole do not, alas, constitute a cassoulet.

Bear in mind, also, that a cassoulet is heavy and filling food, and should be kept for cold winter days, preferably for luncheons when none of the party have anything very active to do afterwards.

The ingredients for say 6 people are 1½ lb. of good quality medium-sized white haricot beans (butter beans will not do, they are too floury), 1 lb. of belly of pork, 1 lb. of breast of mutton, ¼ lb. of fresh rind of pork, or failing that of ham or bacon, 1 lb. of fresh, coarse garlic sausage (not salame, but the kind sold for frying or boiling by French and continental delicatessen shops), 2 or 3 pieces of preserved goose (in England replace this with half a duck, or omit it altogether), 1 lb. of a cheap cut of smoked gammon, 2 or 3 cloves of garlic, herbs, 3 ozs. of goose dripping or pig's lard, an onion.

Soak the beans overnight. Put them in a large casserole or saucepan, add the onion, garlic, pork rind, the piece of gammon, and a faggot of herbs (bay leaf, thyme, parsley). Add no salt at this stage. Cover with fresh water and cook either in a slow oven for 4 to 5 hours or over a direct flame on top of the stove for 1½ to 3 hours (the time of cooking varies a good deal with the quality of the beans).

Meanwhile, roast the pork and the mutton in the dripping (and the duck if you are using this).

When the beans are all but cooked, cut all the meats, the rinds and the sausage into convenient pieces, put them in alternate layers with the beans in a deep earthenware pot and add enough of the liquid in which the beans have cooked to come about halfway up. Put into a fairly slow oven (Regulo 3–4) uncovered, to finish cooking. This final operation can be prolonged to suit yourself by turning the oven right down.

Eventually a brown crust forms on top of the beans. Stir this gently into the whole mass, and leave for another crust to form. Again stir it in, and when a third crust has formed the cassoulet should be ready. Sometimes the top is sprinkled with a layer of breadcrumbs when the pot is put in the oven and this speeds up the crusting of the cassoulet, and if perhaps you have added too much liquid the breadcrumbs should help to absorb it. Serve on very hot plates, with plenty of young red wine, and perhaps a green salad and a good cheese to finish the meal.

FOOL

Fool (brown beans) are the staple food of the Egyptian peasant. 1 lb. of these beans and 6 tablespoons of red lentils are washed and put into an earthen or copper casserole with 3 cups of water. This is brought to the boil and then left for hours and hours—all night usually—on a low charcoal fire. If necessary more water can be added. Salt is not put in until the cooking is finished, and olive oil is poured over them in the plate, and sometimes hard-boiled eggs are served with them. The lid of the casserole should be removed as little as possible, or the beans will go black.

RAGOÛT DE MOUTON À LA CATALANE

2 lbs. of leg or loin of mutton, an onion, 2 cloves of garlic, a tablespoon of concentrated tomato purée or $\frac{1}{2}$ lb. of fresh tomatoes, $\frac{1}{2}$ lb. of bacon, herbs, $\frac{1}{2}$ lb. of chick peas (see p. 139), white wine or port.

Cut the meat and the bacon into thick squares; brown them on each side in pork or bacon fat or oil; add the garlic and the tomato purée or the fresh tomatoes, skinned and chopped, and plenty of thyme or marjoram or basil, and 2 bay leaves. Pour over a glass of sweet white wine, or port. Cover the pan and cook very gently for 2 hours, until the meat is tender.

Have ready the chick peas, soaked and cooked. When the mutton is about ready put the drained chick peas and the meat mixture together into a fireproof dish, put a layer of bread-crumbs on the top and cook in a gentle oven for an hour until a slight crust has formed on the top, and the chick peas are absolutely soft.

Poultry and Game

N.B.—Further recipes for poultry and game will be found in the chapter on Cold Food.

"In came the Grand Priors hand in hand, all three together. 'To the kitchen,' said they in perfect unison, 'to the kitchen, and that immediately; you will then judge whether we have been wanting in zeal to regale you.'

"Such a summons, so conveyed, was irresistible; the three prelates led the way to, I verily believe, the most distinguished temple of gluttony in all Europe. What Glastonbury may have been in its palmy state, I cannot answer; but my eyes never beheld in any modern convent of France, Italy, or Germany, such an enormous space dedicated to culinary purposes. Through the centre of the immense and nobly-groined hall, not less than sixty feet in diameter, ran a brisk rivulet of the clearest water, flowing through pierced wooden reservoirs, containing every sort and size of the finest river-fish. On one side, loads of game and venison were heaped up; on the other, vegetables and fruit in endless variety. Beyond a long line of stoves extended a row of ovens, and close to them hillocks of wheaten flour whiter than snow, rocks of sugar, jars of the purest oil, and pastry in vast abundance, which a numerous tribe of lay brothers and their attendants were rolling out and puffing up into a hundred different shapes, singing all the while as blithely as larks in a corn-field.

"My servants, and those of their reverend excellencies the two Priors, were standing by in the full glee of witnessing these hospitable preparations, as well pleased, and as much flushed, as if they had been just returned from assisting at the marriage at Cana in Galilee. 'There,' said the Lord Abbot, 'we shall not starve: God's bounties are great, it is fit we should enjoy them.' "

The Travel-Diaries of William Beckford of Fonthill

Aleppo Chicken

1 chicken, 1 lemon, carrots, onions, celery, garlic, ½ lb. mushrooms, ¼ lb. blanched almonds, half a glass of sherry, 1 egg, 1 glass cream.

Rub the chicken over with salt, pepper and lemon juice, insert a piece of lemon peel in the inside of the bird. Boil with the vegetables in the usual way and when cooked take the pan off the fire, and with a ladle pour out about a pint of the stock into another pan. Add to this the juice of half a lemon, the sherry, the almonds, and the previously sautéd mushrooms, and when hot pour it spoon by spoon on to the egg beaten up with the cream. When it has thickened put the chicken on a hot dish, and pour the sauce all over and around it.

Sherkasiya (Circassian Chicken)

1 chicken, 3 ozs. each of shelled walnuts, almonds and hazel nuts, rice, red pepper, salt, 2 onions, butter.

Boil the chicken in the usual way, cut it into 4 pieces and arrange it in the centre of a dish of boiled rice.

The following sauce is served with it. Pound the walnuts, almonds and hazel nuts in a mortar with the red pepper and salt. Fry the chopped onion in butter and add the pounded nuts and a little of the chicken stock, and when it is thick pour it over the rice.

Pollo in Padella con Peperoni

Cut a chicken into 6 pieces. Brown them in a braising pan with olive oil, 2 or 3 onions sliced, 3 cloves of garlic, salt, pepper, marjoram and thyme; cover the pan and cook slowly for about 1 hour, taking care that the chicken does not burn.

In the meantime put 4 or 5 large red or green pimentos into the oven until they are soft and the outer skin can be peeled off; remove the seeds, cut them in strips and add them to the pan with ½ lb. of tomatoes roughly chopped and a pinch of basil. When the tomatoes are cooked the dish is ready.

A few slices of orange, peeled and cut in rounds and added at the last moment are a pleasant addition.

POULET ANTIBOISE

Slice 2 lbs. of onions and put them into a deep casserole with a half tumbler of olive oil, a little salt and a pinch of cayenne pepper.

On top of the onions place a cleaned chicken seasoned with salt and pepper. Cover the casserole and cook very gently for about an hour and a half. The onions must not brown, but melt gradually almost to a purée, as in *Pissaladina* (see p. 38). Add a little more oil during cooking if necessary.

When the chicken is tender carve it into pieces and serve on a dish with the onions all round, garnished with a few stoned black olives and squares of bread fried in oil.

If the chicken is of the elderly, boiling variety, it can be cut into joints before cooking, so that it will not take so long to cook, although whenever possible I think that chickens should always be cooked whole to preserve the flavour and juices, and carved into joints for serving.

A Delicate Stuffing for Roast Chicken

1 cup cooked rice, a handful raisins, ½ cup blanched and pounded almonds, ¼ cup finely chopped raw onion, ½ cup chopped parsley, liver of chicken, 2 ozs. butter, a sprig of basil, one whole egg.

Mash the liver and mix all the ingredients together, working the butter well into the mixture, adding the beaten egg last.

Roast Duck

The flavour of roast duck is much improved if the cleaned bird is first put into a pan over a hot fire until most of the fat has been extracted. (Watch to see that it does not burn.) Strain the fat off and repeat the process. When all possible fat has been removed put 3 tablespoons of butter into the pan and place it in a hot oven. Baste and turn frequently for 1¼ hrs.

Oie Rôtie à la Bordelaise

Another recipe from the same French cookery book as the *Gigot de Mouton à la Provençale*.

"Prepare a goose as for roasting; fill the interior with the following stuffing. About 20 fine mushrooms, chopped very finely with the liver of the goose, a pinch of parsley, and a clove of garlic; to this add ½ lb. of fresh butter, and ¼ lb. of anchovy butter.

Knead all very well together before stuffing the bird; sew up the opening and roast the goose on the spit, exactly as for an unstuffed bird.

Even if the goose is not an excessively fat one it will still render an abundance of *jus* while it is roasting, owing to the butter in the interior. The bird should be basted almost continuously while it is roasting with this butter, in order that it may be completely penetrated with the savour of the anchovy butter allied to the garlic. The taste of the goose prepared in this manner is highly esteemed by the gastronomes of the Midi, but apart from the southern *départements*, it is not particularly popular with the majority of gourmets."

Les Perdreaux aux Raisins

In a medium-sized cocotte or braising pan melt a little bacon fat, put in some slices of bacon, a bouquet garni, and two partridges, cleaned and trussed as for roasting. Fill up the pan to the height of the partridges with peeled, somewhat unripe, white grapes. Season with salt and pepper, cover the pan, seal the lid with paste and simmer very gently 1 hour.

Serve very hot with the pieces of bacon and the grapes arranged round the partridges.

Les Perdreaux à la Provençale

Another recipe for those who are very fond of garlic.

Into a thick braising pan put a small piece of butter, 2 ozs. of fat ham or bacon, and 2 cleaned partridges. Fry gently until the partridges are golden, and then add 20 or 30 cloves of garlic chopped with parsley, and fry another 2 or 3 minutes.

Pour over a glass of strong white wine and a glass of thick tomato purée. Cover the pan and cook gently for 1½ hours.

Put the sauce through a fine sieve, squeeze in the juice of a lemon and cook another 30 minutes.

Partridges Cooked Klephti Fashion

Klephtis (from the word meaning "to steal") was the name given to the original Greek brigands, who had their head-quarters in the mountains of Thessaly and harried the Turks (and anyone else who seemed suitable prey) during their 200-years' occupation of Greece—the original Resistance Movement in fact.

Their method of cooking birds and meat wrapped up in paper in a primitively constructed oven has come to be known all over Greece as "Klephti cooking".

The partridges, seasoned with mountain herbs, are wrapped up in paper with a little fat and any vegetables which may be available (in Greece partridges are not treated with the reverence accorded them in England) and placed in an earthen pot, narrowing at the top, called a *stamna*. This pot is then laid on its side in a hollow dug at the edge of a bank of earth, and buried. Underneath the pot the earth is scooped out to make room for a fire of resinous pinewood or charcoal, and this is left slowly burning for 2 or 3 hours.

At any rate, partridges with a piece of fat bacon, wrapped in buttered paper, and cooked in a very slow oven are worth trying. "Klephti cooking" is always a good way of getting the best flavour out of meat or a bird.

Pigeons à la Romanaise

Prepare the pigeons as for roasting. Tie each one in a rasher of bacon and a slice of lemon peel. Put them in a shallow pan with 2 ozs. of butter and sauté them for 10 minutes. Then add a large glass of white wine and the juice of half a lemon and continue cooking slowly until the pigeons are done—about 25 minutes. Remove the pigeons from the pan and keep them hot. Strain the liquor from the pan into a double saucepan and stir in 1 ounce of butter and the yolks of 2 eggs. Stir continuously as for a sauce *béarnaise*. When it has thickened pour the sauce over the pigeons and serve them with a simplified pilaff of rice (p. 102) containing fried onions and raisins or currants.

Piments Farçis de Cailles

Bone the quails, 1 for each person. Stuff them with foie gras. Have ready 4 cups of rice cooked as for a pilaff (p. 102). Remove the core and seeds from as many large red pimentos as you have quails. Roll each quail in the rice until it has a coating all round, insert it into the pimento. Put the pimentos into a deep dish with 2 or 3 ozs. of butter and some tomato sauce to which you have added some brown stock. Cover the dish and braise them on top of the stove for about 30 minutes. They can also be cooked in the oven.

BECFIGUES EN BROCHETTES

The little figpeckers are threaded on skewers, head and all, with the insides left in, about 6 to the skewer, seasoned with pepper and salt and herbs, and grilled.

SNIPE AND MUSHROOMS

In Northern Italy this dish is made with little figpeckers and the beautiful wild red mushrooms called *funghi ovali*. In England any small bird, woodcock, snipe, or plover, can be cooked in this way with very excellent results. For each bird you need one very large mushroom; remove the stalks, and lay the mushrooms, stalk side up, in a baking dish. Pour a little oil over them, and place your small bird on the top, seasoned with salt and ground black pepper, put a sprig of fresh thyme or marjoram on top of each bird, and pour over a little more oil. Cover with a greaseproof paper, and cook in a slow oven for about 30 minutes. The mushrooms take the place of the usual croûtons under the bird, and soak up the juices, but the cooking must be gentle, or the mushrooms will shrivel up. For the last 5 minutes of cooking, remove the paper to let the birds brown.

HARE AND RABBIT

A Farmhouse Dinner

"COME TO Montpazier any time of the year and you will eat well. The thick stone walls are cool in summer and warm in winter, for the wind can whip cruelly about this upland. Then, the low lights of the wood fires seem good after the brilliant grey-green hill-frosts of early winter.

"The food is prepared over a fire in a vast open hearth. The cauldrons, pots and saucepans hang black upon the ratchet. Wood-pigeon and partridge turn on the spits. The dry vine-shoots crisply crackle as the place fills with their blue aromatic smoke and tingling odour.

"This is, indeed, no place to get fussy dishes *à la Cambacérés*,[1] but go when the game is on and you will eat food for outdoor men and it must be, one likes to think, very like the rustic cooking of the Romans.

[1] Cambacérés is one of the sign-posts, like parmentier (potatoes) or florentine (spinach). When one reads upon a menu the name of Napoleon's arch-chancellor then look out for something stuffed with foie gras.

"The kitchen is in the hall and you can eat with an eye upon the spits and sizzling pots. That's the way to enjoy a meal, but, luckily, I have run across nowhere in France that peculiarly Iberian combination that used not to be rare in Spain: stable, kitchen, bedroom and dining-room all in one—that's very Low Latin indeed.

"Maybe the main dish will be *lièvre à la royale*. There are plenty of thyme and herbs and long runs hereabouts. The hare are tasty.

"Now hare done in Royal Style is a real piece into which go not only your hare and a belly of pork but white wine and meat juice, pears and prunes, garlic, herbs, onions, chestnuts, mushrooms, truffles, red wine and ham. It's not a city dish. Like all game (and even that glutinous horror, rabbit), the Royal Style is better experienced in the country.

"But before the main dish you will get a fine, thick soup in a deep bowl. Real soup and nothing like the plash of skilly offered us here. None of your timid soup-plates for this juice of the *civet*. If you like a substantial opening to your meal you will, if wise, pour into the soup a quarter of a litre of red wine and drink the whole from the bowl without any new-fangled soup-spoons. This fashion of lapping it up is called by the men of the South-West *faire Chabrol*. No one seems to know why. Perhaps some member of that ancient southern family was a noted *gourmet*.

"Then, depending upon the days, there may be some fish, but we're a good way inland for anything but trout or crayfish. *Ecrevisses* can be good enough served in a heaped scarlet *buisson*, a veritable Burning Bush of Crayfish. But such things are, as they say, *pour amuser la gueule*—to amuse the muzzle. We get right down to the *civet à la royale*. . . .

"And then come along a brace of *palombes* or wild doves and then the other half of the hare, well grilled. . . .

"The sweet-meats, the *entremets*, will be, as always, the weakest part of this rustic meal. Better eat some home-made jam and fresh cream and then tackle the cheeses of the country. Roquefort is their glory and although there are not here such magnificent soft cheeses as Brie and Camembert (at their best) still, the strong and subtle cheeses of the South are worthy of all respect.

"Down here, after all, one is near the Lot and it may well be that the wine is the fruity, purple southern vintage of Cahors, city of Popes and prelates and prunes and memories of pomp. Nearly all the *Coteaux du Lot* are interesting and well sustain the Périgord cooking that ranks with those of Burgundy, Provence, Bresse and Béarn as the best in the French provinces."

Cross-Channel,
by Alan Houghton Brodrick

Lièvre à la Royale

This famous recipe for Lièvre à la Royale was invented by Senator Couteaux, who contributed regular articles to the Paris newspaper *Le Temps*. On the 29th November 1898, instead of his usual political column, appeared this remarkable recipe. M. Couteaux related at length how he had spent a week in Poitou hunting the right kind of hare; how, the exactly suitable animal at last in his hands, he instantly took the train to Paris, sent out his invitations and hurried off to consult his friend Spüller, who ran a well-known restaurant in the Rue Favart, to arrange the preparation and cooking of his hare for the following day. The dish takes from noon until 7 o'clock to prepare and cook, and Senator Couteaux tells how by 6 o'clock the exquisite aroma had penetrated the doors of Spüller's restaurant, floated down the street and out into the boulevard, where the passers-by sniffed the scented air; an excitable crowd gathered, and the whole *quartier* was "*mis en émoi*". If you ever feel like devoting the time (perhaps you need not after all spend a week catching your hare) and the ingredients to cooking this dish, you will see that the senator was not exaggerating.

I have translated the recipe as faithfully as possible. It is very lengthy and there are repetitions. But in those days there was plenty of space to fill up; and from the senator's precise instructions one can well imagine the delightful old gentleman bending over his "daubière", and the pride with which he presented this beautiful creation to his gourmet friends.

"*Ingredients.*

"You require a male hare, with red fur, killed if possible in mountainous country; of fine French descent (characterised by the light nervous elegance of head and limbs), weighing from 5 to 6 pounds, that is to say older than a leveret but still adolescent. The important thing is that the hare should have been cleanly killed and so not have lost a drop of blood.

"*The fat to cook it:* 2 or 3 tablespoons of goose fat, ¼ lb. of fat bacon rashers; ¼ lb. of bacon in one piece.

"*Liquid:* 6 ozs. of good red wine vinegar. Two bottles of Macon or Médoc, whichever you please, but in any case not less than 2 years old.

"*Utensils:* A *daubière*, or oblong stewing pan, of well-tinned copper, 8 inches high, 15 inches long, 8 inches wide and possessed of a hermetically closing cover; a small bowl in which to preserve the blood of the hare, and later to stir it when it comes to incorporating it in the sauce; a double-handled vegetable chopper; a large shallow serving dish; a sieve; a small wooden pestle.

"*The wine to serve:* Preferably a St. Julien or Moulin à Vent.

"*Preliminary Preparations.*

"Skin and clean the hare. Keep aside the heart, the liver and the lungs. Keep aside also and with great care the blood. (It is traditional to add 2 or 3 small glasses of fine old cognac to the blood; but this is not indispensable; M. Couteaux finally decided against this addition.)

"In the usual way prepare a medium-sized carrot, cut into four; 4 medium onions each stuck with a clove; 20 cloves of garlic; 40 cloves of shallot; a bouquet garni, composed of a bay leaf, a sprig of thyme and some pieces of parsley.

"Get ready some charcoal, in *large pieces*, which you will presently be needing, *burning fast*.

"*First Operation (from half-past twelve until four o'clock)*.[1]

"At 12.30 coat the bottom and sides of the stew pan with the goose-fat; then at the bottom of the pan arrange a bed of rashers of bacon.

"Cut off the head and neck of the hare: leaving only the back and the legs. Then place the hare at full length on the bed of bacon, on its back. Cover it with another layer of bacon. Now all your bacon rashers are used up.

"Now add the carrot; the onions; the 20 cloves of garlic; the 40 cloves of shallot;[2] the bouquet garni.

"Pour over the hare:

(i) the 6 ozs. of red wine vinegar, and
(ii) a bottle and a half of 2-year-old Macon (or Médoc).

"Season with pepper and salt in reasonable quantity.

"*At one o'clock*. The *daubière* being thus arranged, put on the lid and set the fire going (either a gas stove or an ordinary range). On the top of the lid place 3 or 4 large pieces of charcoal in an incandescent state, *well alight and glowing*.

---

[1] These times are given for a dinner to be served at seven o'clock.
[2] In spite of the enormous quantity of garlic and shallots which enter into the composition of Lièvre à la Royale, the remarkable fact is that to a certain extent the two ingredients cancel each other out, so that the uninitiated would hardly suspect their presence.

"Regulate your heat so that the hare may cook for 3 hours, over a gentle and regular fire, continuously.

"*Second Operation (to be carried out during the first cooking of the hare).*

"First chop exceedingly finely the four following ingredients, chopping each one separately:

(i) ¼ lb. of bacon,
(ii) the heart, liver and lungs of the hare,
(iii) 10 cloves of garlic,
(iv) 20 cloves of shallot.

"*The chopping of the garlic and the shallots must be so fine that each of them attain as nearly as possible a molecular state.*

"This is one of the first conditions of success of this marvellous dish, in which the multiple and diverse perfumes and aromas melt into a whole so harmonious that neither one dominates, nor discloses its particular origin, and so arouse some preconceived prejudice, however regrettable.

"The bacon, the insides of the hare, the garlic and shallots being chopped very fine, and separately, blend them all together thoroughly, so as to obtain an absolutely perfect mixture. Keep this mixture aside.

"*Third Operation (from four o'clock until a quarter to seven).*

"*At four o'clock.* Remove the stew pan from the fire. Take the hare out very delicately; put it on a dish. Then remove all the débris of the bacon, carrot, onions, garlic, shallot, which may be clinging to it; return these débris to the pan.

"*The Sauce.* Now take a large deep dish and a sieve. Empty the contents of the pan into the sieve, which you have placed over the dish; with a small wooden pestle pound the contents of the sieve, extracting all the juice, which forms a *coulis* in the dish.

"*Mixing the coulis and the hachis (the chopped mixture).* Now comes the moment to make use of the mixture which was the subject of the second operation. Incorporate this into the *coulis*.

"Heat the half bottle of wine left over from the first operation. Pour this hot wine into the mixture of *coulis* and *hachis* and stir the whole well together.

"*At half-past four*. Return to the stew pan:

(i) the mixture of *coulis* and *hachis*,
(ii) the hare, together with any of the bones which may have become detached during the cooking.

"Return the pan to the stove, with the same *gentle and regular fire* underneath and on the top, for another 1½ hours' cooking.

"*At six o'clock*. As the excess of fat, issuing from the necessary quantity of bacon, will prevent you from judging the state of the sauce, you must now proceed to operate a *first removal of the fat*. Your work will not actually be completed until the sauce has become sufficiently amalgamated to attain a consistence approximating to that of a purée of potatoes; not quite, how-ever, for if you tried to make it too thick, you would end by so reducing it that there would not be sufficient to moisten the flesh (by nature dry) of the hare.

"Your hare having therefore had the fat removed, can con-tinue to cook, *still on a very slow fire*, until the moment comes for you to add the blood which you have reserved with the utmost care as has already been instructed.

"*Fourth Operation (quarter of an hour before serving)*.

"*At quarter to seven*. The amalgamation of the sauce proceed-ing successfully, a fourth and last operation will finally and rapidly bring it to completion.

"*Addition of the blood to the hare*. With the addition of the blood, not only will you hasten the amalgamation of the sauce but also give it a fine brown colour; the darker it is the more appetising. This addition of the blood should not be made more than 30 minutes before serving; it must also be preceded by a *second removal of the fat.*

"Therefore, effectively remove the fat; after which, without losing a minute, turn to the operation of adding the blood.

"(i) Whip the blood with a fork, until, if any of it has become curdled, it is smooth again. (Note: the optional addition of the brandy mentioned at the beginning helps to prevent the curdling of the blood.)

"(ii) Pour the blood into the sauce, taking care to stir the contents of the pan from top to bottom and from right to left, so that the blood will penetrate into every corner of the pan.

"Now taste; add pepper and salt *if necessary.* A little later (45 minutes at a maximum) get ready to serve.

"*Arrangements for serving.*

"*At seven o'clock.* Remove from the pan your hare, whose volume by this time has naturally somewhat shrunk.

"At any rate, in the centre of the serving dish, place all that still has the consistency of meat, the bones, entirely denuded, and now useless, being thrown away, and now finally around this hare *en compote* pour the admirable sauce which has been so carefully created."

Needless to say (concludes the senator) that to use a knife to serve the hare would be a sacrilege. A spoon alone is amply sufficient.

CIVET DE LIÈVRE

This Civet consists of the whole hare carefully cut up, with a garnish of cèpes[1] and croûtons. Do not marinate the hare;

---

[1] Cèpes are not usually obtainable in England, although they do grow in some parts of the country. I have been able to buy them occasionally at Roches or Parmigiani's, both in Old Compton Street. Dried cèpes are also obtainable in Soho and are worth trying. Soak them for a few minutes and then simmer them in oil until they are tender. They have plenty of flavour. I do not recommend the tinned variety, which are woolly and have no taste whatever. For the Civet de Lièvre cèpes can naturally be replaced with mushrooms, or with chestnuts.

in my opinion to do so spoils its fine flavour, and if you have an elderly animal he will do very nicely for a terrine (see p. 150).

In a heavy pan put 4 ozs. of fat bacon cut in squares, 2 onions finely chopped, 2 or 3 shallots and a clove of garlic, also finely chopped. When they start to turn golden, put in the pieces of hare, which you have carefully wiped. Let them brown on both sides, for about 10 minutes, and then stir in 2 ozs. of flour, taking care that it does not burn. Add ½ pint of red wine and ½ pint of brown stock. Cover the pan and leave it to simmer for an hour.

Clean and cut in slices ½ lb. of cèpes, fry them in oil and add them to the hare (when it has cooked for an hour), and simmer a further 30 minutes. Arrange the pieces of hare in the serving dish and keep them hot. Add to the sauce in the pan the blood of the hare, to which you have mixed a teaspoon each of oil, vinegar and wine, the pounded liver and a pinch of parsley, thyme and rosemary.

Reheat the sauce but do not let it boil again, pour it over the hare and garnish with croûtons of fried bread.

Lepre in Agrodolce

A typical Italian way of cooking game. The chocolate sounds alarming, but serves to sweeten and darken the sauce, and in the blending of the whole the taste of chocolate does not obtrude.

A hare, cut up, vinegar, butter, onion, ham or bacon, sugar, chocolate, almonds, raisins and seasoning, stock.

Wash the pieces of hare in vinegar, sauté them in butter with the sliced onion, ham or bacon and seasoning, and add the stock. Simmer slowly. Half fill a wine glass with sugar, and add vinegar until the glass is three-quarters full. Mix the vinegar and sugar well together and add to the hare when it is nearly cooked.

Add a dessertspoon of grated chocolate, a handful of shredded almonds, and stoned raisins, and finish cooking.

LAPIN AU COULIS DE LENTILLES

Cut a rabbit in large pieces, sauté it with bacon and fat. Pour over a glass of white wine or cider, let it bubble a minute or two to reduce, then add seasoning and aromatic herbs. Cover the pan and simmer until the rabbit is tender. Have ready a purée of lentils. Mix the liquid from the rabbit into the purée, reduce until thick, add the pieces of rabbit and bacon and reheat.

Vegetables

N.B.—Many of these vegetable dishes constitute a course in themselves, and are intended to be served as such, after the meat or fish, when their full flavour will be appreciated.

The Vegetable Market at Palermo

"THE NEAR end of the street was rather dark and had mostly vegetable shops. Abundance of vegetables—piles of white and green fennel, like celery, and great sheaves of young, purplish, sea-dust-coloured artichokes, nodding their buds, piles of big radishes, scarlet and bluey purple, carrots, long strings of dried figs, mountains of big oranges, scarlet large peppers, a last slice of pumpkin, a great mass of colours and vegetable freshnesses. A mountain of black-purple cauliflowers, like niggers' heads, and a mountain of snow-white ones next to them. How the dark, greasy, night-stricken street seems to beam with these vegetables, all this fresh delicate flesh of luminous vegetables piled there in the air, and in the recesses of the window-less little caverns of the shops, and gleaming forth on the dark air, under the lamps."

Sea and Sardinia,
by D. H. Lawrence

POTATO KEPHTÉDÉS (a favourite Greek dish)

Sieve 1 lb. cold boiled potatoes, add ½ oz. of melted butter, salt, pepper, chopped parsley, a little chopped green onion and 2 finely chopped tomatoes (without the peel) and 2 ozs. flour. Knead lightly, roll out and shape into rounds. Fry them in a little hot fat or oil, or put them on a greased tin in the oven until golden brown. They should be very soft inside.

POMMES ANNA

A recipe often found in cookery books but less frequently upon the tables of either restaurants or private houses. They make the ideal accompaniment to a Tournedos, or a roast bird of any kind.

For 4 people you need about 1½ lbs. of potatoes (1 medium-sized potato per person), an earthenware terrine or metal pan of 1-pint capacity with a close-fitting lid, 3 ozs. of butter, salt and pepper.

Peel and wash the potatoes. Slice them all the same size, about the thickness of a penny. This is important, in order that they should all be cooked at the same time, and it is laborious to do unless you have a cutter. The perfect instrument is a wooden board with an arrangement of blades, which is also the only quick way of slicing cucumbers thin for salads. It is called a mandolin, and can be found in the shops which sell imported French kitchen utensils.

Having sliced your potatoes, wash them well (this does away with any starchy taste) and dry them in a cloth. Coat the inside of your terrine with butter and arrange the potatoes carefully in layers, building up from the bottom and round the sides, so that the slices are evenly distributed, placing small pats of butter and seasoning with a little salt and pepper at intervals. Over the top place a piece of buttered paper and put the cover on.

Cook them in a slow oven (Regulo 2 or 3) for 40 minutes to an hour. They can either be turned out on to a dish or served from the terrine.

POMMES DE TERRE EN MATELOTE

Cut hot boiled potatoes in half, put them in a casserole with butter, parsley, chives, pepper and salt, cover with stock or water and a glass of wine. Cook about 10 minutes. Bind the sauce with a yolk of egg.

POMMES DE TERRE À LA MANIÈRE D'APT

Potatoes cut in rounds, 3 tablespoons olive oil, 5 tablespoons freshly made tomato purée, salt, pepper, a bay leaf, 6 stoned black olives, breadcrumbs.

Put the olive oil into a shallow gratin dish, add the tomato purée, the potatoes, salt, pepper and bay leaf, and simmer for 5 minutes.

Barely cover the potatoes with boiling water, and simmer another 30 minutes. Now add the black olives, and cover with a layer of breadcrumbs.

Put in a moderate oven for another 30 minutes.

Serve in the same dish.

SWEET POTATOES (Patátés)

When there was a shortage of potatoes in the Middle East during the war, the Army cooks made the fatal mistake of cooking sweet potatoes like chips, with the result that the whole of the Eighth Army grew to detest these vegetables, and it is true that they are not good when treated as an ordinary potato and served as an adjunct to meat.

They should be baked in their skins, and eaten as a separate course with butter and salt, and they are simply delicious.

The Greeks slice them and make them into sweet fritters, served with a honey sauce.

CAROTTES AU BLANC

Blanch carrots in boiling water, slice them and put them in a casserole with butter, salt, pepper and parsley. Cover them with milk. When they are cooked bind the sauce with the yolk of an egg.

COURGETTES AUX TOMATES

Slice the courgettes (very young marrows), peeling them unless they are very small. Salt them and leave to drain for 30 minutes. Put them in a fireproof dish with plenty of butter and 2 sliced and peeled tomatoes. Cook for about 10 minutes on a very low flame.

BEIGNETS D'AUBERGINES (1)

In the big markets of Marseille and Toulon there are always one or two stalls selling cooked food, such as socca and panisse (different sorts of pancakes made of semolina or maize flour), little anchovy pâtés, and these beignets, smoking hot from the pan. They are quite excellent.

Without peeling the aubergines, slice them lengthwise, very thinly. Salt them and leave them to drain on a plate for an hour.

Squeeze out the water, dip the slices in frying batter (see p. 50) and fry them in very hot oil.

Courgettes can be cooked in the same way.

BEIGNETS D'AUBERGINES (2)

Boil 3 or 4 large aubergines in a little water. When they are soft put them through a sieve. Add seasoning and cayenne and a little flour to stiffen the mixture and a beaten egg. Shape into rounds, dredge with flour and drop into smoking oil.

Aubergines à l'Arménienne

Cut the ends of some small aubergines, but leave the skin on. Sauté them in oil, drain them, cut them in half lengthways and take out all the flesh without breaking the skins. Chop the flesh finely and add (for 10 aubergines) about ½ lb. of lean minced lamb, 2 tablespoons of finely chopped onion which has been melted a minute or two in oil, 2 tablespoons of chopped pimentos, salt, pepper, 2 or 3 chopped cloves of garlic, a handful of chopped parsley, a handful of little pine nuts and 2 ozs. of fresh breadcrumbs.

Fill the aubergines with this mixture, arrange them one against the other in a fireproof dish, sprinkle a little more oil over them, cover the pan and cook them in a gentle oven for 10 minutes.

Aubergine Dolmas (a Turkish and Middle Eastern dish)

8 small round aubergines (or 4 large ones), a cup of cooked rice, ¼ lb. of minced mutton (either raw or cooked), 2 tomatoes, salt, pepper, onions, lemon juice, herbs, a few pine nuts or walnuts, olive oil.

Mix the cooked rice with the well seasoned meat, a chopped fried onion or two, the chopped tomatoes, and some marjoram, mint, or basil.

Cut about an inch off the thin end of the aubergines, and with a small spoon scoop out most of the flesh. Cut this into dice and mix it with the prepared stuffing. Fill the aubergines with the stuffing (not too full), put the tops in, inverted, so that they fit like corks, lay them in a pan with a little olive oil; let this get hot and then pour hot water over them to come halfway up. Simmer for 30 minutes, add the juice of a lemon, and cook very slowly another 30 minutes. There should be just a very little sauce left by the time they are ready. If there is any stuffing over, use it to fill tomatoes, which can be baked and served with the aubergines.

AÏGROISSADE TOULONNAISE

Make an aïoli (see p. 193). Cook a mixture of vegetables —green beans, artichokes, dried haricots, chick peas, etc. Strain them, put in a warmed dish and mix the aïoli into them. Do not reheat.

RATATOUILLE

Ratatouille is a Provençal ragoût of vegetables, usually pimentos, onions, tomatoes and aubergines, stewed very slowly in oil. This dish has the authentic aromatic flavour of Provençal food.

2 large onions, 2 aubergines, 3 or 4 tomatoes, 2 red or green pimentos,[1] garlic, oil, salt and pepper.

Peel the tomatoes and cut the unpeeled aubergines into squares. Slice the onions and pimentos. Put the onions into a frying pan or sauté pan with plenty of oil, not too hot. When they are getting soft add first the pimentos and aubergines, and, 10 minutes later, the tomatoes. The vegetables should not be fried, but stewed in the oil, so simmer in a covered pan for the first 30 minutes, uncovered for the last 10. By this time they should have absorbed most of the oil.

POIREAUX À LA PROVENÇALE

3 lbs. leeks, ½ lb. tomatoes, 1 dozen black olives, 2 tablespoons olive oil, juice of 1 lemon, 1 dessertspoon finely chopped lemon peel.

Chop the cleaned leeks into half-inch lengths. Into a shallow heatproof dish put the oil and when it is warm, but not

---

[1] See Stuffed Pimentos (p. 144) for the cleaning of pimentos for cooking.

smoking, put in the leeks, add a little salt and pepper, cover the pan and simmer for 10 minutes. Add the tomatoes cut in halves, the stoned olives, the lemon juice and the chopped lemon peel and cook slowly for another 10 minutes. Serve in the dish in which it has been cooked.

This is excellent cold as a salad.

Pois Chiches (Chick Peas)

These are the *garbanzos* of Spain, where they figure in a great many stews and soups. In Italy they are called *Ceci*, and are sometimes served mixed with *pasta*. They are also eaten a good deal in the Levant (see the recipe for *hummus bi tahina*, p. 159).

Soak $\frac{1}{2}$ lb. of chick peas for 24 hours. Put them in a thick pan and well cover with water. Season with a sliced onion, salt and pepper, sage, and garlic. Put them on the lowest possible flame and while they are cooking do not stir them or let them stop gently boiling or they will never get soft. They will take about 6 hours to cook.

Fennel

This is the Florentine, or sweet fennel, much cultivated in southern Europe for its thick and fleshy leaf stalks, as distinct from the common fennel, which will spread like a weed in any English garden, and of which only the delicate little leaves are used in the kitchen.

An absolutely delicious vegetable.

Cut the fennel roots in half and throw them into boiling water. When they are tender arrange them in a buttered fireproof dish, spread grated Parmesan and breadcrumbs on the top and put them in the oven until the cheese has melted.

In the south of France the very young fennel is cut in half and eaten raw, like celery, with salt and lemon juice.

Fèves au Lard

Throw young broad beans into boiling water. When cooked, fry some chopped bacon, add a little flour and some of the water in which the beans have cooked. When the sauce has thickened put in the beans, add half a cup of cream. The beans must not cook too long in the sauce or they will lose their fresh flavour.

Broad Beans and Artichokes (a Greek dish)

Cook separately 2 lbs. of broad beans and 8 artichoke bottoms. Strain the vegetables, keeping a little of the water in which the beans have cooked.

Heat 2 tablespoons of olive oil in a pan, stir in a very little cornflour, half a cup of the water in which the beans were cooked, the juice of a lemon, some chopped parsley, and add the artichokes and broad beans.

Céleri-Rave Farçi

Celeriac is usually eaten raw. It is peeled, cut into fine strips and mixed in a bowl with a rather mustardy mayonnaise. But it can be cooked as follows:

Peel 2 or 3 celeriac roots, cut them in half and blanch them. Scoop out some of the flesh.

Prepare the following stuffing: chopped mushrooms and shallots cooked a few moments in butter, to which add a sprinkling of flour, a cup of milk and 2 ozs. of any minced cold meat or chicken.

Fill the celeriacs with the stuffing, arrange them in a buttered casserole with more butter on the top, cover the pan and cook them in a slow oven for 45 minutes.

The milk in the stuffing mixture can be replaced by tomato purée.

Cavolfiore al Stracinati

Cavolfiore is the Italian for cauliflower, and "stracinati" means, literally, "pulled". Half cook a cauliflower in salted water; drain it, and discard the thick part of the stalk and the leaves, and divide the flowerets. Have ready a pan with warm olive oil in which you have put a clove of garlic, chopped, and put in the cauliflower; mash it with a fork and turn it over and over until it is browned on all sides.

Onions Agrodolce

Put about 25 peeled small onions in a heavy *sauteuse* with 3 tablespoons of olive oil. As soon as the onions start to brown, add a sherry glass of port, one of vinegar, 2 tablespoons of brown sugar, a handful of raisins, salt and cayenne pepper.

Simmer slowly until the onions are quite soft, and the sauce has turned to a thick syrup.

Stuffed Tomatoes à la Grecque

Displayed in enormous round shallow pans, these tomatoes, together with pimentos and small marrows cooked in the same way, are a feature of every Athenian *taverna*, where one goes into the kitchen and chooses one's meal from the pans arrayed on the stove. It is impossible to describe the effect of the marvellous smells which assail one's nose, and the sight of all those bright-coloured concoctions is overwhelming. Peering into every stewpan, trying a spoonful of this, a morsel of that, it is easy to lose one's head and order a dish of everything on the menu.

Cut off the tops of a dozen large tomatoes, scoop out the flesh and mix it with 2 cups of cooked rice. To this mixture add 2 tablespoons of chopped onion, 2 tablespoons of currants, some chopped garlic, pepper, salt, and, if you have it, some left-over lamb or beef. Stuff the tomatoes with this mixture and bake them in a covered dish in the oven, with olive oil.

TOMATES PROVENÇALES

Cut large ripe tomatoes in half. With a small sharp knife make several incisions crosswise in the pulp of the tomatoes, and in these rub salt, pepper and crushed garlic. Chop finely a good handful of parsley and spread each half tomato with it, pressing it well in.

Pour a few drops of olive oil on each and cook under the grill for preference, or in a hot oven.

To be quite perfect, Tomates Provençales should be slightly blackened on the cut surface.

TOMATES FROMAGÉES

Choose medium-sized tomatoes, cut off the tops, scoop out the flesh, sprinkle them with salt and leave them to drain.

In a double saucepan melt some Gruyère cheese with black pepper, cayenne, a little French mustard and a drop of white wine and a pounded clove of garlic.

Fill the tomatoes with the mixture, which should be about the consistency of a welsh rabbit. Bake for 10 minutes in the oven and finish under the grill.

CHAMPIGNONS À LA PROVENÇALE

½ lb. fresh field mushrooms, a small glass olive oil, parsley, garlic, salt and pepper.

Wash the mushrooms in cold water; slice them, leaving the stalks on. Heat the oil in a shallow pan, and when it is only fairly hot put in the mushrooms, and sauté them for 5 minutes. Add a handful of chopped parsley, a very little garlic, salt and pepper, and cook 2 or 3 more minutes.

Mushrooms à l'Arménienne

½ lb. mushrooms, 2 rashers bacon, garlic, parsley, olive oil, a glass of wine (red or white).

Slice the mushrooms, sauté them in 2 tablespoons of olive oil; add a few very fine slivers of garlic, and the bacon cut in squares.

Let this cook a few minutes before pouring in a glass of wine, then cook fiercely for just 1 minute (to reduce the wine), turn the flame low and simmer for 5 more minutes.

Mushrooms cooked in this way can be served as a separate course, as a garnish for scrambled eggs or omelettes, added to a *poulet en casserole*, or eaten cold as an hors d'œuvre.

Cèpes à la Bordelaise

Wash the cèpes and take the stalks off. If the cèpes are large ones cut them in 2 or 3 pieces. Put a glass of good olive oil in a sauté pan and when it is hot put in the cèpes. Let them brown a little, then turn the fire down very low. In the meantime chop the stalks finely with a handful of parsley and as much garlic as you like. Sauté this mixture in a separate pan, also in oil, then add it to the cèpes. They need about 25 to 30 minutes' cooking.

This method of cooking can be applied to all kinds of mushrooms.

Cèpes à l'Italienne

1 lb. cèpes or morels or other mushrooms, vine leaves, oil, garlic, salt and pepper.

Clean the cèpes, take off the stalks, put them on a dish and sprinkle with salt and leave them a little so that the water comes out of them, then put them in a warm oven a minute or two to dry them.

At the bottom of a fireproof dish lay the washed and dried vine leaves; cover them with a coating of olive oil and put them over the flame until the oil is hot but not boiling, when you put in the cèpes, stalk side up, cover the pan and put in a moderate oven for 30 minutes.

Now cut the stalks into thin pieces, with a clove of garlic, add them to the cèpes, season with black pepper and cook another 10 minutes.

Serve very hot in the dish in which they have cooked.

STUFFED PIMENTOS

No book of Mediterranean cooking would be complete without this dish, so although it is well known, here is a typical way of doing it.

Cut the stalks off the pimentos and make a small slit down the side of each one, through which you extract the core and the seeds. Take care over this operation and wash the pimentos under the tap, or there will be seeds left in, which are very fiery.

Stuff the pimentos with the same mixture as for tomatoes (p. 141) and put them in a deep baking dish with a moistening of tomato purée and a little oil on the top.

Cover the dish and cook in a medium oven for about 30 minutes.

PIMENTS SAUTÉS

Mixed red, green and yellow pimentos, cooked a few minutes in boiling water, then peeled and sautéd in butter. The seeds should be taken out before cooking. Especially good as an accompaniment to Wiener Schnitzel.

TA'AMIA

This Arab way of doing beans makes a delicious *mézé*[1] to serve with drinks.

[1] See p. 155.

1 cup dried and crushed haricot beans, parsley, green coriander, onion, garlic, salt, teaspoon bicarbonate of soda, handful bread soaked in water.

Wash the beans and soak them overnight. Put all the ingredients through the mincing machine and mix them well. To soften the dough pound it a little in the mortar. Mix in the bicarbonate of soda. Leave the mixture to rest for an hour or two, then cut it into small pieces and fry each one in very hot fat.

FASOÙLIA

The Greek name for haricot beans. People who appreciate the taste of genuine olive oil in their food will like this dish. Soak ½ lb. of beans for 12 hours. Heat half a tumbler of olive oil in a deep pan; put in the strained beans; lower the heat; stir the beans and let them simmer gently for 10 minutes, adding 2 cloves of garlic, a bayleaf, a branch of thyme, and a dessert-spoonful of tomato paste. Add boiling water to cover the beans by about one inch. Cook them over a moderate fire for 3 hours. The liquid should have reduced sufficiently to form a thickish sauce. Squeeze in the juice of a lemon, add some raw onion cut into rings, some salt and black pepper, and leave them to cool.

COLD FOOD AND SALADS

Luncheon at Montegufoni

"WHILE WE wandered through the high, cool rooms of the great house or, if it were not too hot, along the three sun-baked decks of the garden, Henry would be unpacking an ample luncheon of cold chicken, and Angelo Masti, the peasant in charge, would hurry in with a large, flat, cylindrical cheese, the *pecorino* of the neighbourhood, with a basket of figs and late peaches, tinged with green, and grapes, all still warm from the sun—some of these being of the kind called *fragole*, the small, plump, blue grapes, so different from others in their internal texture, and in their taste, which recalls that of the wood strawberry, that they might be fruit from the planet Mars or Venus—or a huge flask, covered in dry, dusty rushes, of the excellent red wine of the Castle itself. Presently, too, a very strong, pungent scent approaching us indicated that Angelo had just bought a large clothful of white truffles from a boy outside, who had been collecting them in the woods. (The white variety is only found, I believe, in Italy, and most commonly in Piedmont and Tuscany, and round Parma: it is coarser than the black, and, in its capacity to impregnate a dish, more resembles garlic, a fine grating of it on the top of any substance being sufficient.) His wife would cook for us, and send in a dish of rice or macaroni sprinkled with them. And these things to eat and drink would be placed on a table covered with the coarse white linen used by the *contadini*, under a ceiling painted with clouds and flying cupids, holding up in roseate air a coat of arms, a crown and a Cardinal's hat."

> *Great Morning*,
> by Sir Osbert Sitwell

Aspic Jelly

For many cold dishes aspic jelly is required as a garnish; the following is a good basic recipe.

Into a large saucepan put a knuckle of veal and a calf's foot, cut in convenient pieces, 2 carrots, 2 leeks (white part only), 1 onion stuck with cloves, the rind of about 6 rashers of bacon, 2 cloves of garlic, a small piece of lemon peel, thyme, bay leaves and marjoram, salt, a few peppercorns. Should you have the carcass of a chicken, or even the feet and neck, add these as well. Pour a glass of white wine into the pan, then cover the contents with water (about 4 pints for $2\frac{1}{2}$ pints of jelly). Bring the pan to the boil, take off the scum, and then leave to simmer for 4 to 5 hours.

Strain the liquid into a basin and leave it to cool. The next day, when the jelly has set, remove very carefully all the fat, so that no speck remains. To clarify the jelly, put into a saucepan the slightly beaten white of an egg, with the crushed egg shell, a sherry glass of port, a few leaves of tarragon, and a little lemon juice. Add the jelly, bring to the boil, then leave it barely simmering for 15 minutes. Now strain the jelly through a fine muslin, taking care not to stir up the sediment. To obtain an absolutely clear and limpid jelly it may be necessary to put it twice through the muslin.

POULET AUX NOIX

Prepare a concentrated stock by boiling for 2 hours in 1½ pints of water the insides of the chicken with carrots, leeks, turnips and seasoning. Cut the chicken in pieces, brown in butter; add a few small onions. Cover with the stock, and a spoonful of wine vinegar. Cook for 30 minutes. Meanwhile shell and mince 1 lb. of walnuts. From time to time add a little water to thin the oil which comes from the nuts. Add the minced nuts to the chicken and cook another 15 minutes. The sauce should be fairly thick.

Turn into a shallow dish and serve very cold.

COLD CHICKEN VÉRONIQUE

Divide a carefully boiled chicken into several large pieces. Put ½ oz. of butter in a pan and when it has melted pour in a glass of sherry. Add the pieces of chicken. Beat up 2 yolks of eggs with ½ pint of cream, pour over the chicken and stir until it has only slightly thickened. Sprinkle with finely chopped lemon peel and serve very cold. The sauce will thicken when the dish gets cold. This is far superior to the usual chicken salad with mayonnaise. Serve with the following rice salad:

Rice Salad

Boil some rice and while it is still warm mix in some oil, tarragon vinegar, salt, black pepper and a very little grated nutmeg. Add chopped celery, fresh basil leaves, a few stoned black olives, slices of peeled raw tomato, and red and green pimentos.

LEMON CHICKEN

Poach a chicken with turnips, carrots, onions and a large piece of lemon peel. Leave the chicken to cool in the stock and when cold take all the meat off the bones and cut into fairly large pieces. Strain the stock, keeping aside the vegetables. Take about 3 large ladles of the stock and heat in a pan. Add 2 tablespoons of chopped lemon rind, the juice of half a lemon and a small glass of sherry or white wine. Simmer 5 minutes, then thicken the sauce with a tablespoon or so of cornflour mixed in a teacup of milk, and when it begins to thicken put in your sliced chicken, the vegetables that were cooked with it cut into long strips and a handful of chopped watercress. Cook all together for a few minutes and turn into a glass dish.

Lemon chicken should be served cold, and the sauce, if made correctly and not too thick, should be very slightly gelatinous and have a translucent appearance. Small chunks of pineapple and a few blanched almonds can be added to this dish.

Note: The vegetables to be boiled with the chicken should be put in whole, otherwise they will be overdone and tasteless.

COLD STUFFED DUCK

If you don't know how to bone a duck probably the butcher or poulterer will do it for you. You must also have ready an aspic jelly made from calf's foot and veal bones, flavoured with garlic and port wine. Stuff the boned duck with a mixture of pâté de foie, plenty of chopped mushrooms and a truffle or two. Sew up the skin, wrap the duck in fat bacon, and roast it for about 25 minutes. Now remove the bacon fat, put the duck into a large shallow terrine, pour the melted jelly all round and place the covered terrine in a larger receptacle containing water, and steam in the oven for about 45 minutes.

Squeeze the juice of an orange over the duck and don't forget to remove the thread; serve cold in its jelly.

Pâté of Chicken Livers

Take about 1 lb. of chicken livers or mixed chicken, duck, pigeon or any game liver. Clean well and sauté in butter for 3 or 4 minutes. Remove the livers and to the butter in the pan add a small glass of sherry and a small glass of brandy. Mash the livers to a fine paste (they should be pink inside) with plenty of salt, black pepper, a clove of garlic, 2 ozs. of butter, a pinch of mixed spice and a pinch of powdered herbs— thyme, basil and marjoram. Add the liquid from the pan, put the mixture into a small earthenware terrine and place on the ice.

Serve with hot toast.

Pâté de Lièvre

Mince together 2 lbs. of the raw flesh of a hare with 3 lbs. of fat bacon, 2 onions, and parsley; add 3 liqueur glasses of brandy, salt and black pepper, and knead them all together until they are well amalgamated. Take one large or several small earthenware terrines, fill them with the mixture, place on top a bay leaf, some bacon rashers and a piece of waxed paper. Cover the dishes. Put them in a bain-marie into a slow oven and cook 1 hour for the small terrines, 2 hours for the large. If covered with a thick layer of melted lard, and a piece of wax paper and stored in a cool place, they will keep for months.

This pâté can also be made with rabbit.

Terrine de Campagne

1 lb. of belly of pork, 1 lb. of lean veal, $\frac{3}{4}$ lb. of bacon, a tea-cupful of white wine, 2 tablespoons of brandy, a few juniper berries, mace, 2 large cloves of garlic, thyme and marjoram, salt and black pepper, bay leaves.

Remove the rind and any bones from the pork, and cut it, together with the veal (the meat from a knuckle does very well for a terrine) and $\frac{1}{2}$ lb. of the bacon, into small squares; if you really have to save time, have the pork and veal coarsely minced by the butcher. Chop the garlic, juniper berries (about 8) and herbs and add to the meat. Season with the ground mace or nutmeg and salt and pepper. Not too much salt, as a good deal is already supplied by the bacon. Put all the meat into a bowl, pour over the white wine and brandy, mix thoroughly, and leave to stand for 2 hours.

Cut the remaining $\frac{1}{4}$ lb. bacon into small strips the length of a match and about $\frac{1}{4}$ inch wide and thick. Arrange these strips criss-cross fashion at the bottom of the terrine or terrines, and pack in the meat, fairly firmly. Fill almost to the top. Put a bay leaf on the top. and then more strips of the bacon, in the same criss-cross fashion. Stand the terrines in a baking tin half full of water and cook in a slow oven (Regulo 3 or 4) for $1\frac{1}{2}$ hours for small terrines, 2 hours for larger ones. It is the depth of the terrines which is the point to consider. When the terrines have cooled a little put a piece of greaseproof paper over them and a 2-lb. weight on the top and leave several hours. If to be stored, seal with pure pork lard. Should you have the end of a ham to be used up, 1 lb. can be used instead of the $\frac{1}{2}$ lb. of bacon, but be very sparing with salt.

Jambon Persillé de Bourgogne

This is the traditional Easter dish of Burgundy. The recipe comes from the famous Restaurant des Trois Faisans at Dijon.

Soak a ham for 24 hours, in order to desalt it. Half cook the ham in a large pan of unsalted water, reckoning 10 minutes to the pound instead of the usual 20. Drain it, remove the rind and divide it into large pieces.

Put it to cook again with a knuckle of veal of about 1 lb. in weight cut in pieces; 2 calf's feet, boned; a bouquet garni of chervil and tarragon; 10 grains of white pepper tied in a muslin, a little salt, and cover it with a white Burgundy. Bring it to the boil, and then continue cooking gently, on a steady heat, so as to preserve the limpidity of the stock, which is to become the jelly; skim off the fat which rises to the surface from time to time.

When the ham is cooked, and *very* cooked, mash it a little with a fork, and turn it into a large bowl, pressing it down with a fork. Strain the liquid through a muslin, add a little tarragon vinegar. When the liquid has started to jelly, stir in 2 tablespoons of chopped parsley. Pour this jelly over the ham, and keep it in a cold place until the next day.

Oie en Daube

Put the goose into a thick fireproof casserole with diced bacon, parsley, shallots, garlic, thyme, bay leaf, basil, 2 glasses of water, 2 of red wine, ½ glass of cognac, salt and pepper. Hermetically seal the pan and cook very slowly for 5 hours. Strain the sauce and when it is cool remove the fat, pour back over the goose and serve cold. Chicken can be cooked the same way, either whole or cut into joints.

Bœuf à la Mode à la Provençale

3 or 4 lbs. of round or topside of beef. Lard the beef with small pieces of bacon and cloves of garlic. Tie round with string, season with salt and pepper and brown on all sides in

bacon fat. Put into a deep casserole, cover with a quantity of well-fried onions, 5 or 6 carrots, a piece of celery, a piece of orange or lemon peel, thyme, bay leaf, peppercorns, cloves and a calf's foot or veal bones cut up, cover with half water and half red wine. Cook extremely slowly either on top of the stove or in the oven (Regulo 1 or 2) for 7 or 8 hours.

Remove the meat, which should be so soft it can be cut with a spoon, take off the string and put it into the serving dish. Strain the sauce over and, when it is cold, remove the fat. The meat should be entirely covered with a soft clear jelly.

Serve with potatoes baked in their jackets and a plain salad, but no other vegetables.

FILET DE PORC FRAIS TRUFFÉ FROID

This beautiful recipe is given by Paul Poiret in his *107 Recettes et Curiosités Culinaires*.

You need a fine fillet[1] of pork, cut from a young animal; cut some uncooked *truffes* in pieces about the size of a pigeon's egg. With the point of a knife make a number of deep incisions, a few centimetres apart, in the inside of the fillet. Into each incision introduce a piece of *truffe*, pushing it well in towards the centre of the fillet, to produce a marbled effect. When the fillet is thus piquèd with the *truffes*, season it with salt and pepper, roll it up into a good shape, tie it with string, and roast it.

Leave it to cool in its own fat, and serve it cold the next day.

PICTÍ

Picti is the Greek brawn.

A pig's head is boiled for hours in water strongly flavoured with bay leaves and peppercorns.

[1] See page 90.

When cooked it is cut up into chunks, the juice of 3 or 4 lemons is added to the strained stock, which is poured over the brawn, arranged in large earthenware basins, and left to set. Not very elegant, but usually very good.

CHANFAÏNA OF LIVER (a Spanish dish)

1 lb. pig's liver, 3 tablespoons olive oil, 4 onions, a few mint leaves, 2 or 3 parsley stalks (finely chopped), 2 red pimentos, 3 cloves, a pinch of cumin, a pinch of cinnamon, a pinch of saffron, black pepper, breadcrumbs.

Blanch the liver, cut in pieces, in salted water. In the oil put all the other ingredients, except the breadcrumbs.

Cook them a minute or two, and add the strained liver, and a little of the water it has been cooked in, let it simmer a few minutes, then stir in the breadcrumbs.

Pour the whole mixture into a dish and serve cold.

PIMENTOS TO SERVE WITH COLD MEAT (Escoffier's recipe)

Warm half a wineglass of olive oil in a thick pan. Put in 1 lb. of finely chopped white onions and 2¼ lbs. of pimentos, from which you have removed the core and the seeds; cut in rounds. Cover the pan and let them simmer 15 minutes, when you add 2 lbs. of very ripe peeled tomatoes, a clove of garlic, a teaspoon of powdered ginger, 1 lb. of sugar, ½ lb. of sultanas and a teaspoon of mixed spice. Pour over a pint of good vinegar and continue cooking very slowly for 3 hours.

NOTE ON HORS D'ŒUVRE

As I have not given a separate chapter for hors d'œuvre I have included a few in this section on cold food. In Spain, the south of France and Italy an hors d'œuvre is a very simple affair, consisting usually of olives, salame sausage, a tomato or pimento salad and a few anchovies in oil, or alternatively a plate of fresh shell fish, prawns or *oursins* (those spiny sea-urchins cut in half from which you scoop out the coral with a piece of bread). The Genoese are fond of an antipasto of *Sardo* (a hard ewe's milk cheese imported from Sardinia), young raw broad beans, and the local, rather highly flavoured salame. In Greece your *mezé* (the equivalent of our hors d'œuvre) is eaten while you drink your aperitif and not as part of the main meal. You can sit at a table on the sand with your feet almost in the Aegean as you drink your *Ouzou*; boys with baskets of little clams or *kidónia* (sea quinces) pass up and down the beach and open them for you at your table; or the waiter will bring you large trays of olives, of which there are dozens of different kinds and colours in Greece, dishes of *Atherinous* (tiny fried fish rather like our white-bait), slices of fresh crumbly cheese called *mysíthra*, or *graviera* (the Cretan Gruyère), small pieces of grilled octopus, minute *kephtédés* (little rissoles made of crushed haricot beans and fried in oil), quarters of fresh raw turnip (this sounds doubtful but is in fact delicious for there is no vegetable more vegetable-tasting than these little turnips freshly dug up from the garden), slices of fresh cucumber cooled in ice water; all this accompanied by limes or lemons and a mound of bread. There are also many kinds of smoked or cured fish —*lakerda* (a kind of smoked tunny fish), red caviar or *brique*, *botargue* (pressed tunny fish eggs made into a kind of sausage and eaten in slices with oil and lemon), and *tarama* for which I have given a recipe.

In Turkey and Egypt there is a kind of ham called *bastourma*, of Armenian origin, heavily spiced with garlic and red pepper, and in the Greek islands the peasants make a small fillet of ham called *louza*, strongly flavoured with herbs, which is excellent. The Cypriots have little sausages heavily spiced with coriander seeds, and the Italians dozens of different local salame and country hams, best of which are the *prosciutto di San Daniele* and *prosciutto di Parma* (raw Parma ham) which, eaten with fresh figs, or melon, or simply with butter, must be the most perfect hors d'œuvre ever invented.

BLACK OLIVES

"The whole Mediterranean, the sculpture, the palms, the gold beads, the bearded heroes, the wine, the ideas, the ships, the moonlight, the winged gorgons, the bronze men, the philosophers—all of it seems to rise in the sour, pungent taste of these black olives between the teeth. A taste older than meat, older than wine. A taste as old as cold water."[1]

GREEN OLIVES

Olives to serve with cocktails or as hors d'œuvre are better bought by the pound, not in bottles; prepare them in this way, as they do in Marseille.

Choose the small oblong French or Greek olives. In each olive make an incision with a knife, and put them in layers in a jar with some pieces of cut garlic and 2 or 3 stalks of thyme, and a small piece of chile pepper, fill the jars up with olive oil, and cover them. In this way they can be stored for months.

Black olives can be treated in the same way, or simply put straight into olive oil without the garlic or thyme.

AMBELOPOÙLIA

These are the tiny birds called *beccafica* or figpeckers. In Cyprus they are preserved in vinegar and eaten whole, bones and all.

Pluck a dozen *beccafica*, cut off the feet, and, if they are to be preserved, the heads as well, but do not clean them out.

---

[1] *Prospero's Cell*, by Lawrence Durrell.

Bring a small saucepan of water to the boil, add a teaspoon of salt and boil the little birds in this for 5 or 6 minutes. Take them out of the water, drain them well, and allow them to cool. They can then be eaten cold as they are, or preserved for as long as a year by being put into a glass or earthenware jar and covered with wine vinegar, to which a tablespoon of salt is added or not, as you please.

DOLMÁDÉS

Dolmádés, little rolls of savoury rice in vine leaves, are a favourite first course in Greece, Turkey, and the Near East.

For 3 dozen vine leaves you need about 2 teacups of cooked rice mixed with enough olive oil to make it moist, and a little chopped fried onion. Blanch the vine leaves in boiling salted water. On the back of each leaf spread a teaspoon of the rice, and then fold the leaf up like a little parcel and squeeze it in the palm of your hand; in this manner the *dolmádés* will stay rolled up and need not be tied. When they are all ready put them carefully in a shallow pan, squeeze over plenty of lemon juice and add about a cup (enough to come half-way up the pile of *dolmádés*) of tomato juice or good stock. Cover with a small plate or saucer resting on top of the *dolmádés* to prevent them moving during the cooking and keep them just simmering for about 30 minutes. They are best eaten cold. A good cocktail snack.

SALAD OF AUBERGINES

A good dish from Greece and the Near East, where it is often served as a *mézé*. You dip slices of bread into the salad and eat it while drinking your apéritif.

Grill 3 or 4 large aubergines in their skins. When they are soft, peel them and pound the flesh in a mortar with 2 cloves of garlic, salt and pepper. Add, drop by drop, a little olive oil, as for a mayonnaise. When it is a thick purée, add the juice of half a lemon and a handful of chopped parsley.

The grilling of the aubergines gives the finished dish a characteristic slightly smoky flavour. If preferred they can be boiled or baked instead of grilled.

AUBERGINES IN A MARINADE

Cut the aubergines in half, lengthways, without peeling them. Sprinkle them with salt and leave them for 2 hours. Drain off the water which has come out of them, and fry them lightly in oil.

Then put them in jars, and pour over them a marinade consisting of 2 parts oil to 1 part white wine, or wine vinegar.

They will keep like this for some days, and are served as hors d'œuvre, or can be stuffed or used in a stew.

TARAMÁ

Taramá is the name given to the dried eggs of grey mullet pressed and sold out of a barrel—a favourite *mézé* in Greece and Turkey.

Take about ¼ lb. of *taramá* and pound it in a mortar with lemon juice and olive oil, added very slowly, until the preparation has a consistency of a thick and smooth purée. Add a few drops of water to thin it. It is served with bread and butter or hot toast. The taste is not unlike that of English smoked cod's roe, which can be treated in the same way, the skin having first been removed.

SARDINES MARINÉES À LA NIÇOISE

Fresh sardines are grilled and then put to marinate for a few days in olive oil, with a drop of vinegar, a bay leaf, peppercorns, and herbs, and served as hors d'œuvre.

HUMMUS BI TAHINA

An Arab dish. Tahina is the sesame paste which is to be found in Oriental stores[1] in London, and which is mixed with oil and garlic and thinned with water to make a sauce which in Arab countries is eaten as a salad, with bread dipped into it.

For this hors d'œuvre the ingredients are ½ lb. of chick peas, a cupful each of tahina, olive oil, and water; a little lemon juice, mint, and garlic.

Cook the chick peas in plenty of water, slowly, for about 6 hours. They should be very soft for this dish. Strain them, pound them to a fine paste, or, if you prefer, put them through the food mill. Pound two or three cloves of garlic into the purée, stir in the tahina, the olive oil, the lemon juice, and season with salt and pepper. Thin with water until the mixture is about the consistency of a thick mayonnaise. Stir in about 2 tablespoons of dried or fresh mint. The mixture is poured either into a large shallow dish, or on to saucers, one for each person, and sets fairly firmly when cold.

TAHINA SALAD

Pound a clove of garlic in a mortar; stir in a cupful of the tahina paste, salt, pepper, half a cupful of olive oil, half a cupful of water, lemon juice and coarsely chopped parsley. The tahina should be of the consistency of cream. In Egypt and Syria a bowl of tahina is served either with pre-lunch drinks or as an hors d'œuvre, with pickled cucumbers, pickled turnips, and the flat round bread (Esh Baladi) of the country. The tahina is eaten by dipping the bread into the bowl.

PAN BANIA (a Provençal sandwich)

Cut fresh french rolls in half lengthways. Rub them with garlic. Spread with stoned black olives, pieces of red pimento,

[1] The Oriental Provision Stores, 25 Charlotte Street; John and Pascalis, 35 Grafton Way, Tottenham Court Road; The Little Pulteney Stores, Brewer Street, W.1.

tomato and young raw broad beans. Pour on a little olive oil and vinegar over the rolls, join the two halves together and put them under a heavy weight for 30 minutes.

Pan Bania is served in Provençal cafés with a bottle of wine when a game of *boules* is in progress. The ingredients vary according to what is in season, or what is available. There may be anchovies, gherkins, artichoke hearts, lettuce. Probably it is the origin of *salade niçoise* which is made with the same variety of ingredients, but without the bread.

TIAN

One of the national dishes of Provence, but a family dish; one that the tourist will search for in vain on the menus of restaurants.

It is the container which indicates the contents, and the *tian* owes its name to the vast and heavy terrine of the earthenware of Vallauris, where it is sent to cook on a wood fire in the baker's oven. The dish consists of a gratin of green vegetables, spinach, and chard (*blettes*), sometimes mixed with marrows, all finely chopped, and first melted in—this is essential—olive oil. For this reason the dish is to be found in olive-growing areas. But from one region to another the dish is subject to all kinds of variations, which give it its local *cachet*. Up in the hills they do not despise the addition of salt cod; on the coast this is replaced with fresh sardines or anchovies.

This savoury mosaic can also be enriched with a few cloves of garlic, a cupful of rice, or a handful of chick peas. Another refinement is to thicken it with eggs and cover the top with breadcrumbs and Parmesan.

Tian is one of those ready-made dishes which is eaten cold on picnics. There is a story that six gourmets from Carpentras, having decided to treat each other, each provided at the time fixed for the picnic a surprise dish of a monumental *tian*; all six were devoured with patriotic enthusiasm. Not one of the guests had been able to imagine that there was a better dish in the world.

From *La Cuisine à Nice*, H. Heyraud

PATAFLA (a good recipe for a cocktail party or a picnic)

4 tomatoes, 1 large onion, 2 green pimentos, 2 ozs. black olives, 3 ozs. green olives, 2 ozs. capers, 2 ozs. gherkins, 1 long French loaf.

Peel the tomatoes, stone the olives, take the core and seeds out of the pimentos, and chop them together with all the other ingredients. Cut the loaf in half longways and with a sharp knife remove all the crumb, which you mix with the tomato preparation, kneading it all together with a little olive oil, a pinch of paprika, black pepper and salt.

Now fill the two halves of the loaf with the mixture, put them together and put the loaf into the frigidaire.

To serve, cut into thin slices about a quarter-inch thick, and pile them up on a plate.

Always make *patafla* the day before it is needed.

A PROVENÇAL SALAD

Mix shredded celery with chopped watercress, grated orange peel, parsley, garlic, stoned black olives and slices of tomato. Oil and lemon dressing.

OIGNONS À LA MONEGASQUE

Choose small pickling onions. Peel them and put them into a little boiling water.

When they are half cooked add olive oil, a little vinegar, 2 or 3 chopped tomatoes, thyme, parsley, a bay leaf and a handful of currants. They are served cold.

SALAD OF SWEET PEPPERS

Cold cooked red peppers (or mixed green and red) with oil and vinegar dressing.

LEEKS À LA GRECQUE

Boil some small leeks. When they are nearly cold drain most of the water away, leaving enough to cover them. Stir some of this water into a teaspoon of cornflour, add to the leeks and stir until the sauce thickens a little. Squeeze in the juice of a lemon, stirring all the time, and add a tablespoon of olive oil. Let the leeks get cold in the sauce, which should be slightly gelatinous and shiny.

Serve as it is.

SALADE DE HARICOTS BLANCS SECS

Cold boiled haricot beans, drained and mixed while still warm with oil and vinegar, chopped raw onion, slices of salami sausage and parsley.

SALADE AUX ÉPINARDS

Plunge some cleaned spinach into boiling water for 3 minutes. Drain it, mix with some sliced cold potatoes and thin slices of Gruyère cheese. Dress with a spoonful of cream and the juice of a lemon.

PICKLED CUCUMBER SALAD

Into a bowl of Yoghourt mix a little of the vinegar from pickled cucumbers, a handful of chopped mint and a little sugar. Into this mixture put the sliced pickled cucumbers.

A Few Sweets

"SOMEWHERE round about half-past six that evening I was taken to a famous café at the end of the university boulevard, the name of which eludes my memory. Here faced by the prospect of nothing but boiled rice for days to come I was presented by the waiter with a card on which some thirty different kinds of ices were listed. The temptation was atrocious. My soul responds to a mere vanilla ice smeared out into the thick glass of an Italian ice-cream vendor; but here was an opportunity to sample ices which were to the ordinary vanilla as Hyperion to a satyr. Although I knew nothing could be worse for my complaint than even a moderate indulgence in ices, greed and curiosity were too much for me. I really did feel that life was less important than sampling these ices to discover which were the most delicious. Some of the fervour which has given martyrs to science was mine. I understood and sympathised with the impulse that drives a man to explore the North Pole. I comprehended at last the passionate recklessness of Bluebeard's Fatima. Even without dysentery and cystitis it would have been impossible for any man to sample every ice on that list, and I do not remember that ever in my life I was so anxious to make a right choice. Paris faced by the problem of awarding an apple to the most beautiful of three goddesses was in no predicament at all compared with mine. I looked at the waiter. Could I rely on his taste to direct me aright, so that whatever pain I might suffer on the morrow would not be embittered by the thought that for all I was suffering I had chosen the wrong ices? And while I was trying to decide with what varieties I should make myself that amount more ill than I was already I found myself

being introduced to the wives of various members of the
British Naval Mission whose habit it was to meet here at
dusk. . . . I heard which were the best six ices on the list and
of those six I ate four. Then, thinking of that boiled rice before
me and deciding that I might as well make the most of what
life remained to me, I wound up my last night of freedom
with a mayonnaise of crayfish at dinner."

> *First Athenian Memories*
> by Compton Mackenzie

I have included only a few sweets in this collection. The
sweet course in these southern countries, and particularly in the
eastern Mediterranean, frequently consists of very sweet little
cakes and pastries, and bowls of fresh fruit. The cakes usually
require quantities of eggs, sugar, honey, almonds, pistachio
nuts, rose-water, sesame seeds and other Arabian Night ingredients. Very often little bowls of Yoghourt are handed
round and eaten with sugar and a conserve of quinces or little
oranges, more like jam than our compote.[1] The Greeks are
also much addicted to a slab-like cold rice sweet, called *rizo-
galo*, liberally sprinkled with cinnamon, *loukoumadés*, which
are like very small doughnuts served in a honey syrup, and
baklawá, the honey and almond cakes which originated in
Turkey.

The huge selection of ices which had such allure for Mr.
Compton Mackenzie are still, so far as I know, a speciality of
the large cafés in Athens; one does not find them, though, in
the small *tavernas* and typical Greek restaurants. The Athenians
dine very late, so they sit in these cafés drinking *oúzo* or
Varvaressou brandy until nine o'clock in the evening. After

---

[1] In Greece these conserves are always offered to a stranger arriving at the house,
served on a tray with a glass of water and a small cup of sweet Turkish coffee.
a symbol of hospitality which must on no account be refused.

dinner they will return to the café, to eat ices and sweet cakes with their Turkish coffee.

In the summer fresh fruit is put on the table in bowls of ice, melon is served at the end of a meal, not at the beginning, and the beautiful *pastèque* or water melon is much eaten for its thirst-quenching properties.

In the winter there are the succulent dried figs and raisins of Greece and Smyrna; tender little apricots dried with their stones in from Damascus; *loucoumi*,[1] to accompany sweet Turkish coffee. In Italy there will be Zabaglione, the famous sweet of frothed egg yolks, sugar and Marsala, delicious water ices (*granite*), Sicilian *Cassata* and elaborate ice-creams (although both of these are eaten as refreshments at odd times of the day more than at the end of a meal; they have also become rather Americanized in recent years). The Neapolitans make very beautiful-looking fan-shaped pastries, filled with cream cheese and spices, called *sfogliatelle*, and their Christmas sweet, *pastiera Napoletana*, is a rich and solid confection of eggs, butter, sugar, almonds, spices, and crushed wheat.

The Spaniards serve nougats and *turrons* and quince paste with the coffee; the little town of Apt, in the Comtat Venaissin, in Northern Provence, produces delicious candied apricots and other *fruits confits*, and no one who has seen them will forget the gorgeous displays of crystallized fruits of every conceivable variety in the shops of Nice, Cannes, and Genoa.

In the rose-coloured city of Toulouse there is scarcely a street without a confectioner's window showing little boxes of candied violets, and among the best of all French sweetmeats are the delicate, diamond-shaped little *calissons* of Aix-en-Provence.

Nearly all these delicacies belong rather to the province of the professional pastrycook or confectioner; I have tried therefore to give recipes for the sweet course which will be practical

[1] Turkish Delight.

possibilities for the amateur cook at home, at the same time using the ingredients of Mediterranean cooking, the oranges, lemons, apricots, and almonds, the honey and cream cheese, the eggs and wine and figs of those shores.

HONEYED SOUFFLÉ

Beat 1½ teacups of honey into the yolks of 4 eggs, then heat without boiling, over hot water, and stir until the mixture thickens.

When it has cooled, fold in the well-beaten whites of the eggs and 4 or 5 ozs. (about ¼ pint) of whipped cream.

Keep on the ice.

HONEY PINEAPPLE

Cut some fresh pineapple into chunks, cover them with honey and heat gently until the honey thickens and starts to caramelise.

Serve with cream.

A DISH OF POMEGRANATES

Take all the inside from 6 pomegranates and mash them into a silver bowl. Sprinkle with rose-water, lemon juice and sugar and serve iced.

CRÈME À L'ORANGE

3 ozs. of sugar, 4 yolks of eggs, juice of 4 oranges, 1 lemon and the grated rind.

Mix all together and cook slowly, like a custard. Garnish with slices of oranges.

CRÈME AU CAFÉ

Make some very strong coffee with 2 ozs. coffee. Strain it into 1 pint of milk, add 4 ozs. powdered sugar, 6 yolks of eggs and 3 whites beaten stiffly with a few spoons of cream. Pour this cream into the serving dish, cover it and place on top of a saucepan of boiling water, stirring until it thickens. When cold pour caramelised sugar over the top.

WATER MELON STUFFED WITH BLACKBERRIES

If by any chance you happen to come upon a water melon and some blackberries in the same season try this dish.

Cut the water melon in half, take away the black seeds and cut up the red flesh into pieces. Squeeze lemon juice on to it and mix it with some blackberries. Put them back in the halves of melon, add sugar, and put on the ice.

BAKED BANANAS

Peel and split bananas and cut in half. Place in baking dish with butter, brown sugar, orange and lemon juice, nutmeg, cinnamon, a tablespoon of honey and a glass of rum. Place strips of lemon peel on the top and bake for about 30 minutes in a moderate oven. The sauce should be thick and syrupy.

FRUIT SALAD

Fruit salad can be delicious; it can also be very nasty indeed. Here is a good recipe which includes the making of the syrup which is so important.

2 oranges, 1 apple, 1 pear, 1 grapefruit, 2 bananas, 3 fresh figs, 2 slices pineapple, either fresh or tinned.

For the syrup, bring 2 teacups of water to the boil; throw in 10 lumps of sugar and the peel of an orange cut in strips. Boil for 3 minutes and leave the syrup to cool.

Prepare the fruit carefully, put it into a glass dish and pour over it a small wineglass of maraschino, and the prepared syrup.

It is important that the fruit salad should be very well iced, and it should be prepared several hours before it is needed.

APRICOTINA

½ lb. dried apricots, ¼ lb. butter, 2 ozs. sugar, 4 eggs.

Soak the apricots in water for 2 or 3 hours. Stew them slowly and keep aside 10 or so nice whole apricots for the garnish, and put the rest through a sieve, keeping the juice separately, and reserve 2 tablespoons of the purée, also for the garnish. Now put the purée into a saucepan, and add gradually the sugar, the butter, and the yolks of the eggs, stirring all the time until you have a smooth thick cream. Leave it to cool. Fold in the stiffly beaten whites of the eggs, and pour the whole mixture into a buttered soufflé dish and steam it (on the top of the stove) for 45 minutes. When it has cooled turn the pudding out on to the serving dish. Now spread over the top the purée which you have reserved and on the top of this arrange the whole apricots. For the sauce, mix the apricot juice with an equal quantity of thin cream. This sweet is greatly improved by being made the day before, and kept in the refrigerator, in which case it is preferable not to do the garnishing until an hour before you are going to serve it.

Apricotina is not such a trouble as it sounds: the result should be something between a moist cake and an iced soufflé.

APRICOT SOUFFLÉ

Put ½ lb. of cooked dried apricots through a sieve. Put them in a buttered, sugared soufflé dish. Mix in the stiffly beaten whites of 3 or 4 eggs. Bake in a fairly hot oven for 15 to 20 minutes.

MANDARINETTES

The peel of 2 tangerines, 7 ozs. ground almonds, 4 ozs. sugar, 2 whites of eggs, 2 tablespoons flour.

Mix the sugar, almonds, flour, finely shredded peel and beaten whites of eggs. Put on a buttered baking-tin in the shape of small balls, commence in a moderate oven and finish 8 to 10 minutes in an increased heat.

Serve cold.

COLD ORANGE SOUFFLÉ

1 pint orange juice, about ½ oz. gelatine, 2 tablespoons sugar, 2 eggs.

Soak the gelatine in the orange juice for 30 minutes. Put the orange juice in a saucepan with the sugar and as soon as it starts to boil take it off the fire and pour gently through a strainer over the yolks of eggs. Stir well, and leave to cool. Add the stiffly beaten whites and fold them into the soufflé. Leave to set, and put whipped cream flavoured with sherry on top.

GÂTEAU DE ROCHEFORT

1 lb. flour, 6 eggs, ¼ lb. butter, ¼ lb. soft brown sugar (or Demerara), 1 dessertspoon orange-flower water, 1 tablespoon cognac, 3 ozs. peeled shredded almonds, 2 ozs. angelica.

Knead the flour with the eggs, butter and sugar. Add the orange-flower water, the cognac, the almonds and the angelica cut in small pieces. Work this all well together, adding a little more flour if the paste is too soft.

Roll out very thin—about an eighth of an inch—and cut it in the shape of a round galette. With the point of a knife, make small incisions in the surface, to form a design. Paint with egg and bake in a moderate oven.

ESH ES SERAYA, OR PALACE BREAD (an Egyptian sweet)

Heat ½ lb. of honey with ¼ lb. of sugar and ¼ lb. of butter until the mixture thickens. Add 4 ozs. white breadcrumbs.

Cook all together in a saucepan, stirring until it has become a homogeneous mass. Turn out on to a plate and when cold it will be like a soft cake, and can be cut into triangular portions. This sweet is always served with a cream which is skimmed off the top of quantities of milk cooked very slowly until a thick skin forms on the top, so stiff that when separated from the milk it can be rolled up. A little roll of this cream is placed on top of each portion of Palace Bread.

SIPHNIAC HONEY PIE

These quantities fill 2 medium-sized flat pie dishes.

1 lb. unsalted *myzíthra* (this is the fresh Greek cheese made from sheep's milk; in England ordinary fresh milk cheese can be used), 4 ozs. honey, 3 ozs. sugar, 8 ozs. flour, 8 ozs. butter, 4 eggs, cinnamon.

Make a paste of the flour and butter with some water, roll it out thin and line the tins. Work the cheese and warmed honey together, add the sugar, the beaten eggs and a little cinnamon and spread this mixture on the paste and bake in a medium oven (Regulo 5) for 35 minutes.

Sprinkle the top with a little cinnamon.

BEIGNETS DE PRUNEAUX

Soak prunes in weak tea for 2 hours and then in rum. Make a frying batter[1] with the addition of a tablespoon of rum and fry the prunes. When golden, roll them in powdered chocolate mixed with vanilla sugar.

GÂTEAU DE FIGUES SÈCHES

1 lb. figs, 1½ pints milk, 4 tablespoons rice, 3 eggs, 2 ozs. butter.

Let the rice soften in the milk. When it is well soaked turn into a basin in the bottom of which are the figs cut up. Leave

[1] Page 50

to cool. Add the eggs one by one, then the butter, mix well. Pour into a buttered mould and cook slowly for 2 hours.

FIGUES AU FOUR

In a fireproof dish arrange some fine, unpeeled figs. Put in a little water, sprinkle them with sugar and bake them (as for baked apples).
Serve them cold, with cream.

TORRIJAS

The Spanish version of a sweet well known in most European countries, and designed for using up stale bread. In France it is called *Pain Perdu*.

First prepare a syrup of $\frac{1}{4}$ lb. of sugar, a coffeecupful of water, a small piece of lemon peel, a pinch of cinnamon, all cooked together for 10 minutes or so. When the syrup has cooled add a small glass of sweet white wine or sherry.

Cut 8 to 10 slices of white bread, about $\frac{1}{4}$ inch thick. Soak them in milk (about $\frac{1}{2}$ pint) then in beaten egg (1 large egg should be sufficient).

Fry the slices until crisp and golden in very hot olive oil. Pour the cooled syrup over them and serve. Instead of sugar honey can be used to make the syrup.

CENCI

Cenci are good to serve with a cold sweet, mousse, ice-cream, etc.

$\frac{1}{2}$ lb. flour, 1 oz. butter, 1 oz. castor sugar, 2 eggs, few drops cognac, pinch of salt, grated lemon peel.

Make a rather stiff paste with all the ingredients. Work it well with the hands and then leave it to rest for a little, wrapped in a floured cloth. Take a small piece at a time and roll out very thin, like paper. Cut into shapes—bows, crescents, plaits, or diamonds, etc. Make an incision in each biscuit with a knife. Dip them into a pan of hot fat, turn immediately and then take them out. When they are cool sprinkle them with castor sugar.

This quantity makes a very large number. Half quantities would be enough for 6 people.

YOGHOURT

Throughout the Balkans and the Middle East Yoghourt, or Yaourti, is served as a sweet, or as a sauce (as for the pilaff on p. 102) in salad (p. 162); it is eaten for breakfast or at any meal, and is refreshing and light in a hot climate. Try it with brown sugar and hot stewed fruit. Dried apricots are particularly good, fresh damsons, apple purée, blackcurrant purée, quince or bitter orange marmalade.

ORANGE AND ALMOND CAKE

The juice of 3 oranges, grated rind of 1 orange, 4 ozs. ground almonds, 2 ozs. fine breadcrumbs, 4 ozs. sugar, 4 eggs, ½ teaspoon salt, cream, orange-flower water.

Mix together the breadcrumbs, orange juice and grated orange rind, add the ground almonds, and, if available, a tablespoon of orange-flower water.

Beat the egg yolks with the sugar and salt until almost white. Add to the first mixture. Fold in the stiffly beaten egg whites. Pour into a square cake tin, buttered and sprinkled with breadcrumbs, and bake in a moderate oven (Regulo 4) for about 40 minutes.

When cold turn the cake out and cover the top with whipped cream (about ¼ pint). Very good and light, and excellent for a sweet at luncheon or dinner.

Jams Chutneys
and Preserves

Corfu: Making the Preserves

"Now THAT the *robola*[1] is safely on the way, the Count can turn his attention to the kitchens with their gleaming copper ware and dungeon-like ovens. Here he busies himself with Caroline and Mrs. Zarian in the manufacture of *mustalevria*—that delicious Ionian sweet or jelly which is made by boiling fresh must to half its bulk with semolina and a little spice. The paste is left to cool on plates and stuck with almonds; and the whole either eaten fresh or cut up in slices and put away in the great store cupboard.

"*Sykopita*, Zarian's favourite fig cake, will come later when the autumn figs are literally bursting open with their own ripeness. But for the time being there are conserves of all kinds to be made—orange-flower preserve and morella syrup. While the Count produces for the table a very highly spiced quince cheese, black and sticky, but very good."

Prospero's Cell,
by Lawrence Durrell

[1] A "black" wine made in Corfu.

Poires à l'Aigre-doux

Make a syrup with 1¾ pints of white wine vinegar, 2 lbs. sugar, peel of half a lemon, cinnamon. Cook in the syrup 6 to 8 lbs. of small peeled pears. Pour into a basin, cover and leave a week. Strain, put the fruit into bottles, reheat the syrup and pour it boiling on to the fruit. Cool before covering.

Plums à l'Aigre-doux

Ripe but fine plums. Wipe and prick with needle. Make a syrup as for Poires à l'aigre-doux, adding cloves and nutmeg instead of lemon, put them into the boiling syrup. Take each one out as soon as the skin is lightly broken. Strain them in a sieve, add the juice to the syrup, reboil it and pour on to the fruit in pots.

Melon à l'Aigre-doux

Good for serving with a cold curry.

Peel a 3 lb. melon, throw away the seeds, cut in pieces the size of a nut. Blanch 2 minutes in boiling salted water. Strain. Put in cold water, re-strain. Cook 2 minutes in 8 oz. boiling vinegar. Put into a basin, keep in a cool place for 48 hours. Strain. Cook the vinegar with 1 lb. of sugar and a few cloves. After boiling 15 minutes add the melon. Boil 3 minutes. Pour into a basin. The next day put in pots and cover.

Spanish Quince Paste

Wash the quinces but do not peel them. Quarter them and remove the seeds. Steam them until quite soft, and put through a sieve or food mill. Weigh the resulting pulp and add the equivalent weight in sugar. Cook in a heavy pan and stir frequently until the paste starts to candy and come away from the sides of the pan.

Turn into square or round tins about ¾ inch deep. Leave to cool. The paste should be left to dry in the sun for several days, but the drying process can be achieved by putting it into a warm oven which has been turned out after the joint has cooked, or into the plate drawer of an electric cooker, or in the cool oven of an Aga cooker. The process need not all be carried out at once, but can be done for an hour or two at a time when it is convenient.

The paste can either be stored in the tins, or wrapped in greaseproof paper.

Serve the paste cut into squares, as a dessert, with the coffee.

STUFFED DATES GLACÉ

Remove the stones from 10 ozs. dates. Stuff them with the following mixture: 3 ozs. of ground almonds, mixed with a little hot syrup made with sugar and water. To this add icing sugar until the paste is firm. Stuff the dates with this mixture, and dip in syrup made as follows:

For the syrup: 7 ozs. sugar to half a glass of water and a few drops of lemon juice. Cook without stirring, dip a spoon in cold water and then in the syrup, then in water again; if it is covered with a layer like glass, the syrup is ready. With a hat-pin take each date and dip in the sugar and with a knife dipped in water put each on an oiled plate. When they are dry put them into little paper cases.

Prunes can be treated in exactly the same way.

PEACH JAM

8 lbs. stoned peaches, 8 lbs. sugar, 2 glasses water.

Peel the peaches, break in halves, put into the saucepan with the sugar and water. Cook quickly. When the peaches become transparent the jam is done.

PRESERVED MIXED FRUIT

Into good white vinegar pour enough sugar to make the vinegar into an acid syrup. Leave this for some days. Into it put the fruit,[1] ripe and dry. At the end of 6 or 7 months, they will be ready. Keep in a cool place in earthenware jars, not too cold or hot.

RAISINÉ DE BOURGOGNE WITH PEARS

Put 4 or 5 lbs. of ripe grapes through a sieve and reduce the juice obtained by half, taking care it does not stick. Peel some ripe pears, cut in quarters and put them into the juice and reduce another third. The pears will then be cooked.

QUINCE PRESERVE

Peel and cut the quinces (large ones) in four pieces; carefully core and cut out all the hard inside. Now make a note of their weight. Lay them in a saucepan, cover with cold water containing a handful of salt ($1\frac{1}{2}$ to 2 ozs.). Boil quickly till *soft* (for about 10 minutes), then drain quickly. Take the peels and cores and pips, cover with cold water, boil well and strain. Pour this juice into a basin and add an equal quantity of sugar. Pour this mixture over the quinces, arranged in a preserving pan, now add more sugar, equal to the original weight of the prepared quinces. Simmer gently till the pieces are quite clear, and the juice forms a thick syrup when cold.

TO PRESERVE FRESH TOMATOES

Choose ripe tomatoes, medium size, absolutely whole, perfect and without the slightest crack or bruise. If the tomato has a hole where the stalk is, drop a little wax on it. Roll the tomatoes in a deep cloth and dry well.

---

[1] Plums, peaches, pears, figs, cherries, melon, apricots, etc. To serve with ham, cold turkey or chicken.

Put them carefully into jars with a large mouth, fill the jars with nut oil (huile d'arachide) *without taste* so that the tomatoes are covered with a layer of oil an inch deep. On the oil pour a layer of eau-de-vie (to prevent the oil from going rancid) half an inch deep. Seal hermetically.

The oil can be used afterwards as it will remain quite tasteless.

Stuffed Walnuts in Syrup

This is one of the traditional recipes of Cyprus, kindly obtained for me by Mr. Sigmund Pollitzer, of Kyrenia.

50 fresh green walnuts, 50 almonds, roasted in their skins, 50 cloves, 6 tumblers of water, 4½ lbs. of sugar.

Skin the walnuts, as delicately as possible, and put them in a bowl of water; leave them to soak for a week, changing the water every day. Make a small incision in each walnut, into which you put an almond and a clove (the cloves are optional, depending on your taste).

Make a syrup of the sugar and the water, and leave it to cool, then put in the walnuts, bring them to the boil, and simmer for about 20 minutes. Leave them to cool in the syrup, and the next day boil them again for another 20 minutes.

When they are cool put them into preserving jars. They are delicious.

Sauces

The Good Cook

"ALL CULINARY tasks should be performed with reverential love, don't you think so? To say that a cook must possess the requisite outfit of culinary skill and temperament—that is hardly more than saying that a soldier must appear in uniform. You can have a bad soldier in uniform. The true cook must have not only those externals, but a large dose of general worldly experience. He is the perfect blend, the only perfect blend, of artist and philosopher. He knows his worth: he holds in his palm the happiness of mankind, the welfare of generations yet unborn. . . . If she drinks a little, why, it is all to the good. It shows that she is fully equipped on the other side of her dual nature. It proves that she possesses the prime requisite of the artist; sensitiveness and a capacity for enthusiasm. Indeed, I often doubt whether you will ever derive well-flavoured victuals from the atelier of an individual who honestly despises or fears—it is the same thing—the choicest gift of God."

South Wind,
by Norman Douglas

The first four sauces in this chapter have, strictly speaking, little to do with Mediterranean cooking, but they are classics of the French kitchen, and it is important to know how to make them. Anyone who has mastered the principles of cooking these sauces, and of a mayonnaise, should be able to produce almost any sauce without difficulty, and will be able to improvise to suit themselves.

SAUCE ESPAGNOLE

Sauce Espagnole being the basic brown sauce from which many others derive, it was usually made in considerable quantity, and kept for several days. This being no longer possible, I give the quantities for making about 1 pint.

2 ozs. bacon or ham, 1½ ozs. flour, 1½ ozs. butter, 1 oz. carrots, ½ gill white wine, ½ oz. onion, 1¼ pints good brown stock, thyme, bay leaf, salt and pepper, ½ lb. tomatoes.

Melt the bacon or ham cut in dice in a little of the butter; add the carrots, also cut in dice, the onions and the herbs and seasonings; when they turn golden add the white wine and reduce.

In another pan put the rest of the butter and when it is melted put in the flour; let it brown very gently, stirring to prevent burning. When it is smooth and brown add half the brown stock, bring to the boil, transfer the mixture from the other pan, and let the whole cook very slowly for 1½ hours. Put the sauce through a fine sieve; return to the saucepan and add the chopped tomatoes and the rest of the stock; let it cook slowly another 30 minutes and strain it again; the sauce should now be of the right consistency, but if it is too thin cook it again until it is sufficiently reduced.

SAUCE BÉCHAMEL

Put 1½ ozs. of butter into a thick pan; when it has melted stir in 2 tablespoons of flour; let this cook a minute or two, but it must not brown. Add gradually ½ to ¾ pint of hot milk, and stir the sauce until it thickens; season with salt, pepper and a very small pinch of nutmeg. The sauce should cook very slowly for 15 or 20 minutes, to allow the flour to cook; this precaution is frequently omitted by English cooks, hence the appalling taste of imperfectly dissolved flour. Should the sauce turn lumpy, bring it very quickly to the boil and let it bubble a minute or two; sometimes this eliminates the lumps, but if they still persist pass the sauce through a fine sieve into a clean pan.

Sauce Béarnaise

Even experienced cooks get into a panic when Béarnaise sauce is mentioned. It is not really so fearsome to make, but it does require the cook's full attention.

Any sauce with eggs in it is best made in a double saucepan, but if there is not one available put a Pyrex or china bowl into a small saucepan half-filled with water, and cook the sauce in this; the sauce can be served in the bowl in which it was cooked.

The sauce is made as follows:

In a small saucepan put 2 chopped shallots, a little piece of parsley, tarragon, thyme, a bay leaf, and ground black pepper. Add half a tumbler of white wine, or half white wine and half tarragon vinegar. Let this boil rapidly until it has reduced to 1 tablespoon of liquid. It is this preliminary reduction which gives a Béarnaise sauce its inimitable flavour. Strain what is left of the vinegar into a Pyrex bowl, add a dessertspoon of cold water, and over the saucepan containing hot water, and on an exceedingly gentle fire, proceed to add little by little 4 ozs. of butter and 4 beaten egg yolks, stirring with great patience until the sauce thickens, and becomes shiny like a mayonnaise. If the fire becomes too hot, if the water in the double saucepan boils, or if you stop stirring for one instant the sauce will curdle; when it has thickened take it off the fire and keep on stirring; the sauce is served tepid, and is at its best with grilled tournedos, but can be used with many other dishes. A very little finely chopped tarragon is stirred in before serving.

If all precautions fail and the sauce curdles, it can sometimes be brought back again by the addition of a few drops of cold water, and vigorous stirring; if this fails put the sauce through a fine sieve, add another yolk of egg and stir again.

The addition of a quarter of its volume of concentrated tomato purée to the Béarnaise makes Sauce Choron; 2 tablespoons of meat glaze added to the initial Béarnaise makes Sauce Foyot. Whatever variations are to be made are made at the end when the sauce has already thickened.

Red wine, although unorthodox, makes just as good a sauce as white wine.

SAUCE HOLLANDAISE

The same remarks apply here as for Sauce Béarnaise (see preceding page).

Reduce by two-thirds 2 tablespoons of white wine or white wine vinegar, and 4 tablespoons of water, seasoned with a pinch of pepper and salt. Put this reduction into a double saucepan, and add gradually the yolks of 5 eggs and ½ lb. of butter; stir until the sauce thickens, adding a spoonful or two of water, which keeps the sauce light. Season with a little more salt, and a few drops of lemon juice and put it through a fine sieve. Sauce Hollandaise is usually served with asparagus, or with poached sole, salmon, and so on.

For Sauce Mousseline add 4 tablespoons of cream to a Sauce Hollandaise.

Sauce Tomate

Chop 2 lbs. of good ripe tomatoes; put them into a thick
pan with salt, pepper, 3 or 4 lumps of sugar, 1 clove of
garlic, 1 onion, chopped, 2 ozs. of raw minced beef or, failing
this, 2 rashers of bacon, and half a teaspoon of sweet basil.
Put the lid on the pan and leave the tomatoes to stew very
slowly. When they are reduced to pulp and most of the water
from the tomatoes is evaporated (this will take 20 to 30
minutes) put the mixture through a sieve. If it is still too
liquid put the sauce back into the pan and reduce until it is
the right consistency.

Sauce Bolognese for Spaghetti

½ small tin Italian tomato paste, 2 ozs. mushrooms or mushroom stalks, 2 ozs. minced raw beef, 2 ozs. chicken livers,
1 onion, 1 clove of garlic, basil, salt and pepper, 2 lumps of
sugar, a little oil, butter, or dripping, stock or water, ½ glass
wine.

Into a small thick pan put a tablespoon of oil, butter or
dripping. In this fry the chopped onion until it is golden. Add
the minced beef, the chopped mushrooms and the chicken
livers. Cook until the beef is slightly fried—only about 3
minutes.

Now add a small glass of wine, red or white, and let it
bubble until reduced by half. Put in the tomato paste, add
the basil, the seasoning and the sugar and enough stock or
water to make the sauce of a creamy consistency, but thinner
than you finally require, for it will reduce quite a bit in the
cooking.

With the point of a knife crush the clove of garlic and add
to the sauce. Put the lid on the pan and simmer very slowly
for 30 minutes at least. The longer the better, so that the

essence of the meat penetrates the sauce. You can leave it at the bottom of a slow oven for as long as you like. Be sure to have it very hot before serving with your spaghetti.

TOMATO PASTE

The slightly salty, smoky flavour of this sauce in Greek *stiphádo* (p. 84) and macaroni dishes is entirely characteristic; it may not be to everybody's taste but it blends remarkably well with *retsina,* the *vin ordinaire* of Greece, which seems so outlandish when one first arrives there that it is hard to believe that one could ever become accustomed to it. Sooner or later, though, most people do, and sitting in a village taverna, the wine barrels stacked around, retsina seems the right and proper drink.

Several pounds of tomatoes are chopped up and put in a pan, with a good deal of salt, and cooked until they are reduced to a pulp. They are then put through a sieve, and reduced again over a slow fire. The sauce is then put in bowls and left out in the sun until it has become very dry.

It is stored in jars with a layer of oil on the top to keep out the air.

SAUCE OF DRIED CÈPES[1] TO SERVE WITH SPAGHETTI

2 to 3 ozs. of dried cèpes. Cover them with water, add salt and pepper. Simmer for 30 minutes. Strain them, keeping the water they have cooked in, which you strain again through a muslin.

Put this back in the pan, and melt 2 or 3 ozs. of butter in it.

Serve the sauce and the cèpes over the cooked noodles or spaghetti.

[1] See note on dried cèpes, p. 127.

Sauce Catalane

This sauce is intended to give the taste of partridge to grilled mutton cutlets.

In a tablespoon of pork fat sauté 1 chopped onion and a little ham cut in dice. Sprinkle with flour, stir with a wooden spoon. Add a glass of water and a glass of white wine, a dozen cloves of garlic and a whole lemon cut in slices. Simmer for 30 minutes. In a mortar pound 6 ozs. of almonds and stir them into the sauce 5 minutes before serving.

Avgolémono Sauce

This is simply the Greek way of making a sauce for practically anything.

The juice of a lemon and 2 or 3 egg yolks are beaten together and added to some of the stock in which fish or meat or chicken has cooked, and stirred carefully until it is thick.

Youvarlakia, or little meat rissoles, served in this sauce are not to be despised, and, as the standby of every Greek cook, how different from the bottled horror and the stickfast of English cooking.

Sauce Chevreuil

2 glasses of red wine (Burgundy if possible), $1\frac{1}{2}$ glasses of stock or meat essence, 2 tablespoons vinegar, 2 level tablespoons sugar, 4 or 5 tablespoons red currant jelly, 2 tablespoons flour, 2 tablespoons butter or lard, half a lemon, a good pinch of pepper.

Put into a saucepan $1\frac{1}{2}$ glasses of the red wine, the vinegar, the sugar and the lemon, peeled and cut into dice. Mix the jelly into this preparation and boil until it is reduced by half. Meanwhile prepare a brown *roux* with the butter and flour, add the stock and the rest of the wine and cook slowly for 20 minutes. Mix the two preparations, put through a fine sieve and reheat.

SAUCE PIQUANTE

In oil, butter or dripping fry a sliced onion until it is golden, then add a wineglass of vinegar and 2 cups of the stock of whatever meat the sauce is to be served with. Add herbs, a clove of garlic, salt and pepper and simmer until the sauce is a good consistency.

A few minutes before serving, add a spoonful each of capers and chopped gherkins.

MAYONNAISE

For mayonnaise for 4 people 2 egg yolks are sufficient, and about ⅓ pint of olive oil. I find the best utensils to use are a small but heavy marble mortar which does not slide about the table, a wooden spoon, and for the olive oil a small jug with a spout which allows the oil to come out very slowly.

Break the yolks very carefully into the mortar; add a little salt, pepper and a teaspoon of mustard in powder. Stir well before adding any oil at all; at first the oil must be stirred in drop by drop, then a little more each time as the mayonnaise gets thicker. Stir steadily but not like a maniac. From time to time add a *very* little tarragon vinegar, and at the end a squeeze of lemon juice. Should the mayonnaise curdle, break another yolk into a clean basin, and add the curdled mayonnaise gradually; it will come back to life miraculously.

SAUCE TARTARE

Sauce Tartare is a mayonnaise to which you add finely chopped tarragon, capers, parsley, chives and a very little pickled gherkin and minced shallot.

SAUCE VINAIGRETTE

The basis of Sauce Vinaigrette is olive oil and good wine vinegar; ⅔ oil to ⅓ vinegar, with the addition of a little finely minced onion, parsley, tarragon, capers, chives, chervil and lemon peel, all stirred together with a seasoning of salt and pepper.

Turkish Salad Dressing

3 ozs. of shelled walnuts, a breakfastcup of clear chicken or meat broth, or milk, 4 tablespoons of dried breadcrumbs, salt, cayenne pepper, lemon juice, parsley or mint, a clove of garlic.

Pound the walnuts and garlic to a paste; stir in the breadcrumbs, then the broth or milk, season with salt, lemon juice, and cayenne pepper. The sauce should be about the consistency of cream. Very good with salads of haricot beans and chick peas. Enough to season ½ lb. of either of these vegetables. Sprinkle the salad with fresh herbs before serving.

Aïllade

A mixture of garlic, basil and grilled tomatoes, pounded together in the mortar. Olive oil is added drop by drop, until thick.

Mohammed's Sauce for Fish

Mayonnaise, 2 hard-boiled eggs, 3 anchovies (boned and chopped), juice of onions, capers, celery, fresh cucumber.

Chop all the ingredients finely and stir into the mayonnaise.

Aïoli

Aïoli is really a mayonnaise made with garlic, and sometimes breadcrumbs are added.

It is served usually with salt cod, or with boiled beef, accompanied by boiled carrots, potatoes boiled in their skins, artichokes, french beans, hard-boiled eggs and sometimes with snails which have been cooked in water with onions and fennel, or with baby octopus plainly boiled, and with pimentos; in fact, with any variety of vegetables, but always cooked *à l'eau*. It is one of the most famous and best of all Provençal dishes. The aïoli sauce is itself often called *beurre de Provence*.

Start by pounding 2 or 3 cloves of garlic, then put in the yolks of eggs, seasonings, and add olive oil drop by drop, proceeding exactly as for mayonnaise. Add lemon juice instead of vinegar.

SKORDALIÁ (the Greek version of Aïoli)

2 egg yolks, 2 oz ground almonds, 2 oz fresh white bread-crumbs, ½ dozen cloves of garlic, ¼ pint olive oil, lemon juice, parsley.

Pound the garlic in a mortar, then add the yolks, the olive oil drop by drop as for mayonnaise, and when of the right consistency stir in the ground almonds and the breadcrumbs. Add plenty of lemon juice and chopped parsley. This sauce curdles very easily; if it does, start again with another egg yolk as for mayonnaise (p. 192).

SAUCE À LA CRÈME D'OURSINS

In Provence, *oursins* (sea urchins), as well as being eaten as an hors d'œuvre, are made into a most delicate sauce. The coral is scooped out of 2 or 3 dozen *oursins* and pressed through a fine muslin. There should be about 2 ozs. of purée, which is then incorporated either into a Sauce Mousseline or a mayonnaise, and eaten with plainly cooked fish, or with cold lobster.

TAPÉNADE

Tapénade is a Provençal sauce. The name comes from the word *tapéna*, Provençal for capers. It is a simple sauce, and excellent for hard-boiled eggs, cold fish, or a salad of cold boiled beef.

Pound 2 tablespoons of capers in a mortar with half a dozen fillets of anchovies; add olive oil little by little as for mayonnaise, until you have about a cup of sauce. Add the juice of a lemon and a little black pepper, but no salt, as the anchovies will probably be salty.

Sauce Rouille (a Provençal sauce for fish)

1 clove of garlic, 1 red pimento, breadcrumbs, olive oil.

Grill the pimento whole until the skin turns black. Take out the seeds, rub off the burnt skin, rinse the pimento in cold water, and pound it with the garlic. Soak a handful of breadcrumbs in water and squeeze them dry. Add them to the pimento and then stir in very slowly 4 tablespoons of olive oil. Thin the sauce with a few teaspoons of the stock from the fish with which it is to be served.

Syrian Sauce for Fish

A teacup of fresh white breadcrumbs, 2 ozs. of pine nuts or walnuts, the juice of a lemon, salt.

Soak the breadcrumbs in water, then squeeze dry. Pound the pine nuts or walnuts to a paste. Mix them with the breadcrumbs, add salt and the lemon juice. Press through a coarse sieve. Serve poured over a cold baked fish. If too thick add a few drops of cold water or broth from the fish.

Cappon Magro Sauce

A large bunch of parsley, a clove of garlic, a tablespoon of capers, 2 anchovy fillets, the yolks of 2 hard-boiled eggs, 6 green olives, fennel (either a bunch of the leaves or a slice of the root), a handful of breadcrumbs, a large cupful of olive oil, a little vinegar.

Remove the thick stalks from the parsley, wash the leaves, put them into a mortar with a little salt and the clove of garlic.

Pound until it is beginning to turn to a paste (this is not so arduous a task as might be supposed). Then add the capers, the anchovies, the stoned olives, and the fennel. Continue pounding, and add the breadcrumbs, which should have been softened in a little milk or water and pressed dry. By this time there should be a thick sauce. Pound in the yolks of the hard-boiled eggs. Now start to add the olive oil, slowly, stirring vigorously with a wooden spoon as if making mayonnaise, and when the sauce is the consistency of a thick cream add about 2 tablespoons of vinegar.

This is the sauce which is poured over *Cappon Magro*, the celebrated Genoese fish salad made of about twenty different ingredients and built up into a splendid baroque edifice. The sauce is an excellent one for any coarse white fish, for cold meat, or for hard-boiled eggs.

FRENCH COUNTRY COOKING

FRENCH COUNTRY
COOKING
by
Elizabeth David

decorated by
John Minton

To my Mother

ACKNOWLEDGMENTS

As ANY cook must be, I am deeply in the debt of countless cookery writers. In the case of this book I have drawn on several French cookery books for regional recipes. Chief among these are *L'Art du Bien Manger* by Edmond Richardin, Editions d'Art et de Litterature, Paris, 1913; *Les Plats Régionaux de France* edited by Austin de Croze; *La Bonne Cuisine du Périgord* by La Mazille, Flammarion, 1929; *La Cuisine du Pays: Armagnac, Béarn, Bigorre, Landes. Recettes Recueillies par Simin Palay*, published at Pau, 1937; Pampille's *Les Bons Plats de France*, A. Fayard, Paris; and Reboul's *La Cuisinière Provençale*, Tacussel, Marseille. The last two are the only ones still in print; second-hand copies are exceedingly hard to find, but anyone interested in French regional cookery would find the trouble of searching for them worth while. My grateful thanks are due to Messrs. Allen and Unwin and to Madame Janet Biala for permission to reproduce an extract from Ford Madox Ford's *Provence*. The passage from Gertrude Stein's paper on Raoul Dufy, published in *Harper's Bazaar* for December 1949, is quoted with the permission of Carl van Vechten, Miss Stein's literary executor. I also wish to express my gratitude to the editors and publishers of *Harper's Bazaar* and *Contact* for allowing me to reprint recipes which first appeared in those magazines, and to Messrs. Saccone and Speed for permission to reproduce here the chapter on "Wine in the Kitchen", most of which was originally published by them.

E. D.

PREFACE TO SECOND EDITION (REVISED)

THIS book was written and published at a time when food rationing was still in full force, and of necessity contained suggestions as to what ingredients might be substituted for quantities of bacon, cream, eggs, meat stock and so on. A list of stores to keep handy and where to buy them was also included, and a few recipes for dealing with tinned foods.

Such advice no longer seems necessary, so these chapters have been eliminated, as well as a few of the longer and more elaborate recipes.

I am anxious to stress the fact that this little collection gives no more than an indication of the immense diversity and range of French regional cookery. It is a subject of such scope that half a dozen large volumes of recipes would scarcely exhaust it. Indeed, it would be almost impossible ever to compile a complete collection, because in France regional cookery is very much alive, and therefore perpetually evolving. As modern transport, changing agricultural methods, and new types of kitchen stoves and utensils make old recipes out of date, so resourceful housewives and enterprising chefs invent new dishes to meet the altered circumstances and to satisfy their own creative instincts where cookery is concerned. But many of these new dishes will be based on the old traditional ones; the ingredients used will be those native to the district; the local flavour will be preserved. And so it comes about that for the collector every visit to France will produce some new dish, and those interested enough will find there is always something new to learn about the engrossing subject of French cookery. E. D.

INTRODUCTION

A CERTAIN amount of nonsense is talked about the richness of the food to be found in all French homes. It is true that the standard is much higher than that of most English households, but it will not, I hope, be taken as an ungracious criticism to say that the chances are that a food-conscious foreigner staying for any length of time with a French middle-class family would find the proportion of rather tough *entrecôtes*, rolled and stuffed roast veal, and *sautéd* chicken exasperatingly high. For parties and festivals there would be more elaborately cooked fish and poultry, separate vegetable courses and wonderful open fruit tarts ; but he would not find many dishes were cooked in cream, wine and garlic—it is bad for the *foie*, he would very likely be told. Those who care to look for it, however, will find the justification of France's culinary reputation in the provinces, at the riverside inns, in unknown cafés along the banks of the Burgundy canal, patronised by the men who sail the great petrol and timber barges to and from Marseilles, great eaters and drinkers most of them, in the hospitable farmhouses of the Loire and the Dordogne, of Normandy and the Auvergne, in sea-port bistros frequented by fishermen, sailors, ship-chandlers and port officials; and occasionally also in *cafés routiers*, the lorry drivers' restaurants.

In such places the most interesting food in France is to be found, naturally, because the shopkeepers, the lawyer, the doctor, the curé, the gendarme and even those stony-faced post-office officials are exceedingly addicted to the pleasures of the table ; and, being thrifty as well, you may be sure they know where the cheapest and best of everything is to be

obtained. The peasant farmers are prosperous, and not for
nothing are they known as the thriftiest people in Europe.
Every scrap of food produced is made use of in some way or
another, in fact in the best way possible, so it is in the heart of
the country that one may become acquainted with the infinite
variety of *charcuterie*, the sausages, pickled pork and bacon,
smoked hams, *terrines*, preserved goose, *pâtés*, *rillettes*, and
andouillettes, the cheeses and creams, the fruits preserved in
potent local liqueurs, the fresh garden vegetables, pulled up
before they are faded and grown old, and served shining with
farmhouse butter, the *galettes* and pancakes made from country
flour, the mushrooms, *cèpes*, *morilles* and *truffes* gathered in the
forest, the mountain hares, pigeons, partridges and roebuck, the
matelotes of pike, carp and eel and the fried trout straight from
the river, the sustaining vegetable soups enriched with wine,
garlic, bacon and sausages, the thousand and one shell-fish soups
and stews, the *fritures du golfe*, the *risottos aux fruits de mer* of
France's lovely prodigal coast, from Brittany to Biarritz and
from Spain to Monte Carlo.

Although there is not such a profusion of raw materials in
England, we still have much greater gastronomic resources than
the national cookery would lead one to suppose.

Rationing, the disappearance of servants, and the bad and
expensive meals served in restaurants, have led Englishwomen
to take a far greater interest in food than was formerly considered polite; and large numbers of people with small farms
in the country produce their own home-cured bacon, ham
and sausages ; personal supervision of the kitchen garden induces
a less indifferent attitude to the fate of spring vegetables ; those
who have churned their own butter, fed their chickens and
geese, cherished their fruit trees, skinned and cleaned their own
hares, are in no mood to see their efforts wasted. Town
dwellers, who take trouble over their marketing, choose their

meat and fish carefully and keep a good store cupboard, are equally interested in seeing that their care is repaid in good and interesting meals.

It is for such people that I have collected the recipes in this book, most of which derive from French regional and peasant cookery, which, at its best, is the most delicious in the world ; cookery which uses raw materials to the greatest advantage without going to the absurd lengths of the complicated and so-called *Haute Cuisine*, the *pompeuses bagatelles de la cuisine masquée*, considered the height of good taste and refined living during the nineteenth and early twentieth centuries. Nor is the Technicolor cooking which has partially taken its place in any way an improvement. Good cooking is honest, sincere and simple, and by this I do not mean to imply that you will find in this, or indeed any other book, the secret of turning out first-class food in a few minutes with no trouble. Good food is always a trouble and its preparation should be regarded as a labour of love, and this book is intended for those who actually and positively enjoy the labour involved in entertaining their friends and providing their families with first-class food. Even more than long hours in the kitchen, fine meals require ingenious organisation and experience which is a pleasure to acquire. A highly developed shopping sense is important, so is some knowledge of the construction of a menu with a view to the food in season, the manner of cooking, the texture and colour of the dishes to be served in relation to each other.

The proper composition of a meal being a source of continual anxiety to the inexperienced, I have thought it would perhaps be helpful to include a short chapter on the subject; and as there is no French cooking without wine, its use in the kitchen, unfamiliar to many, is explained in a separate chapter.

The respective merits of *Haute Cuisine, Cuisine Bourgeoise,* regional and peasant and good plain, Italian and German, Scandinavian, Greek, Arab or Chinese food are less important than the spirit in which cooking is approached ; a devoted, a determined, spirit, but not, it is to be hoped, one of martyrdom.

E.D.

CONTENTS

BATTERIE
DE CUISINE

BATTERIE DE CUISINE

DELICIOUS meals can, as everybody knows, be cooked with the sole aid of a blackened frying-pan over a Primus stove, a camp fire, a gas-ring or even a methylated spirit lamp. This book, however, is for those whose ambitions lie in the direction of something less primitive in the way of food, so the question of stocking the kitchen with good pans and the right implements is of the first importance.

If you are starting from scratch, the most satisfactory method is to see that you have the basic necessities to begin with and buy gradually as you find out which style of cooking best suits your talents. (If, for example, you have no particular flair for cakes and pastries, it is pointless to clutter up the kitchen with a whole range of pastry boards, cake tins, tartlet moulds and icing sets.)

One thing is quite certain, and that is that if Englishwomen paid more attention to having the right equipment in their kitchens, we should hear a great deal less about the terrible labour of good cooking. How many times have I been told: " Oh, I haven't time to fiddle about with that kind of thing ", just because a recipe called for putting something through a sieve or chopping up a few vegetables. Don't hamper your cooking and waste time and materials through lack of the right tools for the job.

First, and these are essential to any kitchen, come the very best quality of cook's knives. A small vegetable knife, razor sharp, a medium one for trimming meat and fish (known as a filleting knife), a large one for cutting up meat and poultry, and a long, thin-bladed ham knife for cold meat, and anything which has to be thinly sliced. (For instance it is much more economical to buy a whole salame sausage and slice it as it is

needed, but this is impossible without the sharpest of knives.)
A first-class bread knife goes without saying, so keep it for
bread. Take the greatest care of your knives; don't cut with
them on an enamel- or marble-topped table or a plate; have a
good knife-sharpener; keep your kitchen knives in a special box
or compartment of the knife drawer; wash, dry, and put them
away, with the points stuck into a cork, as soon as you have
finished with them. Let it be understood by all members of the
household that there will be serious trouble if your knives are
borrowed for screwdriving, prising open packing-cases,
cutting fuse wire or any other purpose for which they were not
intended.

Your saucepans will, of course, depend on your cooking
stove. For electricity and for the Aga type of cookers there are
special pans. For gas you can have either enamel or aluminium.[1]
My own preference is for aluminium, as I find it easier to keep
clean and there is no risk of chipping, but this is a question of
taste. Have at least two deep stew pans, one large and one
small, with a small handle at each side ; in these all manner of
soups and stews can be put in the oven as well as on top of the
stove, an essential requirement for anyone who has other duties
than those of a cook to attend to. For boiling potatoes keep one
special pan. Those heavy iron pans, black outside, with an enamel
lining and a long handle, are the best; they are comfortable-
looking and satisfactory to cook in. A small enamel-lined, five-
or six-inch pan with a lip, for milk, is useful, and you will
need two or three medium-sized saucepans for vegetables, one
double saucepan, and a shallow fireproof pan which will go
under the grill or in a very hot oven for dishes which are to
be browned quickly. For cooking rice and spaghetti, for
anything over four people you must have a very large pan,
say 4 or 5 quarts' capacity, and this will do for cooking chickens

[1] The alternative of copper saucepans is discussed on page 18.

and for making stock. Shallow, two-handled braising and sauté pans from seven to ten inches in diameter and about three inches deep for Risotto, pot roasts, various forms of *ragoûts* and vegetable dishes are a blessing. These can now be found in heavy aluminium or better still enamel-lined cast iron.

Earthenware casseroles and terrines for oven cooking should be in every household; for some of the French farmhouse and peasant dishes described in this book they are essential; with time these rustic clay pots acquire not only a patina but an aroma of their own, which in the course of long patient simmering communicates itself to *cassoulets, choux farçis, daubes* and *civets*, which would lose something of their flavour and a good deal of their charm if cooked in an ordinary saucepan. Earthenware pots can be put on the top of gas and electric stoves provided an asbestos mat is put underneath. The important point to remember is never to pour cold water into one of these casseroles while it is hot, or it will crack.

For eggs good frying and omelette pans are obviously needed, and little dishes for eggs *en cocotte*, soufflé dishes, and a small, heavy, double saucepan for sauces made with eggs. Plain white, fireproof porcelain or glass egg dishes can be found in various sizes, and these are the most satisfactory for baked eggs in all forms, as the egg does not stick as it does to earthenware. The larger sizes are useful for an infinite variety of little dishes. Three frying-pans and one omelette pan are not too many and they should all be heavy, with a perfectly flat bottom, or the food will never be evenly fried. Have one ten-inch frying-pan, for all ordinary purposes, with a lip on each side, so that it is easy to pour off the fat; one which is kept for steaks and cutlets and so on; one small one (say six inches) for frying a few croûtons for soup or anything else to be done in small quantities. An omelette pan which will hold an omelette of 3 or 4 eggs (about ten inches) is the best size to choose if you have only one ; heavy iron omelette pans are hard to come by nowadays and nothing else is quite so good. Try Cadec, 27 Greek Street—they sometimes have them. Rangemaster make good heavy aluminium omelette pans in several sizes.

A deep frier with a basket is necessary for chips, but for the deep frying of small quantities of fritters, or fish, any heavy saucepan will do; half a dozen fritters can be done at a time, and lifted out with a perforated spoon.

Frying-pans must be kept scrupulously clean; leaving fat in pans is wasteful and makes good frying impossible, for fat must be clear and clean and free of all burnt specks and sediment. When frying is finished, pour off all fat through a small strainer kept specially for this purpose. Keep different kinds of fat separately—a bowl for bacon fat, another for beef dripping, one for mutton and one for pork fat ; each has its individual use and should never be mixed.

Cadec of Greek Street and Jaeggi's of Dean Street specialise in copper pans; they are fairly expensive, and their upkeep arduous, but they do make for good cooking. These two shops will also re-tin old copper pans, which can sometimes be bought cheaply in second-hand shops. A heavy copper suaté pan, about four inches deep and twelve inches across, with a long handle, is the most convenient pan in the world for braising a whole chicken or duck on top of the stove, for it can be left unattended without fear of disaster, and it can be looked at from time to time without the business of getting the pan in and out of the oven; the same pan is good for the cooking of *matelotes* of fish and *bouillabaisses*.

For poaching large fish, such as salmon or turbot, you need a very big fish kettle with an inner drainer on which the fish rests, so that it can be lifted out of the pan and drained without fear of breaking ; the same pan can be used for cooking hams. They are very expensive, but are to be found now and again at sales and in junk shops. Oval gratin dishes in varying sizes for baking and grilling fish are easy to find, in earthenware, china or metal or enamel-lined cast iron. A long platter for serving fish is important; the appearance of a fine salmon is ruined by being brought to table on too small a dish.

A roasting pan with a self-basting cover is a valuable replacement for the tin usually supplied with the stove, and which is unsatisfactory, as the meat or bird always has to be covered with greaseproof paper, the tin is difficult to handle and tiresome to clean.

The question of kitchen gadgets is one which must depend on personal preferences, and I cannot do more than enumerate those which through long use and the saving of countless hours I regard with especial affection.

First of these is a purée-maker or food mill, usually called a *moulinette* in France. For soups, sauces, fruit and vegetable purées this is absolutely invaluable; in 2 minutes you have a purée which would take 30 minutes' bashing to get through an ordinary sieve. The best and cheapest of these is a French one, called the *mouli*, and the medium size, about £1. 1s., is the one for a small household. (Those who can afford an electric mixer will probably not need a *mouli* as well.) Then there is a vegetable slicer which goes by the charming name of *Mandoline*. If you have ever spent an hour slicing a cucumber paper-thin, or cutting potatoes for *Pommes Anna* or *Pommes Soufflés*, go and buy one of these—a whole cucumber can be done, thinner than you could ever do it with a knife, in a minute or two.[1]

Vegetable choppers are now obtainable in England; called

---

[1] The mandoline, or Universal Slicer as it is sometimes called, can be found at Cadec, 27 Greek Street, Kitchen Supply Stores, 10 Brewer Street, William Page, 87 Shaftesbury Avenue, W. A. Brown & Harris, Oldham Road, New Cross, Manchester, and other shops specialising in catering equipment. The mouli-légumes is stocked by most good stores and ironmongers.

in France an *hâchoire*, in Italy a *mezzaluna*, these instruments are crescent-shaped blades with a small handle at each end. They make the fine chopping of onions, meat, parsley and vegetables the affair of a second.[1] A hand-operated potato peeler called Legumex has recently appeared on the market and proved very satisfactory for a small household.

A good pair of scales, a pint-measuring jug, a first-class pliable palette knife, a perforated slice, a pepper mill and a salt mill are obvious necessities; so are a selection of wooden spoons and a pair of kitchen scissors, two or three fine strainers in different sizes, and a clock. A perforated spoon for draining anything which has cooked in deep fat is a great boon; a good solid chopping-board, at least twelve inches by eighteen inches, you must have, and either a wood or marble pestle and mortar. Wedgwood are making these again. A bread tin with a roll top which stands on the dresser I regard with particular gratitude, for it has saved endless stooping down to lift the lid off an ordinary bread tin.

A rather large selection of cooking and mixing bowls I insist on having—there can't be too many in any kitchen—and two or three Perspex boxes for keeping vegetables and salads in the larder are well worth their rather high price. A supply of muslin squares for draining homemade cheese and for straining aspic jelly, an extra plate rack for saucepan lids, some Pyrex plates which can be put in the oven and made really hot without fear of breakage, a Pyrex or metal omelette dish, and a large collection of glass store jars in all sizes, with glass stoppers, and a supply of greaseproof paper, are all adjuncts of a well-run kitchen. The aluminium foil called "Mirap" has proved to be all that it claims for wrapping food, covering jars and bowls and for paper-bag cookery.

[1] These choppers can be bought at Staines, Victoria St.; and at the shops mentioned above.

As time goes on you accumulate your own personal gadgets, things which graft themselves on to your life; an ancient thin pronged fork for the testing of meat, a broken knife for scraping mussels, a battered little copper saucepan in which your sauces have always turned out well, an oyster knife which you can no longer afford to use for its intended purpose but which turns out to be just the thing for breaking off hunks of Parmesan cheese, a pre-war sixpenny tin-opener which has outlived all other and superior forms of tin-opening life, an earthenware bean pot of such charm that nothing cooked in it could possibly go wrong.

Some sensible person once remarked that you spend the whole of your life either in your bed or your shoes. Having done the best you can by shoes and bed, devote all the time and resources at your disposal to the building up of a fine kitchen. It will be, as it should be, the most comforting and comfortable room in the house.

WINE IN THE KITCHEN

NOBODY has ever been able to find out why the English regard a glass of wine added to a soup or stew as a reckless foreign extravagance and at the same time spend pounds on bottled sauces, gravy powders, soup cubes, ketchups and artificial flavourings.[1] If every kitchen contained a bottle each of red wine, white wine and inexpensive port for cooking, hundreds of store cupboards could be swept clean for ever of the cluttering debris of commercial sauce bottles and all synthetic aids to flavouring.

To the basic sum of red, white and port I would add, if possible, brandy, and half a dozen miniature bottles of assorted liqueurs for flavouring sweet dishes and fruit salads, say Kirsch, Apricot Brandy, Grand Marnier, Orange Curaçao,

[1] I do not know how artificial flavourings are concocted nowadays. This is what a book of household hints and cookery (*Lady Bountiful's Legacy*, edited by John Timbs), published in 1868, had to say on the subject: " *Artificial Flavouring* has increased to a dangerous extent of late years . . . the peculiar flavour of ' pineapple rum ' is obtained from a product of the action of putrid cheese on sugar, or by making a soap with butter, and distilling it with alcohol and sulphuric acid, and is now largely employed in England in the preparation of pineapple ale. Oil of grapes and oil of cognac, used to impart the flavour of French cognac to British brandy, are little else than fusel oil. The artificial oil of bitter almonds, now employed for flavouring confectionery, is prepared by the action of nitric acid on the fetid oil of gas tar. . . ."

Cointreau and Framboise. Sherry is a good addition, but should be used in cooking with the utmost discretion; it is useless to think that the addition of a large glass of poor sherry to the contents of a tin of soup is going to disguise it.

The Cooking of Wine

The fundamental fact to remember about the use of wine in cooking is that the wine is *cooked*. In the process the alcohol is volatilised and what remains is the wonderful flavour which perfumes the dish and fills the kitchen with an aroma of delicious things to come. In any dish which does not require long cooking the wine should be reduced to about half the quantity originally poured in the pan, by the process of very fast boiling. In certain soups, for instance when the vegetables have been browned and the herbs and spices added, a glass of wine is poured in, the flame turned up, and the wine allowed to bubble fiercely for two or three minutes; when it starts to look a little syrupy on the bottom of the pan, add the water or stock; this process makes all the difference to the flavour and immediately gives the soup body and colour.

When making gravy for a roast, abolish the cabbage water, the gravy browning and the cornflour; instead, when you have strained off the fat pour a $\frac{1}{2}$ glass of any wine round the roasting pan, at the same time scraping up all the juice which has come out of the meat, let it sizzle for a minute or two, add a little water, cook gently another 2 minutes and your gravy is ready.

For a duck, add the juice of an orange and a tablespoon of red-currant jelly; for fish which has been grilled add white wine to the butter in the pan, lemon juice, and chopped parsley or capers; to the butter in which you have fried escalopes of veal add a little red wine or Madeira, let it bubble and then pour in a $\frac{1}{2}$ cup of cream.

To Flamber

To *flamber* is to set light to a small quantity of brandy, liqueur or rum poured over the contents of the pan, which are left to flame until the alcohol has burnt away, leaving a delicately composed sauce in which any excess of fat or butter has been consumed in the flames. The brandy or liqueur will be easier to light if it is first placed in a warmed silver spoon, to release the spirit, which will then easily catch fire.

To Marinate in Wine

To marinate meat, fish or game is to give it a bath lasting anything between 2 hours and several days in a marinade usually composed of a mixture of wine, herbs, garlic, onions and spices, sometimes with the addition of a little vinegar, olive oil, or water. A tough piece of stewing beef is improved by being left several hours in a marinade of red wine; it can then be braised or stewed in the marinade, strained of the vegetables and herbs which, by this time, have become sodden, and fresh ones added.

A leg of mutton can be given a taste approximating to venison by being marinaded for several days. It is then carefully dried and roasted, the strained marinade being reduced and used for the sauce.

For a *terrine* I always marinate the prepared meat or game for two or three hours in white wine, but red can be used. Hare, I think, needs no marinade, unless it is ancient and tough, as the meat of a good hare has a perfect flavour which is entirely altered by being soaked in wine before cooking, although a glass or two of good red wine to French *Civet de Lièvre*, and of port to English Jugged Hare, is indispensable.

The Choice of the Wine

There is no hard-and-fast rule as to the use of white or red wine, port or brandy for any particular dish. Generally speaking, of course, red wine is better for meat and game dishes, white for fish, but one can usually be substituted for the other, an exception being *Moules Marinière*, for which white wine is a necessity, as red turns the whole dish a rather disagreeable blue colour, and any essentially white dish such as potato or fish soup, or a delicate concoction of sole, must have white wine.

Incidentally, white wine for cooking should, except for certain dishes such as a cheese fondue, not be too dry, as it may give rather too acid a flavour; and beware of pouring white wine into any sauce containing milk or cream; to avoid curdling, the wine should be put in before the cream and well simmered to reduce the acidity, and the cream stirred in off the fire, and reheated very cautiously.

Don't be discouraged when you read lovely French regional recipes containing a particular and possibly little-known wine; remember that in their country of origin the *vin du pays* is always within arm's reach of the cook, so that while in Bordeaux a *Matelote* of eel is cooked in wine of the Médoc, in Lyons the nuance is altered because Beaujolais is used, and cider in the apple country of Normandy. Here, too, a sweet omelette is *flambéd* with Calvados, in Gascony with Armagnac. In the same way the French frequently employ their own sweet wine, Frontignan, Muscat, or the Vin Cuit of Provence in place of port or marsala.

Cider is excellent for white fish, mussels, for cooking ham, and for rabbit, but it should be either draught or vintage cider.

Cheap wine is better than no wine at all, at any rate for cooking, but the better the wine the better the dish. By this I do not mean that fine old vintages should be poured into the saucepan, but that, for instance, Coq au Vin (see p. 128), cooked in a pint of sound Macon or Beaujolais, will be a much finer dish than that cooked in fiery Algerian wine.

Never discard the heel of a bottle of wine. Keep two large bottles or covered jugs, one for white wine, and one for red into which your bottle ends can be poured; they will keep for weeks, and a few drops of brandy, sherry or port thrown in as well can do nothing but good; they will strengthen the wine and help to preserve it, and even odds and ends of good vermouth will not come amiss.

If you are going to keep wine especially for cooking, it can be bought in half or even quarter bottles.

Liqueurs

A variety of liqueurs in ounce bottles can be bought by the dozen. A word of warning here—liqueurs in fruit salads should be used with some caution and not mixed too freely, or the fruit will simply be sodden and taste like perfumed cotton-wool.

For soufflés use rather more than you think is needed—the taste evaporates with the cooking. Grand Marnier, Mirabelle and Orange Curaçao are particularly good for soufflés and for omelettes (see p. 179) and, owing to their concentrated strength, can be used when a wine such as Madeira or Sauternes would have to be used in too great quantity for the volume of the eggs. As a substitute, however, you can pour a claret glass of a sweet dessert wine (Sauternes, Marsala, Brown Sherry, Port) into a small pan, add a little sugar (about a dessertspoon), a piece of orange rind or a few drops of orange-flower water, and reduce the wine to half. Let it cool and strain it into the egg mixture. The result is a sort of syrup with a pleasant winey flavour.

In this book will be found many recipes for lovely French dishes enriched with wine; it will soon be clear, though, that very few of them involve any alarming expense.

THE MENU

A LIST of menus suitable for spring, autumn, summer and
winter, for family luncheons, formal dinners, christening tea
parties and buffet suppers can never be more than the vaguest of
guides; I should be surprised to hear that anybody had ever
followed any cookery book menu in every detail; all that is
needed to design a perfectly good meal is a little common sense
and the fundamental understanding of the composition of a
menu. The restrictions of the years of rationing have been the
cause of some remarkably unattractive developments in the
serving of food in restaurants, but if some ignorant or careless
restaurant managers still serve chips with spaghetti or boiled
potatoes and cauliflowers heaped up in the same dish with curry
and rice there is no need for us to do likewise at home; we can
plan our dinners round three, or at most four, courses, each one
perfect of its kind. In the days of long dinners there were usually
two choices at every course, and white and brown succeeded
each other monotonously. The idea was right—contrast is important but contrast in texture and the manner of cooking is
more essential than the colour, which was frequently arranged
so that roast beef with brown gravy was followed by roast

chicken with a white sauce and so on through endless expensively dull food.

Whether or not you are your own cook, it is unwise to have more than one course needing last-minute preparation. When opening the meal with a hot soup, it is perfectly reasonable to follow it with a cold main dish, accompanied perhaps by hot baked potatoes. A dish of hot vegetables which have been braising in butter in the meantime can succeed the main course, to be followed by a cold sweet. A cold first course can come before a hot dish, which will be simmering in the oven without being spoilt, and can be brought to table with the minimum of fuss. You can then have a cold sweet, and perhaps a savoury, although the savouries acceptable at a dinner party are extremely few, should be very hot and preferably composed of cheese. None of the fishy mixtures spread on tough or sodden toast are in the least welcome at the end of a good meal, in fact the only fish savoury which seems to me worth bothering with is the delicious Angels on Horseback, oysters wrapped up in the thinnest slices of bacon, threaded on skewers, grilled, and served on squares of freshly fried bread, which rules them out for the cook hostess who does not wish to leave her guests while she disappears to the kitchen for ten minutes, emerging breathless and crimson in the face.

Most people can get as far as deciding of what ingredients the meal shall consist, and indeed this is largely dependent on the food in season; the next consideration is the manner of their presentation. A sole cooked in a rich sauce of cream and mushrooms must be followed by a dry dish of entirely different aspect such as a roast partridge or a grilled tournedos, cold ham, jellied beef or a terrine of duck. It must not be preceded by a creamy mushroom soup, nor followed by chicken cooked in a cream sauce. Have some regard for the digestions of others even if your own resembles that of the ostrich. Should you decide to serve your fish grilled, say with little potatoes and an Hollandaise sauce, don't follow it up with another dish requiring potatoes and two more different sauces. The transatlantic manner of serving poultry, game, meat and ham dishes with dozens of different trimmings is simply pointless; the chances are that not one of them will be quite perfectly cooked or sufficiently hot, everybody will have their plates overloaded with half-cold food, and the flavour of the main dish will pass unnoticed amongst the vegetables, relishes, sauces, and salads. One or at most two vegetables are entirely sufficient, and one sauce, nor need potatoes always accompany a meat course. With a roast saddle of hare, for instance, serve a purée of chestnuts, the gravy from the hare, unthickened, but with the addition of a little red wine or port, and perhaps red-currant jelly. Anything else is superfluous. Avoid hot vegetables with anything served in an aspic jelly; if the aspic has been made as it should be with calf's foot and not with artificial gelatine, hot vegetables on the same plate will melt the jelly and make an unattractive watery mess. Potatoes baked in their jackets should be served on separate plates. A delicate green salad, or an orange salad, is the only other accompaniment necessary.

When starting the meal with a hot soufflé avoid serving a mousse at the sweet course; a mousse is only a cold soufflé, and you will have two dishes of exactly the same consistency. In the days of eight courses this was permissible, but with a small meal much more rigid care must be taken.

For the first course, when soup is unsuitable, eggs *en cocotte*, cold poached eggs in aspic, all kinds of *pâté* and terrines, and all the smoked-fish tribe, salmon, trout, eel, cod's roe, and herring are excellent; each accompanied by its particular adjunct, nicely presented hot toast and butter or fresh French bread for the *pâté*, brown bread and butter, lemon and cayenne for the smoked salmon; a creamy horse-radish sauce is the traditional companion of smoked trout, although to my mind this sauce is detrimental to the flavour of the fish.

Any of the sweets made with cream cheese, given on pp. 185–186, make a good ending to a luncheon or dinner, particularly for the summer. Being refreshing and light, they are also appropriately served after such aromatic and satisfying dishes as the stuffed cabbages, on pp. 97–102. Rich chocolate desserts are better served after very light and simple meals.

For the inexperienced cook it seems fairly obvious to say that it is safer when giving a dinner party to stick to something you know you can do successfully, but this doesn't necessarily mean the food need be stereotyped. A little experimenting before-hand will usually show whether a dish is a suitable one to appear at a party; but showing off, however amiably, may well end in disaster. "Know your limitations" is a copybook maxim which could be applied more often when planning a meal; many a reputation for skilful entertaining has been founded on the ability to cook one dish to perfection; it may be the flair for doing a rice dish, for roasting a duck, or for poaching eggs. The rest of the meal may consist of salad, fruit and cheese, and it will be infinitely preferable to the over-ambitious menu of several dishes, none of which are quite as they should be.

Deep fried food such as soufflé potatoes, cheese *beignets*, and the delicious *scampi* or Dublin Bay prawns in fritters are better kept for days when you have one or two friends who will eat them with you in the kitchen, straight from the smoking fat, the aroma of which is more penetrating than any other cooking smell, permeating the whole house and your own clothes, so it is not for dressing-up days. It should also be borne in mind by the ambitious cook that many dishes served in grandiose restaurants and designed, in fact, for advertisement are not suitable to the small household. Where there is an army of cooks and waiters it may be admissible to make *Crêpes Suzette* at the table and *flamber* them under your dazzled eyes. At home these conjuring tricks are likely to fall flat. Experience, more than anything else, will bring the ability to plan the cooking and serving so that the minimum anxiety and disturbance at the dinner table is compatible with the maximum excellence of the fare.

In this book will be found, I hope, a variety of recipes from which such meals can be composed: soups which can be prepared beforehand and heated up without detriment; a number of simple first-course dishes, always the hardest part of the meal to plan; some noble main dishes in the form of fish, meat, chicken, game and ham cooking, vegetables, eggs, sweets hot and cold, with soufflés for the confident.

A little common sense must be exercised in deciding which dishes can safely be left simmering and which must be served immediately they are ready. It is pointless, for example, to spend time and money on young spring vegetables and then leave them half an hour stewing in the oven; they will have lost all their charm, and it would have been better to serve a purée of dried vegetables. The sterling virtue of punctuality in a cook must give way, if need be, to the greater necessity of keeping guests waiting while last-minute preparations are made.

SOUPS

Soupe de Langoustines d'Orthez

ORTHEZ is in the Béarn, which, with the Pays Basque, made up the ancient Kingdom of Navarre; although Béarnais cooking is much more traditionally French than that of the Pays Basque, their raw materials are similar, and the food has colourful qualities.

Langoustines are the small and delicious shell fish about three inches long, delicate pink, with a very thin shell, resembling Dublin Bay Prawns. They are very plentiful in southern and south-western France, and cheap, costing two to three shillings a pound. In England they are not very often seen, and this soup can equally well be made with a small lobster, crawfish, or even prawns.

For four people:

1 lb. of any white fish, 1 lb. langoustines or lobster, 1 lb. tomatoes, 1 glass white wine or cider, 2 lemons, thyme, 2 carrots, 2 onions, 3 or 4 cloves of garlic, paprika or a red pimento, 2 ozs. rice, 2 eggs, 2 uncooked potatoes, parsley.

Put the white fish, and the shells of the langoustines or lobster (keeping the flesh aside), an onion, the carrots, potatoes, herbs, garlic, wine or cider and a lemon cut in slices all together into a large pan, with 4–5 pints of water. Let this simmer for 2 hours at least, so that you have a strong fish stock. Strain it into a clean pan.

Chop up the second onion and the tomatoes and put them into a shallow pan, adding the pimento or the paprika and seasoning, over a low heat without any liquid or frying medium. Cover the pan and cook them until they are reduced to a pulp, which will take about 10 minutes; put this mixture through a sieve into the fish stock. This operation is done separately in order to preserve the flavour of the tomatoes, which if cooked in the stock would disappear. Stir the soup until it is well amalgamated, bring it to the boil and put in the rice. By the time the rice has cooked it will have thickened the soup a little and softened the taste.

Stir in the flesh of the shell fish, cut into small pieces. Have the 2 eggs beaten up in a bowl with the juice of the second lemon; pour a ladle of the hot soup into the eggs, stirring quickly, then add the mixture to the soup, stirring all the time, without letting the soup boil again or the eggs will curdle. At the last moment add a tablespoon of grated lemon peel and a little cut parsley.

This makes a first-class shell-fish soup, reminiscent of the *bisques* of sophisticated restaurants, but not so cloying and, incidentally, a good deal less hard work, as it involves no pounding of shells and sieving of lobster butter; it is smooth and sufficiently thick without needing the addition of cream. With a glass of white Jurançon, or the Vin de Monein, the topaz-coloured wine of the country, or in England with a dry sherry, there is no better way to start off a good dinner.

Crab or Crawfish Soup

2 lbs. tomatoes, 1 lb. onions, herbs (if possible sweet basil, thyme and fennel), seasonings (coarse salt, ground black pepper, a pinch of nutmeg and saffron), 1 medium-sized cooked crab, crawfish or lobster, 1 wineglass of white wine, a little cream, 1 oz. butter, 2 pints water, a piece of lemon peel, a clove of garlic.

Slice the onions and put them to cook in a little butter; as soon as they are melted put in the chopped tomatoes and all the herbs and seasonings. Cover the pan and leave to simmer for

20 minutes; now add the wine and turn up the flame so that the wine bubbles. After 2 minutes put in half the shell-fish meat, cut in pieces, and add the water. Cook another 15–20 minutes and put all through a sieve. Return the purée obtained to the pan and put in the rest of the shell-fish, finely cut. Reheat the soup, and before serving add the cream or a lump of butter.

Shrimp Soup

> 1 pint cooked shrimps, 2 ozs. butter, 3 tablespoons white breadcrumbs, 1½ pints fish stock made from the shells of the shrimps, a small piece (about ½ lb.) of any white fish, 1 onion, lemon peel, herbs, salt and pepper, 1 teacup cream or milk, 1 egg yolk, a pinch of nutmeg, the juice of ½ lemon.

Prepare the stock by simmering the fish and the shrimp shells, the onion, herbs and lemon peel in 1½ pints of water for about 20 minutes. Strain it, and put the white breadcrumbs into it.

Pound the shrimps in a mortar with the butter, adding the lemon juice and the nutmeg. Add gradually the stock and the breadcrumbs until the mixture is creamy. Heat it up in a pan for 5 minutes and then press it through a wire sieve.

Beat the egg yolk and the cream or milk together, stir in 2 or 3 tablespoons of the hot soup, return the mixture to the pan and stir until the soup is hot, but don't let it boil.

This is a very delicately flavoured soup and at the same time simple to make. Prawns may be used instead of shrimps.

Soupe aux Marrons

This is the real *Soupe aux Marrons* as it is made in the Pyrenees, and a very different dish from the ordinary purée thinned with milk or stock.

You take a cold roast partridge and pound the meat in a mortar. Roast about 40 chestnuts in a slow oven for quarter of an hour, shell and peel them and cook them slowly in stock for 2 hours. Then add the pounded partridge meat, amalgamate this mixture by more pounding, and then put it all through a sieve. Return the soup to the pan and let it boil again.

Serve it with fried croûtons.

Potage Saint Hubert

A fine soup for the days after Christmas, to be followed by the cold turkey or a terrine of game.

1 pheasant, 1 lb. brown lentils, 1 onion, 1 leek, 4 ozs. cream, thyme, bayleaf.

Cook the soaked lentils in salted water with the onion, the white of the leek, the thyme and bayleaf and seasoning.

Roast the pheasant (this may sound wasteful, but an old bird can be used, and at Christmas-time we can surely be a little extravagant), and when it is cooked cut the meat off the bones, and keep aside the best fillets, which you cut into dice.

Pound the meat in a mortar, strain the lentils, add them to the meat; put the mixture through a fine sieve into a saucepan. Moisten it with the lentil stock, adding it until the soup is the right consistency. When it is quite hot add the cream and the diced pheasant.

Any cold game could be used for this soup or the remains of a roast goose. The amounts given will serve eight people.

La Potée

This is the traditional daily food of the peasants of eastern France, particularly in the Haute Marne. It is a simple rustic dish, made from freshly gathered vegetables and home-cured bacon.

It is cooked in a marmite, or heavy iron saucepan; you need a selection of vegetables in about equal proportions, say 12 small potatoes, 12 small carrots, 6 small turnips and 6 small onions, 2 lbs. of French beans or broad beans, 2 lbs. of green peas, the heart of a young cabbage cut in strips, and a piece of home-cured bacon, say about 1 lb. for six people.

Put the root vegetables and bacon on first, covered with water, and let them simmer slowly. Thirty minutes before serving add the green vegetables. The cabbage is put in, cut in strips, during the last 5 minutes.

The soup is served in a large deep dish or tureen, the vegetables almost, but not quite, crumbling, and the rose-pink bacon cut into convenient pieces.

Soupe au Lard et au Fromage

Cut $\frac{1}{4}$ lb. of fat bacon in small pieces and melt it gently in a saucepan; when the pieces have yielded enough fat, and before they are overdone, take them out, keep them aside, and into the fat put 6 small onions cut into thin rounds. Cook them very gently until they are almost reduced to a purée; at this moment season the onions and add about $1\frac{1}{2}$ pints of water and leave it to simmer for 30 minutes.

Meanwhile, get ready a number of thin slices of stale bread. Put a layer of these into a deep earthenware casserole or other pan which will go in the oven. Cover the bread with a layer of grated Parmesan cheese, then a tablespoon of fresh cream and some of the bacon; then another layer of bread, cheese, cream and bacon, and so on until the casserole is half full.

Now pour the onions and their stock in the pan and put into the oven for 5 minutes to heat up.

Choucroûte Soup
(An unusual soup with a pleasant smoky flavour)

1 lb. *choucroûte* (sauerkraut) or the equivalent of tinned *choucroûte*, 2 medium potatoes, 2 rashers bacon, or a bacon bone, or rinds of bacon, pepper, salt, bayleaf, 6 juniper berries, 2 lumps sugar, 1 oz. dried mushrooms, ¼ lb. uncooked salami sausage or 2 or 3 smoked Frankfurter sausages, 2 pints stock or water, 2 ozs. cream.

Put the *choucroûte* into a large pan; add the potatoes, peeled and cut up small, the dried mushrooms, the bacon, or the bacon bone or rind, the herbs and seasonings and the stock or water. Simmer for about 1 hour. Put all through a sieve. Return to the pan.

Cut up the sausage and cook it in the soup for 15 minutes. Before serving, stir in the cream and, if you like, some grated cheese as well.

Mushroom Soup

½ lb. mushrooms, 1 pint water, 1 pint milk, 3 tablespoons flour, 2 ozs. butter, seasoning, a few bacon rinds.

Make a white sauce with the butter, flour and milk; while this is cooking, bring the water to the boil and put in the washed mushrooms, whole, and the bacon rinds, pepper and salt.

Cook them for about 5 minutes. Strain the mushrooms, keeping the water, and add this gradually to the white sauce. Remove the bacon rinds and chop the mushrooms fairly finely. Add them to the liquid mixture, season, and heat up.

This way of making mushroom soup preserves the full flavour of the mushrooms. It is a mistake to use too many, or to ginger it up with sherry, but a little butter or cream can be added immediately before serving.

Elzekaria

(A Basque peasant soup)

In pork or goose fat sauté a large sliced onion; add a small white cabbage cut in thin strips, ½ lb. of dried haricot beans which have been soaked overnight, 2 crushed cloves of garlic, salt and pepper.

Cover with about 4 pints of water and simmer for at least 3 hours, until the beans are ready. In the Basque country they pour a few drops of vinegar into each plate of soup.

Potato and Watercress Soup

Boil 2 lbs. of potatoes and 2 onions in 2 pints of water. When they are very soft, pass through a sieve. Reheat, adding ½ pint of milk, plenty of pepper, and a little nutmeg or mace.

Chop the leaves of 2 bunches of watercress finely and, when ready to serve the soup, add it and stir well in, together with 2 chopped raw tomatoes.

A little white wine, added cautiously so as not to curdle the milk, is a vast improvement.

Chiffonade

1 lettuce, chicken or vegetable stock or water, 1 tablespoon rice, 1 oz. butter.

Shred the lettuce very small. Melt it in a pan with the butter, and after 10 minutes pour in the stock, and the rice, and cook slowly until the rice is tender. Sorrel can be used instead of the lettuce, or half lettuce and half sorrel.

Soupe à l'Ail

This is a soup only for those who like their garlic unadulterated. There are a number of ways of cooking *Soupe à l'Ail* throughout Provence and south-western France. This is a version from the Languedoc.

Put 2 tablespoons of goose or other good dripping into a deep earthenware casserole. In this dripping melt gently 24 cloves of garlic without letting them actually get brown.

Pour over them 3–4 pints of warmed stock or water. Season with salt, black pepper, mace and nutmeg. Cook for 15 minutes. Put the soup through a sieve, return it to the pan to heat up. In a bowl beat up the yolks of 3 or 4 eggs with 3 tablespoons of olive oil. Stir some of the soup into the eggs, then pour the egg mixture back into the soup without letting it boil again.

Have ready prepared some slices of stale bread, toasted in the oven with the whites of the eggs (not beaten) spread over them. Put these slices into the soup plates and pour the soup over them.

Mayorquina

Majorca once belonged to the Catalan province which included the town of Perpignan, where the castle of the Kings of Majorca is still to be seen. This traditional soup probably dates from those days. It has all the characteristics of the combined French and Spanish cooking of this region. It should be made in an earthenware marmite, which can be left to simmer either on top of a mat over the stove or in a slow oven.

For five or six people for this soup you need 5 or 6 cloves of garlic, 2 medium-sized Spanish onions, 1 red pimento, ½ lb. of ripe tomatoes, 2 ozs. of leeks, the heart of a small cabbage, a branch of thyme, a bayleaf finely chopped, a clove, 3 tablespoons of olive oil.

Clean and chop all these ingredients, and peel the tomatoes. Put the oil into the pan, which should not be so large that the oil disappears at the bottom, and when it is warmed put in the finely chopped garlic, then the onions and the leeks. Let this simmer gently for 10 minutes, stirring with a wooden spoon so that the vegetables melt but do not brown. Now add the peeled and sliced tomatoes and the pimento cut into strips, simmer and stir for another 15 minutes.

Now add slowly about 2½–3 pints of hot water and bring it to boiling point, at this moment add the chopped cabbage, the thyme, clove and bayleaf, and salt and pepper, and cover the pan, leaving it to simmer for 1½–2 hours.

In the soup tureen place several large thin slices of brown or wholemeal bread. Before serving the soup, stir in a tablespoon of fresh olive oil and do not allow the soup to boil again. Pour it over the bread in the tureen, and be sure to have a pepper-mill on the table so that each guest can season his soup to his own taste.

La Fricassée and Le Farci

In the south-west of France, particularly in the Perigord district, the soups are nearly always enriched with a mixture of fried vegetables, onion and garlic, called *La Fricassée*, or *le hâchis*.

A ladle of the vegetables which have cooked in the soup, such as carrots, turnips and onions, are taken out, cut up with a tomato or two, a clove of garlic and some parsley, and per-haps some rounds of raw leek or celery, and sautéd in goose, pork or bacon fat, then returned to the soup before serving, imparting a very special flavour to these *garbures*. When making a soup of dried vegetables, such as lentils or haricots, the *fricassée* will consist simply of a slice of bacon chopped up with garlic and onion, and fried; these simple additions give character and savour to the most ordinary soups.

Le Farci is a stuffing consisting of breadcrumbs which have been soaked in stock or milk, mixed with yolks of eggs, chopped meat, home-cured ham or bacon or salt pork, what-ever happens to be available. The mixture is wrapped in cabbage leaves and put into chicken or meat broth to cook for

about 20 minutes before serving, giving an added richness and
savour to the soup. The *farci* comes out a fine golden yellow
from the yolks of the eggs, and is cut into slices, and some
put into each plate.

La Garbure

This soup, which, like the *Potée*, is rather more of a stew
than a soup, is traditional in the Landes, the Béarn, and the
Pyrenees. The recipe has many variations, and this one is given
as typical of its kind.

In an earthenware casserole, or *toupin* as it is called in the
Béarn (a fat comfortable-looking pot, narrowing towards the
top, with a straight handle), put ½ lb. of bacon, in one piece.
Fill the casserole with water, and when it is bubbling throw in
the vegetables—say 2 potatoes, 2 leeks, a ½ lb. each of shelled
peas and broad beans, a turnip, 2 or 3 carrots, all cut into small
pieces, a green or red sweet pepper cut in strips, or some
paprika pepper, marjoram, thyme, several cloves of garlic.
Let all this simmer until the vegetables are half cooked; at this
moment add a small white cabbage cut into strips, and a wing
or leg of *confit d'oie*, as described on p. 135, or else a piece of
confit de porc (p. 116), whichever is being used; the fat adhering
to the *confit* when it is taken out of the jar is left round it, and
imparts its flavour to the *garbure*.

The soup is so thick that the ladle stands up in it; it is served
on slices of brown bread in each plate, the solid pieces of bacon
and goose being put on to a separate dish and cut up. As each
person gets to the end of his soup, he adds a glass of wine to the
remaining *bouillon* in the plate, a custom which they call
faire chabrot in these parts.

Failing either *confit* of goose or pork to add to the *garbure*,
make the *farci* as described on p. 43, wrap it up in some of the
cabbage leaves retained when the cabbage is sliced, and add

these stuffed leaves to the *garbure* at the same time. A few strips of fresh pork rind, tied up in a bunch so that they can be removed, the remains of a roast goose, small garlic sausages, can all go to enrich the *garbure*. In the winter when there are no fresh green vegetables, use ½ lb. of white haricot beans which have been soaked overnight.

A few whole roast chestnuts in the *garbure* are a typically Pyrenean addition, and give a most excellent flavour.

The quantities given are sufficient for six to eight people.

L'Ouïllade

L'Ouïllade is the Catalan national soup, so called after the *oulle*, the earthenware marmite in which it is cooked, the Catalan version of the Spanish *olla*.

In spite of their somewhat ferocious ways with garlic and strong red peppers, the Catalan country cooking is not without its refinements, as witness this soup, which is, in fact, cooked in two pots at the same time, so separating the flavour of haricot beans and cabbage until the moment of serving.

For four or five people soak 1 lb. of white haricot beans; the next day put them to cook with water to cover and let them simmer for about 3 hours. In another pot, with boiling salted water, put a white cabbage cut into strips, 5 or 6 medium-sized potatoes cut in half, 1 or 2 onions, a piece of bacon or a bacon bone, 1 or 2 carrots and a turnip, seasoning and herbs, 1 or 2 cloves of garlic, and a small spoonful of good dripping— bacon or pork fat if possible. The cooking of the second lot of vegetables should be timed so that it is ready at the same time as the beans, which by the time they have cooked should have absorbed nearly all their water. Pour the whole contents of the bean pot into the cabbage and vegetable mixture; remove the bacon bone, stir the soup round, and it is ready to serve.

A little *hachis* of garlic, onion and parsley, fried in bacon fat, can be added with advantage.

La Soupe aux Fèves

Take 2–3 lbs. of broad beans out of their pods, then remove the inner skins from the beans; a fairly long business, but, for those who like the unique flavour of broad beans, well worth it. Bring about 3 pints of water to the boil, salt it, and put in the broad beans. Let the pan simmer slowly. When the beans are half cooked, add a handful of fresh green peas, a few very small white onions and a stick of celery cut in small pieces.

In a separate pan make a little *fricassée* as described on p. 43, with a slice of bacon chopped in small pieces, an onion, a clove of garlic and some good fresh parsley or basil; fry these in bacon fat, and when they are brown add a tablespoon of flour; stir it round two or three times, add a ladleful of the soup, and let it thicken; then return the whole mixture to the soup. Cook it for 10 more minutes. The flour merely gives a little body to the soup, which is not intended to be a thick one.

It is served poured over slices of rye bread in the plates.

Consommé Froid Rose

Put 1 lb. of minced lean beef into a pan with 2 lb. of tomatoes, 3 pints of meat or chicken stock, seasoning, herbs, and the whites of 2 eggs, let it simmer for 1½ hours and then strain and ice.

There will probably be a little fat on the top, which must be skimmed off. The *consommé* can be made with water instead of stock, and comes out a delicate straw colour, with a really exquisite flavour. The meat and tomatoes can be utilised for a sauce for spaghetti.

Iced Shrimp Soup

Make the soup in exactly the way described on p. 37, only omitting the butter and reserving a few of the shrimps whole for the garnish.

When the soup has cooled, add about an inch of peeled cucumber cut into small dice, a little chopped fennel or watercress, and the reserved shrimps. It must be very well iced. Garnish each plate or bowl of soup with a slice of lemon.

FISH

FOR ALL cooking, but particularly for the preparation of fish, vegetables and for salting meat, *gros sel*, or coarse sea salt is infinitely preferable to refined salt. *Gros sel* can be bought by the pound in Soho shops and in packets at Health Food stores, where one can also buy the crisp, flaky Maldon Salt; this comes in 3-lb. packets and is delicious for the table, necessitating no salt mill. This salt can also be ordered direct from the Maldon Crystal Salt Company, Maldon, Essex.

Lobster

" During the early summer months, lobsters are in prime condition, and may be bought either alive or dead. As they are very tenacious of life, and indeed will live on till their substance is utterly wasted, it is clearly better to buy them alive, taking care not to kill them till just before cooking. The heaviest are the best; and if the tail strikes quick and strong, they are in good condition, but if weak and light and frothing at the mouth are exhausted and worthless. In like manner, when buying a boiled lobster put your finger and thumb on the body and pinch it; if it feels firm, and the tail goes back with a strong spring, the lobster—if heavy and of a good colour—is a desirable specimen."

These instructions are given by the cookery expert of *Spons Household Manual*, published in the 'eighties. Nowadays lobsters, except for restaurants, are nearly always bought ready cooked, but, while nobody can be blamed for avoiding participation in the martyr's death they die, the fact remains that a freshly cooked lobster prepared in one's own kitchen makes a very much better dish than one cooked by the fishmonger. It may be of some solace to know that Mr. Joseph Sinel, who made experiments on behalf of the R.S.P.C.A., came to the conclusion that a lobster put into cold water which is slowly brought to the boil collapses and dies painlessly when the heat reaches 70°.

Boiled Lobster

" Lobster is, indeed, matter for a May morning," said Peacock, "and demands a rare combination of knowledge and virtue in him who sets it forth." He would no doubt have considered this dish of lobster, simply boiled and served piping hot, a suitable morsel for breakfast.

Tie up the tail of the lobster to the body with string (the fishmonger will do this for you) and put it into a large pan of cold salted water. After it has come slowly to the boil, cook it for 20–30 minutes according to the size. Take it out of the pan, clean the scum off the shell and rub it over with a little butter or oil. Break off the claws, crack them carefully at each joint so that they come to pieces easily, cut the tail down the middle and leave the body whole. Put all on to a large hot platter and serve with melted butter or a *sauce tartare*.

Buttered Lobster

For six people you need 3 medium-sized cooked lobsters. The tails are cut in half and put under the grill for a few minutes with a little butter. The rest of the meat is cut into dice, seasoned with salt, pepper, a dash of cayenne and a generous sprinkling of lemon juice; heat this in a sauté pan with butter, shaking the pan to prevent the lobster from sticking. Serve in a heap in the centre of the dish with the tails arranged round, garnished with quarters of lemon.

Crawfish, or *langouste*, are not so common in England as lobster, but when they do appear they are cheaper and, in the opinion of many people, more delicate. They have no claws, and sometimes the tails only are sold.

Langouste à la Grecque

Cut 2 medium-sized onions in thin slices, sauté them until golden in a small wineglass of olive oil; then add ½ lb. of chopped tomatoes and stir in for a few minutes. Season with salt, pepper and a handful of chopped parsley, then pour in a glass of white wine. Let it cook fiercely for a few seconds. At this stage put in the cut-up pieces of *langouste* and let the pan simmer until the sauce attains a fairly thick consistency. The dish can be served hot, or cold, when it makes a rich hors-d'œuvre.

Homard à la Crème

 1 cooked lobster, ¼ lb. mushrooms, 4 ozs. cream, 1 liqueur glass each brandy and pale sherry, 2 ozs. butter, lemon juice, salt and pepper, cayenne pepper.

Melt the butter in a shallow pan and put in the pieces of lobster, seasoned with the salt, pepper and lemon juice. When the butter is foaming, pour in the brandy and set it alight, and as soon as it has finished burning add the mushrooms cut in thin slices, the sherry and a suspicion of cayenne. Stir the contents of the pan for 2 or 3 minutes and pour in the cream. Another 5 minutes over a moderate flame and the lobster is ready. This is a simple and delicious dish which is too often spoilt by the addition of tomato sauce, too much sherry and a thickening of flour and milk.

When cream is not available, milk can be used and the sauce bound with the yolk of an egg at the very last minute—do not let the sauce boil after you have added the egg.

Beware of poor quality sherry: I have known even a little ruin the dish with its overpowering flavour, and, failing a reasonably good dry or medium sherry, twice the quantity of white wine can be used.

Langouste en Brochettes

For each person allow 1 medium-sized crawfish tail, a rasher of bacon, 2 ozs. of mushrooms, half a tomato, lemon juice, a little butter.

Cut the cooked meat of the crawfish tail into squares, and each rasher of bacon into about 6 pieces. Sauté the mushrooms for 2 or 3 minutes in a little butter. Put a half tomato on to a skewer, cut side towards the point. Then thread on the crawfish, the bacon and the mushrooms alternately until the skewer is full. Melt the butter in a pan and pour it over the skewers, the contents of which have been seasoned with a little salt, pepper and lemon juice.

Put the skewers on to the toaster, over a fireproof dish, and cook under the grill, turning them once and basting with the butter as you do so. Cook them 5–7 minutes, until they are hot.

Arrange them on a dish, garnished with bunches of watercress and halves of lemon. With them serve either of the following sauces: hot melted butter in which there is a squeeze of lemon juice and some cut-up chives; or fresh cream whipped with a scrap of salt and pepper and mixed with chopped tarragon, served very cold.

Langouste à la Catalane

Into a ready prepared *All Grenat* or *Bouillade* sauce (p. 194) put the flesh of a cooked crawfish or lobster, cut into small squares and seasoned with black pepper and lemon juice. Simmer 3 or 4 minutes only, until the lobster is hot.

Langouste de l'Ile Ste Marguerite

Cold, freshly boiled crawfish or lobster is served with an accompaniment of hot, crisp, fried onions, cooked as described for the *Paillettes d'Oignons* on p. 167.

Indigestible but delicious.

Scalloped Oysters à la Créole

Into individual buttered fireproof dishes, put a layer of breadcrumbs mixed with a little chopped parsley, chopped tomato, a suspicion of chives and cayenne pepper.

On this bed place 6 or 8 oysters for each dish, another layer of the breadcrumb mixture, and some butter in small pieces.

Fill the dishes up with cream and the liquor from the oysters, and bake in a medium oven for 5 or 6 minutes.

Shrimps à la Crème

Butter some shallow individual china dishes, and into each one put 2 tablespoons of peeled shrimps (or prawns). Cover the shrimps with thin cream, a fine sprinkling of breadcrumbs, a knob of butter on the top, and put in a medium oven (Regulo 5) for 6 or 7 minutes, until they are just turning brown on the top.

Esquinado à l'huile

Esquinado is the Provençal name for the Spider Crab.

The crab (a female one is preferable, for the eggs improve the taste of the dish) should be cooked for 30 minutes in water to which is added a few drops of vinegar, salt, 2 or 3 peppercorns and 2 bayleaves.

When cold, take out all the inside including the eggs and the flesh from the claws, and pound it in a mortar, with the yolks of 2 hard-boiled eggs, a teaspoon of dry mustard, the juice of a lemon, salt and pepper. Put the purée through a fine sieve into a basin. Add gradually about 1 gill (5 ozs.) of olive oil, so that the purée is well amalgamated, and finally a little finely chopped parsley.

The purée is served in the crab shell, the outside well cleaned and rubbed over with a little olive oil.

To be served as a sauce with any plainly cooked white fish, with risotto, hard-boiled eggs or as an hors-d'œuvre with slices of toasted French bread.

Scallops Fried in Batter

For the batter:

¼ lb. flour, 3 tablespoons olive oil, a pinch of salt, ¾ tumbler tepid water, 1 white of egg.

Sieve the flour, mix in the olive oil, the salt, and the water. Leave the batter to rest for at least 2 hours. When ready to use, stir in the beaten white of egg. This amount will make about 24 fritters.

Cut 12 scallops into two rounds each. Reserve the coral. Season the scallops with salt, pepper and lemon juice. Dip each one in batter and fry in very hot, but not boiling, deep fat or oil. Drain them on a paper napkin.

Warm the coral in a little butter and garnish the dish with them, and alternate quarters of lemon. Alternatively the slightly cooked coral can be pounded and added to a mayonnaise, but the taste of these scallop fritters is very delicate and they do not really need a sauce.

Mussels

Allow about 1 pint of mussels per person and 1 pint over—there are nearly always a few which have to be discarded. Put them into a bowl of cold water, covered with a damp cloth over which you strew a little coarse salt. Leave them in a cold place for 2 or 3 hours. This process helps to clean them.

When you are ready to cook them, throw away any which are opened or broken, and put the rest in a basin of clean water under a running cold tap. Scrape, scrub and beard each one separately, putting them into a second basin of cold water while you do so. When they are thoroughly cleaned, leave them another 10 minutes in a colander under the running tap, then in cold water again for a further 10 minutes. All this sounds very complicated, but it is most important to remove all grit and sand.

The mussels are now ready to cook, and whether they are to be served *à la marinière, au gratin,* as a garnish, in a salad or an omelette, soup, risotto, or fried in batter, the preliminary method is the same, but the cooking medium differs.

For *moules marinière* they are cooked and served in their shells in a *court-bouillon* of water and white wine or wine only, with chopped shallot and parsley, for *moules poulette* the same *court-bouillon* is thickened with egg yolks while the mussels are kept hot in another dish. For soups and risottos the method is as for *marinière,* the stock being used as a basis for the soup or to cook the risotto in, and the mussels shelled. If to be served in a *gratin,* the mussels can be cooked in very little water, white wine, or cider, for a salad or hors-d'œuvre in olive oil; when the stock or oil in which they have been cooked is to be used again for the sauce, soup, or risotto, it is strained through a muslin, as there is always a little sediment at the bottom, however carefully they have been cleaned.

The method of cooking them is as follows: put the water, the wine, or the olive oil in a wide pan, put in the mussels and cook them on a moderate flame until they open, moving them round from time to time with a wooden spoon so that the top ones get cooked at the same time as those underneath. The process takes about 10 minutes, and when they are opened they are ready. Often there are one or two which refuse to open and these can be left a little longer after the others have been taken out. Over-cooking shrivels them up and spoils them. Salt can be added when they are cooked; sometimes they are salty enough, but it is impossible to tell beforehand.

Moules à la Bordelaise

Clean the mussels, allowing 6 pints for four people; let them open over the fire with a glass of white wine. Strain them and remove the empty half shell.

In a small pan melt 1 oz. of butter, and in this sauté 2 chopped shallots; add 1 lb. of tomatoes, cut up, seasoning, a clove of garlic, a handful of chopped parsley and one of breadcrumbs which have been soaked in milk to soften them and then strained; stir the sauce until the tomatoes are cooked, then add a little of the strained juice from the mussels, and a teaspoon of grated lemon peel. Put the mussels into a gratin dish, pour the sauce over them and simmer for 3 or 4 minutes until the mussels are hot.

Messy to eat, but a dish with character.

Moules Niçoises

For four people you need about 6 pints of mussels; this amount should give about 18 mussels per person, allowing for those which are open or broken and have to be thrown away. Clean them as explained on p. 56, and put them into a wide shallow pan with a glass of white wine or cider; let them open by rapid boiling, removing them the very minute they are opening; they are to be cooked again, so they must not be allowed to dry up. Strain the wine in which they have cooked through a muslin.

Prepare a *Pestou* (p. 194) with butter, and substituting parsley if there is no fresh basil available. Remove the empty half shell from each mussel and put the remaining half shells with the mussels in them into individual metal or china egg dishes, about eight inches in diameter.

Spread a little of the prepared *Pestou* on to each mussel, moisten with a few drops of the strained stock and put the dishes under the grill to melt and brown the sauce, 3 or 4 minutes for each dish.

Moules au Gratin

First prepare 2 ozs. of butter pounded with a clove of garlic and some finely chopped parsley. With an oyster knife open the cleaned, uncooked mussels, at least a dozen per person; put a little of the prepared butter on each mussel, arrange them in a fireproof dish and heat them until the butter is melted.

Pour a cup of fresh cream mixed with about 3 tablespoons of grated Parmesan cheese over them and put them in a hot oven or under the grill to brown.

Gratin of Mussels, Mushrooms and Shrimps

4 or 5 pints mussels, ¼ lb. mushrooms, ½ pint cooked shrimps, 1 glass white wine, 2 ozs. cream, breadcrumbs, 1 small clove of garlic, parsley, 1 oz. flour, 1 oz. butter.

Clean the mussels, put them to cook in ½ pint of water and the white wine. When they are opened, strain them, keeping the stock. Shell the mussels. Strain the stock through a muslin. Make a white *roux* with the butter and flour, add the strained mussel stock and cook until it is smooth. Now add the cream and the mushrooms, previously sautéd a minute in butter, and the shrimps. When the sauce is thick and creamy, stir in the mussels. Turn the mixture into a fireproof gratin dish, well buttered.

Add a little cut parsley, a handful of breadcrumbs, some nuts of butter, and put under the grill until golden and bubbling.

Laitances au Vin Blanc

Soft roes are cheap, plentiful, and can be cooked in a few minutes. They are usually served as a savoury, but are better as a first dish.

Butter a shallow dish, lay the roes in it, and on top 2 chopped tomatoes, a scrap of grated lemon peel, salt, pepper, parsley and a little more butter. Pour over ½ wineglass of white wine, cover with a thin layer of breadcrumbs and cook in the oven for about 10 minutes.

Mackerel en Papillotes

Choose fairly small mackerel, one for each person, and have them split and cleaned. For four, prepare a mixture of a teacup of chopped parsley, ½ teacup of capers, 2 oz. of butter, a strip of lemon peel, a pinch of cayenne, salt and black pepper. If you can get fennel, add ½ teacup of the chopped leaves to the mixture—fennel is particularly good with mackerel—and knead all the ingredients together.

Put a portion of this mixture inside each mackerel. Butter four squares of greaseproof paper, put a mackerel on each one, and fold over the edges so that no butter can escape. Lay them on the grid in the pre-heated oven, as you would a baked potato, and cook (Regulo 4), for 25–30 minutes, putting the ones which have to go on the lower shelf into the oven 5 minutes before the others.

To serve them, turn them out of their paper cases into a hot dish with all the butter and herbs poured over them, and accompanied by slices of lemon. No sauce or vegetable is necessary, but they must be very hot. The mackerel can be prepared in their papillotes beforehand, and even if they are left a little longer than necessary in the oven they will come to no harm.

Filets de Maquereaux Gratinés aux Câpres

Arrange your fillets of mackerel in a flat buttered fireproof dish; salt and pepper them and pour over a small glass of white wine. Cover and cook in the oven.

In the meantime, melt a nut of butter in a saucepan; stir in a spoonful of flour; let it cook a minute and add stock made from the bones of the fish. The sauce should be smooth and creamy, but not too thick. Add a beaten egg and stir again without letting the sauce boil; now add a tablespoon of capers, and pour over the fillets. Sprinkle breadcrumbs on top, and a little melted butter, and put the dish under the grill to brown, but only for two or three minutes or the sauce will curdle.

Grilled Mackerel

Make two slanting incisions on each side of the cleaned mackerel. Into these put a little butter worked with parsley, pepper and salt, fennel, and a few chopped capers. Put the mackerel under the grill with a fire-proof serving dish underneath. Grill them 7–10 minutes on each side; add a squeeze of lemon juice to the butter in the dish. No other sauce is necessary, for the mackerel will be quite delicious cooked in this simple way.

Herrings, mullet, whiting and trout can be grilled in the same way.

Filets de Maquereaux au Vin Blanc

One of the classic hors-d'œuvre of France, but very rarely met with in England.

Prepare a *court-bouillon* with a wineglass of white wine and one of water, an onion, a clove of garlic, a bayleaf, salt and ground black pepper, and a piece of lemon peel. Bring this to the boil, let it cook 5 minutes, then leave it to cool.

Put the cleaned mackerel into the cold *court-bouillon* and let them cook very gently for about 15 minutes; leave them to get cold in the *court-bouillon*. Split them carefully, take out the bones, remove the skin and divide each fish into about 6 or 8 small fillets, and arrange in a narrow oval dish. Reheat the *court-bouillon*, letting it bubble until it is reduced by half. When it is cool, strain it over the mackerel, and garnish the dish with a few capers and some chopped chives or parsley.

Stuffed Baked Herrings

Have the herrings boned; stuff them with a smooth, creamy purée of potatoes, flavoured with pepper and nutmeg and fresh herbs. Wrap them in buttered paper, place them on the grid in the oven and cook at a moderate heat for about 10 minutes.

They can also be cooked under the grill on an electric stove.

Turbot à l'Espagnole

Put a sliced onion to brown in a little olive oil; add 1 lb. of tomatoes, roughly chopped, and seasoning of salt, pepper, sugar, sweet basil, a clove of garlic and a dessertspoon of paprika pepper. Cook slowly until it is almost a purée.

In the meantime poach a fine whole turbot in a *court-bouillon* to which you have added a wineglass of white wine, cider or sherry, an onion, a bayleaf, a piece of lemon- or orange-peel, salt and pepper. When the fish is cooked, drain it carefully and put it on the serving dish. Add a wineglass of the *court-bouillon* to the tomato sauce and go on cooking until it is well amalgamated. Pour the sauce over the turbot, and when it is cold garnish with lemon peel and some green herbs—either tarragon or chives.

Turbot should be cooked the day it is to be eaten and not too long beforehand; it loses its delicacy if left more than an hour or two.

Turbot Normand

First prepare 3 pints of *Moules Marinière* (p. 57) and take them out of their shells. Pour the liquid from the mussels through a muslin. In the meantime slice 5 or 6 onions and sauté them in butter, so that they melt and turn almost to a purée.

Put the onions into an oval fish dish, pour over the liquid from the mussels, put the turbot on the top and add a tumbler of cider. Cover the pan and cook in the oven, basting the fish with the liquid from time to time. When the turbot is cooked, add a lump of butter which has been mashed with a little chopped parsley and a drop of lemon juice, put the mussels all round and leave the dish in the oven just long enough for the mussels to get hot.

A handful of fresh shrimps added to the garnish is an improvement.

Sole au Vin Blanc

For four people:

8 fillets of sole, ¼ bottle white wine, not too dry, 4 ozs. cream, 1 oz. flour, tarragon, 1 oz. butter.

Roll the fillets up and place them in a buttered fireproof dish. Season them with salt and pepper and pour the wine over them. Put a sprig of tarragon into the wine. Cover the pan, and put it in a moderate oven (Regulo 4) for about 10 minutes.

In the meantime, make a white *roux* with the butter and flour, and while this is cooking put the cream into a small pan and simmer it for 3 or 4 minutes until it has reduced and thickened. Add it slowly to the flour and butter mixture, stir it well, and then put it aside while you remove the sole from the oven, pour off the wine in which it has cooked into another small pan, and keep the fish covered and warm in the bottom of the oven. Let the wine simmer until it has reduced by half; you can tell by the delicious aroma coming out of the pan when it is ready. Now add this slowly to the cream sauce, stirring over a very low fire, and cooking for 3 or 4 minutes until it is the right consistency. If too thick, add a little more cream; if too thin, then cook a little longer.

Now pour the sauce (through a sieve if it is at all lumpy) on to the fillets, add a tablespoon of chopped tarragon, a fine dusting of breadcrumbs, a knob of butter, and put under a hot grill to brown.

This really is a delicious creamy dish, and one of the few ways of cooking sole in which the richness of the sauce does not detract from the natural flavour of the sole.

Cheese Soufflé with Fillets of Sole

The yolks of 4 eggs and the whites of 5, 2½ ozs. grated cheese, preferably equal parts of Gruyère and Parmesan, salt, pepper, 1 oz. butter, 4 fillets sole.

Roll up the fillets of sole, seasoned with salt and pepper, and cook in a buttered dish in the oven for 5 minutes. They do not need to be quite cooked, as they are cooked again in the soufflé.

Butter a soufflé dish and place the fillets at the bottom, well drained of any liquid that comes from them while cooking. Separate the eggs. Beat the cheese into the yolks until the mixture is creamy. Whip the whites very stiffly, fold them into the yolks, pour quickly into the soufflé dish and put it straight into a preheated oven (fairly hot). Cook for 12–15 minutes.

The timing of soufflés is entirely a matter of experience and depends upon practice and the knowledge of one's own oven, so that while Regulo No. 7 is the set temperature for soufflés on my own gas cooker, the pressure varies considerably in different districts and according to the age of the stove. So before venturing upon a soufflé for a dinner party, it is wise to carry out a few experiments, noting the time taken and the temperature of the oven for the most successful.

Rouget Flambé au Fenouil

In the market places of Provence they sell bunches of fennel stalks specially for *les grillades au fenouil*. There is no substitute, but fennel is easy enough to grow in any garden or in pots.

Clean out the red mullet but leave in the liver. In the opening put 2 or 3 stalks of fennel. Put them in a bed of dried fennel branches, cover with melted butter and put under the grill.

When they are done on both sides, withdraw the dish from the grill. Pour over a glass of Armagnac and set light to it. Bring the dish to the table while the Armagnac is still burning.

Colin à l'Oseille

Colin is another name for merluche or hake. Saithe or rock salmon can also be used for this dish.

Sorrel is not often seen in England, although I have managed to buy it in London from time to time, and some enterprising people grow it in their gardens.[1] It has a delicious flavour, rather acid, and is a perfect foil for fish, and eggs.

[1] Both the nursery gardens mentioned on pages 155–6 sell sorrel plants.

For *Colin à l'Oseille*, poach a large piece of hake or rock salmon in a *court-bouillon* with an onion, herbs, and lemon peel.

Clean the sorrel (about 1 lb.), and cook it as for spinach, with as little water as possible. Make this into a purée by putting it through a sieve, mix in 2 yolks of eggs, a little French tarragon mustard, a few leaves of raw sorrel which you have reserved, chopped finely with a few leaves of tarragon.

Serve the fish on this green bed, either hot or cold, garnished with lemon. A fine summer dish.

Le Brochet au Beurre Blanc de Vouvray

You need a pike weighing not less than 2 lbs. and the following vegetables and herbs:

A sliced onion, a sliced carrot, a sprig of thyme and one of fennel, a bayleaf, parsley, salt, 2 or 3 peppercorns.

Bring all this to the boil in about 1 pint of water and a glass of white wine, and then leave it to cool. Put the cleaned fish in, bring it to the boil again, and let it poach for 20 minutes.

In the meantime, prepare your *beurre blanc*. In about 5 ozs. of white wine (in Touraine they naturally use the wine of Vouvray, but any light white wine of Anjou would do, or even a Pouilly) put 6 finely chopped shallots, and 3 table-spoons of the *court-bouillon* of the fish. Reduce this over a gentle fire to a fifth of its original volume, then add little by little 6 ozs. of butter which you have already worked a little with a fork to soften it, and 1 oz. of fresh cream. Whatever happens, the sauce must not boil, or disaster will ensue. (It would be wise to do this sauce, after the preliminary reduction of the wine, in a bowl over a pan of hot water.)

Beat continuously with an egg whisk so that the butter "rises" and froths; season with salt if necessary. The sauce must be ready at the same time as the fish is cooked, and must be served immediately.

Accompany this splendid dish with plainly boiled potatoes and the same wine as you used for the sauce.

" It is with tears of gratitude in their voices," writes the author of this recipe, " that your guests will remind you of the *beurre blanc de Vouvray*." Another version of *beurre blanc* is made simply with the butter and shallot mixture, without cream.

Pike is fairly rare in England. It is quite possible to make this dish with a small turbot, a fine whole sole, or a salmon trout.

Carpe à l'Oseille

A carp weighing 3 lbs., salt, pepper, 4 lbs. sorrel, 6 hard-boiled eggs, 3 onions, thyme, bayleaf, 2 ozs. butter.

Put the carp, very well cleaned, into a pan containing a tumbler of water, the 3 onions sliced, salt, pepper, thyme and bayleaf, cover it, and cook in a medium oven for about 30 to 40 minutes.

Cook the sorrel in a little water, drain it and leave it *en branche*, mixed with the butter. Take the carp out of the oven and put it on a hot dish surrounded by the sorrel and the hard-boiled eggs cut in halves.

La Bourride

Bourride is almost as popular a dish in Provence as the *Bouillabaisse*. It is easier to achieve away from the Mediterranean than *Bouillabaisse*, for it does not require any special fish like the *rascasse*, and its success depends on the sauce, which is a feast for anyone fond of garlic.

You require about three different kinds of white fish, such as bass, gurnet and sea bream. Clean them and cut them into thick slices.

Prepare a *court-bouillon* with water, a little white wine, vinegar, onion, bayleaf, orange peel and fennel and the heads of the fish. Bring this to the boil, cook it 10 minutes, and let it cool.

Now prepare an *aïoli*, that is to say, a mayonnaise with garlic. The garlic, say 2 large cloves for four people, is pounded in a mortar, 2 yolks of eggs stirred in, then the oil added drop by drop at first, and faster as the *aïoli* gets thick. For *Bourride* you will need at least ½ pint of *aïoli*. When it is ready, put the prepared fish into the *court-bouillon* and poach it for 10–15 minutes. Prepare 2 slices of toasted French bread for each person and put them into a warmed fish dish.

In a double boiler put half the *aïoli* and stir into it 2 or 3 yolks of eggs, then through a strainer a ladle of the *court-bouillon* from the fish. Stir this, without allowing it to boil, until it is thick and creamy. Pour it over the toast, arrange the drained fish on the top, and serve the rest of the *aïoli* separately.

At the Voile d'Or in St. Raphael, famous for its *Bourride*, they serve a *Sauce Rouille* as well as the *aïoli*. This is made not in the usual way with breadcrumbs, sweet peppers and olive oil but with the grilled, skinned red peppers pounded into the *aïoli*, plus pounded lobster coral and the pink inside of *oursins*, Mediterranean sea urchins. They also serve a green sauce made of a particular kind of seaweed cooked and pounded into the *aïoli* with a flavouring of *Pastis*, or *Pernod*, which gives it an aniseed flavour.

A simpler kind of *Bourride* can be made with one large fish such as bream, cooked whole, and one sauce, the *aïoli* mixed with the extra eggs, and the stock from the fish.

Catigau d'Anguilles

A very old Provençal recipe, given by Madame Léon Daudet, in *La France à Table*, January 1935.

In a sauté pan put a little olive oil with a few strips of bacon, and let them turn very lightly brown. Next add about 1 lb. each of sliced onions and 1 lb. of the white part of leeks cut in rounds. Let these brown slightly and then add 1 lb. of tomatoes cut in pieces and 3 or 4 cloves of garlic crushed, a bayleaf, salt, pepper, and a good pinch of saffron. On top of this put a layer of sliced raw potatoes and the eels[1] cut in thick slices. Add water or white veal stock to cover.

Boil rapidly for 20 minutes, and season with a good measure of freshly ground pepper from the mill before serving. Pour the stock from the *catigau* over pieces of French bread in a deep dish and serve the eels and vegetables on another dish.

Matelote of River Fish, as it is made on the banks of the Seine

You will need a carp, and an eel and, if you can get it, a tench.

Scale and clean the carp carefully, remove the gills and the head and cut it in thick slices; you can either skin the eel or not, as you like, but in any case cut the head off and cut the rest in slices, as also the tench, and roll each slice in flour.

In the meantime, in a large pan, put 20–25 small onions to brown in butter; add a tablespoon of flour and a little water or stock; stir it, and see that it does not get too thick. Now pour into the pan a pint of red Vin Ordinaire, salt, pepper, a *bouquet garni* composed of thyme, bayleaf, parsley and a clove of garlic all tied together.

When the onions are half cooked, add the pieces of fish; cook for 5 minutes, pour in a small glass of cognac, and set light to the sauce; when the flames have gone out, cook another 20 minutes on a fairly brisk flame.

Serve the *Matelote* on slices of toasted French bread and

---

[1] If you prefer to cook the eels without their rather oily skins, first put the slices into cold water, and as soon as it boils strain the eels. The skin will then come off easily.

garnished with quarters of hard-boiled egg. The sauce should be creamy but not too thick.

This is the simple and genuine *Matelote*, and it is excellent.

Trout in Aspic

Make a *court-bouillon* with a large glass of white wine, an onion, garlic, a few rounds of carrot, herbs and seasoning, 1 pint of water and the head of any white fish.

Let this cool, then put in the cleaned trout. Poach them gently until they are cooked, lift them out of the pan and arrange them in a long, fairly deep dish.

Reduce the *court-bouillon*, adding seasoning if necessary; add no salt until the end. This stock is to be poured through a muslin over the fish and should set to a light jelly; decorate with a few leaves of tarragon or some slices of lemon.

Boullinada

This is one of the Catalan versions of *Bouillabaisse*.

Into a wide copper or heavy sauté pan put a tablespoon of pork or bacon fat. Add a cupful of parsley chopped with 3 or 4 cloves of garlic and a red pimento cut into strips. When this has cooked a minute add a layer of raw, thinly sliced potatoes, then a layer of thick slices of fish such as bass, whiting, sea bream and John Dory.

Now another layer of potatoes and fish until it is all used up. The proportions of potatoes and fish should be about equal; about 2½ lbs. of each for six people (it is not worth making any kind of *Bouillabaisse* for less than six people, owing to the different kinds of fish required). Add water up to the top of the fish and potatoes, but don't actually *cover* them.

Cover the pan, bring it very quickly to the boil, add 2 tablespoons of olive oil, put the lid back again and cook it very fast for about 15–20 minutes. The rapid boiling will amalgamate the liquid and thicken it, giving the dish its own particular savour. Serve very hot in heated soup plates.

A few carefully cleaned mussels, put on the top of the last layer in the pan, and served as they are, in their shells, are a good addition to this Catalan *Bouillabaisse*.

Tunny Fish with Sauce Tartare

A small tunny fish is cooked whole in a *court-bouillon*, as you would cook a salmon, allowing about 15 minutes to the pound. Drain the fish and leave it all day on a wire sieve or other strainer which will accommodate it comfortably, in order that the fat may drain off.

The fish can then be put into the refrigerator and served very cold next day with a *Sauce Tartare*.

Slices of fresh tunny can be cooked in the same way.

EGGS

Poached Eggs

THIS is what Dr. Kitchiner, author of the *Cook's Oracle* (1829) has to say about poached eggs: "The cook who wishes to display her skill in Poaching, must endeavour to procure Eggs that have been laid a couple of days, those that are quite new-laid are so milky that, take all the care you can, your cooking of them will seldom procure you the praise of being a Prime Poacher: You must have fresh Eggs, or it is equally impossible.

"The beauty of a Poached Egg is for the yolk to be seen blushing through the white—which should only be just sufficiently hardened, to form a transparent Veil for the Egg."

My own method for poaching eggs I learnt from a cookery book published by the Buckinghamshire Women's Institute, and it has proved infallible.

First boil a saucepan of water, and into this dip each egg whole, in its shell, while you count about thirty, then take it out. When it comes to actually poaching the eggs, have a pan of fresh water boiling, add a dessertspoon of vinegar, stir the water fast until a whirlpool has formed, and into this break the eggs, one at a time. 1–1½ minutes cooks them. Take them very carefully out with a draining spoon. They will be rounded and the yolks covered with a "transparent Veil" instead of the ragged-looking affair which a poached egg too often turns out to be, and the alternative of the egg-poaching pan, which produces an over-cooked sort of egg-bun, is equally avoided.

It is interesting to note that Dr. Kitchiner instructs his readers to place poached eggs on bread "toasted on one side only". How right he is; I have never been able to understand the point of that sodden toast. . . .

Try serving poached eggs on a piece of fresh, buttered bread; alternatively on a purée of some kind—split peas, sweet corn, or mushrooms, with pieces of fried bread around, but not under, the eggs.

Oeufs Bénédictine

Poached eggs served in individual flat dishes, over which you pour a tablespoon of Hollandaise Sauce. Originally the eggs were placed on a bed of creamed salt cod (*brandade de morue*) but nowadays they are more often served on pastry or croûtons.

Oeufs Mollets Fines Herbes

These can be made either with poached eggs or *Oeufs Mollets* or coddled eggs—that is, eggs put in boiling water and boiled for 4–5 minutes, steeped in cold water and shelled. The white is cooked and the yolk soft, without being runny.

Allow 2 coddled eggs per person, a dessertspoon of fresh chopped herbs such as parsley, chives, and tarragon and a tablespoon of butter. Melt the butter, put in the eggs and sauté them without letting the butter burn. Sprinkle in the herbs and a squeeze of lemon juice, and serve immediately.

This is one of those excessively (and deceptively) simple dishes which can make the reputation of a good cook; the process only takes about 2 minutes, so provided that the eggs are prepared beforehand and the herbs ready chopped, they can be made at the last minute.

They are nicest cooked and served in individual metal egg dishes.

Eggs en Cocotte

Have your little fireproof china dishes ready with a good lump of butter in each, and an egg for each person ready broken into a separate saucer. Put the little dishes into the oven (Regulo 5) and take them out as soon as the butter has melted, slide an egg into each, pour a large tablespoon of cream on to the egg, avoiding the yolk, return them to the oven. They will take 4–5 minutes to cook, allowing perhaps $\frac{1}{2}$ minute less for those on the top shelf.

If you leave them too long, the yolks get hard and the dish is ruined, so be on the alert to see that they are taken out of the oven at the exact moment.

Experience and knowledge of the idiosyncrasies of one's own oven are the mediums of success here. No pepper or salt should be added, except at table, but a very little cut fresh tarragon when they come out of the oven is an acceptable addition.

Oeufs à la Monteynard

4 eggs, $\frac{1}{2}$ lb. rice, 4 tablespoons grated Gruyère cheese, 1 tumbler of good stock, 1 oz. fresh butter, salt and pepper.

Boil the rice in the usual way, but for only 10 minutes, drain it and then put it on to cook again with the stock, simmering it slowly.

In the meantime, put the eggs into boiling water and let them boil five minutes, no longer. Take them out and put them in cold water.

Shell them. Butter a fireproof dish. Into this put the rice, which should have absorbed all the stock and be quite cooked. With the back of a spoon make eight indents in the rice, to hold the 8 half eggs. Cut the eggs very carefully in half (if they have been boiled properly the yolks should still be slightly runny). Put them into the places you have made for them; season the eggs and the rice with a sprinkling of salt and pepper then add the grated cheese, putting a double layer on each half egg.

Pour the melted butter over the dish, which then goes into a hot oven for not longer than 3 minutes, so that the yolks of the eggs will remain soft under their coating of *gratin* formed by the butter and the cheese.

Fromage d'Oeufs à la Mayonnaise

Break the eggs whole into a large, well-buttered dish or mould. Place this in a *bain-marie* filled with water and cook until the eggs have set.

When they are cold, turn the eggs out whole on to a round dish, mask them with a well-flavoured thin mayonnaise, and garnish with a mixture of chopped chives, parsley and tarragon.

Ragoût of Mushrooms and Eggs

Put about ½ lb. of mushrooms into a pan with a little water, bring them to the boil and add 1 gill of white wine. Season with salt, and a discreet amount of ground black pepper, nutmeg and herbs.

Let the *ragoût* boil again for 2 or 3 minutes; and meanwhile have hot in a dish 5 or 6 hard-boiled eggs, roughly chopped, and a few plainly grilled whole mushrooms.

Pour the *ragoût* over the eggs, garnish with the grilled mushrooms, and serve at once.

An excellent dish, either to start the meal or as the vegetable course after cold meat or game, or as a main luncheon dish.

Pipérade

Pipérade is the best known of all Basque dishes, and various recipes for it have appeared in English cookery books. It is a mixture of sweet peppers, tomatoes and onions, with eggs added at the end; the final result is a creamy scrambled-egg effect deliciously blended with the vegetables in which the sweet pepper flavour slightly dominates. Sometimes one meets it with the purée of onions, tomatoes and peppers topped with fried eggs, sometimes in the form of an omelette; the scrambled-egg version is the most characteristically Basque.

1 lb. onions, 1 lb. tomatoes, 3 fairly large sweet red peppers or about 6 of the small green ones, in season in the Basque country long before the red ones, 6 eggs.

In a heavy frying or sauté pan melt some pork fat (sometimes olive oil is used for this dish, but pork, or even bacon fat, suits it better). Put in the sliced onions, and let them cook slowly, turning golden but not brown: then put in the peppers, cut into strips; let this cook until it is soft, then add the chopped tomatoes, with a seasoning of salt, ground black pepper and a little marjoram. Cook with the cover on the pan.

When the whole mixture has become almost the consistency of a purée, pour in the beaten eggs, and stir gently, exactly as for ordinary scrambled eggs. Take care not to let them get over-cooked.

With the *Pipérade* are served slices of the famous *Jambon de Bayonne*, most of which is in fact made at Orthez, in the Béarn.

The *Jambon de Bayonne* is something like the Italian *Prosciutto* and imparts its particular flavour to many Basque and Béarnais *garbures* and *daubes*. Brochettes of calf's liver are sometimes served with the *Pipérade* and a very good combination it is.

Oeufs Maritchu
Another Basque dish

For each person allow 1 artichoke, or 2 if they are small, 2 eggs, and 1 lb. of tomatoes for four people.

First cook the artichokes in boiling water for 20–30 minutes, and when they are cool, take off all the leaves, leaving only the heart. Sauté them gently in butter or oil, and in the meantime have ready the sauce made with fresh tomatoes, chopped with an onion and a clove of garlic and simmered in a covered pan; the sauce can be used as it is or put through a sieve.

When the artichokes and the sauce are ready, put them into a serving dish, the artichokes in the centre and the sauce all round, and on top of each artichoke put about 2 tablespoons of very creamy scrambled eggs.

Omelette aux Pommes de Terre

The best potato omelette is made with potatoes cooked as for *Galette de Pommes de Terre* (p. 159). When the *galette* is ready add a little butter to the pan and let it run round the edges; pour in 4 or 5 beaten eggs and shake the pan so that the eggs cook; turn the omelette out flat, like a Spanish *tortilla*.

Another method is to grate 1 oz. of Gruyère cheese into a cup of cream and pour it over the omelette as soon as the eggs have set, making a rich but still simple dish.

Omelette aux Croûtons et Fromage

In butter fry a handful of little squares of bread; keep them hot on a plate.

Pour the beaten eggs for the omelette into hot butter in the omelette pan, put in the croûtons, then 2 tablespoons of grated cheese. Fold the omelette over quickly and slide it on to the hot dish.

The combination of the cheese and the croûtons of bread is particularly good.

Fondue de Franche Comté

Put ¼ pint of white wine into a saucepan with a chopped clove of garlic and cook until the wine is reduced by half. Strain it and leave to cool.

In a bowl beat 6 eggs with ½ lb. of grated Gruyère cheese, 2 ozs. of butter, some ground black pepper and a little salt. Stir in the reduced wine and pour the mixture into an earthenware or other fireproof dish and stir over a low fire until the mixture forms a creamy mass, well amalgamated, but in no way re-sembling scrambled eggs.

Serve at once in the pan in which it has cooked, and boiling hot. Each person should have a supply of squares of bread or toast; with a fork these are dipped into the *Fondue,* which gets increasingly good as the bottom of the dish is reached. Sufficient for 4 or 5 people. This *Fondue* is distinct from the Swiss *Fondue,* in that the Swiss one is made without eggs, and with the addition of Kirsch.

LUNCHEON, SUPPER AND FAMILY DISHES

LUNCHEON, SUPPER AND
FAMILY DISHES

IT IS more often when planning day-to-day meals, with ingredients forced upon one by circumstances rather than specially ordered for a grand occasion, that the general provider and cook is hard put to it to think of something new to put before the family, and at the same time not waste food which may already be in the house. Most of the soups in this book come into the category of dishes which can be made according to whatever ingredients may be most easily obtainable; in this chapter I have endeavoured to suggest a few more out of the ordinary ways of presenting such things as liver, dried vegetables, potatoes, cabbages, and sausages, as main dishes. This is the kind of food which is eaten frequently in thrifty French households, and it is very good.

If we all had cooks (and butchers) such as the charming character described below by Edmond About, I suppose life would be very much easier, but then we shouldn't get quite so much satisfaction out of inventing some excellent dish out of practically nothing at all.

" I must tell you that in 1845 (I am speaking of a long while ago) the servants were part of the family itself. They lived for so long in the same house that people fell into the habit of calling them by the surnames of their masters. Angélique, ladies' maid to the three daughters of the pork butcher, was known as Angélique Fondrin, and the old bewhiskered coachman who drove the mayor's carriage answered locally to the name of Léonard Morand. My worthy Catherine, still in my service, as I am in hers, was at that time a strapping young woman of thirty-four. My parents had taken her on when she was very

young, she had grown up with us, she had become accustomed
to us, without a teacher she had mastered the fine art, so French
and at the same time so rare in France, of roasting a leg of
mutton to a turn, of fricasséing a chicken, of the discreet seasoning of a *salmis* of partridge or woodcock. She could knead a
potato cake before which a professional pastry cook would have
gone on bended knees. Rice, which every housewife of Courcy
reduced to a nauseating glue, was transformed, on her stove,
into golden beads of an exquisite flavour. She excelled above all
at simple dishes, and the tax collector, a worthy man whose
friendship had followed us into the upper town, used to say that
Catherine's *Boeuf aux Choux* was as good as a truffled turkey
at the Crown. At the time of our comparative prosperity the
worthy creature was cited as a model of delicacy; the wits of
the club claimed that, to avoid temptation, she had had the
handle of her shopping basket removed.[1] But, after our ruin
reduced her wages to practically nothing, her probity turned
into cunning and sorcery; for us she would have stolen the
fairy queen's wand. Molière's miser would have found his
ideal in this girl, who borrowed bones from the best butcher in
Courcy to make *consommés* and jellies for my mother. Both
butchers' and household bones were bought indiscriminately,
at the same price, by a travelling rag and bone man. Every
week Catherine took away fifteen or twenty kilos of beef bones
and returned them to the butcher's boy after having extracted a
jar of fat and a mountain of jellied stock by long boiling. This
cost her a few *sous*, a small pie made by herself, or simply a
handshake. The fat which she obtained in this way was better
than butter, and made excellent *friture*.

" This culinary imagination, the desperate pursuit of good
value, and the everlasting search for free nourishment which

[1] A play on the expression "*faire danser l'anse de son panier*"—to cheat one's
employers.

resembled the mediaeval alchemist's dream of the philosopher's stone, did not always come off. She suffered some singular failures, notably with *Choucroûte*, which always turned out to be a very expensive dish, and the famous Tripe vaunted by Rabelais. It can scarcely be imagined how much care and time, how much bacon and spice are needed to succeed with this Pantagruelish dish which our ancestors, the ancient Tourangeaux, ate until it gave them indigestion.

" Catherine was sincerely wretched at not being an accomplished *cordon bleu*; she would ask me why the Minister of Education (M. le Comte de Salvandy, if I remember rightly) did not found a school of cooking in every town, simply in order to conserve the meat and vegetables which everywhere went to waste, to the detriment of the public's nourishment. And perhaps the good girl was right. But even in her mistakes and mishaps she was the object of envy of every housewife in the neighbourhood. If ever she were to write her memoirs, like M. de Talleyrand, a rather less irreproachable cook, she could reveal the flatteries, the promises, and the intrigues of five or six noble ladies who would not have shrunk from crime in order to prise her away from us. Provincial life is subject to these ferocious comedies."

EDMOND ABOUT:
Le Roman d'un Brave Homme.

Foie de Porc Braisé

In a whole pig's liver in one piece make a number of small incisions in rows, and in these put small pieces of bacon rolled in ground black pepper.

Place 4 or 5 rashers of bacon in a casserole and on these put the liver; pour over enough white wine and stock or water in equal quantities to come up to the level of the liver; add 6 carrots, an onion stuck with a clove, a bayleaf, thyme, parsley, a few peppercorns and a crushed clove of garlic. Put another rasher or two of bacon over the top of the liver, cover the casserole and simmer in the oven for about 30 minutes.

Strain off the sauce, remove the excess fat, and put the sauce into a small saucepan to reduce by half; when it is thick enough, add a walnut of fresh butter, pour over the liver, and serve quickly.

Foie de Veau en Brochettes

Buy the calf's liver in one piece, and cut it into pieces about an inch wide and quarter of an inch thick. Season them with salt, pepper and marjoram, and a drop of lemon juice.

Have the same number of small pieces of bacon. Thread the liver and bacon alternately on skewers. Pour a few tablespoons of olive oil on to a dish and roll the skewers in the oil. Grill them, not too fast, for about 7 minutes, turning them over once.

Serve them on the skewers on a bed of vegetable purée such as celery or lettuce, or potato, or buttered rice (p. 89), or Pipérade (p. 76).

Liver and Bacon Pâté

For six people:

1 lb. liver sliced, 6 rashers bacon, ¼ lb. mushrooms, parsley, lemon peel, garlic, bayleaf, pastry, sherry, or port, or white wine.

Sauté the liver gently in good dripping or butter. Add the mushrooms sliced, and when they have cooked a minute or two pour into the pan whatever wine you are using and let it reduce by half.

In a small terrine, or pie-dish, put a layer of chopped bacon, then a layer of the liver mixture, seasoned with salt, pepper, a very little garlic, thyme and lemon peel, another layer of bacon, and so on until it is all used up. Cover with a crust of pastry, stand in a pan of water, and bake in a moderate oven.

This can be eaten hot or cold, and can also be done without the pastry crust, in which case cover it with a buttered paper and the lid of the terrine.

Rognons au Maïs

In south-western France maize is cultivated in great quantity; the pigs and geese are fed on it; the country people have a host of dishes, both sweet and savoury, made from maize flour, which is similar to Italian *Polenta*. Tinned sweetcorn makes quite a good substitute for some of the savoury dishes. The purée should be made as thick as possible.

1 lb. kidneys, 1 oz. dripping, 1 tin sweetcorn (the plain, not the creamed, variety), 1 oz. butter, salt and pepper, 1 cup milk or meat stock.

Remove the skin and the fat from the kidneys and blanch them in boiling salted water. Drain them, cut them in slices and sauté them for 10 minutes in the dripping.

Have ready a purée made from the tinned sweetcorn, simmered in the milk or stock, and put them through the sieve twice. This double sieving is always necessary with sweetcorn, or it will not be smooth enough.

Heat up the purée with the butter, put it on a hot dish and arrange the kidneys on top.

Gnocchi à la Romaine

Although generally supposed to be an Italian dish, these *gnocchi* are also a speciality of the Nice district; having been part of Italy for so long, the cooking of the *Pays Niçois* has much in common with that of Genoa, and it is hard to say exactly where dishes such as this actually originated.

1 pint milk, 4 ozs. semolina, 3 ozs. grated cheese, salt, pepper, nutmeg, 1 tablespoon marjoram and chives, butter, an egg.

Bring the milk to the boil in a double saucepan, with salt, pepper, nutmeg, marjoram and chives. When the milk boils, put the semolina in, and stir it until the mixture has about the consistency of porridge, and a wooden spoon will stand up in it.

Take it off the fire and stir in the beaten egg, 1 oz. of cheese and 1 oz. of butter. Pour the mixture into a buttered tin and spread it out about a quarter of an inch thick and leave it to cool. Cut it into rounds about the size of a half-crown, arrange them overlapping in a generously buttered gratin dish, put more butter on the top and the rest of the grated cheese. Heat under the grill, slowly to start with, until the *gnocchi* are warmed through, then faster to brown them.

If you have some good meat glaze, or chicken *velouté*, a little poured over the *gnocchi* just before you take them from the grill is most delicious. *Pestou*, a basil and garlic sauce pounded with olive oil or butter and Parmesan cheese, also goes particularly well with *gnocchi*. The recipe is on p. 194.

Quiche Lorraine

For six people:

6 ozs. flour, 2 ozs. butter, 1 oz. dripping, 6 rashers bacon, ½ pint cream, 2 fresh eggs, salt and pepper, ½ gill water.

Make a pastry with the flour, the butter, the dripping, a pinch of salt and the water. Give it two or three turns and then roll it into a ball and leave it for 1 hour.

Line a flat buttered pie-tin with the rolled-out pastry. On to the pastry spread the bacon cut into dice and previously fried for a minute. Now beat the 2 eggs into the cream with a little salt and ground pepper; when they are well mixed, pour on

to the pastry, put it into a hot oven at once and bake for
about 30 minutes.

Let it cool a little before cutting and serving.

La Quiche aux Pommes de Terre

Cook 4 large potatoes in their skins, and when they have
cooled put them through a sieve and mix them with 2 tablespoons of flour, 2 ozs. of butter, and salt, until you have a
compact paste. Roll it out a quarter of an inch thick and
spread it in a floured and greased flan tin. Prick the paste here
and there with a fork. Fill up the potato tart with a mixture
of small pieces of bacon (about 2 rashers) and 4 ozs. of good
fresh cream. Season with a scraping of nutmeg and a very
little garlic. Sprinkle the top with grated Gruyère cheese.
Put into the oven (Regulo 6) for about 20 minutes.

This dish is best served cold, and is excellent for a picnic.
If you have to make do with thin cream or top of the milk,
mix it with the yolks of 2 eggs.

Buttered Rice

A simple way of serving rice as an accompaniment to
chicken or meat dishes, or by itself with a bowl of grated cheese.

Boil the rice in the usual way—that is, allowing 2 ozs. per
person, put into a very large pan of boiling salted water, into
which you have also put half a lemon. Boil for 15 minutes,
drain very carefully, and dry in a warm oven for 2 or 3
minutes.

Stir into the rice a beaten egg and 1 or 2 ozs. of butter; a
few chopped chives make a pleasant addition.

Macaroni au Jus de Viande

This is a dish to be made when there is good meat stock left
over from a *daube* or from a stewed duck. The macaroni, or

spaghetti, 2 or 3 ozs. per person, should be put into a very large pan of boiling salted water and cooked for 15 minutes, or until it is tender.

Have ready a warmed fireproof dish, and put the drained spaghetti into this; stir in a breakfast cup of good thick stock (previously reduced, if necessary), a lump of butter, some freshly chopped herbs such as parsley, basil, and chives and some grated Parmesan. Stir over the fire for a minute or two so that the spaghetti is hot. Serve more grated cheese separately.

Good either alone or as an accompaniment to a meat dish.

Tarte aux Asperges

For the pastry:

½ lb. plain flour, 6 ozs. butter, a pinch of salt.

For the filling:

A 2-lb. bunch of asparagus, ¾ pint *béchamel* sauce made with milk or cream, 2 ozs. grated cheese.

Knead the flour and butter together, adding a little water to make a paste. Prepare this 1 hour before cooking, if possible.

Prepare the asparagus very carefully, peeling off the dry outer skin of the stalks. Put them tied in a bunch and heads uppermost into boiling salted water, to which you add also a lump of sugar and cook them for 20 minutes (a little longer if they are very large ones). Drain them and cut each asparagus into 3 or 4 pieces, discarding the hard part at the ends.

Roll out your pastry, line a flat buttered pie-tin with it, cover the inside and the edges with kitchen paper and put the usual beans into the paper to keep the pastry flat. Bake it in a hot oven for 20 minutes. Now add the grated cheese to the prepared *béchamel* and, off the fire, the asparagus.

Take the paper and the beans off the pastry, fill up with the asparagus mixture, put it into the oven to brown, and serve very hot.

Croquettes de Volaille

These croquettes can be very good if well made, crisp on the outside and creamy within; they can be made with left-over chicken, but not in the slapdash way usually reserved for " remains ".

For four people you need:

6 ozs. chicken without skin or bone, 2 ozs. ham or bacon, a sheep's brain (this helps the croquettes to attain the required smoothness), an onion, 3 or 4 mushrooms chopped, a *béchamel* made from 1 oz. butter, 1 oz. flour, ⅓ pint milk. For cooking the croquettes—an egg, breadcrumbs, and deep fat.

If possible, prepare the mixture beforehand, and do the final operations the next day. Melt the butter, put in the finely chopped onion and let it cook without browning; add the ham or bacon, minced, then the flour and the milk, a little salt, pepper, and a pinch of nutmeg. Stir until the sauce is smooth and let it reduce by nearly half.

Blanch the sheep's brain and chop it with the chicken and the mushrooms; add this mixture to the sauce, give it 2 or 3 minutes over the fire and pour it out into a dish, smoothing down the surface.

The next day take a tablespoon at a time of the mixture and roll it in your hands, floured, to the right shape. Dip each croquette first in beaten egg, then in fine breadcrumbs, in the egg again, and lastly the breadcrumbs. This double egg-and-breadcrumbing makes a good coat for the croquettes, so that the hot fat crisps them but does not penetrate the inside.

Drop each croquette in the hot deep fat; they should be cooked in 2–3 minutes; drain them carefully and serve them on a napkin, accompanied, if you like, by a sauce, tomato, mushroom, or Béarnaise.

Tarte à l'Oignon

In nearly every French province, but particularly in Alsace Lorraine, there are recipes for onion tarts, sometimes made with a purée, sometimes with fried onions, green spring onions, leeks. Some people add bacon, some cream. In Provence the equivalent is the *Pissaladina*, where the already cooked onions are baked on bread dough and garnished with black olives. The recipe I am giving here is from Lorraine.

Make a short crust with 8 ozs. of flour, 4 ozs. of butter, a pinch of salt and a little water. Leave it to rest while preparing 1½–2 lbs. of sliced onions; melt them gently in butter, bacon fat, or beef dripping. This will take about 30 minutes, with the pan covered. Take them off the fire, and stir in 2 beaten eggs, and 2 ozs. of grated Gruyère cheese. Roll out the pastry, spread it on the tart tin, fill up with the onion mixture and bake it in a moderate oven for 20 to 30 minutes.

Saucisses aux Pistaches

For 2 lbs. of pork sausage meat, well seasoned with salt, pepper, and 2 cloves of garlic, you need 4 ozs. of pistachio nuts. Put in a pan and pour boiling water over them. After 15 minutes the skins will rub off. Chop them finely, or pound them in a mortar, and add them to the sausage meat, with the yolks of 2 eggs. Fill the sausage skins with the mixture.

To be fried or grilled.

Le Saucisson Chaud au Vin

There are many ways of treating sausages with wine and many varieties of sausages with which to do it. This recipe is best for the uncooked coarsely cut type of sausage, such as the *Saucisse de Toulouse*, which can be bought from Benoit Bulcke, 27 Old Compton St., and Aubin in Brewer Street, Soho, and from Harrods, or else for the Italian *Zampone* or *Cotechini*, to be found at Delmonicos' in Old Compton Street or Parmigiani's in the same street. Smoked sausages of the Frankfurter type can also be used, or the Polish sausages now sold in many delicatessen shops.

Make a *court-bouillon* with 4 carrots, 2 onions, the white part of 2 leeks, a small turnip and 2 tomatoes, all cut up finely. Put all these into a pan, add 2 or 3 branches of any one rather strong herb, either basil, rosemary or thyme, a bayleaf, a branch of parsley, a very little salt and two crushed peppercorns, and pour over them ½ pint of red or white wine and ¼ pint of water. Let this cook until the vegetables are half done.

Make a few small incisions here and there in a sausage weighing about 1 lb. and poach it in the *court-bouillon* for 40 minutes. Serve it in its own liquor, accompanied by potatoes or white haricot beans. Cider can be used instead of wine.

Le Cassoulet de Castelnaudary

"Je veux vous amener chez Clémence, une petite taverne de la Rue Vavin, ou l'on ne fait qu'un plat, mais un plat prodigieux. On sait que pour avoir toutes ses qualités le cassoulet doit cuire doucement sur un feu bas. Le cassoulet de la mère Clémence cuit depuis vingt ans. Elle ajoute de temps en temps, dans la marmite, de l'oie, ou du lard, parfois un morceau de saucisson ou quelques haricots, mais c'est toujours le même cassoulet. La base demeure, et c'est cette antique et précieuse base qui donne au plat une qualité comparable à ces tons ambrés si particulier qui caractèrisent les chairs dans les oeuvres des vieux maitres vénitiens."

So wrote Anatole France of the *Cassoulet*, wonderful dish of south-western France, which through the years has been raised from the status of a humble peasant dish to one of the glories of French cooking. Toulouse, Carcassonne, Périgord,

Castelnaudary, Gascony, Castannau, all have their own versions of the *Cassoulet*. The ingredients vary from fresh pork and mutton to smoked sausages, garlic sausages, bacon, smoked ham, preserved goose or pork, duck, calves' feet, the rind of pork and pigs cheek. The essentials are good white haricot beans and a capacious earthenware pot (the name *Cassoulet* comes from Cassol d'Issel, the original clay cooking utensil from the little town of Issel, near Castelnaudary).

For the *Cassoulet* of Castelnaudary the ingredients are:

1½–2 lbs. medium sized white haricot beans (this amount will feed six to eight people; the *Cassoulet* is a dish to be made in quantity; it can be heated up), a wing and a leg of preserved goose (p. 135) or half a fresh goose, a coarse pork sausage of about 1 lb. or several small ones,[1] ½ lb. bacon, 3 onions, 4 or 5 cloves of garlic, 2 tomatoes, and, if possible, 2 pints of meat stock.

Put the beans to soak overnight; next day put them into fresh water and cook them for about 2½ hours, keeping them just on the boil, until they are three-quarters cooked, then strain them.

In the meantime prepare the stock in which they are to finish cooking. Slice the onions and cut the bacon into squares and melt them together in a pan, add the crushed garlic, the tomatoes, seasoning and herbs, and pour over the stock and let it simmer for 20 minutes. Take the pieces of goose out of their pot with the good lard adhering to them. (If you are using fresh goose, it must be half roasted; have some good pork or goose dripping as well.)

Put the goose, the dripping, the sausage, and the bacon from the stock, at the bottom of the earthenware pot, which has been well rubbed with garlic, and the beans on the top. Add the prepared stock. Bring the *Cassoulet* slowly to the boil, then

---

[1] See preceding recipe for places where these sausages may be bought.

spread a layer of breadcrumbs on the top and put the pot into a slow oven and leave it until the beans are cooked. This will take about 1 hour, during which time most of the stock will be absorbed and a crust will have formed on the top of the beans.

Serve exactly as it is; a good young red wine should be drunk with this dish; a salad and a country cheese of some kind to finish, will be all you will need afterwards.

Duck can be used instead of goose, and at Christmas the legs or wings of a turkey go very well into the *Cassoulet*.

Bacon and Lentils

Put 1½ lbs. of farmhouse bacon into a saucepan, cover it with cold water, bring it to the boil, strain it, rinse it in cold water and dry it in a cloth.

Melt a little dripping in a deep casserole, put in the bacon and a dozen or so small onions, with a seasoning of ground black pepper. When the onions begin to turn brown, add 1 lb. of brown lentils, a carrot cut in two, a stick of celery, a bunch of fresh herbs tied together, and 2 or 3 crushed cloves of garlic. Cover with water, put the lid on the casserole, and cook very slowly for about 2 hours.

When the lentils are cooked take out the bacon, remove the carrot and the bunch of herbs, and strain the lentils. Put them on the serving dish with a lump of butter stirred in, arrange the bacon cut in slices all round and garnish with chopped parsley, and, if you like, some halved hard-boiled eggs.

Sufficient for six people.

La Truffado

This is a peasant dish from the Auvergne, made with *fromage de Cantal*, which is something like English Cheshire cheese, which can be used instead, but it must be real Cheshire, not processed cheese, which will not melt.

Slice 1 lb. of raw potatoes thinly and cook them in a frying pan as for the *Galette de Pommes de Terre* (p. 159), with the addition of a few small dice of bacon and a clove of garlic finely chopped. When the potatoes are almost cooked add the cheese, about 2 ozs., cut in very small pieces and turn the potatoes once or twice so that the cheese spreads all over them.

Cover the pan, turn the fire off, and leave the cheese to melt in the heat of the pan for 5 minutes before serving.

El Pa y All

The breakfast dish of the Catalan peasants in the Roussillon district of France. . . . A piece of bread fresh from the baker (or sometimes fried in oil or pork fat), is rubbed all over with a piece of garlic, as little or as much as you like; then sprinkled with salt, then a few drops of fresh olive oil, and the *Pa y All* is ready.

STUFFED CABBAGE DISHES

To show what can be done with a cabbage apart from the one and only, and far too notorious, way common to railway dining-cars, boarding-schools and hospitals (and, goodness knows, these are all places where we should be offered the maximum of consolation in the way of good food), I am giving several recipes, each with its regional characteristic, for turning cabbage into an acceptable main course dish, inexpensive, but abounding in the rich aromas of slow cooking and careful preparation.

There is a choice of two Provençal recipes, a dish using game, red cabbage served with smoked sausages, and a Catalan stuffed cabbage with pimentos and black olives. There are many more such recipes, but anyone can evolve their own from the ingredients to hand.

All these dishes are admirable for Aga and other cookers of the same type. They can be left in the slow oven for hours, and forgotten until dinner-time.

Chou Farçi aux Câpres

A fine large cabbage, about 6 ozs. each of minced pork or pork sausage meat, chicken livers, and breadcrumbs, 1 yolk of egg, seasonings, spices, herbs, capers, 1 small glass brandy, a *roux* made of 2 ozs. butter, 2 ozs. flour, ½ pint stock or tomato juice.

Put the whole cabbage into boiling, salted water and let it blanch for 5 minutes, when you take it out, drain it, and, placing it on a wooden board, you proceed to unfold the cabbage leaf by leaf, gently, until it looks like an open flower.

Now carefully spread each leaf with the stuffing made from the pork, the chicken livers, the breadcrumbs, all finely minced and amalgamated, bound with the yolk of egg and seasoned with salt, pepper, mace, a little powdered thyme or marjoram, a clove of garlic, nutmeg, and a minced bayleaf. When all the stuffing is used up, press the leaves of the cabbage gently together and tie it into its original shape with tape.

Have ready in a deep earthenware marmite a *roux* made from the flour, butter and stock. Into this put your cabbage, stick 4 cloves into it, cover the pot and put it into a slow oven (Regulo 2 or 3) for about 3 hours.

When the cabbage is cooked, take the tape away very carefully, strew a few capers over the dish and pour over a small glass of brandy.

Gros Chou Farçi à la Provençale

For this version of the stuffed cabbage, the stuffing consists of the meat from a pork cutlet, 1 oz. of lean bacon, ¼ lb. of beef, veal or chicken meat, a sheep's brain, 2 eggs, a few lettuce leaves, 2 ozs. of grated Gruyère cheese, an onion, a clove of garlic, and rice.

Mix all these ingredients together (finely chopped) and add a cupful of cooked rice. Put the stuffing into a pan with a little olive oil and let it cook for 1 or 2 minutes.

Meanwhile blanch the cabbage, then separate the leaves, cutting out the hard part and adding the heart, finely chopped, to the stuffing. Spread the leaves with the stuffing, tie up the cabbage and put it into a casserole with some carrots cut in rounds, sliced onions, garlic and shallots, a branch of thyme, a bayleaf and salt and pepper.

Pour over a tumbler of white wine and one of water or stock, cover the pan, and simmer very slowly for 3–4 hours, moistening the top of the cabbage from time to time with its own juice.

Chou Farçi à la Mode de Grasse

Once upon a time the *Chou Farçi*, or *Sous Fassoun* in Provençal, was the great speciality of the town of Grasse. Here is the old recipe; a dish for the hungry.

Put a large white cabbage into boiling water for 5 minutes. Drain it, and carefully separate the leaves.

Have ready a stuffing composed of 2 ozs. of uncooked rice, 2 ozs. of pork or veal sausage meat, 3 ozs. of bacon, $\frac{1}{2}$ lb. of minced pig's liver, $\frac{1}{2}$ lb. of fresh green peas, the heart of a lettuce, and the white part of 2 leeks, finely chopped.

Mix all the ingredients in a large bowl, bind the stuffing with the yolks of eggs, and season with salt, pepper, mace, nutmeg, a crushed clove of garlic and herbs. Spread each cabbage leaf with the stuffing, laying them one on the other until you have used up all the leaves and the stuffing. Tie the cabbage up with tape.

Line a deep casserole with slices of lean beaf or veal, squares of raw ham or bacon, a pig's trotter,[1] 6 carrots and turnips and a *bouquet garni* of thyme, parsley, rosemary and a bayleaf. Put the cabbage in the centre, pour over a tumbler of stock or water, cover the pan and cook extremely slowly in the oven for 2 or 3 hours.

Serve the cabbage in the centre of a big dish, the meat and vegetables all round, and a tomato sauce separately.

---

[1] If the pig's trotter has been salted, soak it for several hours before cooking, in warm water.

Chou Farçi Catalan

This dish is made with the remains of beef which has been cooked in a *pot au feu*, a *boeuf à la mode*, or the *Estouffat* (p. 112), or the mutton from the *Daube Avignonnaise* (p. 109).

> About 4 ozs. meat, 2 ozs. bacon or ham or salame sausages, 3 or 4 sweet red or green peppers, 12 black olives, ½ oz. dried cèpes or mushrooms, 2 or 3 cloves of garlic, seasoning, mace, majoram, bayleaves, fat bacon, a little of the stock or sauce from whatever meat is being used, 1 egg, 2 small cabbages.

Chop the meat with the bacon, a sweet pepper from which all seeds have been removed, the black olives and garlic, season with salt and pepper (if the olives are salt add very little to the mixture) and the mace, nutmeg and herbs, and stir in the egg. Put the dried mushrooms to soak in a little warm water for 10 minutes.

Put the cabbages whole into boiling salted water for 5 minutes. Strain them, and when they are cool open out the leaves, putting the stuffing in between, until it is all used up. Fold the leaves back again until the cabbages are as nearly as possible their original shape. Tie them carefully round with tape. Place the cabbages in a deep earthenware pot into which they just fit (one for each cabbage, if necessary), slice the 3 remaining peppers into strips and place them with the dried cèpes round the cabbages. Put thin slices of the bacon on the top, pour a ladle or two of the sauce or stock over the cabbages (water, if no stock is available), cover with a greaseproof paper and the lid of the casserole and cook in a slow oven (Regulo 2 or 3) for 3 hours.

To make a more substantial dish, almost any kind of sausages can be added half-way through the cooking, or some home-cured bacon or ham.

The nicest accompaniment to this rustic dish is not potatoes or any vegetable, but a few slices of bread gently fried in the dripping from whatever meat has been used.

Chou Farçi Chasseur

Blanch the cabbage, drain it, and cut out the stalk. Spread out the leaves and in between each put a mixture of cooked chestnuts, chopped smoked sausages (Frankfurters) and the meat of a cooked partridge, pheasant, or 2 pigeons, or some roast hare. Season with salt, pepper, herbs, nutmeg and mace.

Tie the cabbage up, put it into a casserole, and moisten it with a tumbler of white wine and one of game stock. Simmer with the lid on the casserole for about 3 hours.

The proportion of stuffing for all these dishes is 16–18 ozs. for a 2½–3 lb. cabbage.

Chou Rouge Landais

1 medium-sized red cabbage, 1 lb. cooking apples, 1 lb. onions, 2 smoked Frankfurter sausages per person, ¼ pint red wine, 1 gill wine vinegar, 4 tablespoons brown sugar, herbs and seasoning, 2 sweet red peppers, garlic, a piece of dried orange peel.

Slice the cabbage crosswise into thin strips. Peel, core, and slice the apples, and slice the onions.

In the bottom of a deep casserole put a layer of cabbage, then one of onions, then apples. Season with salt, pepper, sugar, herbs, mace, ground cloves, garlic, and add the strips of raw sweet pepper and dried orange peel. Continue these layers until the casserole is full up. Moisten with the wine and the vinegar. Cover the casserole and cook in a very slow oven for 3–4 hours. 20 minutes before serving add the sausages, buried deep into the cabbage.

The aroma which emanates from the cooking of this dish is particularly appetising.

To make the dish more substantial, a few thick slices of bacon can be added. A bacon or ham bone, or even bones from roast mutton cooked with the cabbage and removed before serving, enrich the flavour.

MEAT

WHEN visiting Paris or any large provincial town in France it is an education to watch the housewives doing their meat marketing and to see the butchers at work, preparing a fillet of veal for roasting, or larding a piece of beef for a *boeuf mode*; for in France the butcher does all this for you, and you are not required to explain how the veal must be cut for *escalopes*, or for *blanquette de veau*, or fillet of beef for *tournedos*, and if you wish a *gigot* or shoulder of lamb to be boned it will be done without fuss or argument. Recently, Harrods of Knightsbridge have opened a French butcher's shop where nearly all the French cuts may be bought straight off the counter, and if what you need is not on show, it will be done to order.

It is much to be hoped that this innovation will eventually have widespread effects on our meat marketing in this country, for in the end it is more economical to pay a little more for expertly cut and trimmed meat than to buy it cheaply and cut it inexpertly at home. Most particularly does this apply to the cheaper cuts.

Veau aux Tomates

A piece of roasting veal, fillet for preference, weighing 2-3 lbs., 12 tomatoes, 12 small onions, garlic, shallots, herbs.

Put 2 cloves of garlic inside the veal, rub it all over with salt and pepper, and brown the meat in olive oil or dripping. Turn the flame down and add the whole tomatoes and the whole small onions, 2 chopped shallots, a branch of rosemary and seasoning. Cover the pan and let it cook gently, without any water; there should be enough moisture from the tomatoes, but should the pan get dry add a few spoonfuls of meat or vegetable stock.

Serve the veal on the bed of onions with the tomatoes all round.

Escalopes de Veau Sophie

Have your *escalopes*, 1 or 2 for each person, beaten out very thin and flat, seasoned with salt, pepper and lemon juice. For each *escalope* have a thin slice of ham or bacon and half a hard-boiled egg. Lay the ham on the meat and the half egg on top. Roll up each *escalope* and tie it with thread.

Cook them in butter for 10 minutes, then add a glass of cream and simmer for a few minutes more in the covered pan.

Escalopes de Veau en Papillotes

4 *escalopes* of veal, 4 slices ham, ½ lb. mushrooms, 2 onions, parsley, 2 ozs. butter.

Beat the *escalopes* out thin, season with salt, pepper and lemon juice, fry them very lightly on each side in butter. Take them out of the pan, and in the same butter fry the finely chopped onions and mushrooms; stir in a handful of chopped parsley; spread this mixture on to the *escalopes* and on top of the mixture place the slice of ham.

Now cut a large heart-shaped piece of greaseproof paper for each *escalope*; butter one side of it and place the veal and ham on it. Fold it over and turn down the edges so that no juices can escape. Heat them in a slow oven for about 20 minutes.

The nicest way to serve them, if your guests don't mind getting their fingers messy, is piled up in the dish in their paper bags, so that none of the aromas have a chance to evaporate until the food is ready to be eaten.

Rognons de Veau aux Tomates

Skin the kidneys and soak them in warm salted water to clean them. Put them into a pan with good dripping, and ¼ lb. of bacon for 2 lb. of veal kidneys. Let them roast very gently for about 20 minutes.

In the meantime brown a dozen or so chopped shallots in bacon fat or beef dripping; add 1 lb. of tomatoes chopped, seasoning of salt, pepper, basil or marjoram, a lump of sugar and a glass of port, or sweet white wine, or cider. When this has cooked for 10 minutes, add ½ lb. of mushrooms, and the kidneys and bacon. Cook for another 10 minutes.

This dish can be served quite alone, or with a *galette* of potatoes.

Navarin Printanier

This is a *ragoût* of lamb or mutton to which spring vegetables give special character.

Cut 2 or 3 lbs. of shoulder or breast of lamb into squares. In a large, shallow, sauté pan put 2 or 3 tablespoons of good dripping or butter. In this put 3 small sliced onions, then add the pieces of meat, and when they are golden take them out and put them on a plate; to the dripping in the pan add 2 tablespoons of flour, and stir until you have a light brown roux. To this add about 1 pint of brown stock (vegetable stock made with fried onions, carrots and the usual soup vegetables will do) and go on stirring until the sauce has amalgamated. Put back the meat, season with salt, black pepper, a sprig of rosemary, a crushed clove of garlic and a bayleaf. Simmer with the lid on until the meat is nearly cooked—about 1 hour—but this depends on the quality of the meat.

Now add 1 lb. of new potatoes, a small bunch of new carrots, and a few baby turnips; cook slowly for another 35–40 minutes and then add 1½ lbs. of green peas, freshly shelled; as soon as they are cooked the *Navarin* is ready. If the sauce gets very reduced during the cooking add more stock or water; it should be neither very thick nor very thin; about the consistency of a cream soup.

Gigot aux Flageolets ou aux haricots

This is a standard dish of many Paris *bistros*, and it is excellent if mutton and beans are both cooked *à point*.

Roast the leg of mutton, with a clove of unpeeled garlic underneath it and several sprigs of rosemary strewn over it, in good dripping.

The *flageolets*, or white haricot beans, should be soaked the night before; they will take about 3 hours to cook, well covered with water, with an onion and a bayleaf, salt and pepper. Simmer them until they are soft; this should coincide with the moment the *gigot* is cooked. Remove the *gigot* to a large fire-proof serving dish, strain the fat from the roasting pan.

Add a little white wine to the juice in the pan, a little water, and let this bubble a minute. Pour this gravy over the strained beans, and put them all round the *gigot*. Put into the oven for a few minutes, adding a lump of butter to the beans before serving.

Tinned green *flageolet* beans are very good and can be used for this dish; they need only be heated for 10 minutes.

Selle d'Agneau Basquaise

Roast a saddle of lamb in the usual way, with a clove of garlic underneath it in the pan, and in the meantime brown some whole, small, raw potatoes in goose dripping; they must be cooked slowly, in a heavy pan on top of the stove, or else be baked in a covered pan in the oven at the same time as the meat; they will take about 40 minutes to 1 hour, according to size.

While these are cooking, prepare the almonds, about 2 ozs., which must be skinned and chopped, but not too finely ; 10 minutes before serving add them to the potatoes and keep an eye on them to see they don't burn. Lastly, prepare a *Sauce Béarnaise* to which you add finely chopped mint instead of the usual tarragon.

Serve the saddle of lamb surrounded by the potatoes and almonds, and the sauce separately.

Daube à l'Avignonnaise

4 lbs. leg of lamb or mutton, 4 large onions, 2 or 3 carrots, ½ bottle of red wine, salt, pepper, herbs, 4 cloves of garlic, a piece of orange peel, 4 ozs. bacon, a handful of parsley, 1 small glass of brandy, olive oil.

Cut the meat into fair-sized pieces, each weighing about 3 ozs. Into each piece of meat insert a small piece of bacon which has been rolled in the parsley chopped with a clove of garlic. You will need about 1 oz. of the 4 ozs. of bacon for this.

Put the prepared meat into an earthenware dish with 2 onions, and carrots cut up, salt, pepper and herbs (thyme, bay-leaf, marjoram). Pour the red wine over, and the brandy, and leave to marinate 4 or 5 hours.

Into a heavy stewpan put the rest of the bacon cut in squares and 4 or 5 tablespoons of olive oil, and let the bacon melt a little in the oil. Now add the other 2 onions, sliced, and let them brown, then put in the pieces of mutton, with some fresh herbs and seasoning, the orange peel and 3 cloves of garlic. Pour over the wine in which the meat has marinated and let it bubble until it has reduced by about one third. Just cover the meat with boiling water. Put the lid on the pan and simmer very slowly for 4–5 hours.

The *Daube* can be made the day before it is wanted, any surplus fat skimmed off the sauce when it is cold, and gently reheated. A few stoned black olives and a half ounce of dried cèpes added before the water is put in add to the very southern flavour of the *Daube*.

The nicest accompaniment is a dish of dried white haricot beans, cooked with a piece of smoked bacon and a garlic sausage, and moistened before serving with some of the sauce from the *Daube*.

Châteaubriand en Terrine

Into an earthenware terrine with a lid pour a glass of dry white *vin ordinaire*, a glass of Madeira, and a liqueur glass of brandy and put this to heat gently on a low flame.

Now slice 2 or 3 small onions, the same number of carrots, and sauté them very lightly in a little butter. In the same butter sauté on each side your beef, which should be a fine piece of *filet*, thick and in one piece, seasoned with salt and black pepper.

By this time the contents of the terrine should just be beginning to simmer; place the beef in this liquid, cover it with the carrots and onions, and add a chopped shallot, a suspicion of garlic, 4 fine tomatoes, peeled, and each cut into eight pieces.

Now cover the terrine and seal the lid with a flour and water paste. Place the terrine in a very slow oven (Regulo 1 or 2) for 2 hours. Serve in the dish in which it has cooked.

The juice of the *Châteaubriand*, mingled with the wines and the vegetables, will give forth the most wonderful aroma when you finally open the dish.

You can, if you like, accompany the meat with a very light purée of potatoes.

" I can assure you," says Albert Chevallier, the author of this recipe, " that kings and princes have feasted like gods on this dish, although it is a simple, bourgeois household dish, albeit a gourmand household."

Since fillet is now so difficult to obtain and so expensive, a cheaper cut such as rump steak could be used.

Pepper Steaks

Rump steak is the best for this, about a quarter inch thick. Score the steaks lightly all over with a sharp knife, rub them with garlic and then with a thin coating of pounded peppercorns. Heat a tablespoon of butter and one of olive oil in a thick frying-pan, and when it is hot fry the steaks on each side—about 3 minutes in all.

Serve them with the cooking butter, which should not have got burnt, poured over them.

Paupiettes of Beef

8 thin slices of beef cut from the round, without fat, each weighing approximately 1 oz., 2 ozs. mushrooms, 1 egg, 2 onions, finely chopped, 1 tablespoon French mustard, 1 clove of garlic, 1 dessertspoon finely chopped lemon peel, 1 tablespoon breadcrumbs, flour, dripping, salt and pepper, thyme, a handful of parsley.

Fry the onions, mushrooms and bacon in a little dripping, then mix in the lemon peel, breadcrumbs, parsley and seasoning, and a beaten egg.

Flatten out each slice of beef; season with pepper, salt and thyme. On each slice lay a little heap of stuffing, roll up the meat and secure with a tooth-pick, or tie with string. Roll them in flour and brown them in dripping, in a small sauté pan. Add water just to cover, and simmer very slowly for 30 minutes. Now with the point of a knife crush a small piece of garlic and add this to the sauce, together with the French mustard, and cook for another 30 minutes. The sauce should be creamy and piquant. The dish can be made beforehand and heated up.

Serve with either boiled rice or a purée of potatoes, and grilled tomatoes.

A Wine Marinade for Meat

In a saucepan heat a wineglass of olive oil; when it is hot put in a sliced carrot, one sliced onion, and half a head of celery cut in inch lengths.

Let these vegetables brown lightly and pour in ¼ pint of white wine and a small glass of wine vinegar. Add 4 or 5 stalks of parsley, 4 shallots, 2 cloves of garlic, thyme, bayleaf, a sprig of rosemary, 6 peppercorns and salt.

Simmer this for 30 minutes. Leave it to cool, and then pour it over your piece of meat.

L'Estouffat de Boeuf

This is the Gascon way of doing beef *en daube*, and is one of the traditional dishes eaten in Gascony on Christmas Eve. It is cooked in an oval earthenware casserole.

You need:

1½ lbs. fresh rind of pork (this is used in many soups and *ragoûts* in France, but can be replaced with a pig's foot), herbs, 7 or 8 shallots, 2 large onions cut into four, 1 or 2 carrots, 6 lbs. topside of beef in one piece tied into a sausage shape, 2 claret glasses of Armagnac or brandy, a half-bottle of sound red wine.

Put the pork rind or the pig's foot at the bottom of the casserole and on top of it the seasoned beef. Arrange the vegetables all round and pour over the Armagnac. Warm the red wine a little and pour it over the beef. It should just cover the meat. Cover the casserole with grease-proof paper, so that it is completely sealed, and then put on the lid.

Cook it over a slow fire for 1½ hours. In the farmhouses it is then taken off the fire and the casserole put on to the hearth over the hot cinders and left there for 24 hours. In a modern kitchen it can be left all day in the slowest possible oven.

An hour before serving, take it out, leave it to cool a little so that the fat can be taken off the sauce (if it has been cooked with fresh pork rind this is cut up and served with the meat). Heat it up gently.

The *Estouffat* can be made a day in advance, and it will be easier to remove the fat if the dish has cooled overnight. The Armagnac or brandy gives the sauce a wonderful flavour, but half the amount can be used.

Estouffade de Boeuf à la Provençale

Cut about 3 lbs. of lean stewing beef into large slices; put them to marinate in the marinade described on p. 112 and leave them for 24 hours.

Take the pieces of meat out of the marinade, and sauté them in bacon fat on both sides. Put the meat into an earthenware terrine, pour over the strained marinade, adding a little more wine if there is insufficient, add fresh herbs, 2 or 3 crushed cloves of garlic, ¼ lb. of bacon cut into squares, 3 or 4 carrots, and about ¾ lb. of stoned olives, black and green mixed if possible; if the olives are salt, add no salt to the meat. Cover the casserole with a greaseproof paper, then the lid, and cook in a slow oven for 3 hours. Ten minutes before serving skin the fat from the sauce and add 3 or 4 chopped tomatoes.

Serve with ribbon noodles boiled in plenty of salted water, put on to a hot dish with a little olive oil, grated cheese and a ladle of the sauce from the beef. This way of serving *pasta* with a stew or with the *pot-au-feu* is one of the old Niçois dishes, called *Macaronade*.

Red wine instead of white can be used for the marinade.

Filet de Boeuf en Croûte

Make a pastry crust with 8 ozs. of flour and 6 ozs. of pure beef dripping, mixed with a little water.

Have ready a piece of fillet of beef weighing about 1½ lbs., seasoned with salt and pepper and larded with a few small pieces of garlic; brown the meat lightly on both sides in butter; take it out of the pan, and in the same butter sauté a few mushrooms, 2–4 ozs., cut in slices. Put the mushrooms on the plate with the beef, and to the butter in the pan add a small glass of wine, port or sherry, and let it bubble till it is thick. Roll out the pastry, put the meat on one half of it, the mushrooms and the sauce on the top, cover with the rest of the pastry, making a roll with the ends firmly closed down so that no juice will escape, and bake it on a buttered tin in a moderate oven (Regulo 5) for about 25 minutes. Serve it hot with, if possible, a *Sauce Madère* (p. 193).

Rump steak can be used instead of fillet, but in that case the meat should be larded with a few pieces of bacon as well as the garlic, or it will be dry.

Cold, this *Boeuf en Croûte* makes an admirable picnic dish.

L'Entrecôte aux Huitres

In the Bordelais and the Basque country they eat fresh oysters accompanied by hot grilled sausages. Edouard de Pomiane gives the recipe in *Le Code de la Bonne Chère* for oysters to be served at the same time as grilled steak with a highly spiced sauce. Since steak and oysters are the two foods in the world most acceptable to Englishmen and in the form of steak and oyster pudding a time-honoured tradition, this way of combining the two might well be tried.

First of all prepare the sauce by putting into a casserole ½ lb. of chopped shallots, covered with a whole pint of wine or

Orléans vinegar; let this boil until the vinegar is reduced practically to nothing, and what you have left is in fact almost a purée of shallots.

Now grill the steak, and serve each guest with his helping of meat, a spoonful of the sauce, and a dozen oysters. A mouthful of steak and sauce, then a raw oyster. . . . The sensation, says M. de Pomiane, of freshness following the fiery sauce is indescribable.

Langue de Boeuf aux Champignons

Blanch a salted ox tongue for 15 minutes until the skin can be peeled off, then put it in a pan with an onion, a bayleaf, a piece of celery, salt and peppercorns, cover with water and simmer it until it is tender; it will take 4 or 5 hours.

Prepare a brown *roux* with butter, flour, and a little of the stock from the tongue; stir in a dessertspoon of French mustard, a few mushrooms previously sautéd in butter and 2 or 3 chopped pickled gherkins; pour this over the strained tongue in a casserole and cook together for 10–15 minutes; a little white wine or cider added to the sauce is an improvement, and cream if you like.

Gigot de Porc aux Pistaches

For a leg of pork weighing 6–7 lbs. take about 40 pistachio nuts and 2 cloves of garlic.

Lard the leg of pork with the garlic and the shelled and skinned pistachio nuts.

Roast the pork in the usual way, allowing a good 30 minutes to the pound; put the *gigot* on to the serving dish, drain the fat out of the roasting pan and to the gravy in the pan add a glass of white wine and let this bubble until it has thickened a little. Serve the sauce separately, and a dish of braised celery or baby turnips as an accompaniment.

A leg of pork cooked in this way is also delicious cold, with a potato salad, or a green salad garnished with a few chopped pistachio nuts.

Côtelettes de Porc au Cidre

Brown the pork cutlets on each side in very little dripping or pork fat. Take them out, and add to the fat in the pan a tablespoon of flour; let this turn golden, and when it is smooth add a wine-glass of dry cider, half as much water, and cook it 2 or 3 minutes.

Put the cutlets back in the sauce, seasoned with salt, ground black pepper, a crushed clove of garlic, and a whole sprig of rosemary, which can be removed later. Cover the pan and put it in a very slow oven (Regulo 3) for 30 minutes. Five minutes before serving add a few capers to the sauce.

Confit de Porc

This is made with the fillet of freshly killed pig, not shop meat, prepared and cooked in much the same way as the *Confit d'Oie* (p. 134). When the fillet has been salted 5 or 6 days,[1] it is cut into convenient-sized pieces, about three inches square, *piquèd* with garlic and seasoned with black pepper.

It is then cooked very gently in pork fat and put into pots, covered with the strained fat, and stored away for the summer. It is essential that the jars of *confit* be stored in a *dry* larder.

When it is to be used, the jar is put in a warm place, on top of the stove, until the dripping is sufficiently melted to allow the pieces to be taken out easily. The pork emerges rose-pink (due to the original salting), just sufficiently perfumed with garlic and delicious to eat cold with a potato salad. It can also be used in soups and *Garbures* (p. 44), *Cassoulets*, and in the same way as *Oie en Confit*.

[1] In the English climate 2 days salting is sufficient.

Pâté de Foie de Porc du Périgord

When a pig is killed and cut up for ham and bacon an excellent terrine can be made from the liver.

You will need equal quantities of liver and unsmoked bacon. Chop the liver very finely, so that it is reduced to a purée. Mix it with the bacon, also finely chopped, adding salt (taking into consideration the degree of saltiness of the bacon), black pepper, 1 or 2 cloves of garlic, 2 or 3 shallots, and spices such as mace and a pinch of ground cloves. Put the mixture into an earthenware terrine lined with slices of bacon.

Pour in a small glass of brandy, and on the top of the *pâté* put a pig's foot cut in two, 2 carrots sliced, 2 onions, a bouquet of thyme, rosemary and a bayleaf, a glass of white wine and one of water. Put the terrine into another pan containing water, cover it, and cook in the oven for 3 or 4 hours very slowly.

Remove the pig's foot and the vegetables and leave the terrine to cool. There should be a good jelly round the *pâté* from the pig's foot. Seal the *pâté* with a layer of pure pork lard.

Pieds de Porc Ste Ménéhould

If the pigs' trotters have been salted they must be soaked in water for at least 12 hours before being cooked. Tie them together, two at a time, in opposite ways, with tape, to prevent them falling apart while cooking. Put them into a deep pan and cover them with boiling water in which you have put a glass of white wine and a very little vinegar, an onion stuck with cloves, 2 small carrots, a leek, a branch of thyme, 2 bayleaves, and 2 or 3 peppercorns. Add salt only if the trotters have not been previously salted.

Let them simmer for 3–4 hours until they are tender. Drain

them and leave them to get cold. Untie them, cut each trotter in half lengthways and dip each one in melted pork fat or good dripping, then coat them with fine breadcrumbs. Put them under the grill to brown, turning them over and over until they are evenly done.

A mustard sauce, or a *Sauce Tartare*, can be served with them.

French Recipe for Boiling a Ham

" After having soaked, thoroughly cleansed, and trimmed the ham, put over it a little very sweet clean hay, and tie it up in a thin cloth; place it in a ham kettle or braising pan, or any other vessel as nearly of its size as can be, and cover it with two parts of cold water and one of light white wine (we think the reader will perhaps find *cider* a good substitute for this); add, when it boils and has been skimmed, four or five carrots, two or three onions, a large bunch of savoury herbs, and the smallest bit of garlic. Let the whole simmer gently from 4 to 5 hours, or longer should the ham be very large. When perfectly tender, lift it out, take off the rind, and sprinkle over it some fine crumbs, or some raspings of bread mixed with a little finely minced parsley.

" *Obs.* Foreign cooks generally leave hams, braised joints, and various other prepared meats intended to be served cold, to cool down partially in the liquor in which they are cooked; and this renders them more succulent; but for small frugal families the plan does not altogether answer, because the moisture of the surface (which would evaporate quickly if they were taken out quite hot) prevents their keeping well for any length of time. The same objection exists to serving hams laid upon or closely garnished with savoury jelly (*aspic*) which becomes much more quickly unfit for table than the hams themselves.

" These considerations which may appear insignificant to some of our readers, will have weight with those who are compelled to regulate their expense with economy."

ELIZA ACTON,
Modern Cookery, 1855.

Baked Ham

This way of baking hams is very successful. After the ham is soaked and cleaned, put it into a baking tin in a moderate oven until the ham is warmed through. Then remove the ham, fill the tin with water, and put the ham on a rack or grid standing in the pan.

For a gas or electric oven, cover it with greaseproof paper, and cook it at a medium heat for about 20 minutes to the pound.

If you put cider instead of water into the pan you will have the basis of an excellent sauce.

POULTRY

Roast Chicken

" I came back to Paris after the long sad years of the Occupation. I will tell all about that, and I wandered around the streets the way I do and there in a window were a lot of etchings and there so pleasantly was one by Dufy, it was an etching of kitchen utensils, in an inspired circle and at the bottom was a lovely roasted chicken, God bless him, wouldn't he just have a lovely etching by him in the window of a shop and of lots of kitchen utensils, the factories could not make them, but he had, and the roast chicken, how often during those dark days was I homesick for the quays of Paris and a roast chicken." GERTRUDE STEIN.

To successfully roast your chicken the first requirement is that the bird be young and well fed. Season the chicken inside and out with salt, pepper and lemon juice. Inside put a large lump of butter and a piece of lemon peel. Put a buttered greaseproof paper round the bird, and lay it on its side in the roasting dish, with plenty of good butter all round. Good dripping can be used, but there is nothing like a tender chicken cooked in butter. The oven must be well and moderately heated (Regulo 5 or 6).

After 15 minutes' cooking turn the bird over, and see that the butter is not getting burnt; the oven should now be turned down a little. After another 15 minutes take the paper away, turn the chicken breast upwards, and after copious basting with more butter, if necessary, leave another 10 to 15 minutes to get golden brown.

Serve the gravy from the pan, in a small dish and, separately, more butter, melted and flavoured with lemon juice or fresh tarragon leaves. The classic garnish of watercress is the best one. Instead of the lemon peel and the butter, a piece of bread, fried in butter and rubbed with garlic, placed inside the chicken, gives a delicious flavour.

Poulet au Gratin à la Crème Landaise

First prepare the following sauce:

In a tablespoon of goose or pork fat sauté 4 sliced onions, a clove of garlic, parsley and a little ham or bacon, all finely chopped. Add the livers and giblets of 4 chickens and, if possible, a knuckle of veal. (As chicken giblets and livers cannot always be bought separately the stock can be made with veal bones, the giblets and liver of the chicken you are going to cook, and possibly ½ lb. of stewing beef.) Pour 1½ pints of water over this mixture, simmer it for 1 hour, and then strain it through a sieve.

Now put the chicken on to cook in some good goose or pork fat, but without letting it brown. Season with salt and herbs (thyme or marjoram), and pour over it a claret glass of brandy or Armagnac, and set it alight.

Now pour the prepared sauce over the chicken and cook it for 45 minutes.

Take the chicken out and cut it into four pieces. To the sauce add a cupful of thick cream, a dessertspoon of French mustard and a few small mushrooms which have been previously cooked for 1 minute in butter, and stir in 2 ozs. of grated Gruyère cheese. Put the pieces of chicken back in the sauce, sprinkle with more cheese, and put it to brown for 10 minutes at the top of a very hot oven.

Poulet au Riz

1 good chicken, 2 ozs. butter, 1 lemon, herbs, a carrot, an onion stuck with a clove, a stick of celery, a sprig of tarragon, a clove

of garlic, salt and pepper, rice, the neck and giblets of the chicken.

Put the butter inside the chicken, with salt, pepper, a piece of lemon peel and the tarragon. Rub the outside of the chicken with the juice of the lemon and a little salt. Put it in a deep pan with the onion, carrot and celery, and cover with water.

Cook the chicken over a medium flame, covered. If it is a tender bird it will not take more than 45 minutes to cook. This, however, you can only judge for yourself, so when the chicken feels as if it will be cooked in 20 minutes' time, take out the carrot, onion and celery, and the neck and giblets if you have put them in, and put the rice, 2 ozs. per person, into the pan with the chicken, and let it cook fairly fast until the rice is done (15–20 minutes).

Take out the chicken, cut it in four pieces, and keep it hot while you strain the rice. Have ready a large heated dish, into which you put the rice, and on top of it place the chicken.

A cup of hot cream, into which you have stirred some chopped tarragon and a very small piece of crushed garlic, poured over the chicken in the dish is an added refinement.

Poulet au Riz Basquais

1 fine chicken, 1 lb. tomatoes, 3 or 4 red sweet peppers, 1 lb. coarse pork sausage (the Basques have their own particular sausages, called *Loukenkas*, very highly spiced), ½ lb. rice, herbs, salt and pepper, garlic, spices, a piece of orange peel, onions, paprika.

Brown the chicken, whole, in goose or pork fat, with a sliced onion, a branch of thyme, a bayleaf, salt and pepper. When it is golden all over, pour over warm water just to cover it, add the sausage, in one piece, and the orange peel, and simmer with the cover on the pan until it is tender; this will take about 40 minutes if it is a tender roasting chicken, anything up to 3 hours if it is one of those purple boiling fowls, so if you are not sure of the quality of the bird, better start it early—heating up later can hardly hurt it.

In the meantime make a *ragoût* of the tomatoes and peppers by sautéing the peppers, cut in strips, in goose dripping, and when they are half cooked add the tomatoes, chopped, and seasoned with salt, pepper, and marjoram or thyme. Let them simmer until they are cooked, but don't reduce them to a pulp; stir in a tablespoon of paprika (in the Basque country they have a condiment called *Piment Basquais*, a coarsely ground red pepper stronger than paprika, the colour of cayenne, but nothing like so fiery).

When the chicken is nearly ready, put the rice into a large pan of boiling salted water: cook it for 12–15 minutes, until it is nearly, but not quite, done; strain it and put it in a fireproof pan in which it can be served; now take the chicken and the sausage out of the liquid in which they have cooked; pour a ladle or two of the stock over the rice, and stir it over a very gentle fire; carve the chicken into suitable pieces, and when the rice has absorbed the stock and is quite tender but not mushy put the chicken on the top, pour all round the tomato and pepper mixture, and garnish it with the sausage cut into squares.

The result should be a melting dish of rice, softer than a *pilaff* or a *paëlla*, and not so compact as a risotto, more in fact resembling the classic *Poulet au Riz*, but with the characteristic Basque flavouring of sweet pepper, tomato, and spiced sausage.

A stewing pheasant cooked in the same way is quite excellent.

Poulet à l'Estragon

1 good tender chicken, 2 ozs. butter, the yolks of 2 eggs, 1 cup of cream, a bunch of tarragon, salt and pepper, lemon.

Rub the outside of the chicken with lemon juice. Mash the butter with salt and pepper and a tablespoon of chopped tarragon, and put this inside the bird.

Poach the chicken, with water barely to cover, until it is cooked. Leave it to cool in the stock. Take out the chicken and place it whole in a deepish serving dish; strain the stock. Now beat up the yolks of the eggs with the cream and another tablespoon of chopped tarragon. Heat about $\frac{1}{2}$ pint of the stock in a small pan, pour a spoonful or two on to the egg and cream mixture, and then pour all back into the pan, stirring continuously until the sauce thickens, but do not make it too thick, as it will solidify slightly as it cools.

Pour it over the chicken in the dish, and leave to get cold. Before serving arrange a few whole tarragon leaves along the breast of the chicken.

Poulet à la Sainte Ménéhould (for a tender young chicken)

Truss your chicken as for roasting. Put it into a heavy braising pan with a glass of white wine, $\frac{1}{4}$ lb. of butter, salt, pepper, a sprig of parsley, a few chives or a chopped shallot, a clove of garlic crushed, thyme, a bayleaf, a few leaves of basil and two cloves.

Simmer the chicken slowly, spooning the sauce over the bird frequently, so that it absorbs as much as possible.

When the chicken is cooked you take it out of the pan and anoint it all over with the beaten yolks of 2 eggs, and then with fine breadcrumbs; then pour melted butter all over, and egg and breadcrumbs again. If you have a large enough grill, put the chicken underneath and turn it over and over until it is golden, otherwise put it in a fairly hot oven until it browns, or even into a deep pan on top of the stove, so long as it is accessible enough to be carefully turned without damaging the coating of breadcrumbs.

In the meantime get the sauce ready; this is simply a matter of reducing a little the butter and the wine in which the chicken has cooked, so that it has the consistency of a good gravy; add perhaps a little cream and a drop of brandy. Or you can, if you like, serve a *Sauce Tartare* previously prepared.

Another and easier method with this dish is to use small chickens, split in half as for grilling, allowing half per person. This makes the final cooking in the breadcrumbs much simpler.

Coq au Vin

This is a very old recipe for *Coq au Vin*, and the blood is not in this case added to the sauce as in later recipes.

You need a plump tender chicken (it doesn't *have* to be a cockerel) weighing about 3 lbs., when cleaned and trussed. Season the bird inside and out with salt, pepper and lemon juice; into a deep heavy pan put 3 or 4 ozs. of butter and brown the chicken all over in it; pour over a small glass of brandy and set it alight; when the flames have died down, pour in a whole bottle of good red wine—Macon, Beaujolais or Châteauneuf du Pape. Add the giblets of the bird, cover the pan and simmer slowly either on top of the stove or in a low oven for about 2 hours (an old and tough bird will take twice as long).

In the meantime, prepare 20 or so little onions, browned in butter and glazed with a little sugar and red wine, and $\frac{1}{2}$ lb. of mushrooms, sautéd in butter. A few minutes before the chicken is ready, take out the giblets and add the onions and mushrooms and a crushed clove of garlic.

Remove the chicken on to a hot dish and carve it for serving.

The sauce should by this time be sufficiently reduced to need no thickening, but if it is not, put the pan on to a high flame and let the sauce bubble until it is thick enough. Pour it over the pieces of chicken, and arrange the mushrooms and the onions on the top.

Le Poulet à la Crème

This is the recipe given by Madame Brazier, of the Restaurant Brazier, one of the famous restaurants of Lyon, in Austin de Croze's *Les Plats Régionaux de France*. In those regions the chickens are plump and tender and cook very quickly. When using an older and less well-fed bird it is always advisable to braise it whole, conserving such flavour as it has, carving it for the table when it is cooked, and pouring the cream sauce over the pieces in the serving dish.

"Cut a small chicken in four pieces. Melt a good piece of butter in a thick pan, put in a chopped onion and the pieces of chicken, and cook slowly, so that the chicken does not dry up. When it is nearly done cover the pieces with good thick cream and let it bubble for ten minutes. Take out the pieces of chicken and keep them hot in the serving dish.

"Into the sauce in the pan beat the yolks of 2 eggs and a squeeze of lemon juice, and let it thicken. Pour it through a fine sieve on to the chicken."

Canard aux Navets

At the bottom of a fireproof casserole, of a size to hold the duck comfortably, arrange 3 or 4 slices of bacon, 2 onions cut in rounds, 2 or 3 carrots also in rounds, a bayleaf and a small stick of celery.

Place the trussed and seasoned duck on this bed and braise it gently for 10–15 minutes, then pour a glass of white wine over it and let it reduce, add 2 glasses of brown stock and continue cooking very gently with the lid on. A medium-sized duck will take about 1¼ hours. When the duck is cooked take it out and keep it hot. Put the contents of the pan through a sieve, making a fairly thick brown sauce; skim off the fat as much as possible.

Return the sauce and the duck to the pan, and place all round it 2 or 3 dozen baby turnips which you have prepared while the duck is braising, cooked exactly as for *Navets Glacés* (p. 162).

Let the whole dish get very hot and serve it in the casserole.

Duck with Figs

Put 16 fresh figs to marinate in a half bottle of Sauternes for 24 hours.

Season the duck with salt and pepper and put a piece of butter and a piece of orange peel inside the bird. In a deep earthenware terrine with a lid put 2 ozs. of butter, and put the duck in the terrine, breast downwards, and another 1 oz. of butter on top of the duck. Let it brown in a fairly hot oven (Regulo 6), without the lid, for 15 minutes; now pour the butter off, turn the duck over, and pour in the wine from the figs; let this cook 5 minutes and add about ½ pint of stock made from veal bones, the giblets of the duck, 2 sliced onions, 2 carrots, a clove of garlic crushed, and a branch of thyme or marjoram. Put the cover on the casserole and cook in a slow oven (Regulo 3) for 1 hour, until the duck is tender.

Now take out the duck and remove the vegetables and giblets; leave the lid off the casserole, turn the oven up and let the juice bubble for 15 minutes to reduce it; put in the figs and let them cook 5 minutes if they are the very ripe purple ones, 10 minutes if they are green figs; take them out and arrange them round the duck. Leave the stock to cool. Remove the fat and pour the liquid over the duck and figs; it should set to a light jelly.

Serve the duck with a plain green salad.

Canard en Daube

You need 1 large duck or 2 small ones. One which is old and too tough for roasting will do very well for this dish.

Prepare a number of little strips of bacon and the following mixture of herbs:

A handful of parsley, 2 shallots, chives, a clove of garlic, a bayleaf, a sprig of thyme   few leaves of basil, salt, pepper, a scrap of grated nutmeg.

Chop all these very finely and roll each strip of bacon in this mixture. Make incisions all over the duck and lard it with the pieces of bacon. Truss the duck and put it into a casserole or braising pan into which it just fits, and pour over it two tumblers of white wine, the same quantity of water and a liqueur glass of brandy. Cover the pan and cook the duck very slowly indeed for 3–4 hours. The sauce will reduce and, when cold, should turn to jelly.

When the duck is cooked, place it in the serving dish; leave the sauce to get cold, so that you can take off the fat, warm it again slightly and then pour it over the duck, and leave it to set. The duck will be very well cooked, so it will be perfectly easy to carve at the table.

If you are serving baked potatoes and have guests who like garlic, have a dish of *aïoli* (a mayonnaise which has been made with 2 cloves of garlic crushed in the bowl before putting the egg in) and put this on the potatoes instead of butter.

Cold Duck with Orange and Cherry Sauce

1 duck, carrots, onions, bacon, white wine, seasoning, herbs, garlic, mushrooms, oranges, maraschino cherries.

First of all prepare a stock by browning a sliced onion and the giblets of the duck in a little bacon fat. Add 2 carrots, seasoning and herbs, and a few bacon rinds. When it is all turning brown pour in a glass of white wine and let it simmer 2 or 3 minutes. Add $1\frac{1}{2}$ pints of water and let the stock cook over a moderate fire for about 40 minutes.

In a braising pan put a little more bacon fat, another onion sliced thinly, 2 more carrots, 2 rashers of bacon, a pinch of mace, salt and pepper, a branch of thyme, 2 ozs. of mushroom stalks, and a crushed clove of garlic. Let this mixture melt in the fat, then put in the trussed duck, seasoned with salt and pepper, and with a strip of orange peel in its inside.

Let it brown very lightly in the fat, then pour in a glass of white wine. Let this reduce by half, then add 2 tumblers of the prepared stock, strained. Cover the pan and let it simmer for about 1½ to 1¾ hours, until the duck is tender. It must now be left to cool in its sauce.

Next day take out the duck and put it on a long serving dish. Skim all the fat off the sauce, warm the sauce again, then press it through a fine sieve, vegetables included, but not the bacon, which would give it too strong a flavour.

Put the resulting purée into a small pan, and into it stir the rind of an orange which has been thinly pared, cut into strips and blanched 5 minutes in boiling water. Add the juice of the orange, a dozen maraschino cherries and a tablespoon of the maraschino syrup. Let it all simmer together a minute or two, then leave it to cool.

The duck can be decorated with a few quarters of orange and surrounded by some shiny green watercress. The sauce is served separately. All you need with this duck is perhaps a baked potato, but even this is not essential. Don't overdo it by having an orange salad or green peas.

Canard à l'Albigeoise

In a fireproof casserole large enough to hold the duck put a little olive oil or butter; in this sauté ¼ lb. of bacon cut in pieces, and 20 small onions; put in the duck, trussed as for roasting, and let it brown all over; sprinkle over a little flour, and when it has turned golden add 2 glasses of vegetable stock, salt, pepper, a leek cut in pieces, a stick of celery cut up, a branch of thyme and one of fennel, a small spoonful of paprika, and a tablespoon of sugar. Cover the pan and simmer for 1½ hours, until the duck is tender.

Take the duck out of the pan and keep it hot; remove the fat from the sauce as much as possible and reduce it by letting it boil fiercely, then press it through a sieve.

In the meantime prepare a large piece of bread fried in butter or bacon fat, and spread it with either a purée of apples or with redcurrant jelly; the duck is served on the croûton, with the sauce poured over, and some extra apple purée or redcurrant jelly separately.

Salmis de Dinde à la Berrichonne

First of all prepare a stock with the giblets, neck and feet of the turkey, browned in butter with an onion, a carrot, a clove of garlic, thyme, bayleaf and parsley. Sprinkle with a tablespoon of flour and let it turn golden, then add a claret glass of red wine and 2 of water, and leave to simmer for 1 hour.

In the meantime, cut up the turkey, dividing the legs and wings into two pieces each and the breast into four pieces. Season them with salt and pepper. Put 3 ozs. of butter into a casserole or braising pan, and when it is melted put in the pieces of turkey; let them turn golden on each side, take them out and keep them aside. In the same butter put ¼ lb. of bacon cut into small squares and 1 lb. of small mushrooms. When these in their turn have browned, take them out, and to the butter and juices in the pan add a claret glass of red wine and let it simmer 2 or 3 minutes, then add the prepared stock, through a strainer.

Put back the pieces of turkey, covered with the bacon and the mushrooms, and add 2 tablespoons of brandy. Cover the pan, and cook very slowly for 1½ hours. Serve garnished with triangles of fried bread.

Turkey à la Chevalière

An attractive way of presenting what is left of a cold turkey.

First of all, make a stock from some of the turkey bones simmered with an onion, celery, herbs and mushroom stalks, which you turn into a sauce either with yolks of egg, cream or arrowroot.

You will need about 12 ozs. of the white meat, minced or chopped, and some neat little fillets cut from one thigh and drumstick. Put the mince into a small pan with sufficient of the sauce to bring it to the consistency of jam, warming gently over a low fire. Dip the fillets in the sauce, roll them in bread-crumbs and fry them golden-yellow in very hot fat.

To serve, put the mince inside a circle of buttered rice (p. 89), arranging the fillets on the outside, alternated with rolls of crisply fried bacon, and hand the remainder of the sauce, very hot, separately.

Le Confit (preserved goose)

The south-western region of France, the Languedoc, the Landes and the Béarn, is country which is largely given over to the raising of pigs and geese; the *foie gras* of the Périgord district is as famous as that of Strasbourg; the food is southern in character but quite distinct from Mediterranean cooking in that pork and goose fat replace oil as the basis of all the meat and vegetable dishes, and of the soups. In the winter, when the pigs and the geese are killed, they are made, in every farmhouse, into the famous *confits*, stored in earthenware jars covered with lard and used gradually throughout the year. Great jars of pure pork lard and goose fat are stored at the same time; the use of this good dripping gives a robust and countrified flavour to the cooking of these regions, and makes even a simple piece of fried bread into something entirely characteristic. I am giving the recipe for the *confit d'oie*, as it is done in the Landes district; but it is only really worth doing for those who have their own geese and a dry airy larder in which to store the jars.

Oie en Confit Landaise

Cut the goose into quarters. Put it into a terrine and rub the pieces all over with *gros sel*, both skin and cut side, about ¼ lb. of salt to a goose. Take all the fat from the inside and melt it down in readiness for cooking the goose. As the geese we get in England are not specially fattened as they are in France, one goose may not yield sufficient fat to cover the pieces while they are cooking. Pure pork lard or beef dripping may be added to make up the amount, but not vegetable fat.

Leave the goose for 5 or 6 days (this is for freshly killed geese; birds bought from a shop are better left only 2–3 days), at the end of which you take it out, wash it, and put it to cook in the fat, so that it is completely covered, and cook it very slowly, with the lid on, for 2–3 hours, until, when you test it with a skewer at the thickest part of the leg, the juice comes out pink. If it comes out red it is not sufficiently cooked.

Drain the pieces of goose, put them into a deep earthenware jar. Let the fat in which they have cooked get cool, and then pour it through a strainer over the goose until it is well covered. Tie up the jar with paper.

Goose preserved like this should keep for several months on condition that it is kept, as explained above, in a really dry and cool larder. After removing pieces of goose for use, be sure that the rest is well covered again with dripping.

Oie en Confit aux Pommes de Terre

Put the jar containing the *confit* on the top of the stove or in a cool oven so that the dripping melts sufficiently, and then take out as many pieces as you need; in the dripping which still surrounds these pieces sauté them gently until they are hot. In the meantime prepare some potatoes, either as for the *Galette de Pommes de Terre* (p. 159), or as for *Pommes à l'Echirlète* (p. 158), and serve the goose and the potatoes together.

Oie en Confit à la Purée

Prepare the pieces of goose as for *Oie en Confit aux Pommes de Terre*; serve them on a purée of lentils, or of split green peas, or of dried haricot beans, garnished with quarters of hard-boiled eggs and croûtons of bread fried in the goose fat.

Oie à la Poitevine

For this dish a young goose weighing 6–7 lbs. is the most suitable.

Brown the goose all over in dripping or butter. Add 1 lb. of sliced onions and 10 cloves of garlic; let them brown lightly. Add 6 tomatoes cut up, seasoning of salt, pepper and herbs, and a bottle of white wine. Cover the casserole and simmer for about 5 hours, until the bird is absolutely tender.

Pour off the sauce, and press the onions, tomatoes, and garlic through a sieve; leave the sauce to cool so that the fat, of which there will be a good deal, can be drained off. If the goose is wrapped in paper and kept in a covered dish in the slowest possible oven it will keep hot without drying up and will not get overcooked.

In the meantime prepare 2 lbs. of small pickling onions or shallots, put them into a frying-pan with a little oil and let them brown, turning them over from time to time; when they are golden, add a tablespoon of white sugar and a small glass of red wine or port; let this thicken until it is syrupy. To serve the goose, heat it up gently in the sauce to which you have added a small glass of brandy and the browned onions.

This is one of the best ways of cooking goose. Serve with it a dish of Jerusalem artichokes *à la Provençale* (p. 168), or some chestnuts and bacon (p. 166).

Cou d'Oie Farçi

When the *confits* of goose are being prepared, the necks of the geese are stuffed and cooked at the same time.

The skin of the neck is turned inside out like the finger of a glove and the inside removed. Make a stuffing of a few pieces of trimmings of the goose, an equal quantity of bacon, or of fresh pork, herbs, garlic and spices, the whole mixed with 2 or 3 eggs. Stuff the goose's neck with this mixture (not too full), sew up the ends and cook it in the goose dripping with the rest of the goose.

To be eaten cold, cut in slices like a sausage. A stuffed goose neck is also sometimes added to a *Garbure* (p. 44) or to a *Cassoulet* (p. 93), in which case it is served hot.

Lapin au Gratin

Joint the rabbit, conserving the blood in a small bowl. Marinate the pieces of rabbit for 1 or 2 hours in white wine or cider.

Cut 2 or 3 onions into rounds, sauté them in dripping, add the pieces of rabbit and let them brown. Season with salt, black pepper and a generous helping of fresh thyme or marjoram; add the white wine from the marinade, cover the pan, and simmer gently for 1 hour or so, until the rabbit is cooked.

To the blood in the bowl add as many fresh white breadcrumbs as will absorb it, a handful of chopped parsley and a clove of garlic crushed. Stir this mixture into the sauce of the rabbit, and continue stirring 5 minutes over a low flame. Put a few knobs of butter on the top and brown it very quickly under the grill.

GAME

THE FOLLOWING recipes are mainly for country dwellers who are in a position to tire of partridge and pheasant plainly roasted; they can also be applied to birds no longer in their first youth, and to the quick-frozen variety.

Perdrix à la Purée de Lentilles

Clean and truss the partridges in the ordinary way: put them into a pan just large enough to hold them with 3 or 4 ozs. of butter, a large onion sliced and 2 carrots cut in rounds. When the birds have taken colour pour over them a glass of white wine and let it reduce by half; add seasoning and a glass of good stock, cover the pan, and finish cooking over a very small flame. The exact time depends upon the age of the partridge.

In the meantime, you will have prepared a purée with 1 lb. of brown lentils, an onion stuck with 2 cloves, 2 cloves of garlic, 2 carrots and salt. Cover with water, simmer for 2 hours, and when the lentils are quite soft put them through a sieve. In a saucepan mix the purée with half the sauce from the partridges, and work it over the fire until the purée is smooth and of the right consistency.

Serve the partridges on a dish, with the purée all round and the rest of the sauce poured over. Quantities for 6 birds.

Partridges with Soubise Sauce

Prepare the partridges as for roasting. Fill each with a chopped onion previously boiled in milk, seasoned with pepper, salt and rolled in a slice of bacon. Make a stock with the giblets of the birds, a slice of bacon, an onion, a few pepper-

corns, seasoning and herbs. In this stock simmer your partridges for about 45 minutes.

Now strain the liquor, keeping the partridges hot in the
pan, and add it to a previously prepared purée made with 4
large onions simmered in milk until tender and put through a
sieve. As well as the stock, add butter and a little cream, so
that the purée is thick and rich. Pour it over the birds and
garnish with curls of crisp bacon.

Perdrix aux Choux

Partridges cooked with cabbage is one of the classic recipes
of French household and country cooking.

Allow 1 stewing partridge per person and 1 medium-sized
cabbage for every 2 partridges; ½ lb. of bacon, 4 large carrots,
and 8 small smoked sausages for 4 partridges.

Brown the birds in bacon fat; blanch the cabbages in boiling
water for 7 or 8 minutes; drain them carefully, cut out the
stalks and the hard inner part. Cut the cabbages in fine slices
and put a layer at the bottom of a large earthenware pot; on
top put the bacon, cut in large slices, the carrots, the sausages
and the partridges; season with salt, pepper, a few juniper
berries,[1] 2 or 3 cloves of garlic, 2 lumps of sugar, nutmeg and
a little grated lemon peel.

Cover with the rest of the cabbage, moisten with stock, to
about half-way up the cabbage, cover the casserole, and cook
in a very slow oven for 4 or 5 hours.

Partridge en Papillotes
(For young birds)

Cut a good-sized partridge completely in half, from the
neck to the rump; put some butter into a pan, and sauté
the two pieces in it for 8–10 minutes. Take them out, season

---

[1] To be bought at Soho shops and large stores such as Selfridge's.

them with salt, black pepper, herbs and a little orange or lemon peel; leave them to cool.

Then prepare a piece of greaseproof paper for each half bird, rubbed with butter or oil. Lay a piece of bacon on the paper and the partridges on top. Fold the paper over, with the edges together, and fold down all round to make them airtight. Put them straight on the grid in a medium oven (Regulo 5) and cook for 10–15 minutes.

Perdrix à la Catalane

You don't, of course, use the tenderest little roasting partridges for this dish. More elderly birds, so long as they are nice and plump, will do very well.

Truss your partridges as for roasting and put them into a thick pan, just large enough to hold them, in which you have melted two good tablespoons of pork or bacon fat. Season them with salt and pepper, and brown them all over. Sprinkle them with 2 tablespoons of flour, and stir until the flour and the fat are amalgamated and turning golden.

Now pour over them 2 glasses of white wine—in the Roussillon they use the Rancio wine—an ordinary, not too dry white wine can be used, with a small glass of port added. Add a little water, until the liquid comes a little over half-way to covering the partridges. Cover the pan and simmer over a low fire. Halfway through the cooking add 2 sweet red peppers cut into strips.

In the meantime, peel 24 cloves of garlic (for 4 partridges) and cut a Seville orange into slices, rind included. Throw these into a pint of water, and cook until the water boils. This operation is to remove the bitterness from the orange and the garlic, which are strained and put into a second lot of water and cooked for another 8–10 minutes. The garlic will now taste very mild; anyone who likes their garlic strong can omit this second cooking.

By this time the liquid will be considerably reduced and the whole mixture is added to the partridges, together with the juice of a second orange, and all cooked together another 10–15 minutes, until the partridges are tender.

If the sauce is not thick enough, take the partridges out and keep them hot, turn up the flame and let the sauce bubble until it is sufficiently reduced.

Serve the partridges surrounded with the sauce, the sweet peppers, the orange and the garlic, very hot.

The partridges will take from 2–3 hours to cook, according to how old and tough they are.

The *Galette de Pommes de Terre* (p. 159) is particularly good as an accompaniment to Catalan Partridges.

Pheasant with Celery

Prepare a pheasant in the same way as you would for roasting; braise it with butter, a little stock, some squares of bacon and a glass of port.

Have ready 2 fine heads of celery, cut into thin rounds, blanch them for a few minutes, drain them, and then proceed to braise them, also in butter and stock.

When they are done, stir in a cupful of cream, and add them to the sauce the pheasant has cooked in. If this is too thin, thicken it with the yolk of an egg, and pour it quickly over the pheasant in the serving dish.

Roast Wild Duck

Put a tablespoon of salt and an onion into the cavity of the trussed birds, and if they are of the fishy-tasting variety put boiling water to the depth of a quarter of an inch into the baking pan. Bake for 10 minutes, basting the ducks with the water. This removes the fishy taste. Then drain, sprinkle lightly with flour, salt and pepper, baste well with hot lard or butter and roast for 15–20 minutes. Take care not to over-cook them or they will lose their flavour.

A *Sauce Bigarade* (p. 192), or the Orange Sauce on p. 193, is the accepted accompaniment of roast wild duck.

Les Palombes à la Béarnaise

The wild doves and the wood-pigeons of the Landes and the Béarn are particularly delicious little birds. The ordinary pigeons which one buys in England are rather dull and dry, but cooked *à la Béarnaise* they can be excellent.

First of all, braise the pigeons in butter, in a covered pan, for 30–40 minutes, until they are tender; take them out, cut them in halves and put into a bowl with the juice of a lemon, a glass of white wine or brandy, salt and pepper, and leave them in this marinade while you prepare a purée made from the hearts of cooked artichokes, at least 3 for each pigeon; put this purée into an earthenware casserole with a lump of butter; sauté the livers of the pigeons in the butter in which the birds have originally cooked, adding the wine or brandy marinade, and press them through a sieve, with the liquid, into the artichoke purée; put the pigeons on top of the purée and heat it gently.

Failing artichokes, a purée of broad beans or of Jerusalem artichokes or of celery will serve quite well.

Pluvier aux Olives

Put a few stoned green olives, or green olives stuffed with pimentos, into each plover. Wrap them in bacon and roast them in butter.

Serve them on slices of bread fried in the butter in which the birds have cooked and impregnated with the juice which has come out of them during the cooking.

Bécasse en Cocotte

This way of cooking woodcock differs from the traditional method in that the entrails, which have a very powerful flavour not appreciated by everybody, are first removed from the little birds.

Clean the woodcock, reserving the insides; wrap each bird in a rasher of bacon and place them in an earthenware terrine with a tablespoon of butter or dripping for each one; cover with a buttered paper and the lid of the terrine. Put them into a hot oven and cook them for 20 minutes.

In the meantime fry a slice of bread for each woodcock, and spread them with the entrails of the bird chopped and seasoned with salt, pepper, a pinch of nutmeg, a nut of butter and a scrap of fresh thyme or marjoram. Let these heat 2 or 3 minutes in the oven.

When the woodcock are cooked, put the croûtons underneath them and serve in the terrine. The dripping at the bottom of the terrine will have a most exquisite flavour.

Hare

To make a roast saddle and a terrine from one hare. Hare is cheap, but a whole animal is usually rather large for a small household, and this is a way of combining two delicious dishes without waste and without getting tired of it, for the terrine can be stored for two or three weeks if necessary.

First of all, have the hare cut so that the back is in one piece, and reserve this for the roast.

For the terrine put the rest of the hare in joints into a casserole with a half bottle of red wine, 2 onions cut up, 2 or 3 cloves of garlic, a bayleaf, a tablespoon of marjoram or thyme, and 2 lbs. of fat bacon cut in squares. The bacon serves to lubricate the meat of the hare which is very dry, and also to improve the taste which is very strong by itself. *Add no salt.*

Cover the casserole and cook in a slow oven for about 45 minutes; when the meat has cooled take it all off the bones and, with the bacon, put it through the mincer. Season it highly with more marjoram or thyme, crushed garlic, ground black pepper, salt if necessary, a small piece of chopped lemon or orange peel, and powdered mace.

Put a layer of fat bacon rashers at the bottom of a 2-pint terrine (or two smaller ones) and put in your hare mixture, but don't press it down too much. Put more rashers of bacon on the top and moisten with about half the original cooking liquor of the hare (the other half is kept for the saddle).

Now put a piece of greaseproof paper over the terrine, cover with the lid and stand in another pan of water and cook in a low oven (Regulo 3) for 1–2 hours, according to the size of the terrines you have used.

When the terrines are cooked leave them to cool. Cover with melted lard or clarified butter, and when cool seal with tinfoil or greaseproof paper, and store in a cool larder, or the refrigerator.

The terrine can be eaten either with hot toast as a first course, or as a main course with baked potatoes served on separate plates and a salad such as Orange and Celery, or Orange and Endive (see chapter on Salads). The recipe for this terrine as it appeared in the original edition of this book contained an addition of aspic jelly, but it is simpler to make in the present version. Also I have come to the conclusion that it keeps better without the jelly.

Roast Saddle of Hare. Prepare the saddle for cooking by seasoning with ground black pepper, and wrapping first in rashers of bacon and then in a piece of greaseproof paper, and put it in a self-basting pan with plenty of good beef dripping.

Put it into a hot oven (Regulo 7 or 8) and roast for 20 minutes.

In the meantime, take the strained liquor in which the pieces of hare for the terrine were cooked, put it in a shallow pan and simmer it until it is reduced and thick. (If it has been salted, the reducing process will make it too salt.)

Take the saddle out of the oven, carve it in thin long pieces and put these into the sauce. Strain the fat out of the pan, and to the remaining juices add a little port or red wine and a little water. Cook this a minute or two and add it to the sauce and the pieces of hare. Cover the pan and cook in a slow oven for about 15 minutes until the hare looks quite done.

As an accompaniment serve a purée of chestnuts (p. 167) and redcurrant jelly.

Râble de Lièvre Bourguignon

As in the previous two recipes, the saddle will serve three or four people, the rest of the hare in this case being used for a *civet* or a Jugged Hare.

Put plenty of good dripping or butter over the saddle, cover with a buttered paper and roast for about 40 minutes in a medium to fast oven. When it is done, put in the serving dish to keep hot, pour off the fat, and to the juices in the pan add a cup of cream and half a cup of fine smooth chestnut purée (p. 167).

Pour over the saddle, and serve redcurrant jelly as well.

This is really a first-class dish.

Aïllade de Levraut

1 young hare, ½ lb. fat bacon, 2 ozs. garlic, 2 ozs. shallots, the liver and blood of the hare, half a tumbler of red wine vinegar.

Chop finely the bacon, the shallots, the garlic and the liver of the hare. Add the red wine vinegar, the blood of the hare, and seasoning of salt, black pepper, mace and a little thyme or marjoram. Put this mixture into a small oval copper or earthenware pan and let it simmer very gently for 2 hours. Care must be taken that it does not stick to the bottom of the casserole; should the *aïllade* dry up, add a little warmed red wine or vinegar, so that the mixture remains smooth and liquid.

When the *aïllade* has been cooking for 1 hour, put the hare on to roast (if the hare is not a young one, the saddle only can be used) with plenty of dripping and covered with a grease-proof paper. It will take about 1 hour to cook if it is whole; 40 minutes for a saddle. When it is ready, put the *aïllade* on the serving dish and the hare on top.

A sauce can be made from the juices in the pan, with the addition of red wine or port and a little water.

Civet de Lièvre Landais

Have the hare cut into the usual pieces. Brown them slightly in goose or pork fat. In an earthenware casserole brown 12 shallots chopped fine, 2 or 3 cloves of garlic, and ¼ lb. of bacon or gammon cut in dice (in the Landes they use *Jambon de Bayonne*). Add a glass of red wine, let it reduce a little, add 2 glasses of stock or water and a tablespoon of thick tomato purée (or 6 ripe tomatoes previously grilled and skinned) and an ounce of dried cèpes. Put in the pieces of hare, cover the casserole and cook very slowly for 2–3 hours, until the hare is quite tender.

The sauce should by this time be sufficiently reduced to need no further thickening, but if it is too thin, pour it off into a wide pan, keeping the hare hot in the casserole, and reduce it very quickly for a few minutes.

Les Filets de Lièvre à la Provençale

Cut fillets from the back of the hare in long, fairly thick slices; *piquez* each fillet with a small piece of bacon, season with salt and pepper and sauté them gently in oil or bacon fat, turning them over several times and adding more fat, if necessary. They will take 20 to 30 minutes to cook, as they must be well done.

10 minutes before serving add a wineglass of red or white wine to the pan, 2 tablespoons of thick tomato purée, and a little finely chopped garlic. Continue simmerings with the cover on the pan, and serve garnished with croûtons of fried bread.

VEGETABLES

Garlic

Anyone who may be alarmed by the quantities of garlic used in some of the recipes in this book, particularly in the Catalan and Provençal dishes, may be interested in the following story of the beautiful mannequin who found out how to indulge her insatiable appetite for garlic and at the same time keep her job. That girl was perfectly right. Eating garlic is a question of habit and digestion. There is also the indisputable fact that garlic changes its character according to the amount used. Half a clove crushed into the salad dressing has a more penetrating aroma than a ½ lb. stewed with a chicken.

As a matter of fact, the best way of cooking that *Poulet Béarnais* of which Ford Madox Ford writes, is to place the peeled cloves of garlic (by all means use 2 lbs. if you can face peeling so much) *underneath* the chicken before putting it on to roast. The perfume coming from the kitchen while the roasting is going on is indescribably delicious. The chicken (or, for that matter, a leg of mutton) will be permeated with the flavour, but not unduly so; those who enjoy it may eat the garlic, impregnated with the juice from the roast, while those who do not can do without.

"I came yesterday, also in Fitzroy Street, at a party, upon a young lady who was the type of young lady I did not think one ever could meet. She was one of those ravishing and, like the syrens of the Mediterranean and Ulysses, fabulous beings who display new creations to the sound of harps, shawms and tea-cups. What made it all the more astounding was that she was introduced to me as being one of the best cooks in London—a real *cordon bleu*, and then some. She was, as you might expect, divinely tall and appeared to appear through such mists as surrounded Venus saving a warrior. But I found that she really could talk, if awfully, and at last she told me something that I did not know—about garlic. . . .

" As do—as *must*—all good cooks, she used quantities of that bulb. It occurred to me at once that this was London and her work was social. Garlic is all very well on the bridge between Beaucaire and Tarascon or in the arena at Nîmes amongst sixteen thousand civilised beings. . . . But in an *atelier de couture* in the neighbourhood of Hanover Square! . . . The lady answered mysteriously: No: there is no objection if only you take enough and train your organs to the assimilation. The perfume of *allium officinale* attends only on those timorous creatures who have not the courage as it were to wallow in that vegetable. I used to know a London literary lady who had that amount of civilisation so that when she ate abroad she carried with her, in a hermetically sealed silver container, a single clove of the principal ingredient of *aïoli*. With this she would rub her plate, her knife, her fork and the bread beside her place at the table. This, she claimed, satisfied her yearnings. But it did not enchant her friends or her neighbours at table.

" My instructress said that that served her right. She herself, at the outset of her professional career, had had the cowardice to adopt exactly that stratagem that, amongst those in London who have seen the light, is not uncommon. But when she went to her studio the outcry amongst her comrades, attendants, employers, clients and the very conductor of the bus that took her to Oxford Circus had been something dreadful to hear. Not St. Plothinus nor any martyr of Lyons had been so mis-called by those vulgarians.

" So she had determined to resign her post and had gone home and cooked for herself a *Poulet Béarnais*, the main garniture of which is a kilo—2 lbs.—of garlic per chicken, you eating the stewed cloves as if they were *haricots blancs*. It had been a Friday before a Bank Holiday, so that the mannequins at that fashionable place would not be required for a whole week.

" Gloomily, but with what rapture internally, she had for that space of time lived on hardly anything else but the usually eschewed bulb. Then she set out gloomily towards the place that she so beautified but that she must leave for ever. Whilst she had been buttoning her gloves she had kissed an old aunt whose protests had usually been as clamant as those of her studio-mates. The old lady had merely complimented her on her looks. At the studio there had been no outcry, and there too she had been congratulated on the improvement, if possible, of her skin, her hair, her carriage. . . .

" She had solved the great problem; she had schooled her organs to assimilate, not to protest against, the sacred herb. . . ."

Provence

by Ford Madox Ford (pub. George Allen & Unwin, 1938).

Herbs

People who seriously intend to have good cooking grow as many kitchen herbs as they can, so as to have them always fresh. Where this is impossible an enterprising shop called Country Style, 18 Ship Street, Brighton, Sussex, operates a postal service of fresh herbs such as tarragon, chives, basil, chervil, thyme, lemon thyme, marjoram and fennel when they are in season, and supply them dried in the winter. Harrods, Youngs' in the Brompton Road, Bathgates' in the Kings Road, and Roche, 14 Old Compton Street, W.1., are some of the London shops which sell a selection of fresh herbs.

For seeds and plants of these kitchen herbs, write to George Bunyard, Broadway, Maidstone, Kent, The Herb Farm, Seal,

Kent, or to John Jefferies & Son, The Royal Nurseries, Ciren-
cester, for their catalogues. When ordering tarragon plants, be
very firm about them being the *true French* variety, or you
may be fobbed off with a plant which, although it grows
easily, has no flavour whatever.

Dried herbs should be bought in very small quantities, and
stored in airtight jars, as they quickly lose their flavour.

The Potato

In 1749 the Paris *Journal* declared of the potato "*voilà le
plus mauvais de tous les légumes dans l'opinion générale*". In our
own day we have witnessed the enraged British housewife,
backed up by an indignant press, deprived of her national
birthright, obliged to queue for a pound or two of potatoes.
Too well we know to what base uses those potatoes were put.
Boiled to ruins on the outside, and hard within, battered to a
grey pulp by a blunt instrument, interspersed with lumps
like a boarding-house mattress. Well might the French press
repeat its criticism of two hundred years ago.

Yet the potato can be a lovable vegetable. Its uses are wide;
it can, if well treated, accompany almost any dish with
distinction; makes a most admirable soup, and, richly cooked
with cheese or simply baked in its jacket and eaten with butter
and freshly ground salt, is a dish fit for any *gourmet*.

The Cooking of Potatoes

For *sauté potatoes* cook the potatoes in their skins; peel,
slice and sauté them gently in dripping or butter, adding a
little chopped onion and parsley at the end.

Potatoes for salad should also be cooked in their skins, peeled
and mixed with the dressing or mayonnaise while still warm.

For *Pommes Pailles*, *Allumettes* and all variations of chips,
the raw potatoes should be plunged into plenty of water to

wash away the outer starch which otherwise makes them stick together in the cooking. Drain and dry them thoroughly before cooking.

Put *new potatoes* into boiling water.

Go to the extra trouble of *mashing* potatoes through a sieve and adding *warmed* milk.

To keep *boiled* potatoes hot cover them with a clean tea-cloth instead of the lid of the serving dish. This absorbs the moisture and results in dry and floury, instead of sodden potatoes.

Mashed fried potatoes should be done in bacon fat, very little of it, and watched constantly.

Rub the outside of potatoes for *baking* with a coating of salt.

Baked potatoes are delicious eaten with *aïoli* (p. 67) instead of butter.

Gratin Dauphinois (Escoffier's recipe)

Peel and slice thinly and evenly 2 lbs. of raw waxy potatoes. Put them in a basin and add salt, pepper, grated nutmeg, a beaten egg, a pint of scalded milk, and $\frac{1}{4}$ lb. of grated Gruyère cheese. Mix all well together. Put them into an earthenware dish, rubbed with garlic, and well buttered, spread the surface with a generous coating of grated cheese, add several nuts of butter, and cook in a medium oven for 40–45 minutes.

Gratin Savoyarde is made in the same way, the milk being replaced by *consommé*. But there are those who claim that only the Savoyard dish should be made with cheese, and that the Dauphinois gratin should contain potatoes and cream only. In that case the amount of cream is half a pint to a pound of potatoes.

Potatoes en Papillotes

Nicholas Soyer, grandson of the famous Alexis, spent years perfecting the system of paper-bag cookery and published a book extolling its advantages. Indeed they are many. I can vouch for the excellence of this method for cooking new potatoes.

Scrape 24 very small new potatoes. Put them on a fair-sized piece of greaseproof paper, with 2 leaves of mint, a little salt and 2 ozs. of butter. Fold the paper over and then fold down the two edges so that the bag is completely sealed. Put it into a pre-heated oven, on to the grid (Regulo 5), and cook for about 35 minutes. They will come out perfectly cooked, buttery and full of flavour. Larger potatoes can be cut in half.

Pommes Fondantes

This is the most delicious way of cooking new potatoes. Have them well scraped, washed and dried. Choose a thick pan, either a small frying-pan or saucepan or sauté pan of a size which will accommodate the number of potatoes you are going to cook so that each one lies on the bottom of the pan with very little room to spare, or the butter will be wasted and may burn. For 1 lb. of potatoes (as much the same size as possible) you need about 1½ ozs. of butter. Melt it very gently in the pan, put the potatoes in whole. Cover the pan and cook over a low flame. After 10 minutes have a look at them, and when they are getting brown turn them over very carefully and cover the pan again. Small potatoes will take 20–25 minutes, larger ones 10 minutes longer. They should be golden on the outside (but not hard like roast potatoes) and melting inside. Margarine simply will not do for this kind of cooking; it leaves a sediment at the bottom of the pan, which sticks and burns; in any case the flavour of the butter is essential to the dish.

Pommes de Terre à l'Echirlète

This is a way of cooking potatoes from the Périgord district, first class with grilled steak or roast game or by themselves.

Cook whole fairly small potatoes, in just enough water or, better still, stock, to cover them, adding 2 cloves of garlic; cover the pan. By the time the liquid is absorbed they should be cooked. Now put them in a pan with a tablespoon of goose or pork fat and the garlic and cook them slowly until they are brown all over. Turn them over two or three times.

Large potatoes cut in halves or quarters can also be successfully cooked by this excellent method.

Pommes de Terre au Grain de Sel, Sauce Bouillade

Peel and cut into inch squares 1 lb. of waxy potatoes. Throw them into boiling water salted with *gros sel*; when they are cooked, strain them, return them to the pan and dry them over a low flame, shaking the pan.

Serve them with the *All Grenat* or *Sauce Bouillade* (p. 194) poured over.

Galette de Pommes de Terre

Peel about 1½ lbs. of potatoes and slice them very thinly and evenly. Wash them in plenty of cold water. In a thick frying-pan heat a tablespoon of butter and one of oil (the mixture of butter and oil gives a good flavour, and the oil prevents the butter from burning).

Put the potatoes into the pan and spread them evenly; season with nutmeg, salt and ground black pepper; turn the heat down as soon as they start to cook, cover the pan and leave them cooking gently for 15 minutes; by this time the under surface will be browned and the potatoes coagulated in such a way as to form a pancake; turn the *galette* over and leave the other side to brown for 3 or 4 minutes; serve either turned out whole on to a flat dish or cut into quarters.

Les Epinards du Chanoine Chèvrier

This recipe was given by Jeanne Savarin in August 1905 in *La Cuisine des Familles*, a weekly magazine of the nineteen hundreds, published in Paris and sold for five centimes a copy.

" The Abbé Chèvrier, contemporary of my great-great-uncle, left a reputation in Bresse for being the perfect gourmet; he and Brillat-Savarin were the best friends in the world; the Abbé, however, did not always disclose his culinary secrets to Brillat-Savarin.

" Amongst other delectable things, Brillat-Savarin was excessively intrigued by the spinach cooked in butter of the Abbé Chèvrier. ' Nowhere,' he used to say, ' does one eat spinach, simple spinach cooked in butter, to compare with his. What can be the secret? ' Brillat-Savarin's mind was finally put at rest; he discovered the famous secret. Here it is.

" On Wednesday (for Sunday) choose your spinach, young leaves, neither too old nor in flower, of a good green and with their middle ribs. In the afternoon clean the spinach, removing the stalks, and wash it carefully. When it is tender, drain it in an enamel or china colander; drain out as much water as possible by pressing the leaves firmly down in the sieve; then chop them finely.

" Now put them into a pan (enamel or glazed earthenware) with some fine fresh butter and put on to a very low fire. For a pound of spinach allow ¼ lb. of butter. Let them cook gently for 30 minutes, then take them off the fire and let them cool in the same pan. They are not to be served today.

" *Thursday:* Add another 1½ ozs. of butter to the spinach, and cook again for 10–15 minutes over a very low fire; again leave them to get cold; they are not to be served yet.

" *Friday:* Exactly the same operation as the previous day;

the same quantity of butter, the same length of cooking. Do not be tempted.

" *Saturday:* Again the same operation as Thursday and Friday. Beware of temptation; the spinach will be giving out a wonderful aroma.

" *Sunday:* At last the day for your expected guests has arrived.

" A quarter of an hour before you intend serving the dinner, put the spinach again over a low flame, with two good ounces of butter, for 10–12 minutes. This time, take them out of their pan and put them in a warmed vegetable dish and serve them very hot.

" In the course of five daily cookings, your pound of spinach has absorbed 10½ ozs. of butter. Such was the Abbé Chèvrier's secret."

As well as the 10½ ozs. of butter the spinach has absorbed, it has also reduced to practically nothing. It is certain that the butter does give the spinach a most delicate flavour, but it is advisable to cook at least 2 or 3 lbs. if all this performance is to be gone through. The given amount of butter will still impart a good flavour to the spinach.

Endives au Beurre

These are the Belgian endives or chicory as they are sometimes called in England—the long smooth ones.

Do not cut or wash the endives, or they may turn bitter. Take off the outside leaves, and wipe the endives with a clean cloth. Put them into an earthenware or glass casserole, with 2 or 3 fair-sized pieces of butter, and cook them covered over a moderate flame, or in the oven.

Towards the end of the cooking the butter should be all used up and the endives tender and golden brown. At this stage add a little salt and a squeeze of lemon juice.

One of the best vegetables there is to eat as a separate course.

Braised Celery

Clean 2 or 3 heads of celery and cut each one in half length-ways. Blanch them in boiling water for 10 minutes. Drain them carefully, put them into a fireproof dish with 1 or 2 ozs. of butter, cover the pan and cook slowly until they are tender. 5 minutes before serving add, if possible, 2 tablespoons of meat glaze, which makes all the difference to this dish.

Turnips

It seems a pity that childhood prejudices should have almost banned turnips from our tables. Small young turnips are the most delicious of vegetables, and presumably there *are* people who appreciate them in England, for during their brief youth they cost nearly as much as a hot-house peach.

An excellent soup is made from a purée of turnips, and small dice of cooked turnips are an indispensable ingredient of Russian salad, to counteract the sweetness of carrots and green peas. In Greece baby turnips are cut into quarters and eaten raw, with salt, as a *Mézé*; but for this they must be fresh from the garden. The Egyptian Arabs make a pickle of turnips, done in vinegar and beetroot juice to make them pink.

Duck cooked with turnips is one of the classic dishes of the French Cuisine Bourgeoise. Perhaps the best way of all is glazed turnips, either as a separate vegetable or to accompany a steak, or roast beef, or pork.

Navets Glacés

Put small, whole, peeled turnips (as nearly as possible the same size) into boiling salted water and cook them for 10–15 minutes, until they are nearly ready. Drain them, put them into a small buttered dish which will bear the heat of the flame, sprinkle them with castor sugar, put more butter on the top and 2 or 3 tablespoons of the water in which they have cooked, and put the dish on a very low fire until the sauce turns brown and slightly sticky. Watch carefully to see that it doesn't burn. Spoon a little of the glaze over each turnip and serve as they are, in the same dish.

Mushrooms in Cream

My sisters and I had a Nanny who used to make these for us over the nursery fire, with mushrooms which we had gathered ourselves in the early morning. I don't suppose they will ever taste quite the same, for the sensations of childhood food elude us in later years—but as a recompense nothing will surely ever taste so hateful as nursery tapioca, or the appalling boiled cod of schooldays.

In the days when cream was plentiful (and nothing but fresh, thick cream will do), I experimented often with this mushroom dish, and the best way of doing it is this:

For four people you must have 1 lb. of mushrooms, and they must be medium-sized, white, button mushrooms, perfectly fresh from the fields. Do not wash or peel them, but carefully rub each one with a clean cloth, and take off the stalks. Put about a teacup of water into a pan and bring it to the boil; add a teaspoon of salt. Put the mushrooms in and cook them for 3 or 4 minutes.

In the meantime, heat your cream, 8 to 10 ozs. (10 ozs. is ½ pint) in a small pan, and as it cooks it will reduce and get thicker. Now strain the water off the mushrooms, put the mushrooms back in their pan, and pour the hot cream over them. Cook for 2 or 3 more minutes and serve immediately, extremely hot, on hot plates, in solitary splendour. To have anything else with them would be absurd, but see that there is a pepper-mill on the table, as you cannot add pepper while they are cooking for fear of spoiling the look of the dish.

Grilled Mushrooms

For grilling, the large flat mushrooms are best. Wash them, remove the stalks, and put them on a dish sprinkled with a little salt. This brings out the flavour. Put them into a flat, buttered dish, stalk side up, with a small piece of butter in the centre of each mushroom and grill them gently for about 10 minutes, basting now and again with the butter and adding more if they are beginning to look dry.

Mushrooms, especially field mushrooms, are at their best cooked this way, either alone, with grilled bacon, with steak, or with roast pork.

Champignons Cévenols

Clean 1 lb. of medium-sized mushrooms by wiping them with a clean cloth; put aside the stalks. In a thick pan warm some olive oil, enough to allow the mushrooms to cook comfortably without actually frying. The mushrooms should be put in when the oil is warm, not smoking, and cooked gently for 10 minutes.

Remove them with a draining spoon on to a dish, then in the same oil sauté the stalks cut into small pieces; spread these over the mushrooms, adding a sprinkle of finely chopped garlic and parsley. Still into the same oil throw a handful of fresh white breadcrumbs, and when these are golden, pour oil and breadcrumbs over the mushrooms.

Serve the dish cold the following day; if carefully cooked, without the oil having been overheated, they will be excellent.

Truffles

Most French gastronomic writers make a great to-do about truffles; and they are indeed a most remarkable fungus, imparting their delicate flavour to terrines of *foie gras*, stuffed capons and turkeys, fillets of beef, omelettes, and fine sauces; towards the end of the nineteenth century and until 1914, however, their use in what was regarded as *Haute Cuisine* became ridiculously excessive, and no dish was considered really refined without a garnish of sliced truffle; more often than not this garnish consisted of parsimonious slices of inferior truffles (there are several varieties, and not all of them have the fine flavour of *truffes du Périgord*) added after the dish was cooked and having scarcely any taste at all. The fact is that the most valuable property of the truffle is its capacity to flavour any dish in which it is cooked for some time with its perfume; the truffle itself then loses the greater part of its virtue, having given it to the sauce; it follows that the cutting up of an already cooked truffle, particularly a tinned one, which is the only way we ever get them in England, to decorate a dish, is an expensive and fairly pointless pastime.

Fresh truffles, cooked by themselves, in a sealed terrine with Madeira or champagne, or in a closed crust in the ashes of a wood fire are very delicious, but none of their flavour must be allowed to escape during the cooking. The recipe for cooking them in bacon will be of academic interest only to English readers, except perhaps for a few, fortunate enough to be able to bring them back from France. It is said that one of the most exquisite ways of enjoying their flavour is to leave fresh truffles overnight in a basket of new-laid eggs; next day the eggs, when eaten lightly boiled, will be found to have absorbed the aroma of the truffles.

Les Truffes au Lard

" This recipe is best carried out over a wood fire. The truffles are peeled, salted, and each one is wrapped up in a rasher of bacon which is also lightly salted. Wrap each truffle up in an oiled paper, then in another and yet another. In front of the fire arrange a heap of embers, and on this put the little packets of truffles and cover them with more embers, and a few small branches on the top. Leave them to cook for about half an hour.

"Remove the paper and put the truffles on a dish with their bacon. They will give off an exquisite aroma, perfuming the air of the dining-room and leading the guests into the sin of greed. Tasting them, it is hard to decide which is the better, the bacon, which has absorbed the flavour of the truffle, or the truffle impregnated with the fat of the bacon. . . .

"They may be cooked in the oven in the same way, but they will not be quite so good."

La France Gastronomique.

Aubergines en Gigot

A recipe from the Catalan coast of France, and perhaps the very best way of eating aubergines.

In each whole, unpeeled aubergine, make two rows of small incisions; into these put alternatively small pieces of bacon and cloves of garlic which have been rolled in salt, pepper and herbs, either marjoram or basil.

Put the aubergines in a roasting dish with a little oil poured over them, cover the dish and roast them in a slow oven for about 1 hour.

To be served as a separate course. They are also very good cold, split open, salted, and with a little fresh oil poured over.

Les Châtaignes au Lard

Score the chestnuts across on the round side and roast them in a low oven for 15 minutes until both shell and skin can be peeled off. For 2 lbs. of chestnuts put $\frac{1}{4}$ lb. of bacon cut in pieces into a casserole, add the chestnuts and water to cover. Cook for about 30 minutes.

Serve with turkey, roast hare, or as a separate dish.

Purée of Chestnuts

Make a small incision in each chestnut and put them into a tin in a moderate oven for about 20 minutes, when both the skins should peel off fairly easily. Put the peeled chestnuts into an earthenware pot with water to cover and a little pepper, and cook them very slowly either in the oven or on top of the stove for about 1½ hours, until they are soft enough to put through a sieve.

To serve, heat the purée with a lump of butter, a little cream if possible, and a ladle of meat or game stock.

Paillettes d'Oignons Frits

Slice large onions into very fine rings. Put them into a bowl containing a little milk, then on to a paper on which you have spread a coating of flour. Fry them in very hot olive oil or dripping. As soon as they are golden and crisp, drain them and serve them with freshly ground *gros sel*.

Roast Onions

Put medium-sized onions, unpeeled, into a roasting pan. Cook them in a moderate oven, in the same way as baked potatoes, for about 2–2½ hours. The skins then come off, and the onion inside is delicious and full of flavour, to be eaten with salt, pepper and butter.

They are also good cold, as an hors-d'œuvre, with a little oil dressing poured over.

Concombres à la Crème

Cut peeled cucumbers into fingers and steam them, seasoned with salt, pepper and chopped mint. Prepare a *liaison* of butter and flour with a little milk or cream and stir in the cucumbers when they are cooked.

Topinambours en Daube

In a little oil or beef dripping brown a sliced onion, sprinkle in a tablespoon of flour and stir until it is golden; add a small glass of white wine or cider, let it bubble, then put in 1 lb. or so of small peeled Jerusalem artichokes, salt, a crushed clove of garlic, a scraping of nutmeg, black pepper, and water just to cover. Simmer until the artichokes are cooked, taking care they don't turn to purée. Before serving stir in a good tablespoon of chopped parsley.

Les Topinambours à la Provençale

Boil the artichokes in salted water, straining them before they are quite cooked. Cut them in halves and sauté them gently in a little olive oil with 2 or 3 tomatoes cut up, a chopped clove of garlic, and chives and parsley.

Haricots à la Gasconne

Put 1 lb. of haricot beans, of the large variety called butter beans, to soak overnight.

Strain the water off and put them into an earthenware pot with several pieces of fresh pork rind, a little salt and water to cover. Cover the pot and cook them in a slow oven (Regulo 3) for about 3 hours, when they should be quite tender.

With a perforated spoon take them out and put them into a heated dish in which you have melted a tablespoon or so of *Beurre de Gascogne* (p. 195), sprinkle a little parsley or chives on the top and serve them either separately, with a stew such as the *Daube Avignonnaise* (p. 109), or with bacon.

La Courge au Gratin

In slightly salted water cook a piece of pumpkin weighing about 1 lb. Put the pulp through a sieve and then into a pan in which you have melted 1 oz. of butter; add $\frac{1}{2}$ cup of milk, a whole egg and the yolk of another; season with salt, pepper and nutmeg; stir in the beaten white of the egg and put the dish in a very hot oven, with small pieces of butter on the top, to brown. Leave it in for 5 minutes only.

SALADS

Tomates Provençales en Salade

Take the stalks off a large bunch of parsley; pound it with a little salt, in a mortar, with 2 cloves of garlic, and a little olive oil.

Cut the tops off good raw tomatoes; with a teaspoon soften the pulp inside, sprinkle with salt and turn them upside down so that the water drains out. Fill the tomatoes up with the parsley and garlic mixture. Serve them after an hour or two, when the flavour of the garlic and parsley has permeated the salad.

Tomato Salad with Cream

Put the required number of whole tomatoes into boiling water to remove the skins. Arrange them in a shallow salad bowl or silver dish.

Pour over them a dressing consisting simply of thick fresh cream into which is stirred a little salt and a tablespoon of chopped tarragon or fresh sweet basil.

A splendid accompaniment for a cold or, for that matter, a hot chicken.

Salade Armènienne

You will need $\frac{1}{2}$ lb. of mushrooms, a couple of rashers of bacon, garlic, parsley, pimentos, celery, olive oil and a glass of wine. Slice the mushrooms, sauté them in 2 tablespoons of oil, add a few very fine slivers of garlic, and the bacon cut in squares.

Let this cook a few minutes before pouring in a large glass of red wine; cook fiercely for just 1 minute, then turn the flame low and simmer for 5 more minutes. Stir in a handful of chopped parsley. Leave this preparation to cool.

In the meantime, fill a shallow salad bowl with sliced pimento and celery, dressed with oil and a drop of tarragon vinegar. When the mushroom mixture is cold, pile it on the top. Keep it cool, but don't spoil the flavour by putting it in the icebox.

Iced Cucumbers

A pleasant way of serving cucumbers is to have a bowl in front of each place containing salted iced water, a few cubes of ice, slices of peeled cucumbers cut lengthways, and a few cut leaves of mint. This treatment makes the cucumbers deliciously cool and crisp.

Carottes Marinées

Prepare a marinade of ⅓ pint each of water, wine vinegar, and white wine (or cider), a teaspoon of salt and a teaspoon of sugar, a sprig each of parsley and thyme, and a bayleaf, a small clove of garlic crushed, a pinch of Cayenne pepper and 8 tablespoons of olive oil.

Bring the marinade to the boil and throw in 1 lb. of young carrots cleaned and cut in halves, or quarters if they are large. Let them boil fairly fast until they are cooked, but not too soft. Drain them, and mix about a dessertspoon of French mustard into the marinade. Pour this over the carrots and leave them to cool.

Serve them cold either as hors-d'œuvre or salad. They can be prepared 2 or 3 days in advance.

Boeuf en Salade

To use up a piece of cold spiced beef or *Boeuf à la Mode*, or beef from an *Estouffat*.

At the bottom of a salad bowl put a layer of sliced tomatoes, seasoning them with salt and pepper, then a layer of small slices of beef, then a layer of cooked potatoes, also seasoned with salt and pepper. Pour over a *Vinaigrette* dressing (oil, tarragon or wine vinegar, French mustard, a little sugar, capers, chopped chives, parsley and lemon peel).

Garnish the salad with quarters of hard-boiled egg.

Fennel Salad

The raw fennel roots are washed and cut into small strips, dressed with oil and lemon juice, preferably 2 or 3 hours before serving.

Orange and Celery Salad

Inch-long pieces of celery and quarters of orange, with a very little dressing of oil and lemon. Especially good to accompany a terrine of hare or rabbit.

Salade de l'Ile Barbe

1 lb. potatoes cooked in their skins, peeled and cut in slices, 2 cooked red or green sweet peppers in strips, 2 ozs. ham cut in dice, 1 lobster or crawfish tail cut into rounds, a few rounds of truffle, and a few olives.

Mix all together, seasoned with olive oil, salt, pepper and lemon juice. The truffles can be replaced by a few blanched mushrooms, cut across in thin slices.

A very attractive salad, to be eaten as a separate course.

Salade Japonaise

This fantasy is the recipe given by Alexandre Dumas *fils* in his play *Françillon*. Without taking it too seriously, the combination of mussels and potatoes with white wine and herbs in the dressing produces an excellent salad.

Cook some potatoes in a meat stock, cut them in slices, and while they are still warm season them with salt, pepper, fine olive oil, Orléans vinegar, and, if possible, half a glass of Chateau Yquem. Chop very finely a large handful of fresh herbs.

In the meantime, cook some large mussels (a third of the quantity of potatoes) in a *court-bouillon* of white wine and water to which you have added a stick of celery; drain the mussels, take them out of their shells and add them to the potatoes. Mix all the ingredients lightly.

When the salad is ready, cover it with a layer of sliced truffles which have been cooked in champagne. The salad must be made 2 hours before serving.

Salad of Lettuce Hearts with Melted Butter

Use only the tenderest of lettuce hearts for this exquisite salad; arrange them in a salad bowl, season them very lightly with salt and a scrape of sugar, and at the last moment pour over them warm melted butter into which you have pounded a very small piece of garlic and a squeeze of lemon juice.

La Salade au Chapon

A *chapon* is a piece of bread or toast rubbed with garlic sprinkled with olive oil, and placed at the bottom of the salad bowl. The salad, lettuce, curly endive, or dandelion, is put on the top of the *chapon*, and mixed with the dressing in the usual way. For those who like garlic it is one of the most delicious of salads. Rubbed on bread, garlic retains its full flavour and wonderfully permeates the whole dish.

Les Cerneaux au Verjus

An hors-d'œuvre from Touraine, made with green walnuts.

Cut the walnuts in half and take them out of their green skins. Put them into a bowl and cover them with the juice of white grapes, pressed through a sieve; season with a little pepper and a finely chopped shallot; leave them to marinate at least 1 hour before serving.

SWEETS

Gâteau de Marrons

Roast about 2½ lbs. of scored chestnuts for 20 minutes in a slow oven, so that both the shell and skin will peel easily. Finish cooking them in water to cover, strain them and put them through a sieve.

To this purée add about ¼ pint of milk, 2 ozs. sugar and 1 oz. of brandy. Fold in the beaten white of 6 eggs. Prepare a caramel of ¼ lb. of sugar with 3 tablespoons of water, and coat the bottom and the sides of a cake tin with it. Pour in the chestnut mixture and cook it in a moderate oven for 1 hour. When it is cold, turn it out and serve it with cream.

Gâteau de Marrons au Chocolat

Cook 2½ lbs. of chestnuts as in the previous recipe and put them through a sieve.

Melt ¼ lb. of chocolate in a very little water or black coffee, stir in ¼ lb. of butter and ¼ lb. of sugar, timing this operation so that the chestnut purée is still warm, and stir the two mixtures together. Pour it into an oiled cake tin, square for preference, and leave it on the refrigerator or in a cold place for 24 hours. Turn it out on to the serving dish.

As this sweet is rather rich, a small amount, with cream separately, is enough for most people. Half quantities work out quite successfully.

Marrons à la Lyonnaise

Make a purée from 1 lb. of skinned chestnuts (start off with about 1½ lbs.), cooked in very slightly salted water to which you have added 1 or 2 cloves. Add to the purée 4–6 ozs. of sugar (according to how sweet you like the chestnuts), 3 ozs. of butter, 3 yolks of eggs, and finally the whites of the eggs stiffly beaten. A little brandy or rum (added before the whites of eggs) will do no harm.

Pour the mixture into a cake tin and cook for about 40 minutes in a moderate oven. When cold, turn it out, and serve with cream.

This is a very filling sweet, and, although it does not look very large, this amount is ample for eight people.

Coffee Chestnuts

For four people you need about 36 shelled and skinned chestnuts. Put them in a pan with enough water to cover and 2 tablespoons of sugar. Simmer until they are soft.

In another pan (preferably a double saucepan) put the yolks of 2 eggs, a tablespoon of sugar, a teacup of strong black coffee, 2 tablespoons of cream or top of the milk and a liqueur glass of rum. Stir the sauce over a low flame until it thickens and pour it over the strained chestnuts in a silver dish.

Lemon Soufflé (1)

3 yolks of eggs, 4 whites, 1 lemon (juice and rind), 1½ ozs. plain flour, 1 breakfast-cup milk, 2 tablespoons castor sugar, 2 ozs. butter.

Melt the butter, stir in the flour, cook until it is smooth, then add the warmed milk and cook again until you have a smooth white sauce. Add the sugar, the grated rind, the 3 yolks, stir off the fire, then add the lemon juice. When it is cool fold in the beaten whites.

Pour it into a buttered soufflé dish, with a buttered paper band round the top, and cook for about 15 minutes in a Regulo 6 or 7 oven.

Lemon Soufflé (2)

4 eggs, 3 tablespoons castor sugar, the juice and rind of one lemon.

Beat the yolks of the eggs with the sugar, the grated rind of the lemon and the juice, for several minutes. Whip the whites and fold them in. Pour into a buttered soufflé dish and cook for 10–12 minutes in a medium–hot oven.

Soufflés made without the addition of flour are very light and creamy, but the whole operation should be performed with speed, and, as already explained on p. 64, the exact heat of the oven and the timing can only be learnt by experience.

Omelette Soufflé au Grand Marnier

For two people you need 3 eggs, 2 tablespoons of sugar, a sherry glass of Grand Marnier, butter.

Separate the eggs; into the yolks stir the sugar and the Grand Marnier, amalgamating them well. Beat the whites very stiffly.

In the meantime heat a ten- or twelve-inch omelette pan, and have your hot plates and a hot omelette dish in readiness.

Now fold the whites into the yolks, put a small nut of butter in the pan—if the frying-pan is properly heated it will melt instantly. Quickly pour in the egg mixture and give the pan a shake. The outer surface next to the pan will brown at once and the rest puff up. Now take your omelette dish in one hand and the pan in the other, and, holding the pan close to the dish, slide the omelette out, folding it over once as you do so.

An omelette soufflé must be eaten immediately, while it is still frothy and creamy, and as it has only been cooking *one minute* it will soon be cold.

Don't attempt to make more than the quantity given in one pan; for four people double the mixture and make 2 omelettes.

Buttered Apples

One of the nicest and simplest ways of serving apples. Bramleys are best as they turn fluffy when cooked. Put the sliced and peeled apples into a fireproof dish. For 1 lb. of apples put 1 oz. of butter cut in pieces on the top, 2 tablespoons of brown sugar, and a piece of lemon peel.

Put the dish uncovered, and without any water, into the top of a medium oven, for about 30 minutes. Have a look at them from time to time and turn them over so that all get equally cooked.

They are nice hot or cold, for an open tart or for the filling of an omelette soufflé.

Gouère aux Pommes

A country sweet from the Berry district of France.

Peel and slice a pound of apples, and put them in a dish with a little sugar and 2 tablespoons of brandy.

Make a batter with ½ lb. of flour, 2 eggs, a pinch of salt, 3 tablespoons of sugar and a tumbler of milk.

Stir the apples into the batter and pour it into a shallow buttered tin and cook for 45 minutes in a moderate oven.

Apples in Cider

Peel and slice 2 lbs. of apples. Put them into a fireproof dish with brown sugar, the amount depending on what apples are being used. Add cider to about a third of the height of the apples.

Cover the dish with a buttered paper and cook for about 30 minutes in a moderate oven; at the end of this time baste the apples with the cider and leave a little longer without the paper, so that the top will get lightly browned. These apples are very good hot or cold.

Jacques

(These pancakes are a speciality of the country districts of Périgord.)

¼ lb. flour, 1 gill milk, 1 dessertspoon olive oil, a pinch of salt, 1 teaspoon sugar, ½ glass water, 2 eggs, 2 or 3 apples.

Make a pancake batter with the flour, oil, salt, milk, water and eggs; stir it very well, then let it rest for several hours.

Peel the apples and cut them in very thin slices; sprinkle a little castor sugar over them and a squeeze of lemon juice. Heat a small, thick frying-pan and coat with a thin film of oil or butter; drop in a tablespoon of the batter and let it spread out as much as possible; on top of the pancake place 2 slices of apple, cover them with a little more of the batter and turn the pancake over; let it cook a little longer than the ordinary pancake on account of the apples; the pancakes are served flat, sprinkled with sugar, and, of course, as quickly as possible. The apples can be soaked in a little rum or brandy should it be available.

Apricot Compôte

Apricots are exquisite to eat raw when they are slightly overripe, sun warmed and straight off the tree. Otherwise they gain by being cooked, and this *compôte* brings out their slightly smoky, delicious flavour.

Halve the apricots and take out the stones. Cook them gently with water half-way to covering them and about ¼ lb. of sugar to 2 lbs. of apricots. Watch them to see that they do not dissolve into a purée. Take the apricots out of the pan and put them into a dish. Reduce the remaining syrup until it is thick, then pour it over the apricots.

Serve cold. Cream is unnecessary; it would disguise the taste of the apricots.

Chocolate Mousse

1 egg per person, 1 oz. plain or vanilla chocolate per person.

Melt the chocolate in a thick pan over a low flame with a tablespoon of water. A tablespoon of rum added will do no harm. Stir the chocolate until it is smooth. Separate the eggs and beat the yolks. Stir the melted chocolate into the yolks.

Whip the whites very stiffly and fold them over and over into the chocolate, so that they are perfectly blended, or the chocolate may sink to the bottom. Put the mousse into a soufflé dish so that the mixture just about comes to the top (nothing is sadder than a small amount of mousse hiding at the bottom of a huge glass bowl) and leave it in a cool place to set. Unless in a hurry, don't put it on the ice, as this tends to make it too hard.

Instead of water, the chocolate can be melted in a tablespoon of black coffee.

Saint Emilion au Chocolat

¼ lb. butter, ¼ lb. sugar, 1 egg, ½ lb. chocolate, 1 teacup milk, 12 to 16 macaroons.

Cream the butter and the sugar until they are well amalgamated. Scald the milk and let it cool, then mix it with the yolk of the egg. Melt the chocolate over the fire, with a very little water, then stir in the milk and egg mixture, then the butter and sugar. Stir this cream carefully until it is absolutely smooth.

In a soufflé dish arrange a layer of macaroons, soaked in a little rum or brandy; over these pour a layer of the chocolate cream, then put another layer of macaroons and so on until the dish is full, finishing with macaroons. Leave the dish in a cold place for at least 12 hours.

Honey and Hazel Nut Cake

This is not really a cake, but a kind of soufflé eaten cold, a Périgordine speciality.

Put $\frac{1}{2}$ lb. of honey in a jar in a saucepan of hot water so that it is easy to manipulate. Pour it over 5 or 6 yolks of eggs beaten in a large bowl; add gradually a teacup of sifted flour and a teacup of hazel nuts pounded in a mortar with a little castor sugar; bind the mixture either with a little milk or cream (about $\frac{1}{2}$ cup) or the equivalent amount of butter.

Lastly, add the beaten whites of the eggs, and pour the whole mixture into a buttered cake tin or soufflé dish, and cook it for 40 minutes in a moderate oven. When cold, turn the cake out.

It is also excellent made with walnuts instead of hazel nuts.

Caramel Rice

This sweet is inspired by the famous *Crème Brûlée*, one of the loveliest sweets in the world, made with eggs and cream, and burnt sugar on the top. There is no possible substitute for it, but Caramel Rice makes a pleasant, attractive finish to a simple luncheon or dinner.

For four people you need:

1 teacup rice, 1 pint milk, 1 vanilla pod or a large piece of lemon peel, 4 ozs. cream, 6 ozs. sugar, the juice of a lemon or an orange, 2 ozs. candied peel.

Put the milk in the top half of a double saucepan, and put in the rice, 4 tablespoons of sugar and the vanilla pod or the lemon peel. Cover the pan and simmer until the rice is cooked; this takes $1\frac{1}{2}$–2 hours, at the end of which time the rice should have absorbed nearly all the milk and be very creamy without being a cloggy mass. Turn the rice into a soufflé dish, add the lemon or orange juice, and the cream which should be fairly thick, and the finely chopped candied peel. Chill this mixture thoroughly.

Now spread on the top of the rice a layer of sugar about a quarter of an inch thick. Have the grill already hot and put the dish underneath it, fairly close to the heat. In about 2 minutes or even less the sugar will have turned to toffee on the top; the surface should be even and smooth, but with a gas grill this is not very easy. Turn off the grill the second the sugar looks set, as it burns in no time. Serve very cold.

Croûtes aux Prunes

Not exactly a dish for a grand party, but, all the same, an excellent countrified sweet.

For each person cut 1 or 2 slices of new bread into slices, half an inch thick, leaving on the crust. Butter them on one side, and on this side put 5 or 6 half raw plums, stoned, pressing them down and into the bread with a knife; put a little butter and brown sugar into each half plum, and put the slices into a generously buttered fireproof dish, plum side up; put them into a moderate oven (Regulo 4) near the top, with a piece of buttered paper over them, and in about 30 minutes the bread will be golden and crisp and the plums cooked with a coating of sugary syrup on the top.

Apricots can be cooked in the same way with good results.

Tourte de Citrouille

1 lb. pumpkin, 2 ozs. sugar, 1 teacup fresh cream, 20 prunes, 2 ozs. butter.

Cook the pumpkin in the butter until reduced to a purée. Add the soaked and stoned prunes, the cream and sugar, and keep aside. Make a short crust with ½ lb. of flour, ¼ lb. of butter, a pinch of salt and a little milk. Leave to rest 2 hours.

Roll out and cut two rounds the size of the piedish. Line the tin with one round, put in the pumpkin mixture, cover with the second round of pastry. Cook in a fairly fast oven to start with, turning it down after about 10 minutes.

Les Crémets d'Angers

For every ½ pint (10 ozs.) of fresh cream, allow the whites of 2 eggs; whip the cream until it is stiff, then whip the whites of eggs separately. Mix the two together gently. Pour it into little baskets lined with muslin and leave them to drain in a cool place overnight.

Serve them turned out in a bowl, with fresh liquid cream poured over, and a bowl of sugar separately.

La Tarte au Petit Suisse

Make a paste with 6 ozs. of flour, 4 ozs. of butter, an egg, 3 tablespoons of sugar and a pinch of salt. Work the paste as little as possible, and roll it out on a clean floured cloth to the size of the pastry tin; the pastry breaks easily, so turn the cloth gently upside down on to the tin. Fill it with beans, and bake it in a moderate oven (Regulo 4) for 20 minutes. This makes a very crisp pastry, but the sugar in it is apt to burn, so it is advisable to cover the edges of the pastry with a buttered paper; it will brown during the second cooking with the filling.

In the meantime pound 6 ozs. of Petit Suisse (Pommel) or Demi-Sel (Gervais) cheeses with ½ teacup of cream or milk, 2 yolks of eggs, 4 tablespoons of sugar, a teaspoon of orange-flower water or grated orange peel, and, lastly, the whites of eggs beaten to a stiff froth. Spread the mixture on the cooked pastry, put it in a moderate oven (Regulo 4) for 15–20 minutes.

A beautiful golden crust should form on the top, but look at it from time to time to see that it does not burn.

To be eaten cold.

Tourteau Fromagé

Make a pastry with ½ lb. of flour, 4 ozs. of butter, an egg and a pinch of salt. Knead it with a little water and leave it to rest 1 or 2 hours.

Mix together 6 ozs. of fresh cream cheese (in Poitou, where this recipe comes from, they use goat's cheese; home made milk cheese or *Petit Gervais* will do), 3 eggs, 4 ozs. of sugar, 2 tablespoons of cream (or top of the milk), and 2 tablespoons of chopped angelica.

Line the tart tin with the rolled-out pastry, fill it with the cheese mixture, and bake it in a slow oven (Regulo 4) for about 40 minutes.

To be eaten cold.

Raspberry and Redcurrant Tart

These flat open tarts are made on Sundays and fête days in a great many French households both in the towns and in the country. They are also to be bought in *patisseries*, of a better quality than anything we could buy ready-made in England. They are usually baked in a large shallow tin about ten inches across, and served cold. They are not difficult to make and are one of the nicest possible dessert dishes. The point to remember is that fruit which gives out a great deal of juice when cooking should be prepared first, the pastry also baked in advance. When the pastry is cooled it is filled with the fruit and put back in the oven for a few minutes. In this way the pastry does not become sodden with the juice of the fruit.

Make the pastry as described for the *Tarte au Petit Suisse* (p. 185), and bake it in the same way.

Put 1½ lbs. of raspberries and ½ lb. of redcurrants into a pan with 6 ozs. of white sugar and let them cook for a few minutes only; the fruit should not lose its shape. When the pastry has cooled, fill it with the fruit, strained, and put it in a moderate oven for 10 minutes.

To the juice of the fruit add a tablespoon of redcurrant jelly. Stir this mixture until it is a thick syrup and pour it over the fruit when this has cooled. It will give a fine glaze and a firm consistency. The quantities given will fill an oblong tin ten inches by eight, or a ten-inch round flan tin.

Tarte aux Pêches

This is made in the same way as the *Raspberry and Redcurrant Tart*, the peaches being skinned, sliced and very lightly stewed before being put into the cooked pastry. The syrup can be made in the same way, with the addition of a small glass of peach brandy.

Tarte aux Pommes

Make a crust as for the *Tourteau Fromagé* (p. 186), spread it on a buttered tart tin and make a few incisions here and there with a fork.

On top of the pastry arrange 2 lbs. of apples peeled and cut in fine slices, adding about 4 ozs. of white sugar in between the layers of apple. Bake in a moderate oven for 30 minutes.

The apples should be slightly browned on the surface and moist inside. A little syrup, made from the peel of the apples, sugar, and a flavouring of either lemon peel, brandy, *calvados*, or sweet cider, can be poured over to form a glaze when the tart has cooled.

Tarte aux Abricots

This is made in the same way as the Apple Tart above, the apricots being cut in half and stoned but not skinned.

Put a little sugar in each half apricot. Remember that the fruit shrinks considerably in the cooking, and if there seems to be too much to start with it is all to the good.

Stew a few extra apricots with a little sugar and water. Strain off the liquid, reduce it, and use this as a syrup for glazing the tart. If available, a few drops of kirsch or apricot brandy can be added.

SAUCES

Very few of the dishes described in this book need the addition of any elaborate sauce. Meat, chicken or game simmered in wine with vegetables, onions, herbs and garlic need no further adornment. For vegetables, good butter is nearly always the best accompaniment. Chicken and fish *veloutés*, lobster butter, and so on, belong rather to the methods of restaurant cooking and professional chefs than to country and household meals; nor are such sauces always an embellishment of the food with which they are served, although nobody would deny that plenty of fresh cream and butter help enormously in the preparation of good food.

Sauce Béarnaise and *Sauce Hollandaise* are classic and delicious accompaniments to grilled meat and fish; I have already described these in some detail in a previous book, so they are not repeated here. As, however, the *Sauce Bordelaise* for fillet of beef, and the *Sauce Bigarade* for roast duck, are both made on a foundation of *Espagnole*, I am giving an easily made version of this sauce, suitable for a small household. These recipes, with meat glaze, the brown and white *roux* given in this chapter, and various sauces explained at the same time as the dishes with which they are to be served (such as the *Beurre*

Blanc de Vouvray, or the sauce for roast saddle of hare on p. 148), should give plenty of ideas about the composition of simple sauces to anyone who is at all imaginative about food. Further explanations of the use of wine in sauces will be found in the chapter "Wine in the Kitchen".

It will be seen that only a very few of these regional recipes contain flour for the thickening of sauces; whenever possible the consistency should be achieved either by reduction, as explained for the meat glaze (another example is the *Coq au Vin*, p. 128), or with a *liaison* of egg yolks (after adding egg yolks to a sauce it must never be allowed to boil, unless there is flour in the sauce, or it will curdle). Cream should also be thickened by reduction (see *Sole au Vin Blanc*, p. 62).

When a sauce is to be made with a basis of a brown or white *roux*, it must cook for a minimum of 15 minutes, or it will taste of raw flour; and remember that flour should always be sieved before being added to a dish. When flour is used (as in the *Perdrix à la Catalane*) at the beginning of the cooking, the sauce has had plenty of time to absorb the flavours of the bird (or meat) and the wine and seasonings by the time the dish is ready to be eaten. When a sauce such as this seems too thin, don't panic and add a lot more flour at the last minute; let it thicken by fast boiling and reduction.

Brown and White Roux

A *roux* is simply the composition of butter and flour which is the basis of a great many sauces such as *Espagnole*, which is made with a brown *roux*, and *Béchamel*, made with white *roux*.

Melt 2 ozs. of butter in a small saucepan, and when it barely begins to bubble add 2 ozs. of sieved flour. Stir carefully over a gentle fire until the mixture amalgamates (2 or 3 minutes in the case of a white *roux*), when it is time to put in the milk or stock or whatever is to be the foundation of the sauce. For the brown *roux* the mixture is cooked about 5 minutes, stirring all the time until it takes on a nut colour; it must not burn, or it will have a bitter flavour. The quantities given will serve to thicken about 1 pint of sauce.

Meat Glaze

In the old days meat glaze or *glace de viande* was made with huge quantities of beef and veal and probably 2 chickens as well, the resulting stock being reduced until it was a thick jellied sauce; it was then stored for use. There is no doubt that a small quantity of meat glaze in the larder adds enormously to the joy of good cooking. To make certain sauces, added to the butter in which steaks or cutlets have been cooked, to a simple egg *en cocotte*, to glaze a piece of cold beef, a chicken or duck, for *salmis*, for vegetables such as celery, endive or baby turnips which have been braised in butter, a little meat glaze transmutes ordinary household dishes into the realm of fine cooking.

For a small family it is quite possible to make enough meat glaze to store for a few days without extravagance, and it is worth trying it now and again.

You will need 1–2 lbs. of stewing steak, shin of veal or marrow bones, a glass of red wine, 2 or 3 onions, garlic, herbs.

Fry the onions in dripping, then add the beef, in one piece, and brown on each side. Pour over the wine, let it bubble for 2 or 3 minutes and then pour in about 4 pints of water. Add the veal bones, the garlic, and the herbs, but no salt.

Simmer in a covered pan very slowly (this is best done in a low oven) for 6 or 7 hours. Strain the stock into a bowl and leave it to cool. The beef will not be wasted; it will make a good *Boeuf en Salade*, as described on p. 172.

When the fat has solidified, remove it from the stock, which should be jellied. Put the stock in a wide and shallow pan and simmer it until it starts to look syrupy and shiny—something like undiluted Bovril.

It can be stored in little jars with a layer of fat on the top and used as it is needed.

Salt is not added during the cooking, as the reducing process would make it too salty, so it can be added as you use the glaze.

Easily made Espagnole Sauce

Make a brown *roux* with 3 tablespoons of butter and 4 of flour; when this has cooked add gradually 2½–3 pints of very good beef stock, made as for the meat glaze already described, but not reduced.

Let this mixture simmer, stirring from time to time, for at least 1 hour, until it is well reduced. You then have a foundation on which to make the *Sauce Bordelaise* and the *Sauce Bigarade*, given in this chapter.

Sauce Bordelaise

Reduce a wineglass of white Bordeaux by half, with a pinch of black pepper and a finely chopped shallot.

Stir in ½ pint of *Espagnole Sauce* and let it bubble 5 minutes. Before serving add a tablespoon of chopped parsley.

Sauce Bigarade

Bigarade is the French name for bitter or Seville oranges. The sauce is made with a foundation of *Espagnole*.

Reduce ¾ pint of *Espagnole* to about ½ pint. In the meantime cut the peel of 2 Seville oranges into strips and put them into boiling water for 5 minutes. Drain them and add them to the sauce with the strained juice. Heat up gently.

Orange Sauce (a simpler way than the preceding recipe)

When you are going to serve orange sauce with a roast duck or pheasant, have ready the peel of an orange cut into fine strips and blanched 5 minutes in boiling water, and squeeze the juice of the orange.

When the duck is cooked take it out of the roasting pan and keep it hot on a fireproof dish in the oven. Pour the fat out of the roasting pan, and to the remaining juices in the pan add a small glass of port, Madeira or Malaga, or a little of the Burgundy you are going to drink with the duck. Let this bubble over a low flame a minute or two while you scrape the juices up and blend them with the wine. Now add a very little water, let it bubble again, and put in the orange peel and juice, and let it cook another minute.

The whole process does not take 5 minutes and can in fact be done while someone else is carving the duck. It is a thin sauce and does not need thickening of any kind.

Sauce Soubise

Cut up 2 lbs. of onions and cook them in boiling water for 20–30 minutes. Strain them, put them through a sieve, and stir this purée into half its volume of *béchamel* sauce, or thick cream; if to serve with game or poultry, some of the stock in which the bird has cooked is amalgamated into the sauce.

Sauce Madère

Slice an onion and a carrot finely, and put them in a pan with 1 oz. of butter. Let them melt slowly, then add ½ pint of water and a chopped tomato or a tablespoon of tomato purée, a dessertspoon of meat glaze or a small cube of *Maggi*,[1] a *bouquet garni* of parsley, thyme and bayleaf, and leave this to cook for 20 minutes.

[1] The best substitute for meat glaze or meat stock. It can be bought at large stores.

Now mix 3 teaspoons of flour with a small glass of water and pour it through a strainer into the sauce, stirring all the time. Cook until the sauce thickens and strain into a clean pan. Add a sherry glass of Madeira.

In a small frying-pan melt 2 ozs. of butter, let it just turn golden, but don't let it burn. Add this to the sauce—it gives a characteristic flavour.

Pestou

This is the garlic and basil butter added to soups and used as a sauce for *pasta* and for fish in the Nice district and in Genoa.

Two medium-sized cloves of garlic, 1½–2 ozs. of butter, about 6 sprigs of fresh basil, a pinch of salt, 2 tablespoons of Parmesan cheese.

Pound the garlic in a mortar, then add the basil, then the butter and the cheese.

It is also, of course, made with oil instead of butter with the addition of pine nuts and makes a sauce more like a thick purée.

To serve with *spaghetti* or *lasagne*, this version is better, but for *gnocchi à la romaine* (p. 87) it is best with butter.

Bouillade or All Grenat

This is the Catalan sauce in which snails are cooked in the Roussillon district, and also fish, making a kind of *Bouilla-baisse*.

In a tablespoon of olive oil and one of pork fat, sauté 2 or 3 chopped sweet red peppers; when they are soft add 4 or 5 cloves of garlic crushed with the point of a knife, and simmer 2 or 3 minutes. Pour over a small glass of white wine and let it reduce for 1 or 2 minutes; stir in a tablespoon of flour to bind the sauce and cook gently for 10 minutes, adding a little water if the sauce gets too thick.

Beurre de Gascogne

In a small pan of salted water boil about 6 cloves of garlic. Let them cook for 15 minutes, then strain them, pound them in a mortar and add 1 oz. or so of good dripping. In Gascony, of course, they use pork lard, but any good meat dripping will do. When the garlic and the dripping are well amalgamated, add a tablespoon of chopped parsley.

This sauce is stirred into cooked haricot beans, lentils, stewed mushrooms, aubergines, or can be added to soups before serving.

L'Aïllade Toulousaine

Pound 3 ozs. of skinned walnuts in a mortar with 2 or 3 cloves of garlic; season them with a little salt. Add drop by drop at first, and then more quickly, about 1 gill (5 ozs.) of olive oil, stirring until you have a thick sauce.

To be served as an hors-d'œuvre with fresh bread and raw celery to dip in the aïllade, or as a sauce with any cold meat. Goes particularly well with tongue.

PRESERVES

Redcurrant and Cherry Jam

Put 4 lbs. of redcurrants into a pan without any water and stir them over a gentle flame until the juice comes out. Strain through a muslin without pressing the fruit so that the juice is clear. There should be about 2 lbs. of juice.

For this amount stone 4 lbs. of cherries, and make a syrup with 6 lbs. of sugar and 3 glasses of water; put the cherries into the syrup and let it boil gently until the syrup sets when put on to a cold plate. Now add the redcurrant juice, let the whole mixture boil again, and the jam is ready to put into pots.

These jams made of mixed fruits are very much liked in France, and are often served, with fresh cream, as a dessert.

Water Melon and Orange Jam

Remove the seeds from a water melon and cut the flesh into squares; for 2 lbs. of fruit add $1\frac{1}{2}$ lbs. of sugar and leave this in a basin for 2 or 3 hours, then put it all into a pan and cook slowly for about 1 hour.

At the same time prepare enough oranges to give 2 lbs. when the skin and pips have been removed. Divide the

oranges in quarters, and put them, with the thin peel of
2 oranges cut into strips, into a syrup composed of 2 lbs.
of sugar and a tumbler of water; let this boil gently for 1
hour.

When the two jams are nearly cooked, mix them carefully
together, and boil for another 6 minutes before putting the
jam into pots. A slice or two of lemon can be added to the
water melon while it is cooking, and removed afterwards.

Le Confiture de Pastèque de la Dordogne

Peel the water melon, take out the pips and cut in thin
slices. Weigh the pulp, and for 10 lbs. add 8 lbs. of sugar.
Leave it to marinate in a bowl with 4 sticks of vanilla and 2
lemons cut in thin slices.

After 24 hours put it all into a preserving pan (removing
the vanilla), and cook very slowly for 8–10 hours. Before
taking the jam off the fire add a claret glass of rum. Let it boil
a few minutes before putting it into pots.

Cotignac Orléanais

Peel, core and slice 4 lbs. of quinces. Put them into a preserving pan with water not quite covering them. Bring them
to the boil and cook for 30 minutes. Strain them through
a muslin, pressing them so as to extract as much juice as
possible.

In the juice cook another 3 lbs. of quinces, peeled, sliced and
cored, and 1 lb. of oranges, skinned and quartered, with the
pips removed. Simmer for 1 hour, and put the mixture through
a sieve, so as to obtain a thick purée; weigh the purée, add an
equal quantity of sugar, return to the pan and cook until the
mixture begins to come away from the sides.

The *cotignac* can be stored in jars or tins.

Excellent eaten with soft cream cheese.

Prunes in Cherry Brandy

Into a large glass jar put a quantity of the best French prunes or Carlsbad plums. Pour over them some good cherry brandy. The next day pour in some more, as the plums will have absorbed the brandy; and so on for a day or two.

Finally cork it down for a fortnight or so, then serve at dessert. Refill the jar as the plums are eaten.

Cherries in Brandy

3 lbs. morello cherries, 1 bottle brandy, ½ lb. sugar.

Prepare the cherries, which must not be too ripe, by cutting the stalks, so that there is a small piece left in each cherry. Put them in wide jars, pour over the brandy and screw down the covers. Leave them for 6 weeks in a warm place (in France they are left in the sun).

At the end of this time strain off the brandy and mix it with a syrup prepared with the sugar and 2 or 3 tablespoons of water. Pour this back over the cherries through a muslin or a filter paper and leave them another fortnight before they are ready to eat.

Spiced Peaches

These are to serve with ham or with cold turkey. The proportions are 3 lbs. of ripe peaches, 1 lb. of castor sugar, ½ pint of water, 6 ozs. (just over ¼ pint) of Orléans or other white-wine vinegar, cloves, cinnamon, ginger.

Drop the peaches into boiling water for a few minutes, drain them, and peel off the skin, which comes off very easily if the peaches are ripe. Stick a clove into each peach.

Make a syrup of the water and sugar and add a half teaspoon each of ground cinnamon and ginger. Put the peaches in and cook for 10 minutes, then leave to cool. After a few hours drain off the syrup, put it back in the pan and add the vinegar, bring to the boil and simmer for 20 minutes, add the peaches again and simmer until they are just tender, by which time the syrup should have thickened. Leave the peaches to stand overnight in the syrup.

Next day pack them into jars, reheat the syrup and pour it over the peaches. They will keep a long time, but once a jar has been opened it is advisable to keep it in the ice-box.

Olives

Both black and green olives are best bought loose, whenever possible, and stored in jars, covered with olive oil. Small olives are usually better than large ones.

SUMMER COOKING

SUMMER COOKING

by

ELIZABETH DAVID

CONTENTS

INTRODUCTION

BY summer cookery I do not necessarily mean cold food; although cold dishes are always agreeable in summer at most meals, however hot the weather, one hot dish is welcome, but it should be a light one, such as a very simply cooked sole, an omelette, a soup of the young vegetables which are in season—something fresh which provides at the same time a change, a new outlook. . . . My object in writing this book has been to provide recipes for just such dishes, with emphasis on two aspects of cookery which are increasingly disregarded: the suitability of certain foods to certain times of the year, and the pleasure of eating the vegetables, fruits, poultry, meat or fish which is in season, therefore at its best, most plentiful, and cheapest.

A couple of years ago an advocate of the tin and the deep freeze wrote to a Sunday newspaper explaining that frozen or tinned vegetables were better than fresh ones, as the "pick of the crop" goes straight to the factories to be frozen or tinned. Can this be a matter for congratulation? I am not unappreciative of modern marvels, and in its way the deep freeze is an admirable invention, particularly for the United States, where fresh produce has to be transported great distances. Some foods, game, for example, stand up remarkably well to the freezing process, but let us not pretend that frozen green peas and broad beans, strawberries, raspberries, and blackberries are as "good as fresh". They may indeed be quite adequate, and are an incontestable blessing to people pressed for time or space, or having to provide meals at very short notice, but is it necessary for those not in such circumstances to eat all this food out of season? Frozen peas seem to have become the almost obligatory accompaniment to every meal, whether in private houses or restaurants; yet how often during the season of fresh peas, which is quite a long one, do we get a dish of those really delicate, fresh, sugary green peas? Is it because the "pick of the crop" has gone to the factory instead of to the market and we are therefore unable to buy them, or is it because people no longer know how to shell them and cook them and have forgotten what they taste like?

The deep freeze appears to have gained over the minds of the English housewife and restaurant keeper a hypnotic power such as never was exercised by the canning factories. Even leaving out of consideration the fact that the pleasure of rediscovering each season's vegetables and fruits at the appropriate time is thereby quite blunted, this method of marketing seems to me an extravagant one.

As I write, there are lovely little South African pineapples in the greengrocer's down the road for 1s. 6d. each, sweet, juicy oranges at seven for a shilling, yet people are crowding round the deep freeze in the same shop paying four times as much for a few strawberries in a cardboard packet. As soon as strawberries and raspberries are in season they will be clamouring for frozen pineapple and cartons of orange juice.

Then there are those people who in restaurants insist upon ordering a certain dish although some essential ingredient is not in season, and then complain that the truffles were tinned, or the *sole Véronique* made with the wrong kind of grapes. In a London restaurant which claims to serve Provençal food I found Ratatouille on the menu in February. Upon inquiring how this could be when there are neither pimentos nor aubergines nor courgettes at this time of year I was informed that it was made with cabbage and tomatoes. The fact that restaurant keepers can and do rely upon the ignorance of the customers is to blame for these absurdities.

Almost as perverse a situation seems to prevail in the choice of suitable dishes for the time of year; anyone who has spent a summer in India will remember the famous New Delhi hotel where oxtail soup, Irish stew and treacle pudding as well as all the routine curries were served all through the summer, with the temperature round about 110 degrees. "Turtle Soup, plum pudding and champagne for an August Sunday luncheon in a seaside villa would be to say the least, incongruous, but have been experienced," writes Lady Jekyll in *Kitchen Essays*.[1] This was in 1922, before ice cream all the winter and frozen game all summer had become a matter of routine and it is hardly surprising that inexperienced cooks and hostesses do not stop to think whether a cassoulet of haricot beans,

[1] Nelson. 1922.

sausages, pork, and bacon, or an enormous dish of *choucroûte garnie* are suitable for a hot summer evening. It would be absurd to pretend that there are not a good many summer days in England when such dishes would be welcome barriers against the cold, but I still think it is rather dull to eat the same food all the year round; these heavy foods should be kept for the winter, and cooler, lighter dishes served in the summer; dishes which bring some savour of the garden, the fields, the sea, into the kitchen and the dining room. It is this kind of food, as well as methods of dealing with the fruits and vegetables and herbs of summer in a manner in which their freshness and flavour may be best appreciated, which I have tried to describe in this book. I have also given a few suggestions and recipes for summer occasions such as picnics and outdoor parties, and for presenting those foods available all the year round in ways appropriate to spring and summer.

ACKNOWLEDGMENTS

I AM indebted to Messrs. Methuen & Co., and to Messrs. Constable & Co., for permission to quote passages from T. Earle Welby's *The Dinner Knell* and from Logan Pearsall Smith's *All Trivia* respectively. The editor and publishers of *Harpers Bazaar* have kindly allowed me to reproduce recipes originally published by them, and Messrs. Evans Brothers a recipe which first appeared in *The Traveller's Year* by Elizabeth Nicholas. One recipe has been reproduced from my own *Italian Food*, published by Messrs. Macdonald & Co.

N.B. The quantities given for each recipe are for 4 persons unless otherwise stated.

CHAPTER 1

FRESH HERBS

THE use of herbs in cooking is so much a matter of tradition, almost of superstition, that the fact that it is also a question of personal taste is overlooked, and experiments seldom tried; in fact the restriction of this herb to that dish is usually quite arbitrary and because somebody long ago discovered that basil works some sort of spell with tomatoes, fennel with fish, and rosemary with pork, it occurs to few people to reverse the traditional usage; to take an example, fennel is an excellent complement to pork, adding the sharpness which is supplied in English cookery by apple sauce, while basil enhances almost anything with which it is cooked; for ideas one has only to look to the cooking of other countries to see how much the use of herbs as a flavouring can be varied. In England mint is considered to have an affinity for lamb, new potatoes, and green peas; the French regard the use of mint as a flavouring as yet another sign of English barbarism, and scarcely ever employ it, while all over the Middle East, where the cooking is far from uncivilized, mint is one of the most commonly used of herbs; it goes into soups, sauces, omelettes, salads, purées of dried vegetables and into the sweet cooling mint tea drunk by the Persians and Arabs. In Spain, where the cooking has been much influenced by the Arabs, it is also used in stews and soups; it is usually one of the ingredients of the sweet sour sauces which the Italians like, and which are a legacy from the Romans, and in modern Roman cooking wild mint gives a characteristic flavour to stewed

mushrooms and to vegetable soups. The Indians make a
fresh chutney from pounded mint, mangoes, onion and
chillies which is an excellent accompaniment to fish and
cold meat as well as to curries. Mint is one of the cleanest
tasting of herbs and will give a lively tang to many
vegetables, carrots, tomatoes, mushrooms, lentils; a little
finely chopped mint is good in fish soups and stews, and
with braised duck; a cold roast duck served on a bed of
freshly picked mint makes a lovely, fresh-smelling summer
dish; a few leaves can be added to the orange salad to
serve with it. Dried mint is one of the most useful of herbs
for the winter, for it greatly enlivens purées and soups,
ragoûts of meat and vegetables and winter salads of beetroot, potatoes, and other cooked vegetables.

In England basil is one of the traditional herbs for
turtle soup, and it is well known that it brings out the
flavour of tomato salads and sauces; although it was
common at one time in English kitchen gardens it is now
extremely hard to lay hands on fresh basil, a state of
affairs which should be remedied as fast as possible, for,
with its highly aromatic scent, it is one of the most
delicious of all herbs. In Provence, in Italy, in Greece,
basil grows and is used in great quantities. The Genoese
could scarcely exist without their *pesto*, a thick compound
of pounded basil, pine nuts, garlic, cheese and olive oil
which is used as a sauce for every kind of pasta, for fish,
particularly red mullet, and as a flavouring for soups and
minestrones. The Niçois have their own version of this
sauce called *pistou* which has given its name to the Soupe
au Pistou made of french beans, potatoes and macaroni,
flavoured with the *pistou* sauce. To the Greeks basil has
a special significance, for the legend goes that basil was
found growing on the site of the Crucifixion by the
Empress Helena, who brought it back from Jerusalem to
Greece, since when the plant has flourished all over the

Greek world; scarcely a house in Greece is to be seen without its pot of basil in the window. Once you have become a basil addict it is hard to do without it; Mediterranean vegetables such as pimentos and aubergines, garlicky soups and wine flavoured dishes of beef, salads dressed with the fruity olive oil of Provence or Liguria and all the dishes with tomato sauces need basil as a fish needs water, and there is no substitute.

Of that very English herb sage I have little to say except that, and this is where the question of personal taste comes in, it seems to me to be altogether too blatant, and used far too much; its all prevading presence in stuffings and sausages is perhaps responsible for the distaste for herbs which many English people feel. The Italians are also very fond of sage, and use it a great deal with veal and with liver; it seems to give a musty rather than a fresh flavour, and I would always substitute mint or basil for sage in any recipe. The same applies to rosemary, which when fresh gives out a powerful oil which penetrates anything cooked with it; in Southern France it is used to flavour roast lamb, pork and veal, but should be removed from the dish before it is served, as it is disagreeable to find those spiky little leaves in one's mouth; in Italy rosemary is stuffed in formidable quantities into roast sucking pig, and in the butchers' shops you see joints of pork tied up ready for roasting wreathed round and threaded with rosemary; it looks entrancing, but if you want to taste the meat, use only the smallest quantity, and never put it into stock destined for a consommé or for a sauce.

Thyme, marjoram and wild marjoram are all good and strong flavoured herbs which can be used separately or together for robust stews of beef in red wine, for those aromatic country soups in which there are onions, garlic, bacon, wine, cabbage; the *garbures* of South Western

France and the minestrones of Northern Italy; one or
other of these herbs should go into stuffings for chicken,
goose and turkey, for pimentos and aubergines, into meat
croquettes (accompanied by grated lemon peel), terrines
of game, and stews of hare and rabbit; either thyme or
marjoram is almost essential to strew in small quantities on
mutton, pork and lamb chops and liver to be fried or
grilled; wild marjoram is called *origano* in Italy and Spain
and is used for any and every dish of veal and pork, for
fish and fish soups, and is an essential ingredient of the
Neapolitan Pizza, that colourful, filling, peasant dish of
bread dough baked with tomatoes, anchovies and cheese.
The marjoram which grows wild in Greece and Cyprus,
called *rigani* is a variety which has a more powerful scent;
the flowers as well as the leaves are dried and no kebab
of mutton, lamb or kid is thinkable without it.   Lemon
thyme is at its best fresh rather than cooked and is particularly good in a buttery potato purée, and in salads;
there are dozens of varieties of thyme each with its particular scent, the best for cooking being perhaps the
common thyme which grows wild on the downs.   A
curious thyme which has a scent of caraway seeds is good
with roast pork.

Fennel, both the leaves and stalks of the variety which
grows rather too easily in English gardens, and the roots
of the Florentine fennel which is imported from France
and Italy, has many uses besides the sauce for mackerel
which is found in all old English cookery books.   For the
famous Provençal *grillade au fenouil* the stalks of the fennel
are used as a bed on which to grill sea-bass (*loup de mer*)
or red mullet; there is a Tuscan chicken dish in which the
bird is stuffed with thick strips of ham and pieces of fennel
root and pot-roasted; in Perugia they stuff their sucking
pig and pork with fennel leaves and garlic instead of the
rosemary prevalent elsewhere in Italy; one of the best of

Italian sausages is *finocchiona*, a Florentine pork salame flavoured with fennel seeds; if you like the aniseed taste of fennel use it chopped up raw in soups, particularly iced soups, and in vinaigrette sauces, in rice salads to give the crisp element so necessary to soft foods, in mixed vegetable salads, in fish mayonnaises, in the court-bouillon in which fish is to be poached, in stuffings for baked fish, in chicken salads, and mixed with parsley and juniper berries for a marinade for pork chops which are to be grilled. The leaves of dill are not unlike those of fennel, but the aniseed flavour is less pronounced; it is a herb much used in Scandinavian and Russian cooking, particularly to flavour pickled cucumber and for soups.

Tarragon is essentially a herb of French cookery; *poulet à l'estragon* and *oeufs en gelée à l'estragon* are classics of the French kitchen; without tarragon there is no true sauce Béarnaise; with chives and chervil (which also goes well with carrots, potatoes, and in salads) or parsley it is one of the *fines herbes* for omelettes, sauces, butters, and many dishes of grilled meat and fish. It is a herb to be used with care for its charm lies in its very distinct and odd flavour and too much of it spoils the effect, but a few leaves will give character to many dishes and particularly to smooth foods such as sole cooked in cream, eggs en cocotte, cream soups, bisques of shell fish, stewed scallops, potato purées and also to tomato salads. In Italy, tarragon is to be found only in and around Siena, where it is used in the stuffing for globe artichokes, and to flavour green salads. When buying tarragon plants be sure to insist on the true French tarragon. Common tarragon, sometimes called Russian tarragon, has a rank taste and no scent at all.

The classic bouquet garni of French cookery consists of a sprig of thyme, parsley, and a bay leaf (which besides its well-known use in soups and stews and marinades gives a good flavour to béchamel sauce if put in the milk while it is heated, and then removed). Chives, with their delicate onion flavour and brilliant green colouring, are one of the best of summer garnishes for eggs, vegetables, salads and soups. Borage is used by the Genoese to mix with the stuffing for ravioli, and to make fritters; the finely chopped leaves give a delicate cucumber taste to cream cheese, and its use in wine cups is traditional. The Sardinians flavour roast pork with myrtle, the French consider savory (*sarriette*) indispensable as a flavouring for broad beans; lovage, a member of the Umbelliferae family, has a peppery leaf with a faint hint of celery and gives an interesting taste to a salad of haricot beans and to fish soups. Among its thousands of uses in the kitchen, parsley is the perfect foil for garlic; the fresh leaves of angelica can be used in salads, while the translucent green stalks have a very strong fresh scent, which when candied give such a delicious flavour and elegant appearance to sweet creams and cream cheese puddings; the leaf of the sweet scented geranium gives a lovely scent to a lemon water ice and an incomparable flavour when cooked with blackberries for jelly. The fresh leaves of coriander are much used in Oriental, Spanish and Mexican cookery, while the dried seeds are one of the essential ingredients of nearly all curries and Oriental cooking; with their slightly burnt orange peel taste they are also good to flavour pork, mutton and venison, and in sauces for coarse fish; they can also be used to flavour milk and cream puddings and junkets. All these herbs and many others, tansy, balm, marigold petals, nasturtium flowers and leaves, pennyroyal, burnet, rocket, sorrel, rue, were familiar ingredients of country cookery all over Europe until the twentieth century brought such a battery of chemical flavourings and synthetic essences that the uses and virtues of fresh plants have been almost forgotten. But when you are accustomed to their presence in food they are as necessary as salt; during the summer months while their flavours are fresh and their leaves green they add enormously to the appearance as well as to the flavour of food.

The quantity in which any given herb is to be used is a matter of taste rather than of rule. Cookery books are full of exhortations to discretion in this matter, but much depends on the herb with which you happen to be dealing, what food it is to flavour, whether the dish in question is to be a long simmered one in which it is the sauce which will be ultimately flavoured with the herbs, or whether the herbs are to go into a stuffing for a bird or meat to be roasted, in which case the aromas will be more concentrated, or again whether the herbs will be cooked only a minute or two as in egg dishes, or not cooked at all, as when they are used to flavour a salad or a herb butter. Whether the herbs are fresh or dried is an important point. The oils in some herbs (rosemary, wild marjoram, sage) are very strong, and when these dry out the flavour is very much less powerful. But in the drying process nearly all herbs (mint is an exception) acquire a certain mustiness, so that although in theory one should be able to use dried herbs more freely than fresh ones, the opposite is in fact generally the case.

Some fresh herbs disperse their aromatic scent very quickly when in contact with heat; a few leaves of fresh tarragon steeped in a hot consommé for 20 minutes will give it a strong flavour, whereas if the tarragon is to flavour a salad considerably more will be necessary. Lemon thyme and marjoram are at their best raw, or only slightly cooked, as in an omelette; the flavour of fennel stalks is brought out by slow cooking; basil has a particular affinity with all dishes in which olive oil is an ingredient, whether cooked or in salads. Knowledge of the right quantities, and of interesting combinations of herbs can be acquired by using egg dishes, salads, and soups as a background. Even if the herbs have been dispensed with a less cautious hand than is usually advised the result will not be a disaster, as it can be when some musty dried herb has completely permeated a roast bird or an expensive piece of meat. You may, no the contrary, have discovered some delicious new combination of tastes, and certainly the use of fresh herbs will be a startling revelation to all those people who know herbs only as something bought in a packet called "'mixed dried herbs", and for which you might just as well substitute sawdust.

It is particularly to the dishes in which fresh herbs are an essential rather than an incidental flavouring that I would like to call attention, for it is this aspect of cookery which is passed over by those writers who enjoin so much caution in the use of herbs. Sometimes it is a good thing to forget that basil, parsley, mint, tarragon, fennel, are all bunched together under the collective word "herbs" and to remember that the difference between leaf vegetables (sorrel, spinach, lettuce) and herbs is very small, and indeed at one time all these plants were known collectively as "salad herbs". Nobody tells you to "use spinach with caution", and neither can you be "discreet with the basil" when you are making a pesto sauce, because the basil is the essential flavouring (so for that matter is mint in mint sauce).

In a slightly different way, a plain consommé or potato soup can be used as a background for a flavouring of herbs, tarragon being a particularly good one for this purpose. An *omelette aux fines herbes* relies on the herbs for its flavour. So do many sauces; the classic *sauce verte* and *sauce ravigote* are two of them; the wonderful Sauce Messine (the recipe is on p. 167) is another. There are many recipes in this book calling for fresh herbs, for they can be enjoyed only in the summer (with the exception of parsley, mint, and the thymes, which go on until Christ-

mas), and for quick reference they will be found in the
Index listed both under their own names and under the
particular herb which is an essential or important ingredient of that dish.

For the dispensing of fresh herbs into salads and soups
it is advisable to keep a pair of kitchen scissors handy, and
for chopping larger quantities a two-handled, crescent-
shaped chopper such as may now be obtained in the
larger kitchen equipment stores. Small French wooden
bowls complete with a little axe shaped chopper are also
now obtainable in some stores and are invaluable in any
kitchen where fresh herbs are frequently in use.

Most of the herbs mentioned in this book may be
ordered and will be sent fresh by post from Country Style,
35 Windsor Street, Brighton, Sussex, as long as the season
lasts. In the winter they can be ordered dried.

Other places where a selection of fresh herbs are sold
are Harrods, Young's, 126 Brompton Road, Blake's,
78 Kings Road, Roche, 14 Old Compton Street.

The wooden herb bowls with choppers are to be found
at Madame Cadec's, 27 Greek Street, W.1.

CHAPTER 2

HORS D'OEUVRE AND SALADS

HOW one learns to dread the season for salads in England. What becomes of the hearts of the lettuces? What makes an English cook think that beetroot spreading its hideous purple dye over a sardine and a spoonful of tinned baked beans constitutes an hors d'oeuvre? Why make the cold salmon, woolly enough anyhow by mid-summer, look even less appetizing than it is by serving it on a bed of lettuce leaves apparently rescued from the dust bin? What is the object of spending so much money on cucumbers, tomatoes, and lettuces because of their valuable vitamins, and then drowning them in vinegar and chemical salad dressings?

Cookery books are full of instructions as to the making of a plain lettuce salad but it seems to me that there are only three absolutely essential rules to be observed; the lettuce must be very fresh; the vinegar in the dressing must be reduced to the absolute minimum; the dressing must be mixed with the lettuce only at the moment of serving. Wash the lettuce (ideally of course it should not be washed at all, but each leaf wiped with a clean damp cloth) under a running cold tap, don't leave it to soak. Drain it in a wire salad basket, or a colander, or shake it in a clean teacloth in which it can then be hung up to dry; or it can be put, still wrapped in its cloth, into a refrigerator until half an hour before it is to be served (don't put a freshly picked garden lettuce in the re-frigerator, but it will do no harm to the average bought lettuce). The salad dressing can be prepared beforehand,

and when it is time to mix the salad, do it gently, taking your time, and ensuring that each leaf has its proper coating of oil. The French dressing most commonly used consists of 3 parts oil to 1 of vinegar, but to my mind this is far too vinegary, and I never use less than 6 times as much oil as vinegar, although even then, and however mild the vinegar, I prefer lemon juice, and very little of it. First class olive oil is of course essential, and given this the flavour of the lettuce and the oil, with a little salt and garlic, is quite enough to make a perfect salad without any further seasoning. The grotesque prudishness and archness with which garlic is treated in this country has led to the superstition that rubbing the bowl with it before putting the salad in gives sufficient flavour. It rather depends whether you are going to eat the bowl or the salad. If you like the taste of garlic but don't actually wish to chew the bulb itself, crush it with the point of a knife (there is really no necessity to fuss about with garlic presses and such devices), put it in the bowl in which the dressing is to be mixed, add the other ingredients and stir vigorously. Leave it to stand for an hour and by that time the garlic will have flavoured the oil, and it can be left behind when the dressing is poured on to the salad. A piece of bread or toast, what the French call a *chapon*, can be thoroughly rubbed with garlic, sprinkled with oil, and placed at the bottom of the salad bowl. Put the lettuce on the top and let it stand for a little before mixing it with the dressing. The garlic flavour will be powerful, and the bread will be as delicious as the lettuce.

To keep lettuces fresh wrap them in newspaper and put them in a covered saucepan in a cool larder. Don't remove the outer leaves until the lettuce is to be prepared for the salad. Porothene food bags, which are now sold in most large stores and in stationers' shops are also excellent for keeping all greenstuff fresh, whether in the refrigerator or larder. To keep watercress, which so rapidly withers, put it in a deep bowl, and completely cover it with water.

A good many of the salads I have given in this chapter may be served as an hors d'oeuvre. It is so very easy to make an attractive first course from vegetables, eggs, prawns, rice, and simple sauces, that it is only a question of taste, imagination, and the most elementary knowledge of cooking to avoid alike the everlasting grapefruit, the woolly melon, and the awful little collection of obvious left overs. The simplest hors d'oeuvre are the best, looking clean and fresh; leave those huge spreads of twenty-five different dishes to pretentious restaurants, where as a matter of fact all the dishes taste exactly the same because they are all dressed with the identical over-vinegared sauce. When devising a mixed salad be careful not to overdo the number of ingredients, or chop everything into small pieces, or mash them all up together into one indistinguishable morass; one of the nicest of all country hors d'oeuvre is the Genoese one of raw broad beans, rough salame sausage, and salty sheep's milk Sardo cheese; each of these things is served on a separate dish, and each person peels his own beans and cuts his own cheese; if the same ingredients were all mixed up together in a bowl the point would be quite lost. In the same way a salad of tunny fish piled up on haricot beans or french beans dressed with oil has two quite contrasting but compatible flavours, whereas if the tunny fish is mashed up among the beans, the flavours and textures of both are sacrificed, and the appearance of the dish messy as well.

Apart from all the little dishes which can be cheaply made at home there are now so many products on the market which make delicious hors d'oeuvre that to anyone who can afford them the first course need be no bother whatever. All the smoked fish, trout, mackerel, buckling, salmon, sturgeon, eel, need no accompaniment other than lemon, and bread and butter; red caviar, which is made from salmon roes, is comparatively cheap, but not sufficiently appreciated; smoked cod's roe pounded into a paste with olive oil and lemon juice (see p. 25) is excellent served with hot toast (eaten straight, it is good but disconcertingly sticky). If you are serving salame, buy the best (ask in Italian shops for the kind they call *casalinga*, which is usually better than the mass produced Milan salame) and have plenty of it, and with it some olives, french bread, and good fresh butter. Raw Parma ham with fresh figs is a combination scarcely ever, alas, obtainable in this country, but there is the smoked fillet of ham usually called *filet de Saxe* which is excellent with melon, there is smoked turkey, smoked pork fillet, good quality tunny fish in tins, and for people who can shop in Soho such delightful things as Greek stuffed vine leaves, Calamata olives, spiced, peppery Spanish sausages, Cyprus sausages flavoured with coriander seeds, the Arab *Tahina* sauce, and that salty Greek cheese called Fetta which goes so well with rough wine and olives and plenty of thickly cut coarse bread. With all these things serve inexpensive wines; whether white, rosé, or red does not really matter, but any delicate wine would be overpowered by their salty, smoky flavours.

A SUMMER HORS D'OEUVRE

A dish of long red radishes, cleaned, but with a little of the green leaves left on, a dish of mixed green and black olives, a plate of raw, round, small whole tomatoes, a dish of hard (not too hard) boiled eggs cut lengthways and garnished with a bunch of parsley. A pepper mill and a salt mill, lemons and olive oil on the table; butter, and

fresh bread. Not very original perhaps, but how often does
one meet with a really fresh and unmessed hors d'oeuvre?

Eggs in Aspic with Tarragon

One or two eggs, either poached or *mollet* per person,
approximately a coffee cupful of aspic jelly per egg, a few
leaves of tarragon, a small slice of very mild ham per egg.

Put a slice of ham at the bottom of each small china or
glass ramekin (large enough for one egg). On top of the
ham put the egg. Put a few leaves of tarragon into the
melted aspic and let them infuse for an hour. Pour the
strained aspic very carefully over the eggs, and when it
has nearly set decorate each egg with two fresh tarragon
leaves.

Instead of the ham a layer of chicken mousse (p. 214)
or a little slice of smoked turkey or half a poached fillet of
sole, very well strained, can go underneath the eggs. There
is no point in bothering about this dish unless it is made
with genuine aspic. Gelatine will not do.

It is I think one of the best of summer hors d'oeuvre.

Eggs with Skordalia

Skordalia is the Greek garlic mayonnaise. Pound 4 large
cloves of garlic in a mortar; stir in the yolks of two eggs.
Add a little salt, and ground black pepper. Stir
thoroughly. Add a ¼ pint of olive oil, drop by drop at
first as for a mayonnaise, more rapidly as the sauce
thickens. When the oil is all used up stir in 2 ozs. of fresh
white breadcrumbs, then 2 ozs. of ground almonds, then a
little lemon juice, then a handful of finely chopped
parsley. This is a sauce which easily curdles, so be prepared to use another egg yolk if necessary, putting into a
clean bowl, adding the curdled Skordalia spoonful by

spoonful until it has thickened again. It is worth the trouble. Serve it in a separate bowl to accompany a dish of halved hard-boiled eggs, quartered raw tomatoes, some black olives and some radishes.

PÂTÉ OF TUNNY FISH

Pound the contents of a small tin of tunny fish in a mortar; work in half the weight of the tunny in butter; when the mixture has become a smooth paste season very lightly with a drop of lemon juice and a little black pepper. Turn into a small dish and put in the refrigerator, or a cold larder. Garnish with a few capers and a little parsley or chives. Serve with hot toast.

SMOKED COD'S ROE PASTE

Pound a clove of garlic in a mortar, add ¼ lb. of smoked cod's roe, having first removed the outer skin. Pound or mash till it is soft then stir in, a drop or two at a time, about 4 tablespoons of olive oil; add the juice of half a lemon, and a few drops of water to make the paste of a manageable consistency.

This paste very much resembles the Greek *Taramásalata*, with the difference that *Taramá* is tunny fish roe, and much more garlic and lemon is added to the paste. It is served as an hors d'oeuvre, with bread or toast.

FRENCH BEAN AND PRAWN SALAD

Season cooked french beans (whole, or cut in half across, but not lengthways) with olive oil and lemon. Arrange them in a mound, and on top put peeled prawns, also seasoned with oil and lemon. Garnish with halves of hard-boiled eggs. Serve as an hors d'oeuvre.

MAURITIAN PRAWN CHUTNEY

4 ozs. of peeled prawns, a green or red pimento or half a small hot green or red chilli pepper, olive oil, salt, cayenne, green ginger or ground ginger, lemon or fresh lime juice, 4 spring onions.

Pound the peeled prawns in a mortar with the chopped spring onions. Add the pimento or chilli chopped very finely. Stir in enough olive oil (about 3 or 4 tablespoons) little by little, to make the mixture into a thick paste. Add a pinch of ground ginger, or a teaspoonful of grated green ginger, and, if mild peppers have been used, a scrap of cayenne. Squeeze in the juice of a fresh lime if available, or of half a lemon. Although this is a chutney to be served with curries, it makes a delicious hors d'oeuvre served with hard boiled eggs, or even by itself with toast.

MACKEREL WITH GREEN SAUCE

Poached mackerel, filleted and skinned when cold, and served as an hors d'oeuvre with a green, or vinaigrette sauce (pp. 166 and 168) poured over.

MACKEREL WITH SORREL PURÉE

Cold fillets of mackerel on a bed of sorrel purée (p. 148). Garnish with chopped parsley or tarragon, and capers.

HORS D'OEUVRE OF MUSHROOMS, CUCUMBERS, AND FRENCH BEANS

½ lb. of mushrooms, ½ lb. of french beans, half a cucumber, olive oil, garlic, lemon.

Cook the prepared french beans in a little salted water, in the usual way. Take care not to overcook them. Strain them, and while still hot season with olive oil and a little lemon juice. Wash the mushrooms, cut them into thinnish slices, put them into a dish with the cucumber, unpeeled, cut into little squares; season with ground black pepper, a little chopped garlic, plenty of olive oil and lemon juice. A little while before serving sprinkle with salt and pile this mixture on top of the french beans, in a shallow dish. Garnish if you like with hard boiled eggs, or radishes, or shelled prawns.

Tomatoes with Horseradish Mayonnaise

Cut the tomatoes in half; scoop out the insides, sprinkle them with salt, and turn them upside down to drain. Fill with a horseradish mayonnaise (p. 165) and serve as an hors d'oeuvre or as an accompaniment to roast or grilled chicken, or cold beef, or tongue.

Ham and Sausages

An equal number of Frankfurter sausages and thin slices of ham, butter. Wrap each sausage in a slice of ham (when obtainable raw Parma, Bayonne or Westphalian ham is best, but cooked will do). Arrange them on a long dish, with a pat of fresh cold butter on each. Particularly nice for a quick luncheon, or for a car or train picnic.

Pan Bagna i

Pan Bagna is simply a slice of *pain de ménage* moistened with good Niçois olive oil (sometimes the bread is rubbed with garlic) covered with fillets of anchovy, slices of tomatoes, capers and gherkins; vinegar is optional. It is rare that a game of *boules* in the country (and every one knows how addicted the Niçois are to this sport) comes to

an end without having been interrupted for a few bottles
of Bellet and a Pan Bagna.

From *La Cuisine à Nice*, H. Heyraud.

PAN BAGNA 2

For 4 people: ¼ lb. black olives, ½ lb. tomatoes, a celery
heart, 2 ozs. of mushrooms, 1 artichoke, a small tin of
anchovies in oil.

Cut a long pound loaf of French bread in half, right
through. Soak these two halves first in a little salt water
then in olive oil. When the bread is well impregnated, on
one half put slices of tomato, small pieces of the cooked
artichoke heart, slices of the mushrooms (cooked as for
champignons à la grecque), the celery heart cut into small
strips, then the stoned black olives and a few fillets of
anchovies. Cover with the second half of the loaf, put a
fairly heavy weight on the top for half an hour.

Cut into thick slices for serving.

Recipe from *Recettes et Paysages*.
Sud-Est et Mediteranée.

PAN BAGNA 3

A large round, flat country loaf, ½ litre (about ¾ pint) of
olive oil. Anchovies, fillets of salt herring, rounds of
tomato, green and black olives, a lettuce.

Cut the loaf through the centre, into two rounds. Put
it on a dish and cover with olive oil. Leave to marinate
for an hour. Strain off the oil, spread one half with all the
ingredients; cover with the other half of the loaf. Put on
a dish with a weight on top. Serve the next day, cut into
slices, on an hors d'oeuvre dish.

CRAB AND RICE SALAD

The claw meat of a large crab (the soft meat from the body can be used for soup), 2 cupfuls of boiled rice, a green or red sweet pepper, garlic, half a dozen black olives, lemon, olive oil, nutmeg, a few walnuts, 3 or 4 raw mushrooms, lemon.

Season the boiled rice while it is still warm with nutmeg, lemon juice, and enough olive oil to make it moist but not sodden. Stir into it the crab cut into squares, the stoned olives, the raw pepper cut into strips, the raw sliced mushrooms, the chopped garlic. Strew the chopped walnuts on the top.

CHAMPIGNONS À LA GRECQUE

Bring to the boil the following mixture: $\frac{1}{4}$ pint water, juice of half a lemon, $\frac{1}{2}$ coffeecupful olive oil, sprig of thyme, a bayleaf, and a piece of celery tied together. ground black pepper, a little salt, a dozen coriander seeds. When boiling put in $\frac{1}{2}$ lb. very small white mushrooms washed but not peeled. Simmer 5 minutes. Serve cold as hors d'oeuvre, with a little of their stock and a little fresh oil.

GLOBE ARTICHOKES

If the artichokes are to be served in the ordinary way, boiled, one for each person, buy the large cone-shaped ones, with very close leaves. Wash them and boil them in salted water, with a little lemon juice added, for about half an hour.

Serve them cold with oil and lemon, or hot with sauce hollandaise, maltaise, mousseline, or simply melted butter.

Artichoke Hearts, Sauce Maltaise

The artichokes can either be cooked as above, and the leaves and chokes then removed, or they can be prepared as follows: Pare off all the outer leaves, cut the remainder right down to within half an inch of the choke, and boil them for about 20 minutes. When cold, remove the rest of the leaves and the choke, fill with a sauce maltaise (p. 163) and serve cold.

Avocado Pears

Avocado pears from South Africa and from Madeira are now imported nearly all the year round. They vary considerably both in quality and price. In Soho markets I have sometimes paid as little as 6d. each for them, while the same fruit in the Kings Road will be 1/9, in Piccadilly luxury shops 3/- and often much more. Generally speaking the green variety seem to be better than the red, although not invariably so. They are, I think, at their best served alone, as a first course, with nothing but a dressing of salt, pepper, oil and lemon. Some people like to stuff them with mixtures of mayonnaise, ham or even lobster, which to my mind diminishes their flavour, and makes them sickly. In Jamaica they are sometimes served with a dressing of rum and fresh lime juice.

Sir Francis Colchester Wemyss, writing in *Pleasures of the Table*, advocates cold salt beef as the ideal meat with which to serve an Avocado salad. They are also excellent with smoked turkey (p. 31).

In the West Indies they make a soup from Avocados and in Mexican cooking avocados also go into sauces, soups and into stuffings for turkey and red peppers, and into mixed salads, and are also used as a garnish for meat hashes and stews.

When Avocados are to be served as an hors d'oeuvre cut them in half lengthways, take out the stone, and fill up the cavities with the prepared dressing. Get them ready only just before they are needed, as the flesh tends to turn black when they are left standing for any length of time. Avocados are very filling and a half for each person is usually enough.

SMOKED TURKEY[1]

Smoked turkey, comparatively new to this country, makes an excellent hors d'oeuvre. Serve it cut in thin slices, brown and white meat mixed, quite plain.

SMOKED TURKEY SALAD

Boil ½ lb. of previously soaked small dried green flageolet beans (obtainable in Soho shops) for 1¼–1½ hours; drain them, season with salt, pepper and olive oil; on top of them put a ¼ lb. of raw sliced mushrooms dressed with olive oil, pepper and a very little garlic, and over these arrange a cupful of smoked turkey cut into fillets; garnish with halves of hard-boiled eggs, and serve as an hors d'œuvre.

This is a charming summery looking salad, pale green, cream, pink and yellow. The flageolet beans are a perfect combination with the turkey, but if you can't get them, make the salad with rice instead, or with green peas.

RILLETTES

1½–2 lbs. of belly of pork, with a good proportion of lean

---

[1] Can be ordered through H. A .West Ltd., 22 The Green, Edmonton, London N.9. Edmonton 2616. Prices are about 11/6 per lb. for birds of from 8 lbs. to 25 lbs.

to fat, a clove of garlic, a sprig of fresh thyme or marjoram, salt, pepper, a pinch of mace.

Remove bones and rind from the meat, and cut it into small cubes. Put these into a thick pan with the chopped garlic, the herbs and seasoning. Cook on a very low flame, or in the slowest possible oven for 1½ hours, until the pieces of pork are quite soft without being fried, and swimming in their own fat. Place a wire sieve over a bowl, and pour the meat into the sieve so that the fat drips through into the basin. When the meat has cooled, chop or pound it finely, press into small earthenware or china pots, and cover them with their own fat. Cover with greaseproof paper or tin foil. Rillettes will keep for weeks, and make an excellent stand by for an hors d'oeuvre or for sandwiches.

Chicken Liver Paté

½ to 1 lb. of chicken livers, or duck, turkey, chicken and goose liver mixed, butter, brandy, port, garlic, thyme.

Clean the livers carefully, making sure that the little bag containing the bile is removed; also pare off any parts of the livers which look greenish, as they will give a bitter taste to the pâté. Melt 1 oz. of butter in a frying pan; put in the livers, whole, and let them cook gently for about 5 minutes. They must remain pink inside. Take them from the pan and put them into a marble mortar. To the butter in the pan add 2 tablespoonfuls of brandy and let it bubble; then 2 tablespoonfuls of port or madeira, and cook another minute. Add half a clove of garlic, salt, ground black pepper and a small pinch of thyme to the livers and pound them to a paste; pour in the butter mixture from the pan, and 2 ozs. of fresh butter. When all is thoroughly amalgamated and reduced to a paste, put it into an earthenware terrine in which it will come to within ½ inch of the top. In a clean pan melt some pure pork, duck or goose dripping, or butter. Pour it through a strainer on to the pâté; there should be enough to form a covering about ¼ of an inch thick, so that the pâté is completely sealed. When the fat has set, cover with a piece of tinfoil and the lid of the terrine. Store in the larder or refrigerator. The pâté should not be eaten until two or three days after it has been made, and as long as it is airtight will keep a week or two in the larder and several weeks in a refrigerator. Serve it very cold, in the terrine, with toast. This is a rich pâté, and butter is not necessary with it. 1 lb. of chicken livers makes enough pâté for 8 to 10 people.

TERRINE OF RABBIT

A rabbit weighing about 1 lb. when skinned and cleaned, 1 lb. of belly of pork, ¼ lb. of fat bacon, thyme, pepper, juniper berries, a little lemon peel, 2 tablespoons of brandy, mace, garlic.

Have the rabbit cut into pieces, and simmer it in a little water for 20–30 minutes. When cold, take all the flesh off the bones, and chop it on a board with the pork (uncooked) 2 or 3 cloves of garlic, a good sprinkling of fresh thyme, about 8 juniper berries and a small strip of lemon peel. (If you have not a double-handled chopper, which makes this operation very easy, the meat will have to be put through a coarse mincer, but chopping is infinitely preferable.) Season the mixture fairly highly with ground black pepper, salt, and mace. Stir in the brandy. Line the bottom of a fairly large terrine, or 2 or 3 small ones with little strips of bacon. Put in the meat mixture. Put a bayleaf on top, and cover with another layer of strips of bacon.

Steam, covered, in a slow oven for 1½ to 2½ hours,

according to the size of the terrines. When they come out of the oven put a piece of greaseproof paper over the terrines, and lay a fairly heavy weight on top of them and leave them overnight.

Next day, the terrines can either be filled up with ready prepared aspic jelly, or simply sealed with pork fat. They are good either way, and make an excellent and inexpensive hors d'oeuvre.

TERRINE OF PIGEONS

3 pigeons, 1 lb. of fat pork, ¼ lb. bacon, garlic, 6 juniper berries, 2 tablespoons each of port and brandy, thyme or marjoram.

Proceed exactly as for the terrine of rabbit above and cook for about the same length of time.

Another method is to reserve the breasts of the pigeons cut in small fillets, to add about 2 ozs. of chicken liver pâté to the rest of the chopped pigeon and pork meat mixture, and arrange the fillets and the chopped mixture in alternate layers. Cook as before.

RATATOUILLE EN SALADE

Ratatouille is the well-known Provençal mixture of Southern vegetables stewed in oil. When it is to be served cold, it is cooked with the vegetables cut up very small and with the addition of garlic and coriander seeds. For a dish of cold Ratatouille for four people if it is to be served as a separate dish or for eight if it is to be one of the constituents of an hors d'oeuvre, you need 2 onions, 2 aubergines, 2 large red pimentos, 4 ripe tomatoes, 2 cloves of garlic, a dozen coriander seeds, parsley and olive oil.

Chop the onions fairly small and put them to stew in a

sauté-pan or deep frying pan in half a tumbler of olive oil. In the meantime cut the aubergines, leaving on their skins, into ½ inch-squares and put them in a colander, sprinkled with coarse salt, so that some of the water drains away from them. When the onions have cooked about 10 minutes and are beginning to get soft (but not fried) add the aubergines, and then the pimentos, also cut into small pieces. Cover the pan and let them simmer for 30 to 40 minutes. Now add the chopped tomatoes, the garlic and the coriander seeds. Continue cooking until the tomatoes have melted. Should the oil dry up, add a little more, remembering that the juice from the tomatoes will also make the Ratatouille more liquid, and the final result must not be too mushy. When cold, garnish it with chopped parsley or basil. Drain off any excess of oil before serving.

MUSHROOM SALAD

½ lb. of mushrooms, olive oil, lemon juice, garlic, parsley, salt and pepper.

Buy if possible the large rather shaggy looking variety of mushrooms. Wash them but do not peel them. Cut them in thinnish slices, leaving the stalks on. Put them in a bowl, squeeze lemon juice over them, stir in a little chopped garlic, season with ground black pepper, and pour a good deal of olive oil over them. Immediately before serving salt them and add more olive oil, as you will find they have absorbed the first lot. Sprinkle with parsley, or, if you have it, basil, or a mixture of fresh marjoram and lemon thyme.

This is an expensive salad to make, as mushrooms absorb an enormous quantity of oil, but it is extremely popular, and particularly good with a grilled or roast chicken. Variations can be made by mixing the mushrooms with a few strips of raw fennel or with a cupful of cooked green peas.

For an hors d'oeuvre, mix the mushrooms with large cooked prawns.

SALADE NIÇOISE

There is no precise recipe for a salade niçoise. It usually contains lettuce hearts, black olives, hard-boiled eggs, anchovies, and sometimes tunny fish. There should be garlic in the dressing.

In *La Cuisine à Nice*, Lucien Heyraud gives a salade niçoise composed of young globe artichokes cut in quarters, black olives, raw pimento, quarters of tomato, and anchovy fillets. There are however as many versions of it as there are cooks in Provence, but in whatever way it is interpreted it should be a simple and rather crude country salad, with plenty of garlic, and the ingredients should be put in the bowl in large pieces, nicely arranged so that the salad looks colourful and fresh, and the dressing should be mixed in at the table.

SPICED RICE SALAD

6–8 ozs. rice, a piece of green ginger[1] or dried ginger root, a handful of mixed raisins and currants, a shallot, coriander seeds, nutmeg, olive oil, lemon, almonds or pine nuts, 3 or 4 fresh or dried apricots.

Boil the rice in salted water for 14–15 minutes; drain very carefully; while still warm season with ground black pepper, grated nutmeg, half a teaspoon of pounded coriander seeds, a little lemon juice, and the shallot cut into fine rounds; stir in enough olive oil to make the rice moist but not mushy, then add the raisins and currants, previously simmered a few minutes in water to make them

[1] See Footnote on page 118.

swell, then drained, and the apricots, raw, if fresh ones are being used, soaked and lightly cooked if they are dried. Garnish with roasted almonds or pine nuts.

TOMATO SALAD

Slice the tomatoes into thick rounds and arrange them on a large flat dish. Season with ground black pepper, and strew over them plenty of chopped fresh herbs, tarragon, chives, basil, parsley, whatever is available, and a little garlic. Just before serving sprinkle with salt and olive oil. Made in this way a tomato salad is fresh and crisp and aromatic; it is the salting and dressing of tomatoes several hours before they are to be served which makes them watery and clammy.

PIMENTO SALAD

Grill the pimentos until the skin turns black and will flake off. This takes about 20 minutes under a gas grill, the pimentos being turned as soon as one side is done. When they have cooled a little, peel off the skin, take out the seeds, wash the pimentos under the cold tap, cut them into strips and dress with olive oil, lemon juice, chopped garlic and parsley.

PIMENTOS STUFFED WITH PRAWNS

Grill and skin 3 or 4 large red or yellow pimentos in the way described in the preceding recipe. Cut each pimento into three or four wide strips.

Have ready a prawn chutney mixture as described on page 26. Put a small spoonful of this mixture on each strip of pimento, and roll it up into the shape of a sausage. Pour a little olive oil and lemon juice over. Arrange on a bed of watercress or shredded lettuce on a long dish. This makes a very beautiful and very excellent hors d'oeuvre. Instead of prawns, tunny fish can be used as a basis for the stuffing, either spiced in the same way as the prawn chutney, or simply mixed with a little butter, as for tunny fish pâté (p. 25).

CUCUMBER AND CHIVE SALAD

A cucumber, a few chives, and for the dressing a small cupful of cream, a teaspoonful of sugar, olive oil, salt and pepper, a teaspoonful of tarragon vinegar.

Slice the cucumber paper thin (with the special instrument which the French call a *mandoline* or *coupe-julienne*, and which can now be bought in London shops, this is a matter of less than a minute). Sprinkle coarse salt over the cucumber and leave it in a colander to drain for half an hour.

Mix the sugar and vinegar together, then add the cream, pepper and salt. Add about 2 tablespoons of olive oil and the chopped chives, and pour the dressing over the cucumber in a shallow dish.

CUCUMBER SAMBAL

Cut a cucumber into thin strips an inch long; with them mix a teaspoon of finely chopped onion, one of green chilli, one of parsley. Moisten with a dessertspoon of vinegar mixed with sugar, olive oil, salt and pepper.

Serve with cold meat, or the spiced chicken on page 124.

SALADE LORRAINE

Dandelions, shallots, garlic, chives, olive oil, pepper, salt, bacon, vinegar.

Mix the cleaned dandelions in a bowl with a little chopped shallot, garlic, chives, ground black pepper and a very little salt. Add enough olive oil to moisten the salad.

Cut the bacon in small dice, fry it, and pour it hot with its fat over the salad; in the frying pan heat a tablespoon or so of wine vinegar, and stir into the salad. The system of adding hot fried bacon to salads is typical of Alsace and Lorraine cookery; it is also German. It is applied also to raw shredded cabbage, and to potato salad.

Cream can be added, previously heated in the pan.

Salad of Broad Beans, Cucumber and Oranges

½ lb. small new raw broad beans, ½ a cucumber, 2 oranges, a few radishes.

Shell the beans, cut the unpeeled cucumber into small squares, the oranges into quarters, and the radishes into thin rounds.

Mix them with a *vinaigrette* sauce made with an egg (see p. 168). Good with cold duck.

Salade Espagnole

Sliced boiled potatoes, mixed with oil and lemon, salt and pepper, and a little chopped shallot. Cover completely with slices of tomato; garnish with fine rings of raw green peppers.

Potato Salad

Opinions differ about the making of potato salad. My own method is to boil waxy potatoes in their skins, taking care that they are not overdone. As soon as they can be handled, peel and slice them, and season them with salt and pepper and chopped chives or the green top of an onion. While they are still warm pour over them a freshly made mayonnaise thinned with a little milk, and mix them carefully so that each slice receives its coating of mayonnaise without being broken. On the top of the salad strew a good handful of chopped parsley and mint mixed together.

Laitue à la Crème

A salad for people who cannot eat olive oil. Make a cream dressing in the following way: mix together in a cup half a teaspoon of made English mustard, a teaspoon of sugar, 2 teaspoons of tarragon vinegar, half a crushed clove of garlic (this *can* be left out) and the yolk of a hard-boiled egg. Stir in a teacupful of fresh cream.

Pour the dressing, very cold, over the crisp hearts of cos lettuces, and over the salad sprinkle the chopped white of the egg. Serve very cold. A very beautiful summery looking salad. If you have fresh tarragon or chives add some, chopped, to the dressing.

Lettuce and Almond Salad

Another salad without oil.

The best lettuce for this one is the crisp curly kind known as Iceland or Arctic Prince or Webb's lettuce. The heart of a cos lettuce can also be used.

In the bottom of the salad bowl put the quarters of two oranges. (To prepare oranges for salad, cut them in half lengthways, then into quarters. It is then very easy to cut the pulp from the skin with a sharp knife.) On top of the oranges put the lettuce, then a few roasted, salted almonds. Sprinkle with a very little sugar.

At the last moment pour over a dressing consisting of a

piece of butter melted with a scrap of garlic and a squeeze
of lemon juice, and mix the orange, lettuce and almonds
together as you pour the dressing over.

Goes particularly well with chicken dishes.

LAITUE AU JUS

Cold crisp lettuce with the rich gravy from a roast poured
over it, hot. Exquisite with the hot meat or bird, especially
if it has been cooked in butter and flavoured with garlic
and wine.

Dandelions or Batavian endive can also be used for this
salad.

LENTIL SALAD

Stewed lentils, lentil soup, lentils and bacon are filling
winter dishes. They also make a first class salad for the
early summer, before the lettuces and new vegetables have
started; the flavour of good olive oil combined with lentils
is excellent.

Soak 6 to 8 ozs. of brown lentils in cold water for an
hour or two. Any pieces of grit which they may contain
will then have come to the top, and can be removed. Cook
the lentils, covered with fresh water, for an hour to an hour
and a half. Strain them, stir in a few finely cut rounds of
raw onion and plenty of olive oil. See that the seasoning
is right and when the salad is cold garnish it with quarters
of hard-boiled egg.

AUBERGINE PURÉE

Grill or bake 4 aubergines until their skins crack and will
peel easily. Sieve the peeled aubergines, mix them with
2 or 3 tablespoons of yoghourt, the same of olive oil, salt,

pepper, lemon juice. Garnish with a few very thin slices of raw onion and chopped mint leaves. This is a near Eastern dish which is intended to be served as an hors d'oeuvre with bread, or with meat, in the same manner as a chutney.

AUBERGINE CHUTNEY

Boil 2 aubergines in their skins; leave them to get cold. Peel them and put the pulp through a food mill. Stir a crushed clove of garlic into the purée, add a little minced onion, green chilli and grated green ginger, and season with salt, pepper and lemon juice.

PURÉE OF HARICOT BEANS

Cook ½ lb. of previously soaked white haricot beans in plenty of water. When they are very tender pour off the liquid and sieve the beans. To the resulting purée add two tablespoons of olive oil and two of chopped mint. Serve cold.

CHAPTER 3

SOUPS

A SOUP is often the only hot dish to be served at a summer dinner; it is also, unless at a long dinner at which hors d'oeuvre are served, the first dish, so it is important that it should be very good, attractive, light, well-seasoned, promising even more delicious things to come. The pulses and dried vegetables, the cabbage and bacon and haricot beans which make the warming, comforting soups of winter are replaced in the summer by green peas, french beans, new carrots, spring onions; in France there would be the sorrel which makes one of the most delicious and refreshing of country soups; in Italy consommés with a garnish of little egg and breadcrumb *gnocchi*, or broths thickened with eggs and cheese take the place of heavy dishes of pasta. In the days of the Czars Russian cooking was famous for its luxury, and the summer soups the Russians liked were acid flavoured with pickled cucumbers, fermented beetroot juice and sour cream; a liquor called kwass, made from buckwheat flour or barley and fermented with yeast took the place of stock in these soups; little chunks of ice were floated in the soup, and often slices of cold sturgeon or cold salmon, shell fish, or smoked meats were handed round with the soups. The Spaniards have their famous Gazpacho, compounded of tomatoes, ground red peppers, garlic and cucumber, with ice added, and in Jewish cookery there is an admirable cold beetroot soup thickened with eggs.

In England soup appears to be exactly the same summer and winter, except for the occasional appearance of an

iced consommé; often alas not sufficiently clarified, of a depressing colour, and the wrong consistency; a good consommé does indeed require patience and application to produce in its first class form—the only acceptable one, so those who have not much time to devote to cooking would be wiser to stick to fresh vegetable soups which can be made very quickly, thickened at the last minute with eggs and cream, and served either hot or cold.

Cream soups for the summer give plenty of scope for the addition of attractive garnishes in the form of fresh chopped herbs, a few raw broad beans, little squares of salmon for fish soups, grated lemon peel, grated horseradish; the same soups can be served iced, made rather thinner than if they are to be hot; yoghourt can be mixed into them when they are cold, instead of cream. Quartered hard-boiled eggs, diced cucumber, tarragon, fresh mint, raw fennel, little strips of ham, squares of highly spiced Spanish sausages are additions which go to make a cream soup interesting.

In warm weather never leave unstrained stock standing overnight; the onion is liable to turn it sour. If the stock is to be kept, it should in any case be boiled up every day. If stored in a refrigerator keep it in a covered bowl or jar, or it will freeze, and then turn watery.

POTAGE PRINTANIÈRE

Make a potato soup with 1 lb. potatoes cooked in about 2 pints of water. Sieve, and season the resulting purée with salt and pepper and a scrap of nutmeg. Add ½ cupful of hot milk. In this purée cook gently a handful of shelled green peas, and half a dozen very small carrots cut into dice.

Before serving, stir in some chopped parsley or chives and a nice lump of butter.

BROAD BEAN SOUP 1

1 lb. of young broad beans, 2 potatoes, a little milk or cream, 1 leek, butter.

The beans should be very new ones, so that both beans and pods can be used. Simply cut off the little black piece at the stalk end, and put the beans into a pan with the leek and the potatoes, cut in small pieces. Cover with water, season with a little salt, sugar and pepper, and simmer for about an hour. Strain the beans, keeping aside the liquid. Put them through a sieve (do not attempt this soup unless you have a moulinette or food mill, as the pods are not easy to get through an ordinary sieve) and add enough of the water they were cooked in to make a thin purée. Heat it up, add about half a cupful of hot milk or rather less cream, and a small piece of butter before serving.

Enough for six.

BROAD BEAN SOUP 2

2 lbs. of broad beans, a few lettuce leaves, 2 or 3 spring onions, 1 pint of light veal or chicken stock, butter.

Boil the broad beans in salted water with the shredded lettuce leaves and onions. Be careful to take them from the fire the minute they are cooked or the skins will turn brown and spoil the colour of the soup. Strain them reserving a small cupful of the water. Sieve them, put the purée into a clean pan and stir in the stock and the water which was reserved. Heat up and before serving stir in a small lump of butter, or 2 or 3 tablespoons of cream.

FRESH GREEN PEA SOUP

A teacupful of shelled green peas, 1 oz. of ham, half a small onion, 1½ pints of veal or chicken stock, the juice of a lemon, mint, 2 eggs, 2 ozs. of cream, butter, salt, pepper, sugar.

Melt the butter; put in the finely chopped onion. Do not let it brown, only soften. Add the ham cut into strips, then the peas. Let them get thoroughly impregnated with the butter. Season with salt, pepper, sugar, and add a little sprig of mint. Pour over hot water just to cover and simmer until the peas are tender. Stir in the boiling cream. Remove from the fire and stir in the eggs beaten up with the lemon juice. Pour the boiling stock over this mixture, stirring all the time, or the soup will curdle. Serve at once. A lovely soup.

CREAM OF GREEN PEAS

3 lbs. green peas, a few lettuce leaves, a small slice of ham, 2 or 3 spring onions, sugar, salt, pepper, butter.

Put the shelled peas in a pan with all the other ingredients except the butter. Cover with 3 pints of water. Boil until the peas are quite soft and sieve. See that the seasoning is right, heat up and before serving stir a lump of butter and a scrap of fresh mint into the soup.

A little cream added to the soup while it is heating is an improvement.

SOUP OF PRAWNS AND GREEN PEAS

Add half a teacupful of shelled prawns to the fresh green pea soup described on the top of this page.

To make a cheaper soup add, instead of prawns, half a

dozen soft herring roes poached and cut into strips, or little strips of filleted sole, or rock salmon.

Mushroom Soup

1½ pints of good chicken or meat broth, ¼ lb. mushrooms, 2 eggs, 2 ozs. of cream, fresh mint, butter, lemon juice.

Heat ½ oz. of butter in half a teacupful of water with the juice of half a lemon. When the mixture boils put in the mushrooms and cook for 3 or 4 minutes. Season with salt, pepper and a little chopped fresh mint. Add the mushroom mixture gradually to the beaten and strained eggs in a basin; then add the cream, boiled in a separate pan, then the boiling broth. Stir until the soup is amalgamated and reheat but do not boil or the eggs will curdle.

Soupe Menerboise

½ lb. courgettes (baby marrows), 1 lb. tomatoes, 2 onions, several cloves of garlic, 2 small potatoes, a handful of shelled and peeled broad beans, fresh basil, 1½ ozs. of small pasta or broken up spaghetti, olive oil, 2 yolks of eggs, Parmesan cheese.

In an earthenware casserole warm a coffeecupful of olive oil. Into this put the sliced onions and let them melt but not fry. Add the little marrows, unpeeled, and cut into squares (it is best to prepare them an hour before cooking, salt them lightly, and leave them in a colander so that some of the water drains from them). Let them melt in the oil slowly for 10 minutes before adding all but 2 of the tomatoes, roughly chopped. When these have softened put in the potatoes cut into small squares and pour about 2 pints of hot water over the whole mixture. Simmer gently for 10 minutes until the potatoes are nearly cooked then add the broad beans, the pasta and seasoning of salt and pepper.

In the meantime grill the remaining tomatoes, remove their skins; in a mortar pound 3 cloves of garlic, then the tomatoes, and a small bunch of basil. Add the yolks of the eggs, so that you have a sauce somewhat resembling a thin mayonnaise. The pasta in the soup being cooked, stir a ladleful of the soup into the sauce, then another. Return the mixture to the pan, and let it heat gently, stirring all the time to prevent the egg curdling. At the last minute stir in two large spoonfuls of grated Parmesan cheese.

A substantial soup for 4 people.

CLEAR BEETROOT CONSOMMÉ

4 pints of good beef stock, 2 lbs. of uncooked beetroots, 2 carrots, 2 turnips, cream, vinegar.

Peel the beetroots, cut them into small pieces and simmer them, with the carrots and turnips, in the stock. When they are soft, and the soup a good clear red, strain through a sieve, without pressing the vegetables at all.

When heating up the consommé add about 2 teaspoonfuls of Orleans vinegar, and see that the seasoning is correct. Serve a bowl of cream, either fresh or sour, separately. The quantities given will make 4 helpings; 4 pints of stock sounds a lot for four people, but a good deal is absorbed during the simmering of the vegetables.

SORREL SOUP

To a sorrel purée made as described on page 148 add gradually 1½ pints of light chicken or veal stock, or half stock and half hot milk. Stir all the time, and serve as soon as the soup is hot.

SORREL AND TOMATO SOUP

1½ lbs. of peeled and chopped tomatoes, 1½ pints of chicken stock, a handful of sorrel leaves, 1 oz. of butter.

Melt the tomatoes in the butter until they are soft but not completely disintegrated; five minutes will be long enough. Add the chopped sorrel; give it a stir round, pour over the heated stock, season with salt, pepper and sugar. Serve as soon as the soup is hot; do not overcook, or the tomatoes and sorrel will lose their fresh flavour.

This soup can also be served iced, but do the original cooking of the tomatoes in olive oil instead of butter.

SORREL AND LENTIL SOUP

Make a purée with about ¼ lb. of brown lentils cooked for 1½–2 hours in about 3 pints of water, adding the salt towards the end of the cooking. Put the lentils through the sieve, add enough of the water they have cooked in to make a thin purée.

Chop a handful of sorrel leaves (about ¼ lb.) fairly finely, cook them in the lentil soup for 10 minutes. Immediately before serving stir in 2 or 3 tablespoons of cream. Enough for 4 helpings. This is one of the best of the sorrel soups.

WALNUT SOUP

¼ lb. shelled walnuts, 1½ pints of meat or chicken stock, ¼ pint of cream, a small clove of garlic, salt, pepper.

Pound the walnuts with a little of the stock and the garlic. Gradually add the rest of the stock. Heat up this mixture, and add to it the cream previously boiled until it has thickened a little. Season with salt and pepper.

Enough for 4 helpings.

Tarragon Soup

Clear chicken or meat or fish broth, and for each pint of broth about 2 teaspoons of finely chopped fresh tarragon and 1 tablespoon of grated Parmesan cheese.

Heat the broth very gently with the chopped tarragon, and stir in the cheese just before serving. Nothing could be simpler, and at the same time more attractive and original, but if you like a richer soup can be made with the addition of cream or eggs, or if you have no good stock to hand a thinnish potato soup can be used as a background for the tarragon and the cheese, and is excellent.

Marrow Flower Soup

In Southern France and Italy, the golden yellow flowers of the marrow are sometimes made into fritters, sometimes stuffed with a rice mixture, stewed in oil and served cold as an hors d'oeuvre. In Mexico, they are stuffed with pounded beans and fried, and also made into a soup. For those people who have vegetable gardens, here is the recipe for soup made from marrow flowers, from the *Mexican Cook Book* by Josefina Velasquez de Leon. (Mexico City, 1947.)

2 ozs. lard, 1 lb. marrow flowers, 2 ozs. butter, 1 oz. flour, 2 ozs. bread, 2 quarts milk, 1 onion, ½ cup cream, 2 yolks, salt and pepper.

In a tablespoon of lard fry the chopped marrow flowers and onion, season with salt and pepper. Cover the pan, and let them simmer in their own juice until they are quite soft. When they are cooked pound them to a paste, pour the milk over them. Heat up. In another pan melt the butter, stir in the flour, when it starts to thicken gradually pour in the strained milk and marrow flower mixture. Stir until all the milk is poured in, and when the soup has thickened slightly and is very hot, pour it into the soup tureen in which the yolks and the cream have been beaten up together.

Serve the bread cut into small squares and fried in the rest of the lard.

A pound of marrow flowers is quite a quantity, and the amounts given are enough for at least 8 people, so they can be halved.

FRENCH BEANS AND ALMOND SOUP

In about 2½ pints of mild flavoured stock (chicken is best) cook three quarters of a pound of french beans, cut into half inch lengths and with all the strings carefully removed. Have ready two ounces of almonds, skinned, and browned lightly in the oven or with a little butter in a frying pan. Chop them or pound them roughly in a mortar.

See that the beans are sufficiently seasoned with salt, pepper, and a little lemon juice, and stir in the almonds a minute or two before serving. If you want to serve a more luxurious soup, beat up two yolks of eggs with a little of the hot broth, return the mixture to the pan and let it reheat without boiling.

Sufficient for 4 people.

CRAB SOUP

A medium sized cooked crab, ¼ lb. of rock salmon or other white fish, a small onion, 2 cloves of garlic, 2 tomatoes, lemon peel, mace, cayenne pepper and black pepper, salt, parsley, 3 tablespoons cream, a small glass of white wine, fresh herbs, 2 tablespoons of rice.

Put the rock salmon into a saucepan with the onion,

tomatoes, garlic, a very small piece of lemon peel, salt, pepper, a sprig of parsley and the white wine. Cook for a few minutes until the wine is reduced. Add the rice and pour over 2 pints of water, simmer for 20 minutes, then add all the crab meat, and cook another 5 minutes. Sieve, having first removed the onion and any bones from the fish. Heat up the resulting purée, seasoning with mace and cayenne pepper, and when hot add some fresh herbs such as chives, fennel, marjoram, or lemon thyme, chopped with a little piece of lemon peel. Add the cream just before serving. Enough for 4 or 5.

WHITE FISH SOUP

A large sole, 2 ozs. peeled cooked prawns, an onion, bay leaf, slice of lemon, lemon juice, pepper, salt, 2 eggs, 2 ozs. cream, parsley, garlic, a small glass of white wine.

Have the sole filleted and keep the carcass. Put the latter, with the onion, bay leaf, slice of lemon, pepper, salt, garlic, sprig of parsley and the white wine into a pan with two pints of water. Simmer gently for 40 minutes. Strain. Return to clean pan. Put in the fillets. Cook for 10 minutes and sieve. Heat up, add the prawns and the heated cream. In a basin beat the eggs with the juice of half a lemon. Strain this into the soup, and stir vigorously. Do not let the soup boil again.

COCKLE SOUP

4 pints of cockles, 2 tomatoes, a leek, a piece of celery, 2 potatoes, 2 ozs. of lean bacon, 1 oz. of butter, 2 eggs, lemon juice.

Cook the cleaned cockles[1] for 10 minutes in about 2½

---

[1] See page 91.

pints of water. Remove them from the pan and strain the liquid through a muslin.

Melt the butter in a saucepan, and add the bacon, the chopped leek and celery and the peeled and sliced tomatoes. When the vegetables have softened pour over the strained liquid from the cockles, and add the diced potatoes. Simmer until the potatoes are tender, and add the shelled cockles. See that the soup is properly seasoned; thicken it with beaten eggs and lemon juice in which a little of the hot soup has been stirred. Return this mixture to the pan and heat without letting it boil. Serve with rounds of fried French bread.

JELLIED CONSOMMÉ

2 lbs. of shin of beef, 2 pigs' feet, an onion, 2 or 3 carrots, a clove of garlic, a bay leaf, a small piece of lemon peel, 2 tomatoes, salt, pepper, 3 pints of water, 2 tablespoons sherry or port.

Put the beef in one piece at the bottom of the saucepan, then the pigs' feet split in halves and washed, the onion, unpeeled, (the skin helps to give a golden colour to the consommé), the tomatoes whole and also unpeeled, the seasonings (very little salt to start with). Cover with the water and bring very slowly almost to the boil; if there is any scum skim it off. Keep the liquid barely moving, not boiling, for at least 4 hours; if it doesn't taste strong enough, leave it a little longer. Strain it through a fine sieve and leave until next day. Skim off the fat. The consommé should be clear, golden, and set to a light jelly, much softer than aspic, and if it has not been allowed to boil it will be quite clear, and will not need clarifying.

When every particle of fat has been removed heat it very gently, adding the sherry and a little extra salt if necessary. As it is about to come to the boil turn off the flame, and pour the consommé into a clean bowl to set again. If it is to be kept in the refrigerator, keep it covered, and as far away from the ice trays as possible. Serve in cups. There should be 2 pints of consommé, enough for 4 large helpings or 6 smaller ones.

If the consommé has boiled, and turned cloudy, clarify it as described for the aspic jelly on page 171.

If you want to make do with less meat, use a pound and cut it into small pieces, so that it gives the maximum flavour to the consommé; the meat can be used for a sauce.

If you like the consommé to have a slightly gamey taste, use only 1½ lbs. of beef and substitute a small pigeon for the other half pound. Do not add strong vegetables like turnips or penetrating herbs such as rosemary or sage to consommés. The beef which has been used for the consommé makes an excellent salad as described on page 106.

Zuppa Ebrea (Hebrew Soup)

This recipe comes from *Il Gastronomo Educato*, an imaginative and practical book on the subject of civilized eating by Alberto Denti di Pirajno (Editions Neri Pozza, Venice, 1950). The author recalls eating this soup in a Jewish house in Livorno, and recommends it to all his friends "baptized christians, circumcized moslems, idolaters or fire-worshippers".

Peel and chop half a kilo (a little over a pound) of cooked beetroots. Put this beetroot into three pints of salted water, with the addition of a little vinegar. Cook for 20 minutes and put the mixture through a sieve.

In a soup tureen beat three whole eggs, pour the beetroot broth over the eggs, stirring all the time, see that the seasoning is right, press the soup once more through a sieve, and put it on ice until it is perfectly cold.

Serve the soup iced, and for each guest have a bowl or saucer of hot boiled potatoes which have been stirred in a pan with very hot goose fat. The guests take a spoonful of potatoes, mix them with the cold beetroot soup and consume this ambrosia with little sighs of satisfaction.
(The goose fat can be replaced by butter, the juice from a roast, good beef dripping.)

PICKLED CUCUMBER SOUP

½ lb. pickled cucumbers, 2 pints of clear meat stock, 2 lumps of sugar, mace, ginger, allspice, pepper, salt, ¼ pint of cream.

Chop the pickled cucumbers and simmer them for 30 minutes in the stock. Put through a sieve. Heat up and add the sugar, a pinch each of mace, ground ginger and allspice, ground black pepper and salt. The soup should have a definitely spiced, oriental flavour about it. Stir in the cream, already boiled in another pan.

Serve iced, garnished with a little chopped fennel, or mint. For a special occasion add a few strips of smoked sturgeon immediately before serving, or prawns, or chopped hard-boiled eggs.

ICED RUSSIAN SOUP

This is a very simplified version of a Russian summer soup called Swekolnik.

½ lb. of the leaves of young beetroots, 4 small beetroots, half a fresh cucumber, 2 or 3 small pickled cucumbers, a few leaves of tarragon, chives, mint, fennel, ¼ pint of cream, salt, pepper, tarragon vinegar.

Wash the beet leaves, remove the stalks. Cook the leaves in a little salted water for a few minutes. Drain, squeeze perfectly dry, chop finely. Put them in a bowl.

Cut the cooked beetroots into small squares, salt them, add them to the leaves, and pour in a coffeecupful of tarragon vinegar. Add the diced fresh and pickled cucumber, and a little of the liquid from the pickle. Pour in the cream.

Put the bowl in the refrigerator, and before serving add the chopped herbs, thin with iced water, and serve with little pieces of ice floating in the soup tureen.

This soup comes out a rather violent pink colour, but is very good on a really hot evening.

GAZPACHO

There are many versions of this Spanish summer soup; the basis of it is chopped tomato, olive oil and garlic, and there may be additions of cucumber, black olives, raw onion, red pepper, herbs, eggs, and bread. The following makes a very good and refreshing gazpacho.

Chop a pound of raw peeled tomatoes until almost a purée. Stir in a few dice of cucumber, 2 chopped cloves of garlic, a finely sliced spring onion, a dozen stoned black olives, a few strips of green pepper, 3 tablespoons of olive oil, a tablespoon of wine vinegar, salt, pepper, and a pinch of cayenne pepper, a little chopped fresh marjoram, mint or parsley. Keep very cold until it is time to serve the soup, then thin with ½ pint of iced water, add a few cubes of coarse brown bread, and serve with broken up ice floating in the bowl. A couple of hard-boiled eggs, coarsely chopped, make a good addition.

ICED HADDOCK SOUP

Take half a pint of the milk in which smoked haddock has been cooked, and about 2 tablespoons of flaked haddock. Into this mix a quarter pint of yoghourt, and a cupful of cucumber in dill, 2 raw tomatoes, a handful of parsley,

2 small pickled onions, half a fresh cucumber, a table-spoon of capers and a tablespoon of chives or the green part of leeks, all chopped up. Add black pepper but no salt, and a few drops of the vinegar from the pickled cucumber.

To be made some hours before serving, and iced. Two tablespoons of red caviar added to the mixture makes this a soup for a special occasion.

ICED CREAM SOUPS

Heat good clear chicken, meat or fish broth and stir in a little thin cream (about 3 tablespoons per half pint) and a small quantity of very finely chopped parsley, chives, tarragon or whatever herbs are available; add a scrap of grated lemon peel. A thin soup to be drunk iced from large cups.

It is very simple to think of variations on this theme. Thin purées of green peas or french beans, or tomato juice, can be used as a basis. Flavour can be varied with spices (grated green ginger, pounded coriander seeds, a pinch of curry powder, or a little white wine, and instead of lemon peel a little chopped pimento or pounded salt almonds or walnuts.

The important point is to keep the soup thin and light; a thickening of flour would make it pasty and cloying.

CHAPTER 4

EGGS

EGGS provide perhaps the best and most nourishing quickly prepared meal in the world, at quite a small cost; for a luncheon dish an omelette or a couple of eggs baked in cream can scarcely be bettered; a new laid, boiled egg, with good butter and fresh crusty bread is every bit as much a treat as any sophisticated dish with a cream and wine sauce.

Although I, for one, never tire of eggs, it *is* dull to have them always cooked in the same way, and in this respect English cookery is curiously restricted; one of the reasons, I fancy, is that so many kitchens lack dishes and utensils in which to cook the *oeufs sur le plat*, the *oeufs en cocotte* and the egg sauces of which there is such a huge variety in French cooking. These utensils are now freely available in considerable variety, from the remarkably inexpensive Pyrex ramekins or *cocottes* large enough for one egg, to flat, two handled dishes in earthenware or porcelain lined cast iron in which 8 to 10 eggs can be cooked and served; these last are particularly useful as they can be used over a direct flame as well as in the oven; but beware, for they retain the heat to such an extent that the eggs go on cooking long after they have been taken from the fire. Perhaps the most useful egg dishes for general use are fireproof porcelain ones, measuring about 5 inches across, intended for 2 eggs; they can be bought at most large stores; the cream-lined blue Denby earthenware makes a good background for eggs.

As well as a good heavy 10 inch omelette pan for

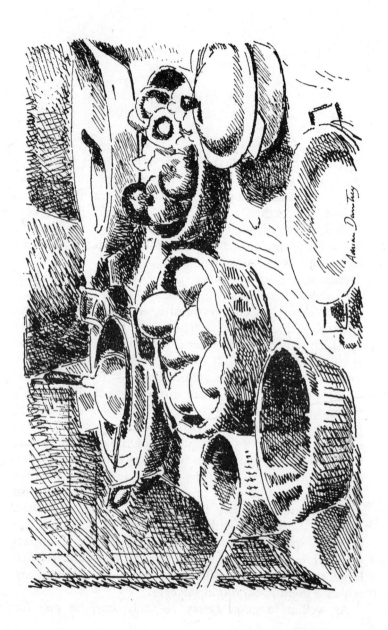

omelettes of three or four eggs, a smaller pan, such as the Rangemaster 6 inch heavy aluminium pan is an invaluable asset in any kitchen, and especially for people who often have solitary meals; it is the right size for an omelette of 2 eggs and useful for frying or sautéing a small quantity of onions, bacon, mushrooms or croûtons. The Pyrex flameware frying pan, which goes over direct heat is useful, as it can be used for omelettes, for frying, and for eggs *sur le plat*.

In this chapter are suggestions for a few egg dishes which will vary the usual routine of fried, scrambled, and poached on toast. Variations in the recipes can always be made, but the addition of too many dabs of this and that will spoil them; their charm lies in their simplicity and freshness.

Cold egg dishes will be found in the chapter on hors d'oeuvre, and dishes which require whites or yolks only are listed in the index.

POACHED EGGS

Here is an easy method. Bring a small saucepanful of water to the boil. Add a small spoonful of vinegar. *As* the water boils remove the pan from the fire and drop in your egg. Leave it in the pan for two or three minutes according to whether it is a large or small egg and whether you want it well or lightly poached. Take it out with a perforated spoon. By this method the white of the egg sets as the egg is put in the water, instead of whirling around. You will have a neat and white veiled poached egg. Provide yourself with a long-handled perforated spoon for getting poached eggs out of the saucepan.

OEUFS POCHÉS À LA PROVENÇALE

Cut ½ lb. tomatoes into smallish pieces. Heat a little butter or olive oil in a metal egg dish. Put in the tomatoes. Add a chopped clove of garlic, salt and pepper, and a little parsley. When the tomatoes have cooked 5 minutes (they must retain their fresh flavour) add 4 to 6 poached eggs; cover these, but not the tomatoes, with grated Parmesan cheese, and put in a hot oven (No. 7 or 8) for 3 minutes, until the cheese has melted.

EGGS AND SPINACH

½ lb. of spinach, 2 eggs, 2 tablespoons of cream and 2 of grated Gruyère or Parmesan for each person. Butter.

Clean and cook the spinach in the usual way. Drain it, and chop it, but not too finely. Arrange it in buttered fireproof egg dishes and heat it gently. Then put two eggs, either poached or *mollets* (eggs put into boiling water and cooked exactly 5 minutes, then shelled) into each dish. Cover with the cream and the cheese. Put in a hot oven for about 3 minutes.

This is a simplified version of the well-known *oeufs Florentine*, in which the poached eggs are thickly covered with sauce Mornay (cheese flavoured béchamel) which is then browned in the oven; a dish which always seems to me rather cloying, but there are those who prefer white sauce to fresh cream.

POACHED EGGS IN CHEESE SOUFFLÉ

For the soufflé mixture melt ½ oz. butter, stir in a dessert-spoonful of flour and add 6 ozs. (just over ¼ pint) of warmed milk. Season with salt and a little cayenne pepper and ground black pepper. When the sauce has thickened, add, off the fire, the yolk of one egg. Return to the fire and stir for a minute, then add 1 oz. of grated Gruyère cheese. When cool, and when you are ready to cook the soufflé, fold in the whipped whites of two eggs.

Have ready, in buttered metal or fireproof egg dishes, (about 5 inches diameter) slices of bread fried in butter, or toast, and on top of each a lightly poached egg. Over this pour the soufflé mixture. Put immediately in an oven preheated at the usual temperature you use for cooking soufflés (mark 7 or 8 in a gas oven). Cook for about 6 minutes, and serve at once.

The quantities given are enough for two people.

The first time this recipe was published was, I believe, by Alfred Suzanne in his *Egg Cookery*, 1893. Marcel Boulestin gave a version of it in *The Finer Cooking*, 1937, and a similar dish is now one of the specialities of a London hotel known for good food. The recipe I have given is that of Alfred Suzanne, except that his instructions are to cook the eggs on toast, not fried bread, the eggs ranged on a baking sheet for 15 minutes.

Another method is to half fill small soufflé dishes with the soufflé mixture, put the poached egg on top, fill up nearly to the top with the rest of the mixture and cook in a very hot oven for 7 to 8 minutes.

Instead of a cheese soufflé, the dish can be made with the crab soufflé mixture described on page 88 and instead of a poached egg a 4 minute *oeuf mollet* can be used.

All these little dishes require some practice, but are very attractive when successful.

Oeufs sur le Plat and Oeufs en Cocotte

Oeufs sur le plat are eggs cooked in butter in a shallow enamel, aluminium, earthenware or fireproof china dish. They can be cooked either on top of the stove or in the oven, but the cooking must always be very gentle, so that

the whites remain white and do not get frizzled round
the edges. Various sauces can be added to them, or they
can be covered with cheese.

Oeufs en cocotte are much the same, except that a
cocotte usually only holds one egg, is deeper than the dishes
used for eggs *sur le plat*, and cream is nearly always added
to them.

Oeufs en cocotte are cooked in the oven, or on top of the
stove with the little dishes standing in a pan of hot water,
and a cover over the whole. The addition of a very small
amount of chopped tarragon, chives, basil, marjoram or
any other herbs you fancy when the cream is poured over
them makes these eggs perfectly delicious.

The timing is important, and practice is necessary to
get it right, as half a minute too long may ruin them.
On no account must the yolks of eggs *en cocotte* be hard, a
fact which is not always grasped in this country. They are
to be eaten with a spoon.

Oeufs au Plat au Beurre d'Escargots

Prepare a snail butter by pounding 2 ozs. of butter with
2 cloves of garlic, a shallot, a little salt, ground black
pepper, and parsley.

Cook your eggs in butter, in fireproof egg dishes, either
on top of the stove or in the oven. A minute or so before
they are ready, add a little of the snail butter to each dish;
it will just start to melt as you eat the eggs.

Delicious for garlic eaters and for those who like snails
and cannot get them in England.

Oeufs au Plat aux Echalottes

Butter, flour, stock, shallots, white wine, parsley, eggs.

Melt ½ oz. butter, add the same quantity of flour. Stir

until it turns golden; add ¼ pint of meat stock, and when the sauce has thickened 4 or 5 finely chopped shallots. After 5 minutes add two tablespoons of white wine, season with salt and pepper and add a little chopped parsley. Cook another 10 minutes, gently. Pour this sauce over the eggs cooked in butter, in metal egg dishes.

OEUFS AU PLAT BRESSANE

In each buttered egg dish put a slice of bread fried in butter; over this, pour a tablespoon of heated cream, and then break the eggs very carefully over the bread. Add another two tablespoons of the hot cream and cook in a moderate oven for 5 minutes.

If this is to be served as a first dish, one egg is usually enough, as the fried bread makes it fairly filling. Instead of butter, I have sometimes fried the bread in dripping from roast pork, which gives the dish quite a different flavour. If you like garlic, rub the fried bread with a cut clove before putting it into the egg dish.

MOONSHINE

"Break them in a dish, upon some butter and oyl, melted or cold; throw on them a little salt, and set them on a chafing-dish of coals; make not the yolks too hard, and in the doing cover them, and make a sauce for them of an onion cut into round slices, and fried in sweet oyl or butter; then put to them Verjuice grated nutmeg, a little salt, and so serve them."

The Accomplisht Cook. Robert May. 1660.

Omitting the Verjuice (the juice of white grapes), Moonshine is an admirable way of cooking eggs *au plat.*

In those days, the dish used would have been a pewter
plate.

Oeufs en Cocotte à la Crème aux Asperges

Pour a little melted butter into each ramekin, put in a few
cooked asparagus tips and break an egg into the centre.
Add 2 or 3 tablespoons of cream and cook 4 or 5 minutes
in a moderate oven.

Oeufs en Cocotte Bercy

Over each egg broken into a buttered ramekin pour a
little sauce Bercy (p. 168). Cook in the oven, or covered on
top of the stove.

Eggs Cooked in Cream with Game Sauce

When you have stock from a casserole grouse or partridge, made as described on page 132, boil a little in a
saucepan until it is reduced to a syrupy glaze.

In china or metal ramekins, or *cocottes* melt a little
butter. Break two eggs into each, pour fresh cream round
the yolks but not over them, cook them for four minutes in
a moderate oven, then add a dessertspoon of the prepared
sauce. Put the dishes back in the oven for another minute.
By this time the eggs should be ready, the whites cooked
and the yolks still soft.

Oeufs Mollets

Oeufs mollets are eggs boiled for five minutes, so that the
whites are firm and the yolks still slightly runny. Naturally, common sense must be exercised in the cooking of
these eggs; if they are very small, cook them a little less, if

large a little longer. As soon as they are taken out of the pan, pour a little cold water over them to stop them cooking any more, but they are easier to shell while still warm. This is a process which is perfectly easy as long as it is not attempted in a hurry, with shaking hands. Handle the eggs gently and don't try to peel off the whole shell at once as you can with a hard-boiled egg.

If you have to cook a number of *oeufs mollets* at a time, put the eggs into a saucepan and pour the boiling water over them. The incidence of cracked eggs is neither more nor less by this method than when they are put straight into boiling water, but it facilitates the timing. (Five minutes from the moment the eggs are covered with the water.)

There are also now available metal stands with a handle which will hold 4 eggs, to be lowered into the pan when the water is boiling. With this device (which is a very old one revived) the eggs do not touch the bottom of the pan, and the risk of cracking is almost eliminated.

Oeufs Mollets à la Crème aux Fines Herbes

Allow 2 eggs for each person, put them into boiling water, and cook them for exactly 5 minutes. Shell them when they have cooled.

For 8 eggs prepare half a teacupful of chopped fresh herbs, such as basil, chives and parsley, with a scrap of garlic, salt and pepper. Put a piece of butter into a fireproof egg dish, and when it has melted add the eggs, then the herbs, then a cupful of fresh cream. Cook 2 or 3 minutes only, turning the eggs over so that they heat on each side. Serve quickly.

Tarragon is a wonderful herb with this dish, instead of, but not with, basil; a combination of sweet marjoram, lemon thyme, parsley and chives, or a very little of the green part of spring onions, is also very good.

Instead of *oeufs mollets*, you can cook your eggs *en cocotte*, having mixed the herbs into the cream before pouring it over the eggs.

OMELETTE AUX FINES HERBES

Fresh eggs, fresh butter, fresh herbs, what more delicious combination can there be? A great luxury for people who live in towns. For an *omelette aux fines herbes* use the same mixtures of herbs as described in the preceding recipe, allowing a large tablespoon of chopped herbs for an omelette of 3 eggs, with a little extra to sprinkle over the omelette before serving. Instead of stirring the herbs into the ready beaten eggs, add them only when the eggs are already in the pan; in this way they will have greater flavour, and there is no risk of little bits sticking to the pan or burning while the omelette is cooking.

TOMATO OMELETTE

For an omelette of 3 or 4 eggs, cook 2 or 3 chopped tomatoes for about two minutes only in butter, adding a little garlic, salt, ground black pepper and some fresh parsley or basil. Add to the omelette when already in the pan.

Provided the tomatoes are cooked just sufficiently to soften them, retaining all their flavour, this makes one of the nicest of summer omelettes.

OMELETTE BERRICHONNE

The white part of a small leek, raw and finely sliced, one shallot, a little mint and a tablespoon of cream, added to the omelette in the pan.

Omelette Savoyarde

A rasher of bacon or a small slice of ham (chopped), a little raw leek, a small diced cooked potato, cooked a minute in butter. Add to the eggs in pan, cover with two tablespoons of coarsely grated Gruyère cheese.

Kidney Omelette

Cut a cleaned sheep's kidney into dice; sauté it in butter; pour over a tablespoon of port or madeira, let it bubble. Add a teaspoonful of meat glaze, or a dessertspoonful of good stock. When the sauce is thick the kidney mixture is ready to add to the omelette.

Omelette à l'Oseille

One of the nicest of summer omelettes. Wash a handful of sorrel; chop it. Melt it in butter; add salt. In five minutes it is ready to add to the eggs.

Omelette Paysanne

Sorrel, 1 oz. ham, a small cooked potato. Cook the sorrel as above (use rather less) add the ham cut in strips, and the potato in dice. Add to the eggs.

Matelote sans Poisson

"You have promised your guests a *matelote*. Like Grouchy at Waterloo, the fish has not arrived. The main body of your well laid plans is lacking. You have, like Louvois, organized victory, and you are faced with defeat. Visions of Vatel begin to haunt your brain . . . But I am there; the harm will go no further.

"In butter brown two dozen small onions, which you leave whole. Remove them, and to the butter add sufficient flour and water to make a white roux. Then add red wine, a bouquet of parsley, thyme and bay leaf, a clove, salt and pepper, a large clove of garlic crushed, 3 chopped shallots, the browned onions and a pound and a half of mushrooms. Leave to reduce.

"Prepare a rather firmly cooked omelette; cut into slices into a deep dish, and pour over it your sauce *matelote* after having removed the bouquet of parsley.

"At dinner, recount your anguish and your success; cite the English proverb 'Fish must swim thrice—namely, once in the water, once in the sauce, and a third time in wine in the stomach.' "

Translated from *Cuisine Messine*,

Auricoste de Lazarque, 1909.

Cheese Pancakes

Make some small thin pancakes, allowing two or three for each person. For 12 pancakes make a béchamel with 1½ ozs. of butter, 2 tablespoons of flour, 1¼ pints of warmed milk, salt, pepper, and nutmeg.

When it has cooked sufficiently, stir in 2 ozs. of grated Parmesan. Divide the béchamel into two separate bowls. Into one half stir ¼ lb. of Gruyère cheese cut into small squares. Put a tablespoon of this mixture into each pancake. Roll them up. Butter a shallow fireproof dish and spread a layer of the other half of the béchamel on the bottom. Arrange the pancakes on the top, pour a little more of the béchamel over them, then a thin coating of grated Parmesan, then a few knobs of butter. Cook them in a hot oven for 10 minutes, until the dish is browned.

The contrast of the Gruyère cheese with the Parmesan, both in taste and texture, is important. A light white wine accords particularly well with the soft flavour of the Gruyère in this dish.

GNOCCHI ALLA GENOVESE

This dish is simply an excuse for eating *pesto*, the wonderful Genoese basil sauce.

The preparation of the *gnocchi* is the same as that for *gnocchi à la romaine*, but the final cooking is different, as they are poached instead of gratiné.

For the gnocchi: 6 ozs. of fine semolina, a pint of milk, nutmeg, salt, pepper, 2 ozs. of grated Parmesan, 2 eggs. Bring the milk to the boil, having seasoned it with salt, pepper and grated nutmeg. Pour in the semolina, and stir until you have a thick, smooth and stiff mass. Add the cheese off the fire and stir in the eggs. Pour the whole mixture into an oiled shallow tin, in one layer about ½ inch thick. Leave to cool for several hours. Cut into small squares, and with floured hands roll each square into a cork shape. Lay on a floured board until all are ready.

Bring a large pan of salted water to a gentle boil. Drop in the gnocchi one by one. Have ready a perforated spoon and a colander and a hot buttered oven dish. As the gnocchi rise to the top (3 or 4 minutes) take each one out and drain in the colander. Put them all in the hot buttered dish, put more butter on the top and leave them in the oven for 5 minutes.

The *pesto* sauce (see following page) can either be spooned lightly on top of the gnocchi, with more butter on top of that, or it can be served separately. A bowl of grated cheese should also be on the table.

Pesto

A large bunch of fresh basil, garlic, a handful of pine nuts, a handful of grated Sardo or Parmesan cheese, about 2 ozs. of olive oil.

Pound the basil leaves (there should be about 2 ozs. when the stalks have been removed) in a mortar with one or two cloves of garlic, a little salt and the pine nuts. Add the cheese. (Sardo cheese is the pungent Sardinian ewe's milk cheese which is exported in large quantities to Genoa to make *pesto*. Parmesan and Sardo are sometimes used in equal quantities; or all Parmesan, which gives a milder flavour.)

When the *pesto* is a thick purée start adding the olive oil, a little at a time. Stir it steadily and see that it is amalgamating with the other ingredients, as the finished sauce should have the consistency of a creamed butter. If made in larger quantities, *pesto* may be stored in jars covered with a layer of olive oil.

This is the famous sauce which is eaten by the Genoese with all kinds of pasta, with gnocchi and as a flavouring for soups.

An imitation of this sauce can be made with parsley or sweet marjoram, and although the flavour is totally different, it is still good. Pine nuts are very hard to come by in England, and walnuts can be used instead, or they can be omitted altogether, but the result is a thinner sauce.

CHAPTER 5

FISH

BOILED salmon with cucumber and mayonnaise is an admirable dish, but anyone visiting this country for the first time and dining out frequently, might well be excused for supposing that salmon is the only fish procurable in England during the whole of the summer. In fact, salmon is àt its best in the very early spring; later, it scarcely justifies its high price. Salmon trout, in season in May and June, is an exquisite fish, and although nearly as expensive as salmon, a small whole one is an occasional possibility for a small household; although again what can possibly induce people to pay something like 14/- a pound for a frozen salmon trout which has quite lost its flavour is beyond my comprehension. If it is a cold dish that is needed and there is money to spend, fillets of sole make a very welcome change (see the recipe for soles *à la juive*, p 76.) from the eternal salmon. Then there are some excellent lesser known fish, such as john dory, sea bream, Cornish bass and grey mullet which are occasionally to be found at the fishmonger's and are comparatively cheap; so it is well worth knowing how to deal with them.

Rock salmon and mackerel make good cheap cold dishes, and red mullet, although more expensive, makes one of the best and most beautiful of summer fish dishes when grilled on a bed of dried fennel stalks. Fresh brown trout fried or grilled and served with plenty of melted butter are a rare treat, but the little rainbow trout usually to be found at the fishmongers' are often rather disappointing. An interesting sauce, however, does a great deal for them. A grilled herring has always seemed to me one of those cheap luxuries of which there are all too few; herrings are out of season in May and June, but later in the summer they can be enjoyed with fresh herbs and butter and perhaps French mustard instead of pasty mustard sauce. Remember soft herring roes too; with a little ingenuity they make most excellent little dishes, at a very small cost.

There is not much in the way of shell fish in the summer except cockles, although in the Mediterranean mussels are eaten all the year round, but the crustaceans—lobsters, crayfish and crab—are at their best in the summer, and there are prawns and Dublin Bay prawns; with the exception of crabs, these are all very expensive and with the same exception, are all best served very plain. The difference between Dublin Bay prawns bought alive, cooked at home and eaten at once and the same fish when it has been boiled and then recooked, is as the difference between fresh coffee and boiled up coffee. The frozen ones (called frozen scampi—the word evidently has some magic for the English public) have just a very faint flavour.

Crabs are useful for all sorts of soups, salads and soufflés, but a little, unlike other crustaceans of which one needs a lot, goes a long way. Unless you know your fishmonger pretty well, it is not advisable to buy "dressed" crab from him; it is often mixed with bread, and sometimes not of the first freshness. In the soup chapter there are ideas (which can be varied according to what is available) which may be helpful to those whose families and friends will eat fish only if it is spoon fed to them.

For those who like fish plain grilled, fried, baked or poached, there are the delicious classic French sauces, Hollandaise, Maltaise, Bercy, Remoulade, and a few lesser known sauces made with herbs, almonds, walnuts, avocado pears, which will often liven up a rather dull fish. Of all vegetables, I think perhaps sorrel is the one which goes best with coarse fish, but in England it is only available to those people who grow it themselves (and at one or two shops in Soho); spinach not being a good substitute, the next best vegetables are tomatoes, and, for more delicate fish, mushrooms.

Paupiettes of Sole in Lettuce Leaves

4 fillets of sole, 2 ozs. of peeled cooked prawns, 8 lettuce leaves, butter, lemon juice, 2 eggs, nutmeg.

Choose 8 good lettuce leaves, not the coarse outside ones, but large enough to roll up. Wash them and blanch them 2 minutes in boiling salted water, drain them. Season the fillets of sole with salt, pepper and lemon juice. In the centre of each arrange a few prawns, also seasoned; roll the fillets up. Arrange the lettuce leaves overlapping each other two by two, so that you have 4 leaves instead of 8. Put a rolled fillet in the centre of each, and roll the leaves round the soles. Squeeze them in the hand, so that each forms a little parcel, which need not be tied. Grate a little nutmeg on to each paupiette. Melt 1 oz. of butter in a small shallow pan. Put the paupiettes in and cook very gently for 30 minutes, with the cover on the pan.

Beat two eggs in a bowl and add the juice of half a lemon and a little salt. Remove the paupiettes to the serving dish. Strain the egg and lemon mixture through a sieve into the butter remaining in the pan, and stir very fast until the sauce has thickened and frothed. Pour over the paupiettes and serve at once.

FILETS DE SOLE EN COCOTTE

Fillets of sole folded, cooked in butter in egg dishes with salt, pepper, lemon juice, small chopped mushrooms, parsley.

Allow 2 fillets of sole per person.

SOLES À LA JUIVE

2 large soles, 1 onion, 2 lemons, parsley, bayleaf, pepper, salt, the yolks of 4 eggs.

Have the soles filleted. With the bones, the onion, a piece of lemon peel, parsley, bayleaf, pepper and salt and 1¼ pints of water, make a court-bouillon. Cook it 15 to 20 minutes, strain, and leave to cool. In this poach the fillets for 10 minutes. Put them in a serving dish. Add a little of the hot court-bouillon to the beaten eggs and lemon juice. Stir to prevent curdling. Return this mixture to the rest of the court-bouillon and heat up, but do not let it boil. Pour over the fillets and serve cold.

SOLE AU VERT

Fillets of sole, sorrel, tarragon, chives, parsley, flour, butter, salt and pepper.

Salt and pepper the fillets, dust them with flour, cook in hot butter. When both sides are lightly browned, throw over them a handful of the chopped herbs, in which sorrel should predominate. Add a little more butter and simmer 3 or 4 minutes.

Filets de Sole Véronique

Wait until the muscat grapes come into season in August to make this dish. No other grapes will really do.

8 fillets of sole, a large wineglass of medium dry white wine, 4 ozs. cream, 3 teaspoons of flour, 1 oz. of butter, ¾ lb. of muscat grapes, a little fennel or tarragon if available.

Poach the fillets of sole (seasoned with salt, pepper, and lemon juice) in the white wine with the fennel or tarragon. Meanwhile heat the butter, stir in the flour, and when it has amalgamated add the boiling cream. Season with salt and pepper.

Remove the poached fillets to a narrow oval buttered fireproof dish. Reduce the wine in which they have cooked by a minute's fast boiling, add it to the prepared sauce, and stir until it is the consistency of thick cream. Arrange the peeled and seeded grapes at each end of the dish.

Pour the sauce over the fish, and brown under a very hot grill for about 3 minutes.

Bar à la Marseillaise

Bar or *loup de mer* is one of the most delicate fish of the Mediterranean; grilled on a bed of fennel stalks it makes the famous Provençal *grillade au fenouil*. The bass which come from Cornwall are the English equivalent; they

don't appear very often, but are well worth buying when
they do.

The ingredients for this dish are a bass weighing 2½/3
lbs., a coffeecupful of olive oil, a small glass of dry white
wine, a little bouquet of fennel leaves, 2 cloves of garlic,
½ lb. of mushrooms, ½ lb. of onions, 1 lb. of yellow waxy
potatoes.

Put the fish in a baking dish, pour over it the oil and
wine, cover with the chopped fennel and garlic, round it
arrange the sliced onions, mushrooms and potatoes.
Season with salt and pepper, add a pint of water and cook
in a fairly hot oven.

Serve with an aïoli or pimento mayonnaise (see recipe
for Rougets à la Provençale).

BAKED BREAM

Marinate a sea bream for an hour in olive oil and lemon
juice, with a bayleaf, parsley, thyme, salt and pepper.

Cook it in an open baking dish in a fairly hot oven so
that the skin gets nicely golden and crackling.

Serve with the following sauce: a chopped shallot in a
glass of white wine reduced to half; add a coffeespoonful
of French mustard, 2 ozs. of butter, 2 pounded egg yolks,
salt, pepper and chopped parsley.

A large grey mullet may be cooked in the same way,
but make sure it is very well cleaned, and washed
under running water, as these fish sometimes have a
slightly muddy taste.

JOHN DORY

A fish of alarming aspect, with a very ugly head and good
solid white flesh. It is something of a rarity in English
fishmongers', but very common in the Mediterranean. In
France, it is called *St. Pierre*, in Italy, *Pesce San Pietro*.

When it does appear in England it is fairly cheap, although there is a good deal of waste as the head is so large.

Have it filleted by the fishmonger; there will be two large triangular fillets which can each be cut into two. The head and carcass make good stock for fish soup. Cook the fillets in a court-bouillon and serve with a green sauce, or a mayonnaise, or on a bed of sorrel purée, or on chopped tomatoes melted in butter.

John Dory can also be cooked in the same way as the Bar or Bass à la Marseillaise (p. 77).

FILLETS OF JOHN DORY MARECHIARO

This recipe comes from the Gritti Palace Hotel in Venice where the *Pesce San Pietro*, or John Dory, is highly esteemed.

Having seasoned and floured your fillets of John Dory, fry them in butter until golden on both sides. Put them in the serving dish and pour over them plenty of bubbling butter, then a sauce made of 4 or 5 tomatoes chopped and cooked with finely sliced onions in butter; garnish the dish with shelled prawns, clams, mussels and chopped parsley.

ROUGETS À LA PROVENÇALE

Score large red mullets obliquely, twice, on each side, and paint them with olive oil. Grill them for about 10 minutes on each side and serve with the following sauce, which is a combination of two Provençal sauces, aïoli, and *sauce rouille*: for the aïoli, two large cloves of garlic pounded in a mortar, two yolks of eggs, a little salt, a third of a pint of olive oil, mixed exactly as for a mayonnaise. For the red part of the sauce, pound the contents of a half pound tin of red peppers (the roasted ones are best for the purpose, as they are already skinned), or the equivalent in fresh peppers, grilled and skinned, with a teaspoon of paprika; add a teacup of fresh breadcrumbs, softened in water, then pressed dry, to the pounded pimentos. At the last minute amalgamate the two sauces, adding the aïoli gradually to the pimento mixture. Grey mullet may be served in the same way.

TURBOT

Turbot cooked whole, poached, steamed or baked, is such a fine fish that it always seems to me a mistake to fillet it or cut it into steaks, but as such a very large fish is not often practical, and since hardly anybody now possesses a proper turbot kettle for cooking it, here is a method of cooking turbot fillets which keeps the fish moist.

Poach the fillets in milk previously simmered with salt, pepper, nutmeg and fresh green herbs (tarragon or fennel or mint).

Serve the fillets quite plain, accompanied by a *vinaigrette aux oeufs* (p. 168) or a sauce *à la crème* (p. 167) or with a little of the milk in which it has been cooked, strained, thickened with yolk of egg and flavoured with lemon.

COLD STURGEON IN OIL

Recently there have been imports of sturgeon from the Caspian Sea to this country, and it is occasionally to be bought at Harrods and other large stores. It is a magnificent looking fish, weighing sometimes as much as 100 lbs. It is sold in steaks, like salmon, and is about half the price.

Steamed and seasoned with good olive oil, it makes a good hors d'oeuvre.

Have it cut in rather thin slices; season it with salt and pepper and steam it, allowing about 25 minutes for it to cook. While it is still warm, pour some olive oil and a very little lemon juice over it.

Serve it cold.

FISH KEBABS

For each person you need a medium sized mackerel or grey mullet, a rasher of bacon, a little onion, two or three bayleaves, a mushroom. Olive oil, salt, pepper, lemon juice, thyme or marjoram.

Have the backbone removed from the fish; cut each one through into about 6 slices; thread these slices on to skewers, alternating with slices of onion and bacon, with an occasional bay leaf and slice of mushroom. Put the prepared skewers on a dish and season them with salt, ground black pepper, lemon juice and a good sprinkling of thyme or marjoram. Pour olive oil over them and leave them to marinate for an hour or so. Put the skewers under the grill and cook them fairly fast, turning them over from time to time, for 10/12 minutes.

Serve on a long dish, on their skewers, on a bed of parsley, or shredded lettuce, garnished with halves of lemon and half tomatoes.

Fennel or mint can be used instead of thyme or marjoram.

MACKEREL WITH SAUCE REMOULADE

Poach the mackerel simply in water to which you add two bay leaves, a few peppercorns, salt, and a slice of lemon. They will take about 12 minutes, cooked gently. Leave them to cool in their juice. Drain carefully and serve on a bed of parsley or watercress, with the Remoulade (p. 165) served separately.

Rock Salmon and Tunny Fish Mayonnaise

1½ lb. of rock salmon, a lettuce, mayonnaise, a small tin of tunny fish, lemon, cucumber.

Poach the fish in salted water with an onion and a bay leaf for about 15 minutes. Leave to cool, then carefully remove all bones and cartilaginous pieces. Arrange the fillets on a bed of chopped lettuce, and cover it with a mayonnaise into which has been incorporated 3 or 4 ozs. of pounded tunny fish and the juice of half a lemon.

Surround the dish with rounds of very finely sliced cucumber.

Grilled Herrings

A plain grilled herring really fresh is one of the most delicious of fish. Unfortunately by the time herrings reach the shops their flavour is somewhat diminished, but they still make an excellent and cheap luncheon. Have them boned by the fishmonger, and to make them more interesting, buy a few extra soft herring roes, which are sold separately. Salt and pepper the fish, and add an extra roe to each herring. Put a little piece of butter into each fish, close it up and grill them in an oiled dish for about 7 minutes, turning them over half way through the cooking.

Instead of the traditional mustard sauce, have a pot of French mustard on the table.

Laitances à la Provençale

½ lb. soft herring roes, flour, butter, parsley, garlic, lemon.

Dust the washed roes lightly with flour. Fry them gently in melted butter. Two minutes on each side should be enough. Sprinkle chopped garlic and parsley over them, cook another half minute, put them on a hot dish and sprinkle a little lemon juice over them.

FRITTERS OF SOFT ROES, MUSHROOMS AND FENNEL

½ lb. of soft roes, ¼ lb. of firm mushrooms, a large root of fennel.

Prepare a frying batter (see below).

Slice the washed and well dried mushrooms into ¼ inch slices, the fennel into 6 or 8 lengthwise pieces. Dip the fennel into the batter and fry in deep, very hot, olive oil or fat. Drain on to blotting paper. Then fry the mushroom slices in the same way; then the soft roes.

Pile up on a dish, sprinkle coarse salt over the fritters, garnish with parsley and lemon.

This is obviously a dish which can be varied according to taste; prawns or Dublin Bay prawns can replace soft roes, celery can replace fennel and so on, but remember to fry the vegetables before the fish.

The smell of deep frying is a very penetrating one, so this method of cooking is not much to be recommended for people who eat in the kitchen.

Frying Batter

4 ozs. flour, 3 tablespoons of olive oil, ¾ of a tumbler of tepid water, a pinch of salt, the white of one egg.

Mix the flour and the oil to a thick paste, add the water gradually, and the salt. Stir very vigorously until the batter is quite smooth. Leave it for at least 3 hours and before using it stir in the beaten white of the egg.

To Boil Salmon and other Fish

Meg Dods' recipe for boiling salmon (from the *Cook's &
Housewife's Manual*, 1829) is so clear and precise that it
cannot be bettered. I have used it with perfect results.

"There are many excellent ways of dressing this
favourite fish, but perhaps none equal to plain boiling
when well performed. Scale and clean the fish without
unnecessary washing or handling, and without cutting it
too much open. Have a roomy and well-scoured fish-
kettle, and if the salmon be large and thick, when you
have placed it on the strainer and in the kettle, fill up and
amply cover it with cold spring water, that it may heat
gradually. Throw in a handful of salt. If a jole or quarter
is boiled, it may be put in with warm water. In both
cases take off the scum carefully, and let the fish boil
slowly, allowing twelve minutes to the pound; but it is
even more difficult to fix the time fish should boil than
the length of time that meat requires. Experience, and
those symptoms which the eye of a practised cook alone
can discern, must fix the point, and nothing is more dis-
gusting and unwholesome than underdone fish. It may
be probed. The minute the boiling of any fish is completed, the fish strainer must be lifted and rested across
the pan, to drain the fish. Throw a soft cloth or flannel in
several folds over it. It would become soft if permitted
to soak in the hot water. Dish on a hot fish-plate under a
napkin. Besides the essences to be used at discretion,
which are now found on every sideboard of any preten-
sion, shrimp, anchovy, and lobster sauce are served with
salmon; also plain melted butter; and where the fish is got
fresh and served in what is esteemed by some the greatest
perfection—crisp, curdy, and creamy—it is the practice
to send in a sauce-tureen of the plain liquor in which it
was boiled. Fennel and butter are still heard of for

salmon, but are nearly obsolete. Garnish with a fringe of curled green parsley and slices of lemon. The carver must help a slice of the thick part with a smaller one of the thin, which is the fattest, and the best-liked by those in the secret. Sliced cucumber is often served with salmon, and indeed with all boiled fish."

GRILLED SALMON

Have the salmon cut in steaks, each weighing 5 to 6 ozs. Season them lightly with salt and pepper, coat them with olive oil, and grill them under a moderate flame for about 7 minutes, turning them over two or three times and basting with a little more oil.

Serve with a *sauce verte* (p. 166).

SALMON TROUT

Salmon Trout is one of the most delicate of all fishes, and is best cooked very simply and gently, in order that its flavour shall be retained. If you have no fish kettle, cook it lying in a baking-tin in the oven, in a little salted water, allowing about 15 minutes to the pound in a medium to slow oven.

If to be served cold, let it cool before lifting it out and it will be easier to handle. Serve it on a long dish with a ring of finely sliced and lightly salted cucumber all round it, and, better than Hollandaise, a Sauce Maltaise (p. 163) or Sauce Verte (p. 166).

If the fish is too big to go into the baking-tin, wrap it up in copiously buttered grease proof paper and lay it on the bars in the oven, cooking it rather more gently, and allowing 20 minutes to the pound, and serve it hot straight out of its paper with fresh melted butter, or the same Sauce Maltaise or Sauce Messine (p. 167).

Truites à la Crème

Arrange the trout in a shallow pan; cover them with very thinly sliced onions, season with salt and pepper and a sprinkling of fresh herbs. Pour over a glass of white wine and one of water. Poach gently (about 10–12 minutes for small trout). Put them in the serving dish, reduce the cooking liquid to half by fast boiling, add half its volume of boiling cream and pour over the fish through a strainer. Garnish with parsley or tarragon.

Can be served hot or cold.

L'Anguille au Vert
(A Belgian Dish)

Skin, behead and wash some small eels. Cut them in slices 5 centimetres (about 2 inches) long. Put them into a casserole with a good proportion of finely chopped aromatic herbs—sage, mint, savory, sorrel, chervil and parsley. Add a piece of butter, salt and pepper and let the eel and the herbs melt. Cover with a quarter of water to three quarters of white wine.

The cooking should be carried out at a good pace and for not longer than 10 to 15 minutes, according to the size of the eels. While the eels are cooking prepare the following sauce: 6 yolks of eggs to a kilo (just over 2 lbs.) of eels, the juice of 3 lemons, 6 tablespoons of cold water, and a few nuts of fresh butter. Having carefully mixed all these ingredients, take the casserole from the fire, giving it several rotating movements as you do so. Incorporate the egg mixture very gradually and gently. Turn the eels and their sauce into a china or earthenware dish and leave to cool. Some people prefer the dish hot or tepid; it is no less delicious.

Paul Bouillard's recipe.

Eliza Acton's Lobster Salad

First prepare a sauce with the coral of a hen lobster, pounded and rubbed through a sieve, and very gradually mixed with a good mayonnaise or remoulade. Next, half fill the bowl or more with small salad herbs, or with young lettuces finely shred, and arrange upon them spirally, or in a chain, alternate slices of the flesh of a large lobster, or of two middling sized ones, and some hard-boiled eggs cut thin and evenly. Leave a space in the centre, pour in the sauce, heap lightly some small salad on the top and send the dish immediately to table. The coral of a seasoned lobster may be intermingled with the white flesh of the fish with very good effect.

Modern Cookery. 1861 Edition.

This is the recipe I always follow for making lobster salad, and is very successful.

Gratin de Langoustines

For 2 people. 10–12 Dublin Bay prawns, ¼ pint milk, 1 oz. flour, yolks of 2 eggs, 2 ozs. cream, butter, grated Gruyère cheese, a tablespoon of brandy, 1 onion, lemon peel.

Shell the cooked prawns. Put the shells and claws into a pan with an onion, a piece of lemon peel, a glass of water, salt, pepper, and a tablespoon of brandy and simmer for 10 minutes. Strain the resulting stock.

Make a thick béchamel with a tablespoon of butter, the flour, the warmed milk. Season it well, let it cook 10–15 minutes. Add 2 or 3 tablespoons of the prepared fish stock, the cream, and off the fire the well beaten egg yolks. Lastly add the prawn tails. Turn into a shallow gratin dish, sprinkle with grated Gruyère and brown in the top of a very hot oven for about 7 minutes.

All except the final cooking can be done beforehand, but before putting the mixture into the gratin dish heat it up in a double boiler so that it is already hot when put into the oven. Otherwise it will have to cook too long and the eggs may curdle the sauce. Nervous or preoccupied cooks can leave out the eggs altogether, make a rather thicker béchamel, and use double the amount of cream.

GRILLED DUBLIN BAY PRAWNS

To grill scampi or Dublin Bay prawns, cut the tails off the uncooked fish; wash them in cold water, flatten them out slightly with a rolling pin, paint their shells with oil and put them, shells nearest the heat, under the grill for 5 or 6 minutes. Serve at once with salt and a little melted butter.

This is worth trying when uncooked Dublin Bay prawns can be obtained; the flavour is really fresh and enjoyable, but it is no use attempting it with already cooked or frozen fish. The heads can be used for making stock for a fish soup, but they should be cooked at once.

CRAB SOUFFLÉ

1 medium sized cooked crab, ½ pint milk, 3 dessertspoons flour, 2 ozs. cream, 2 whole eggs and 2 extra whites, 1 oz. butter, pepper, cayenne pepper, salt, nutmeg, 2 ozs. grated Parmesan.

Make a thick béchamel with the butter, flour and heated milk. Add all the meat extracted from the shell and claws of the crab. Stir in the cheese. Season fairly highly. Add the cream then the beaten yolks of the eggs. Heat over the flame, stirring all the time, but do not allow to boil after the eggs have been put in. Leave to cool. Immediately before the soufflé is to be cooked stir in the four beaten whites. Fill a buttered soufflé dish with the mixture to within an inch of the top. Put in the top of a No. 8 oven, preheated for at least ten minutes. Cook for about 15 minutes.

You can nearly always tell when a soufflé is ready by the smell which comes from the oven. Unfortunately the perfect-looking soufflé, with that blown up crust on the top almost separated from the rest of the dish is not usually the perfect soufflé inside; by the time the top of the soufflé has risen that much, the inside is usually too dry. So it is best to be content with a slightly less spectacular look and have the inside of the soufflé still a little creamy.

The extra whites in this soufflé make it rise well and quickly, the cream helps it to remain moist.

A nice way to serve a soufflé is to cook it in small dishes, one for each person. Special small soufflé dishes are not necessary. Any little fireproof dishes, about 2 inches deep, will do. (Very cheap ones can often be bought at Woolworth's.)

Experiment to find out the correct timing is absolutely essential. Every oven is different and much also depends on the size of the dish. A small soufflé for one person takes about 6 or 7 minutes.

MOUSSE OF CRAB

1 large crab, ⅛th pint (2½ ozs.) of thick cream, a tea-cupful of aspic (see p. 171), lemon, salt, cayenne pepper, 1 tablespoon of grated Parmesan cheese, the whites of 2 eggs.

Extract all the meat from the body and claws of the cooked crab. Pound it in a mortar with the grated Parmesan (this adds both to consistency and flavour) season with salt, a little cayenne pepper, a squeeze of lemon juice. Stir in the melted aspic and the cream. Put in the refrigerator or in a cold place until it is all but set, then fold in the stiffly beaten whites of the eggs. Turn into a soufflé dish just large enough to hold the mousse, so that it is completely filled right up to the top. Leave to set.

This makes a very good creamy mousse, which does not set too hard, so if the weather is exceptionally hot, use a little more aspic.

A cucumber *sambal* (p. 38) goes well with crab mousse.

A salmon mousse made in the same way, allowing a large cupful of cooked salmon, is very successful. A cooked mousse of crab or salmon, or of lobster, sole or prawns can be made in the same way as the ham mousse described on page 110. Although it is not quite so creamy or delicate, many people may prefer it, as no aspic jelly is required.

COCKLES

While mussels are to be found during the winter months at most London fishmongers', cockles are sold only ready cooked and shelled, and that rarely (although some London fishmongers have them once or twice a week). Only on the coast can they be bought in their natural state. The cost and trouble of transport is presumably responsible, for they are excellent little shell-fish when cooked in the manner of *moules marinières*, and in summer, when mussels are not sold in England, make a good substitute in sauces and soups.

On the east coast of England and in Scotland and Wales cockles are often eaten for tea, plain boiled. A way of eating them in South Wales is to shell them when they have been boiled, fry them in bacon fat, and serve them on hot buttered toast. An old North of England rhyme mentions "cocklety pie" and "musselty cake". Cocklety pie sounds an excellent dish, consisting of cooked shelled cockles stirred into a white sauce, baked in a dish lined with bread-crumbs and covered with a pie crust.

Cockles live in the sand and must therefore be most carefully washed under a running cold water tap for about ten minutes; then leave them in cold salted water, changed several times, until there is no more sand. Cockles bought ready cooked are seldom properly cleaned and are also inclined to be over-salted, so before putting them into a soup or stew put them in a colander under a running cold tap for at least an hour. Cockles in their shells can be cooked in a little unsalted water, and as soon as the shells open they are ready. They can also be laid on an iron sheet or griddle, over a flame, and eaten straight from the stove, when they have opened, with bread and butter

If cockles or mussels are bought the day before they are wanted, keep them in a bowl of cold water, in a cool larder, covered with a cloth, over which coarse salt has been sprinkled.

Several Victorian cookery books give recipes for cockles. Here is one from Cassell's *Dictionary of Cookery* (1877).

Cockle Sauce

Prepare a gallon of cockles as for boiling. Set them in the fire and when the shells open strain the liquid from them, throw the shells away, and strain the liquid through muslin, to clean it from sand. Stir in a pint of good melted butter (remember this is for a large quantity of cockles) and add a tablespoonful of white pepper.

Stir the sauce over the fire for two or three minutes, but do not let it boil, and serve it with cod or haddock. Sufficient for 4 lbs. of fish.

CHAPTER 6

MEAT

GRILLED steaks or lamb cutlets with young vegetables make the most delightful of summer meat dishes, but it is not always easy to get the best quality meat which is needed for grills, it is expensive, and in any case few people would want them every day. Home killed veal and lamb are both at their best during the summer months, and it is worth remembering that joints of both are very much more economical to carve (for so long there was nothing to carve that very few people know anything about this art) if they are boned, trimmed and tied by the butcher, who will do it with the minimum of waste. It is useless to be timid when buying meat; the butcher gives the best service and the best meat to the people who insist on getting exactly what they have asked for.

When buying escalopes of veal, which make very agreeable summer dishes, light, quick to prepare and cook, and susceptible of great variation, see that they are cut from the leg, the bone having been taken out, cut very thin and flattened out for you by the butcher, and when ordering a loin of veal or pork ask for the kidney to be left in. Although meat is abundant again, a watchful eye still has to be kept on your butcher to see that when you have asked for fillet steaks you do not get a badly cut hunk from which there will be a lot of waste. Tournedos are small round steaks cut from what is called the eye of the fillet and they should be at least an inch thick.

Cheaper joints allow for plenty of scope in the matter of flavouring with herbs, wine and spices, and all the vegetables of summer, peas, carrots, little turnips, new potatoes, can be cooked with them.

People who have lived in the East think highly of curries as summer dishes; as every other amateur cook in England has his special recipe for curry I have not included any here, but have given instead two or three Oriental dishes which are deliciously spiced without resembling in any way an English-Indian curry; the flavour of these dishes and the methods by which they are cooked, may be new to many people; they also give scope for the compounding of attractive fresh chutneys and sauces to be served with them.

For cold meat dishes my own favourites are the classic *boeuf à la mode* (p. 211), a boned loin of pork flavoured with fresh herbs and garlic and cooked so gently that all the flavour and moisture are retained (p. 107), and a cold leg or loin of veal (p. 101) stuffed with kidneys. Boiled beef can be made into a lovely salad but cold lamb and mutton are best chopped or minced and made into croquettes, or later in the season for the stuffing of aubergines, pimentos and small marrows; fortunately mutton, the least attractive of meats to eat cold, also responds better to re-cooking than any other meat.

EPAULE DE MOUTON À LA BOURGEOISE

A boned and rolled shoulder (or leg) of mutton, butter or dripping, 2 cupfuls of stock (this can be made from the bones), 1 lb. new turnips, 1 lb. new carrots, herbs, seasoning, garlic, a little flour.

Put at least one clove of garlic into the meat, season it, and brown it in the butter or dripping, sprinkle with flour, and when this has amalgamated with the fat pour over the heated stock. Add herbs (thyme, bayleaf, marjoram) and the carrots and seasoning, cover the pan and cook very gently either in the oven or on top of the stove for about 2 hours (for a piece of meat weighing 2 lbs. when boned).

Blanch the peeled turnips in boiling salted water for 5 minutes, cut them in quarters, sauté them in butter and about fifteen minutes before serving add them to the meat.

There should be enough sauce left with the meat for the turnips to finish cooking; if there is too much fat, pour it off before adding the turnips.

Potatoes instead of turnips can be used, treated in the same way.

GIGOT D'AGNEAU À LA FERMIÈRE

A piece of leg of lamb weighing about 3 lbs., a wineglass of white wine and one of stock, ½ lb. each of new turnips and carrots, 1½ lbs. of green peas (weighed before shelling) a dozen or so small new potatoes, 4 ozs. of cream, 2 ozs. butter, salt, pepper, sugar.

Melt the butter in a thick pan; put in the meat, let it turn golden all over; pour over the wine and let it bubble

a few minutes; add the stock; cover the pan and cook it
in a medium oven for 30 minutes; now add the carrots,
the turnips, and the potatoes and five minutes later the
peas. Season with salt, pepper, a little sugar. Cook gently
for 40 minutes, by which time the meat and all the vegetables should be ready: pour off excess fat, sprinkle the
meat and vegetables with flour, stir, and add the boiling
cream; see that there is sufficient seasoning and simmer
10 more minutes. If mutton is used instead of lamb cook
for an hour at least before adding the vegetables.

GIGOT D'AGNEAU À LA PROVENÇALE

A boned and rolled leg (or shoulder) of lamb, 3 aubergines, 1 lb. of tomatoes, ¼ lb. of green olives, a teacupful
of olive oil, 2 cloves of garlic, parsley, salt, pepper.

Stick a clove of garlic into the meat and roast it in the
ordinary way. Cut the unpeeled aubergines into thick
slices, salt them and leave them to drain for an hour or
two.

Skin the tomatoes, chop the second clove of garlic.

Heat the olive oil in a thick frying pan, and sauté the
sliced aubergines. Drain them, put them in the roasting
pan with the almost cooked meat and add the stoned
olives. In the same frying pan cook the tomatoes, cut into
quarters, for 4 or 5 minutes, adding the chopped garlic
and salt and pepper. Slice the meat for serving, put the
aubergines, tomatoes and olives all round in the serving
dish, garnish with chopped parsley.

LAMB ROASTED WITH CORIANDER SEEDS

Make a few incisions in a leg of lamb or mutton and into
them put cloves of garlic and crushed coriander seeds—
about two tablespoons altogether. Rub the meat with

salt and pepper, and roast it in the usual way, adding some potatoes half way through the cooking. The coriander seeds give a perfectly delicious flavour to the meat. Cut it in thick slices to serve, so that everybody gets some of the garlic and coriander. The meat should be very well done, moist and tender.

CÔTELETTES D'AGNEAU BOULANGÈRE

2 onions, 1 lb. new potatoes, a teacupful of good stock, 6 lamb cutlets, butter. Slice the onions finely, and cut the potatoes into two or four pieces each according to size. Arrange them in a buttered fireproof dish, cover with the stock, season lightly, and cook in a slow oven for about an hour. Now brown the cutlets on each side in butter, and put them in the dish with the potatoes. Cook another 20 minutes.

LAMB CUTLETS WITH MINT BUTTER

Make a mint butter as described on page 170. The quantities given will make enough for 8 cutlets. Score the meat lightly on both sides and coat it with the butter. Leave for an hour. Grill the cutlets, first on each side close to the grill, then turn them over twice again, cooking further away from the flame. They will take about 10 minutes altogether. At the same time, if there is room, grill some half tomatoes, and serve with some of the butter poured over them.

NOISETTES D'AGNEAU EN BROCHETTES

8 lamb cutlets, 6 rashers of lean bacon, salt and pepper, Béarnaise sauce, butter.

Cut all the meat from the cutlets, so that you have 2 or 3 small rounds of meat from each cutlet. Cut each rasher of bacon into 3 or 4 pieces. On small skewers thread alternate pieces of bacon and meat, starting and finishing with bacon. Season with salt, pepper and lemon juice, sprinkle over them some chopped fresh marjoram, and grill for 8–10 minutes, turning the skewers round two or three times. Serve on a bed of whole, crisp lettuce leaves, with lemon and the Béarnaise sauce, having added to it if you like chopped mint and chives instead of the usual tarragon.

A very excellent luncheon dish.

POLPETTE OF MUTTON

Polpette are the Italian version of rissoles or croquettes. In Italy they are usually made with veal, but the recipe also provides one of the best ways of using up cooked mutton or lamb.

Mince ½ lb. or so of cooked lamb or mutton with a strip of lemon peel, a clove or two of garlic, a few sprigs of parsley. Mix with a slice of white bread which has been soaked in milk and then squeezed dry. Season with salt, pepper and nutmeg, and stir in 2 eggs. On a floured board form the mixture into little round rissoles no larger than half a crown in diameter. This operation should be performed quickly and with a light hand, or the polpette will be heavy. Roll them lightly in flour and fry them in hot oil or good clear dripping. Drain them on to blotting paper. Serve with a salad. If carefully drained, not at all greasy, these little rissoles make very nice picnic food.

FILLET OF VEAL WITH MUSHROOMS
AND CREAM

A piece of leg of veal weighing about 2 lbs. when boned and rolled, ½ lb. of small mushrooms, 1½ ozs. butter, ¼ pint of thin cream, a little flour, seasonings, herbs, garlic, lemon juice.

Rub the veal with salt, pepper and lemon juice. Melt the butter in a thick braising pan. Put in the meat, let it turn just golden all over, add a clove or two of garlic, some fresh marjoram or thyme, cover the pan and cook on top of the stove or in a gentle oven for 1½ hours. When it is tender, add the mushrooms, whole, and cook 5 minutes. Now sprinkle with flour, stir until the sauce has amalgamated and add the cream, which has been boiled in another pan. Cook very gently for another five minutes, and serve on a long, hot dish.

COTELETTES DE VEAU AU VIN BLANC

4 veal cutlets, or escalopes, 2 ozs. ham, 2 ozs. bacon, the white parts of a few large spring onions, a glass of white wine, flour, butter. Season the meat, dust it with flour, brown it lightly in butter. Add the ham and bacon cut in strips and the whole small onions. Cook 2 minutes, pour in the white wine. Cover the pan and simmer for 10 minutes. Take out the cutlets, keep them hot. Scrape up the juices in the pan, add a little more white wine and a small lump of butter. Give a quick stir and pour it over the cutlets.

ESCALOPES DE VEAU À LA CRÈME

Escalopes of veal, butter, cream.

Season the escalopes and brown them gently in butter, turning them over and over. When they are tender move them to a hot dish, quickly add a ¼ pint (for 6 escalopes) of boiling cream. Give a quick stir so that the butter, cream and juices in the pan are amalgamated and pour over the escalopes.

Escalopes de Veau à la Crème aux Champignons

4 escalopes of veal, ½ lb. of small mushrooms, butter, cream, garlic, salt and pepper, lemon juice.

Season the escalopes with salt, pepper and lemon juice, and flatten them out a little, not too much. Melt an ounce of butter in a frying pan, brown the meat slightly on each side. Add the thinly sliced mushrooms, a scrap of chopped garlic, salt and pepper. Cover the pan and cook gently for 5–7 minutes, until the mushrooms are done. Transfer to the serving dish. Into the pan, but off the fire, pour ¼ pint of boiling cream. Scrape up the juices in the pan so that they amalgamate with the cream and form a pale coffee coloured sauce. Stir a few seconds over the flame, and pour over the veal and mushrooms.

Escalopes de Veau en Aïllade

4 escalopes of veal cut from the leg, 1 lb. of tomatoes, olive oil, 4 or 5 cloves of garlic, a handful of dried bread-crumbs, salt, pepper, a bunch of parsley.

Cover the bottom of a thick sauté pan with olive oil. When it is hot (but not boiling) put in the seasoned escalopes. Cook them gently so that they are just golden on each side. Add the skinned and chopped tomatoes and as soon as they have melted, the breadcrumbs, the chopped garlic and parsley, and cook another 8–10 minutes, by which time most of the oil should be absorbed, and the tomatoes turned to a thick sauce.

Escalopes de Veau au Fenouil

Brown escalopes of veal in pork dripping or butter. Add 2 or 3 spring onions for each escalope; cover the pan and simmer for 7 or 8 minutes. Throw in a handful of finely chopped fennel leaves; stir, add a squeeze of lemon. Excellent.

A Veal and Ham Pie

1½ lbs. of lean veal, ½ lb. ham, ½ lb. bacon, 4 hard-boiled eggs, ¼ lb. mushrooms, fresh thyme, parsley, mace, salt, pepper, ½ pint of very good beef or veal stock which will jelly when cold, pastry.

Cut the veal in thin slices about 3½ by 2½ inches. Season with salt, pepper, mace and chopped herbs, lay a rasher of bacon on each slice and roll it up. Arrange these rolls in layers in the buttered pie dish, and over each layer strew more herbs, slices of mushroom, hard-boiled egg and ham, and on top of the final layer put rashers of bacon. Pour in the stock. Cover with pastry and cook in a moderate oven for an hour and a quarter. Can be eaten hot but is best cold.

Vitello Tonnato

This is one of the standard summer dishes of restaurants all over Italy. The following recipe is from an Abruzzesi *trattoria* in Rome, where the *vitello tonnato* was particularly good, although not the classic version.

Make a good cupful of mayonnaise with 2 yolks of eggs, olive oil and lemon juice. Pound or sieve about 2 ozs. of best quality tunny fish in oil, and add this to the mayonnaise. Thin slightly with juice from the roast fillet of veal. Cut the cold fillet of veal (which should have been boned before cooking) into slices, and pack it into a deep dish into which it will just fit. Pour the prepared sauce over and leave till next day.

Cold Loin of Veal with Kidneys

2½–3 lbs. of loin of veal with the kidneys, white wine, carrots, onions, garlic, herbs, an extra ¼ lb. of veal kidneys or 2 lambs' kidneys.

Have the loin of veal boned, but leave the kidneys. Lay the boned meat out on a board, trim off most of the fat from the kidneys, spike the meat with little pieces of garlic here and there, lay the extra kidneys, trimmed of fat and skinned, on top of the meat, season with salt and pepper, add a sprig of fresh marjoram or thyme, roll the meat up, enclosing the kidneys, and tie into a round. Put it into a braising pan or roasting tin, pour over a wine glass of white wine and 2 of water. Add 2 or 3 carrots and a small onion, and the bones which were taken from the meat. Cover the pan, and cook in a moderate oven (Regulo 3 or 4) for 2–2½ hours. During the last 15 or 20 minutes of cooking, remove the lid, so that the meat browns.

Take out the meat and leave it to cool. Cook the stock, with the bones, gently for another 30 or 40 minutes. Strain it, leave it to cool. It should set to a jelly. Take off the fat.

To serve, carve the veal into slices, and garnish with squares of the jelly. A truffle, even a tinned one (there are no fresh ones in the summer) sliced and put on to the meat before it is rolled up makes this dish even better. Pour the juice from the tin into the sauce during the final cooking.

Tournedos Béarnaise

A tournedos is a small round steak, nearly an inch thick, cut from the fillet and trimmed of all fat. Ask your butcher to cut them from the eye of the fillet. This is the genuine tournedos. A tournedos can be either grilled or fried. If to be fried, first heat a thick frying pan without any fat.

When it is very hot put in the seasoned steaks and let them sizzle until the meat is sealed and brown on one side, then turn them over and brown the other side. Now turn down the flame, put a lump of butter in the pan and cook gently another 2 or 3 minutes, allowing about 5 minutes altogether for a 4 oz. steak. If the steak is to be grilled, put it, seasoned, very close to the very hot grill, and brown it on each side. Then move it further away from the flame, baste it with a little butter, and cook approximately another 3 minutes.

Serve on a very hot dish, garnished with watercress, and the Béarnaise sauce (p. 161) separately.

Some cooks contend that steak should be salted only after cooking, as the salt tends to make the juice run. If the pan or grill is really hot before the meat is put to cook the juices are immediately sealed, so that salting it before cooking does no harm, and usually makes for a better flavour.

TOURNEDOS À L'ESTRAGON

Cook small fillet steaks in a little butter, in the usual way. When they are browned on both sides, and little beads of juice begin to filter out into the pan, pour over a large tablespoon of madeira or port (for each two fillets). Let them bubble for a little under a minute, stir in a dessertspoonful of chopped tarragon and ½ oz. of butter. Put the steaks on the serving dish and pour the sauce over.

TOURNEDOS À LA NIÇOISE

Chop the leaves of a few sprigs of fresh basil and pound it with a small piece of garlic and a little salt; work it into an ounce of butter. Put a portion of this basil butter on top of each grilled or fried fillet steak before serving.

Entrecôte Grillée à la Maître d'Hôtel

An entrecote is usually a rump steak cut about ½ inch thick, weighing 4 to 6 ozs. for each person.

Remove skin, gristle, and most of the fat from the steaks. Flatten the steaks out a little, but don't beat them heavily, it spoils the meat. Score the edges lightly with a sharp knife, which will prevent them turning up and hardening during the cooking. Paint the steaks lightly with olive oil. Heat the grill and put the steaks under it, close to the flame, and cook on each side for a minute, then remove the grid a little further away from the flame, and cook about 2 more minutes on each side. One minute per ounce is about the right timing to get a ½ inch steak grilled à *point*; if you want them well done leave them an extra minute. Put the steaks on the prepared hot dish on which you have already placed the maître d'hôtel butter (see p. 169). It is the juice from the meat combined with the butter, just melting, which makes this very simple sauce so good. Salt and pepper the steaks only when they are ready to serve.

Entrecôte Bercy

Cook the entrecôtes as for the above recipe, and when they are ready on the serving dish, with a bunch of watercress at each end, pour over them the Sauce Bercy (p. 168).

Le Boeuf à la Bordelaise

Pour 2 glasses of white wine over a piece of round of beef weighing about 3 lbs. Add thyme, bayleaf, peppercorns, a sliced onion and clove of garlic. Leave it to marinate for 12 hours. Remove the beef next day, wipe it with a cloth, season with salt and put it into a roasting pan with good dripping; cook it fairly slowly, basting from time to time.

In the meantime make a roux with flour and butter and moisten it with the strained marinade; let it cook 15 minutes. When the beef is ready, put it on the serving dish, drain off the fat in the pan, add a little water to the remaining juice and pour this into the prepared sauce, which is served separately.

Daube à la Corsoise

2 lbs. of rolled rib or round of beef, ¼ lb. of bacon cut into small thick strips, ½ lb. of small mushrooms, 4 large ripe tomatoes, ¼ lb. stoned black olives, 1 lb. of new potatoes, a small glass of brandy, garlic, olive oil, fresh thyme.

Warm a little olive oil in a deep, narrow casserole, put in the beef, which has been rubbed with salt and pepper. Let it brown gently on both sides; add the bacon, the tomatoes peeled and cut in quarters, 2 or 3 cloves of garlic, seasoning, the thyme, and the olives. Pour over the brandy. Cover the pan and cook in a very slow oven for 2 hours. When the meat is all but cooked, add the mushrooms, and the potatoes which have been cooked in olive oil or butter until nearly tender. Cook another 10 to 15 minutes. There is no need to add any liquid to this stew; the tomatoes make sufficient. Take care not to add too much salt to start with.

Farso Magro

(A Sicilian dish)

2 lbs. of lean beef, rump steak for preference, in one piece, 1 lb. of minced beef, 6 eggs, 1 lb. of green peas, 3 ozs. of

tongue, 3 ozs. ham, an onion, a clove of garlic, 2 table-spoons of breadcrumbs, 3 tablespoons of grated Parmesan, celery leaves, a carrot, olive oil, salt, pepper, nutmeg, parsley, 2 teaspoons of concentrated tomato purée, a small glass of red wine.

Chop the parsley and the garlic together and mix them in a bowl with the minced meat. Add the breadcrumbs, which should have been softened in a little water and then pressed dry, the grated cheese, salt, pepper and nutmeg, and two beaten eggs.

Hard boil the remaining 4 eggs; cut them, with the ham and the tongue, into strips.

Flatten out the piece of rump steak on a board, cover it with the prepared stuffing; on top of this arrange the sliced tongue, ham and hard-boiled eggs; roll up the meat like a sausage and tie it round with string, but not too tightly. See that the ends are closed so that the stuffing does not escape.

In a pan which will just about hold the rolled meat, warm the olive oil; put in the chopped onion, carrot and celery leaves; on top of the vegetables put the meat; let it brown all over; add the red wine and let it bubble a little. Stir in the tomato purée, then add about ½ a tea-cupful of water. Cover the pan and cook gently for an hour; if the pan is not too big the liquid will not dry up, but if it does add a little stock or water. When the meat is all but cooked add the shelled peas and cook another 20 minutes, or until they are tender. Remove the string and serve the Farso surrounded by the sauce and the peas.

To serve cold (and it is really at its best this way) omit the peas, do not untie the meat until it is cold and remove the fat from the top of the sauce.

SIKH KEBAB

1½ lbs. lean meat without bone, either beef, mutton, or veal, 1½ tablespoons of curry powder, 1 tablespoon of curry paste, lemon juice, a cupful of curds or yoghourt.

Mix the curry powder and curry paste together, moisten with lemon juice, and mix it with the curds or yoghourt.

Score the meat deeply across in several places, and steep it in the curry mixture for an hour; then cut it up into inch squares, and leave it another hour or so. Now thread the meat on skewers, and grill for about 10 minutes, basting once or twice with a little dripping. If you have green ginger, which is fresh ginger root, a few thin slices on each skewer, between the pieces of meat, give a delicious flavour.

This form of curry is usually eaten not with rice but with chappattee, flat bread made on a griddle. The skewers can also be served on a bed of shredded lettuce, dressed with oil and lemon, and a chutney or a cucumber sambal makes a nice accompaniment.

BEEF SALAD

The beef which has been boiled for a consommé or stock is better made into a salad rather than reheated in a hash or rissoles; cut it into thinnish slices, arrange in a shallow dish, and pour over it a vinaigrette sauce made with plenty of olive oil, a little lemon juice, chopped *fines herbes* (parsley, tarragon, chives, or whatever fresh herbs are available), a few capers, a little garlic, salt and pepper, and, if you like, a little mustard.

Leave the meat to marinate in the sauce for an hour or two, then add 3 or 4 boiled, skinned and sliced potatoes, well seasoned with the same vinaigrette sauce; garnish with slices of hard-boiled eggs, or tomatoes, radishes, or sliced cucumbers.

Paupiettes of Beef Braised with Game Stock

1½ lbs. of good quality lean beef, preferably rump steak, a casserole grouse, a glass of port, butter, a 4 oz. tin of liver pâté, or home made chicken liver pâté (see p. 32) or minced pork, parsley, herbs, garlic.

Cook a casserole grouse as described on page 132. Chop the breast of the bird and mix it with the liver pâté or minced meat, the chopped garlic and fresh herbs. Cut the beef into four slices, trim off the fat and skin, beat them out flat, season with salt and pepper, and cover each with a thin layer of the prepared game and liver mixture. Roll them up and tie them. Heat an ounce of butter in a thick pan, brown the paupiettes all over, pour over the port. Let it bubble, then add just enough of the grouse stock to come half way up the meat. Cover the pan and simmer very gently for 1 to 1½ hours. Take out the paupiettes, remove the string and transfer to the serving dish. Reduce the sauce if necessary, pour over the paupiettes, garnish with parsley.

Cold Roast Pork

A joint of pork always seems to me better cold than hot. It is usually a fat meat, so when cold is moist, but firm and easy to carve. (The crackling is the great attraction about hot roast pork to most English people, but if you are going to serve the meat cold, the rind must be cut off, and if you like roasted with the meat and served at the same time. It is just as delicious cold. In France pork is always bought from the butcher with the rind already cut off, and the rind, called *couenne*, is sold separately for adding to soups and *daubes*.)

To get a really perfectly cooked piece of cold pork get the butcher to bone a piece of leg or loin, and cut off the rind. Make a few incisions in the meat and in these put a little garlic mixed with chopped fresh herbs (fennel, or lemon thyme, or a very little rosemary mixed with parsley) and ground black pepper and salt. Put the meat in a baking tin, cover it with the rind, put the bone in the tin, add water to come half way up the meat and cook in a slow oven (about Regulo 4), allowing at least 35 minutes to the pound. When it is cooked pour off all the liquid into a bowl, and when it is cold take off the fat. It should have set to a light jelly to serve with the cold pork. If it has not, reduce it by fast boiling for a few minutes, and let it cool again. If the rind is not crisp enough let it go on cooking in a gentle oven. It is delicious to serve in little pieces with drinks.

A good accompaniment to cold pork, instead of the usual potato salad, is honey dew or sugar melon, cut into cubes, and served very crisp and cold, but with no sauce or seasoning.

Terrine of Veal and Pork

1 lb. of veal, 1 lb. of pork, 6 ozs. bacon, 2 cloves of garlic, thyme, a bay leaf, mace, salt, ground black pepper, a glass (about 4 ozs.) of white wine, 1 pint of aspic jelly prepared from calf's or pig's feet.

Chop the meat fairly coarsely with the bacon and garlic. Season with herbs and spices, stir in the white wine. Put into a terrine, add melted aspic to come just level with the meat. Put a bay leaf on top, cover the terrine, and cook in a bain-marie in a moderate oven for two hours. When cold cover with the rest of the aspic. If to be kept, seal with melted dripping when the aspic has set.

Ingredients can be varied—for instance, ham can be used instead of bacon, more or less garlic can be used, and port or red wine instead of white; spices and herbs can be varied according to taste.

Pig's Head in Jelly

Half a pig's head, about ¾ lb. of pork meat (loin chops, or a piece of leg), 2 or 3 carrots, garlic, white wine, pepper, salt, a teaspoonful of coriander seeds, a small piece of orange peel, parsley or tarragon, thyme.

Have the pig's head cleaned and the rind cut off. Rub it lightly with salt. Put the pork meat at the bottom of a deep pan, strew it with a little salt, ground pepper, the pounded coriander seeds, a sprig of thyme, the orange peel and 2 or 3 cloves of garlic. Put the pig's head in the pan with its rind on the top, and the carrots round it. Pour over a small glass of white wine and 1½ pints of water. Cook in a slow oven for about 3 hours until the meat is falling from the bones. When cool strain off the stock into a basin, and remove every scrap of bone from the head. Cut all the meat into fairly large rough pieces, and arrange them in a deep bowl with the sliced carrots, taking care that there are absolutely no chips of bone, and no hard pieces of gristle or skin. See that the pieces of tongue are well distributed amongst the rest of the meat. When the stock in the basin has set take off the fat, heat it up, clarify it if you like, leave it to cool again, and just before it sets stir into it about two tablespoons of finely chopped tarragon or parsley mixed with one or two chopped cloves of garlic. Pour this over the meat and leave to set. This is not intended to be an elegant dish, it is coarse country food, but with plenty of flavour, and rather more interesting than the ordinary brawn. Serve a good green salad with it, or boiled new potatoes.

HAM

A good ham is so delicious cold, served quite plain or with a potato or green salad, or with a mild fruit chutney or a Cumberland sauce, that it seems unnecessary to do anything further about it. Twice cooked ham is always disappointing, and even for ham and eggs the ham is best, to my way of thinking, cold; it dries up and tastes salty when grilled or fried. The end of a ham however can be made into a very successful mousse or mixed with veal and pork for a terrine; there are soups, sauces, vegetable and meat dishes described in this book which require small quantities of ham in their composition, and they will be found listed under ham in the index, as well as under the actual names of the dishes.

HAM MOUSSE

¾ lb. ham, 3 ozs. of cream, a tablespoon of meat glaze, or of madeira or port reduced to a syrup by fast boiling, nutmeg, pepper, the whites of 3 eggs.

Mince the ham, stir in the meat glaze or wine, season with black pepper and a scrap of nutmeg, add the cream, then the beaten whites of egg. Turn into an earthenware terrine, or china soufflé dish and cook in a bain-marie in a moderate oven (covered) for 30 to 40 minutes. Can be served hot or cold.

TERRINE OF HAM, PORK AND VEAL

1 lb. each of ham, pork and veal, white wine, brandy, garlic, bayleaves, herbs, ¼ lb. bacon, mace, pepper, salt, juniper berries.

Mince the pork and the veal, cut the ham into small squares. Mix all together, add a clove of garlic chopped with 5 or 6 juniper berries, a little fresh thyme, marjoram, coarsely ground black pepper, about half a teaspoon of mace, and a very little salt, as the ham will probably be salty. Put the whole mixture into a bowl and pour over a small glass of white wine and 2 tablespoons of brandy. Leave for an hour or two. Cover the bottom of a fairly shallow terrine with little strips of bacon about 2 inches long. Put in the meat mixture, cover with more little strips of bacon and put a bayleaf or two in the centre. Put the terrine in a baking dish filled with water and bake in a slow oven for 2½–3 hours. Leave to cool.

Serve with toast and a salad.

Cervelles de Veau à la Provençale

Blanch and strain the whole calf's brains. When cool put them to marinate for an hour in olive oil highly seasoned with salt and pepper and a clove of garlic. Turn them over two or three times so that they are well impregnated with the oil. Drain them from the oil, cook them in white wine, leave to cool. Cut them in even slices, arrange them in a ring. Fill the centre with mayonnaise, and garnish with a ring of stoned olives. To be served as a cold luncheon dish.

Recipe from *Le Cuisinier Européen*.

Kidneys and Mushrooms

½ lb. kidneys (even ox kidney is good cooked in this way), ¼ lb. mushrooms, port or marsala, garlic, parsley, butter, flour.

Soak the kidneys in warm salted water for 2 or 3 hours. Cut into slices about ¼ inch thick, salt and pepper them and roll them in flour. Sauté them in butter. Pour over them a small glass (about 2 ozs.) of port or marsala, let it bubble a few seconds and add enough water to come just about level with the kidneys. Stew very gently for an hour. Now add the mushrooms, which should if possible be the medium sized flat kind; wash them and leave them whole. At the same time add a chopped clove of garlic. Simmer for another half-hour. Before serving add a little cut parsley. This is an excellent way of dealing with tough kidneys, and the appearance of the dish, black and dark red, is beautiful.

A purée of potatoes, into which some fresh herbs (lemon thyme is especially good) have been mixed goes well with it. Enough for two.

Paupiettes of Liver

½ lb. of calf's liver, ½ lb. of bacon, 4 tomatoes or a coffee-cupful of freshly made tomato sauce, a small glass of port or marsala, a coffeecupful of chicken or meat stock, 1 oz. of butter, flour, fresh thyme or marjoram.

Buy the liver in one piece, and cut it into very thin slices, a little smaller than the rashers of bacon. On each rasher of bacon lay a slice of liver, season with a very little salt, ground black pepper, and lemon juice; add 3 or 4 leaves of marjoram or thyme. Roll up the paupiettes with the bacon on the outside, secure with little skewers. Heat the butter, sauté the paupiettes in it, sprinkle sparingly with flour; stir, and add the marsala; let it bubble, then add the tomatoes, skinned and chopped small, or the tomato sauce, then the stock. Cover the pan and cook gently for about 10 minutes. Remove the skewers, and serve.

Foie de Veau Fines Herbes

Season the slices of calf's liver with salt, pepper and lemon juice. Dust with flour. Brown on each side in butter. Pour over a little stock, or two tablespoons of marsala, cover the pan, and lower the heat. Simmer 4 or 5 minutes. Sprinkle with 2 tablespoons of fresh herbs (lemon thyme, marjoram, parsley, fennel, whatever is available) chopped with a little piece of garlic and a little strip of lemon peel. Squeeze a little lemon juice over and serve.

Calf's liver can also be cooked in any of the ways described for escalopes of veal.

Ox Tongue with Purée of Peas

An ox tongue, 2 carrots, an onion, a leek, 3 lbs. of green peas, 2 ozs. of butter, herbs. Soak the tongue for several hours in cold water. Blanch for 20 minutes in boiling salted water. Strain, and skin the tongue. Put it to cook with the onion and carrots and herbs and salt and pepper, just covered with water. Simmer very gently for 2 hours.

In the meantime cook the shelled peas and the cleaned and chopped leek in water, sieve them. Heat up the resulting purée with the butter. Put in the middle of a heated dish, and round the purée the tongue cut in slices, with a little Sauce Bercy (p. 168) poured over them. Serve more sauce separately.

CHAPTER 7

POULTRY AND GAME

THE quality of poultry for the table has greatly improved during the past year or two; prices are considerably lower than they were during the immediate post-war years, and there is far more variety, so that any respectable poulterer should now be able to supply the customer with the size and type of bird required; it is important therefore to know what kind of bird you need for the dish you intend to cook. A roasting chicken has not necessarily a better flavour and texture than a boiling chicken, but it is much more tender, so that it is not suitable for slow cooking; it will be ready before the vegetables, herbs and wine which go into a stew have contributed sufficient flavours to the dish.

Apart from roasting, a tender bird can be cut into pieces for frying, grilling, for a fricassée or for braising in butter with quickly cooked vegetables such as tomatoes, mushrooms or green peas.

A boiling fowl is always best cooked whole, so that its juices and flavour are preserved. It can always be carved when ready and kept hot in its sauce in a bain-marie. In spite of lengthy simmering the flesh of a boiling chicken does not disintegrate and there is usually plenty of breast meat, so it is suitable for cold dishes.

Whereas a young roasting chicken is mild and delicate food which repays cooking with good butter, cream and wine with a light handed addition of herbs (tarragon and fresh basil are particularly good for chicken) an older and tougher bird serves for more aromatic stews flavoured with

bacon, garlic and coarse red wine, or as a background for sauces compounded of oriental spices, oil, almonds, walnuts. A boiling fowl also makes a very excellent mousse and the possibilities of cold chicken salads are endless.

The tray-packed, ready cut up roasting chickens now sold by many poulterers are quite practical. The relative cost is the same as for the whole bird, and they have been carved by experts, so there is no waste.

Duck makes beautiful cold summer dishes; in fact, being a fat bird, it is always better cold; you get more flavour from it and better value; it will produce lovely jellied sauces, particularly when a calf's foot has been stewed with it; it can be cooked with red, white, or dessert wines, brandy, curaçao, kirsch, and various fruits, oranges, cherries, peaches, figs (not all at once) can be incorporated in some way to make a dish of great character; for those who don't care for the combination of fruit with meat, broad beans, baby turnips, mushrooms, the classic green peas, go with duck. Mint, tarragon, and other fresh green herbs can go into the sauce, or into the accompanying salad.

Wild rabbits (if there are any left after the ravages of the current rabbit plague which is wiping them out by the million) and pigeons are not exactly elegant party food, but all the same make good and savoury countrified dishes, and first-class terrines and pâtés.

The only summer game, technically, is the grouse, although venison, wild duck and teal from the deep freeze may make an occasional variation for summer meals; they appear to suffer very little from the freezing process, and for pies or terrines or sandwiches do very well indeed.

Grilled Chicken

A grilled chicken is perhaps one of the nicest foods at any time; everybody likes it, it needs very little preparation, is quickly cooked, and although expensive, there is nothing to be spent on extras, so it could be much less rare than it is. It is true that the grill on the normal household cooker is only large enough for one chicken cut in half, but even this inadequate arrangement produces a very delicious meal for two people.

To make a good grilled chicken, you need a really first rate quality spring chicken (not a petit poussin. I do not quite understand why these flabby, insipid little birds are considered such a luxury) weighing about 1½ lbs. when plucked and cleaned and ready to cook. Split them down the back, and then right through, into two halves. Rub them over with lemon juice, season with ground black pepper, strew over them a few fresh herbs such as thyme, lemon thyme or marjoram (no sage or rosemary), paint them with olive oil, and leave them for an hour.

Heat the grill, put the bird on the wire grid, skin side uppermost, and pour over it a little melted butter. Let the skin brown, which will take about 5 minutes; turn it over, baste the inside with a little more melted butter, and grill another 5 minutes. Now move the chicken from the wire grid on to the grilling tray, so that it is further away from the heat. Turn it over again, and strew a little coarse salt on it, and baste again; leave it about 4 minutes, turn it over again and salt the inside, and again baste it (there should be a certain amount of liquid in the pan by now). In 4 minutes it should be ready, golden, crackling and tender, although the exact timing must be determined by the heat of the grill, which varies in every cooker.

Have ready a long dish liberally spread with a bed of

watercress, lettuce, mustard and cress, corn salad, whatever green stuff happens to be in season. Put the grilled
chicken on this, a half lemon at each end of the dish and
serve at once on very hot plates. Any sauce or vegetable
is unnecessary and would distract attention from the
chicken; anyhow there is no room for anything else on the
plate, but serve afterwards a salad—not a green salad, as
there has been enough with the chicken, but raw mushrooms, or tomatoes, or in the season, a little dish of fresh
green peas, or artichoke hearts; or simply a very good and
not too heavy cheese—Pont l'Évêque is the ideal, particularly if you are drinking claret or burgundy with the
chicken; if white wine, then Gruyère or a fresh cream
cheese.

Spiced Grilled Chicken

For 2 small spring chickens weighing about 1 lb. each
when cleaned, the spices required are 2 teaspoonfuls of
coriander seeds, 12 cardamoms, 1 oz. of green ginger,[1] ½
teaspoon of ground cloves, salt, black pepper, with à little
butter and olive oil.

For the sauce, 2 onions, ½ teaspoon of turmeric, ½ teaspoon of pounded green ginger, a pot of yoghourt, 2 ozs. of
cream, a handful of currants, a little butter and oil.

To serve with the chicken: lemons, mustard and cress,
chutney.

Put the coriander seeds to roast for 2 or 3 minutes in a
warm oven. Pound the cardamoms and remove the husks
as they split; add the coriander seeds and the peeled and
sliced green ginger, the cloves, a little salt, and a few black
peppercorns. Pound all these spices together, then work
them into a paste with a little olive oil and butter.

---

[1] Obtainable at Indian grocers, and essential to the flavouring of these
spiced Oriental dishes.

Have the chickens each split in half down the centre. Lift up the skins, and with the point of a knife score the flesh very lightly. Rub the prepared spice mixture into the flesh, draw the skin of the bird carefully back into place, and rub also the cut side of the chickens with the spices. These preparations should be made 2 hours before the chickens are to be cooked. Put a little piece of butter on each half of the chicken and grill them as described in the preceding recipe. Serve on a long dish, on a bed of mustard and cress, with halves of lemon, the prepared sauce, and a mild chutney.

To make the sauce, melt a little olive oil and butter in a frying pan; fry the sliced onions slowly until they turn golden; stir in the turmeric and the green ginger, salt and pepper. Cook another 5 minutes, then add the yoghourt, and stir until thick, then add the cream and the currants. The sauce can be prepared in advance and heated up in a double saucepan.

This recipe is a variation on the Indian kubab chicken, and if preferred, the chickens can be fried in butter, or pot-roasted, the sauce being added towards the end of the cooking.

La Poule au Pot

One of the simplest and best of all chicken recipes when you have a boiling fowl to cook. A large deep saucepan or earthenware pot is essential, so that there is plenty of room for a variety of vegetables and a good covering of water, or the broth will boil away and its goodness be lost.

The chicken, a large boiler, is first stuffed with a mixture of the pounded liver of the bird, a good handful of bread-crumbs and a little chopped bacon, garlic and parsley, into which you stir an egg or two. Brown the chicken all over in good dripping or butter, add carrots, a couple of turnips, an onion, a sliced leek, a piece of celery, and salt and pepper. Pour in boiling water to cover the bird and the vegetables, and when the water comes to the boil again remove any scum which has risen to the top. Cover the pan and simmer very slowly for about three hours. Thirty minutes or so before serving, the vegetables which have been cooking in the pot and which will probably be rather sodden, can be removed, and fresh ones added.

Serve with the sauce *vinaigrette aux oeufs* described on page 168. The broth can either be served as a first course, or kept for another meal. In this case a little rice can be boiled in it to give it body.

Chicken Salad

A cold roast or boiled chicken, with all the flesh taken from the bones and cut into nice fillets, ¼ lb. of mushrooms, cooked as for champignons à la grecque (p. 29) or sliced raw mushrooms, 1 lb. of cooked new potatoes, 2 cos lettuce hearts, a few tails of Dublin Bay prawns, or ordinary prawns, cooked and shelled, the yolk of a hard-boiled egg, about ¼ pint of mayonnaise flavoured with grated horseradish (see p. 165).

Put the pieces of chicken with the sliced potatoes and the mushrooms into a bowl and mix them with half the mayonnaise. Cover them with the rest of the mayonnaise. On top put the lettuce hearts, cut into quarters, the prawns, and the egg yolk put straight through a sieve on to the salad, so that it rests lightly and decoratively on the top.

This obviously is not a cheap dish, but using a 3 lb. chicken the amounts given should be enough for 7 or 8 people. For 4 people use half a chicken, ½ lb. of potatoes and the rest of the ingredients in the quantity given.

Poulet Celestine

A 2–2½ lb. roasting chicken, 1½ ozs. butter, a liqueur glass of brandy, 4 ozs. of white wine, 3 ozs. of cream, 2 slices of ham, ½ lb. of tomatoes, ¼ lb. of mushrooms.

Season the chicken inside with salt and pepper; melt the butter; add the slices of ham; on top of this put the chicken, breast side downwards; when it is golden on both sides add the brandy, and set it alight; when the flames have gone out add the wine; leave to bubble a couple of minutes, then put in the peeled tomatoes, and the whole mushrooms, then the heated cream. Season the sauce, cover the pan and cook gently for 30–40 minutes (25 if cut up chicken is used). By the time the chicken is cooked the tomatoes should have melted into the sauce but if it is too thin remove the chicken to the serving dish and reduce the sauce by fast boiling for a minute or two. Serve with the mushrooms all round and the sauce poured over the chicken.

A chicken of this size is always supposed to feed 4 people, but personally I find it enough only for 2 with a little left over, or possibly 3 not very hungry people.

Poulet à l'Estragon

A simple version of chicken cooked with tarragon, one of the nicest of chicken dishes, and essentially a summer one, as it can be successfully made only with fresh tarragon.

Work a tablespoon of chopped tarragon leaves with 2 ozs. of butter, season with salt and pepper, and stuff a 3 lb. roasting chicken with this mixture. Cook the chicken in butter in a thick, covered casserole. The bird should be laid on its side, not breast upwards, and should be turned over half way through the cooking, and basted now and again with the tarragon flavoured butter which comes out of it.

When it is tender remove to a serving dish and stir into the juices in the pan a walnut of butter worked with a teaspoon of flour. When this has amalgamated, add a quarter pint of cream and two tablespoons of chopped tarragon. Bring to the boil and when it has thickened pour it over the chicken.

POULETS AU FENOUIL

Prepare two small chickens as for roasting. Line a small deep pan as for braised veal (i.e. sliced carrots and onions and a little bacon all melted in butter). Put in the chickens, add the usual seasonings, with a little bunch of fennel. Cover the pan. Cook over a moderate fire without liquid. Take out the chickens when they are cooked, press the juices and vegetables through a fine sieve. Blanch some small, tender hearts of fennel, add them to the sauce together with a good piece of butter worked with flour. Let the sauce thicken, taste for seasoning, and serve poured over your chickens.

Recipe from *Les Dons de Comus*, 1758.

POULET EN GELÉE

A chicken of about 4 lbs., a calf's foot or 2 pigs' feet, 2 or 3 onions, 4 cloves of garlic, a leek, a carrot, 2 bayleaves, salt, pepper, a lemon and a half bottle of medium dry white wine.

First of all clean the calf's foot and blanch it in boiling water for 10 minutes, cleaning it of the scum which will come to the top.

Rub the chicken all over with the cut lemon, then with salt and pepper. Wrap the bird in a piece of muslin. Put it in a capacious pot with the vegetables, the bayleaves, a few whole peppercorns, and the calf's foot. Cover with about 3 pints of water. Bring it to the boil and after it has simmered for an hour add the white wine.

Cook for another hour, or a little longer if the chicken is a tough one. Remove the bird from the pan and leave it to cool. Cook the rest of the contents of the pan for another hour, then strain the liquid into a bowl. Next day take off all the fat, heat the jelly a little, see that the seasoning is right and pour it through a fine muslin on to the chicken, which can either be left whole or cut up ready for serving. Leave to set. A mild dish which will in no way obtrude upon any wine which is to be served with it.

To make the dish more elegant, the jelly can be clarified in the following manner: when the fat has been removed, put the jelly into a saucepan with the very slightly beaten white of an egg. Bring gradually to the boil. Let it boil a minute, and when the egg has formed a kind of crust on the top of the liquid, turn off the flame. Let it settle. When the liquid has cooled, pour it through a double muslin over the chicken. All the little particles which have come from the chicken and vegetables during the cooking adhere to the white of egg, and the jelly emerges clear and soft.

POULE EN DAUBE

A good cold dish, the slow cooking of which will break down the oldest and toughest of hens. At the bottom of a deep oval fireproof casserole, put two or three rashers of bacon; on these lay the chicken, season with salt and pepper, rub over with lemon juice, and lay another rasher of bacon over the breast. Round the bird put three or four carrots, two onions, two cloves of garlic, a bouquet of thyme and bayleaf and a calf's foot cut in four pieces. (Failing the calf's foot, a pig's foot will do.) Pour a tumbler of white wine over the bird and just cover it with water. Put it to cook, covered with greaseproof paper and the lid of the casserole, in a very slow oven, for about four hours. When it is quite tender, remove it carefully to a serving dish, with the carrots round it. Strain the stock over it, and next day when it has set remove the fat.

Spiced Chicken Cooked in Milk

A small boiling chicken, a pint of milk to every pound which the chicken weighs when ready for cooking, an ounce of green ginger,[1] a teaspoonful of coriander seeds, a teaspoonful of cardamoms, $\frac{1}{4}$ teaspoonful of ground cloves, salt, pepper, lemon.

Roast the coriander seeds for 2 or 3 minutes in the oven; peel the green ginger; pound both in a mortar with the cardamoms and the ground cloves; remove the husks of the cardamoms. Add salt and ground black pepper. Prick the chicken all over with a fork, rub it with lemon then press some of the spices into the chicken, and put some more in the inside. Leave for an hour or two. Bring the milk to the boil with the remainder of the spices. Pour it over the chicken and cook very slowly for about 2½ hours, for the first hour on top of the stove, with the pan covered, for the remainder of the time in the oven, without the lid. When the chicken is quite tender, take it out and leave to cool. When cold, cut all the flesh from the chicken in nice sized pieces; measure about 1 pint of the sauce, heat it up. Add to two whole beaten eggs, through a sieve, and heat it in a double boiler till thick and pour it over the chicken. Serve cold, garnished with a few halves of pistachio nuts or roasted almonds and

[1] See footnote on page 118.

quarters of lemon. Serve with it the spiced rice salad described on page 36.

ITALIAN FRICASSÉE OF CHICKEN

The breasts and livers of 2 tender chickens, an onion, parsley, 1 oz. of pine kernels, 1 lb. of new green peas, 2 cupfuls of chicken stock, a lemon, the yolks of 2 eggs, 1 oz. of butter.

Melt the butter and soften the chopped onion in it without letting it brown. Add chopped parsley. Put in the chicken breasts (4 fillets to each bird) and let them fry golden on each side. Add the pounded pine nuts. Pour the hot stock over, put in the uncooked peas, and cook gently for 10–15 minutes, until the peas are tender. Add the sliced livers and cook them two or three minutes. Remove the fillets to a serving dish, and stir a little of the liquor into the eggs beaten with the juice of the lemon. Return the mixture to the rest of the stock, stir till it thickens. It must not boil, and the operation must be carried out quickly.

Serve if you like with rice.

PARSLEY PIE

A Devonshire and Cornish dish. From the *Cookery Book* of Lady Clark of Tillypronie (Constable & Co. 1909).

Prepare 2 chickens for the pie jointed as for a fricassée. Lay in the bottom of a pie dish a layer about an inch deep of very young parsley (nipped off the stalks and squeezed in a cloth, as the juice is very bitter). Season the joints of chicken, mince a little blanched Portugal onion and 2 shallots, and strew over the chicken with a seasoning of pepper, salt, a breakfast lump of white sugar powdered, and a *very little* mace and nutmeg also, if you like spices.

Lay the joints on the bed of parsley; cover with another layer of parsley, and add more chicken and more parsley in alternate layers till the pie-dish is full.

Pour in a very little good veal stock, and cover all with an ordinary pie crust made so: ½ lb. flour, 4 ozs. butter, 1 egg, a little salt, and enough water to make into good stiff paste; work it well.

In Cornwall they cover the bottom of the pie-dish with a few slices of veal and bacon (to flavour it only, *not to eat*) and the yolks of hard-boiled eggs cut in half, with bacon or ham or tongue cut in dice, are laid in with each layer of chicken and improve the pie much. When the pie is baked, make a small hole in the centre of the crust and pour in ½ pint of double cream, *boiling hot*.

The spices and shallots are often omitted, and only ½ an onion used.

Foies de Volaille Sautés

¼ lb. of chicken livers, 3 ozs. of ham, butter, flour, port, a cupful of chicken or light meat stock, parsley, salt, pepper.

Cut the carefully cleaned livers in half. Season, dust with flour. In the melted butter sauté the ham cut into strips. Add the livers. After two minutes, pour in a small glass of port (or madeira or marsala). Let it bubble a few seconds, add the stock. Cook gently for 5 minutes, stirring frequently. Stir in 2 tablespoons of cut parsley, and serve either with fried croûtons or on a dish of white rice.

Turkey Stuffed with Herbs and Roasted in Butter

A young turkey weighing about 7 to 9 lbs.,[1] roasted in

[1] If your dealer cannot supply small turkeys they can be ordered from P. P. Poultry Ltd., The Bury Farm, Chesham, Bucks, at 30/- for a 7 lb. bird, ready to cook.

butter with a fresh herb stuffing makes a delightful change both from the more usual roast chicken, and from the 25 lb. monsters which are such a tyranny to cook at Christmas time. Turkey breeders have been experimenting for some time in England with the supplying of small birds all the year round, and they are becoming more plentiful on the market.

For the stuffing for a 7 lb. turkey the ingredients are 4 ozs. each of breadcrumbs and butter, the grated rind of a lemon, 3 or 4 tablespoons of chopped fresh parsley, thyme or lemon thyme, and marjoram, 2 eggs, a small clove of garlic, salt, pepper, a squeeze of lemon juice. To make the breadcrumbs put slices of white bread in the oven until they are dry, but not browned, then pound them. Mix all the ingredients together. What makes this stuffing so good is the use of fresh herbs as opposed to packet herbs, and the absence of sage. When the bird is stuffed rub it all over with butter and put it on its side in the roasting pan, covered with liberally buttered greaseproof paper. Put in a preheated fairly hot oven (Regulo 4 or 5) and cook it for about 15 minutes to the pound, and 15 minutes over. After the first hour turn the bird over and baste with more butter. For the last 20 minutes or so remove the greaseproof paper and turn the bird breast upwards so that it browns. This way of cooking a small turkey gives it a very delicate taste, and it will be moist and tender.

The only sauce necessary is the juice and butter in the pan poured off into a small pan and brought to bubbling point, with the addition of a very small glass of white wine.

LE CANETON AUX PETITS POIS

A *caneton aux petits pois* and a duckling with green peas are not so alike as they sound. The two dishes demonstrate

one of the fundamental differences between the cooking of
France and England. The English dish consists of a roast
duckling served with boiled and buttered green peas, and
there the matter ends.

In the French version, the peas are added to the duck
while it is cooking, with little pieces of smoked bacon and
small onions, good stock is added, all is simmered together
sufficiently long for the peas to absorb the stock and some
of the fat from the duck.

You will need 4 lbs. of small new peas. Blanch them in
boiling water. Brown some small whole onions in butter.
Put them together with the drained peas in the pan with
the duckling which has been two thirds roasted (allow
15 minutes to the pound) and from which you pour off the
fat. Add ¼ lb. of smoked bacon cut into thick strips, in
about half a cupful of very good stock (made from the
giblets of the duck if you have no meat stock) and leave
to cook very gently for about 20 minutes more, or until
both duckling and peas are tender.

SALMI OF DUCK

A duck, ¼ pint of jellied stock, 2 shallots, garlic, a small
wineglass each of port and brandy, salt, pepper.

Roast the duck and when it is all but cooked, carve the
breast into fillets. Separate the legs and wings and leave
them in the roasting pan to cook gently a little longer while
the sauce is prepared in the following manner.

Crush the carcass in a mortar and put the juice which
comes out of it into a pan with the giblets of the bird, a
clove of garlic, 2 chopped shallots, ground black pepper, a
bayleaf and the port. Reduce the liquid by half. Add the
stock, cook 10 minutes. Strain, see that the seasoning is
right and heat the fillets in this sauce, which should emerge
in the final stages quite syrupy and shiny. Now warm

the brandy, set light to it and pour it flaming into the sauce. Put the legs and wings of the bird in a serving dish and in the centre the fillets with the sauce.

DUCK WITH CHERRIES

A 4 to 5 lb. duck, $\frac{1}{2}$ lb. morello cherries, red wine, carrots, onions, garlic, herbs, seasoning, veal bones.

Put the seasoned duck into a braising pan with 3 or 4 carrots, a small onion, a clove of garlic, a bayleaf, a sprig of fresh marjoram or basil, the giblets of the bird and 2 small veal bones. Pour a wineglass of red wine over the duck, and two of water. Add a little salt, sugar, and pepper. Cover the pan and cook in a slow oven (Regulo 3–4) for 2 hours. When the duck is tender take it out, put the pan with the rest of its contents over a fast flame and reduce the sauce by about half. Strain into a bowl, leave to cool, take off the fat. Reheat the sauce, which should have jellied, and pour it hot over the stoned cherries.

Serve the cold duck surrounded with squares of the jellied sauce in which the cherries are embedded.

If preferred, the duck can be carved for serving and the sauce either poured over or served separately in a bowl.

DUCK IN ORANGE JUICE

A 4 lb. duck, $\frac{1}{2}$ pint of orange juice, $\frac{1}{2}$ lb. of tomatoes, an onion, 2 cloves of garlic, a sprig each of marjoram and parsley, a bayleaf, 1 oz. of ground almonds, 1 oz. of raisins, 2 tablespoons of vinegar, half a teacupful of water, salt and pepper.

Put the seasoned duck into a casserole or deep pan with all the ingredients, and the giblets of the bird. Cover the pan and cook gently either on top of the stove or in a slow oven (Regulo 2 or 3) for $2\frac{3}{4}$–3 hours. Take out the duck,

strain the sauce; if to be served hot, carve the duck and
put back to heat in the sauce, from which you have
poured off as much fat as possible. If to be eaten cold,
pour the sauce into a bowl and remove the fat when it is
cold.

A very good dish, adapted from a Mexican recipe.

Lapin à la Fermière

A wild rabbit weighing about 1¼–1½ lbs. and cut in pieces,
1½ lbs. young broad beans, a leek, ½ lb. green peas, 2
potatoes, butter, a vinaigrette sauce.

Melt the butter in a large pan, brown the seasoned
pieces of rabbit gently on each side. Add the shelled peas
(unless you have *mange tout* peas which do not have to be
shelled) the leek and potatoes cut in pieces, and the broad
beans in their pods, the black ends near the stalks having
been cut off (if the beans are too old for the pods to be
cooked twice the quantity at least will be needed). Just
cover the vegetables with water, season with salt and
pepper and 3 lumps of sugar and cook at a moderate pace
for 1½–2 hours.

Take out the pieces of rabbit, and while they are still
hot pour over them a vinaigrette sauce made with olive
oil, lemon, a little garlic, and chopped herbs, which
should if possible include fresh thyme or lemon thyme.

Sieve the vegetables (you need a food mill for this).
There should be a thick and fairly firm purée (the liquid
in which they have been cooked should of course be kept
for soup).

Arrange the purée in the middle of a large shallow dish
with the pieces of rabbit all round. Serve cold. If you
like, serve more vinaigrette sauce separately, or a mayonnaise if you prefer. The dish can be garnished with a few
quarters of hard-boiled eggs.

If you prefer to serve the dish hot, simply pour a little oil, pepper and salt over the pieces of rabbit when they are taken from the pan, and while you are heating up the purée, fry the rabbit gently or heat it under the grill. The reheating process will not harm it.

COLD PIGEON FILLETS WITH CHERRIES

2 pigeons, ½ lb. cherries, ½ pint of aspic jelly (p. 171) kirsch, herbs, seasoning.

Put salt and pepper inside the pigeons and place them in a roasting tin with water half way up. Add a bouquet of parsley, thyme and bayleaf, cover the pan and cook in a very gentle oven for about 1½ hours. (Pigeons can be very tough, and need careful slow cooking.) Meanwhile, stone the cherries (morellos if possible) and put them in a bowl to macerate with a small glass of kirsch poured over them. When the pigeons are tender take them from the oven and leave them to cool. Cut each side of the breast of the pigeons into two fillets. Put them in a shallow dish. Arrange the cherries round them. Cover with the melted aspic and leave to set.

If there is no aspic jelly to hand, do not spoil the dish by using gelatine, but cook a calf's or pig's foot with the pigeons, in a little more water. Cook it an extra half hour or so after the pigeons have been taken out, then strain it and remove the fat when cold.

GROUSE

As grouse shooting starts on August 12th, grouse can be counted as summer food. Young grouse are at their best wrapped in a piece of bacon and very carefully roasted, served either hot or cold, but in either case *without* game chips, which are usually sodden and always dull, and no wonder, as they usually come out of a packet.

Old grouse, sold in the shops as "casserole grouse" are usually so dry and have so powerful a flavour that they are all but uneatable, however carefully and patiently simmered. They can however make quite an acceptable dish if first marinated and then stewed in wine, and stock from grouse can be used in several very delicious ways, notably for stewing mushrooms; a little added to a dish of eggs *sur le plat* also makes a lovely dish, and the beef stuffed with chopped grouse and stewed in the stock (recipe on p. 107) is quite excellent. These are really dishes for those people who have their own game to be used up, as few people will care to buy a casserole grouse simply in order to use the stock, although as far as the mushroom dish is concerned it is really worth the trouble and expense.

Lady Clark's recipe for a grouse pudding (p. 133) is also worth a trial; the idea of using old game birds to flavour beef is a fairly common one in old English cookery.

STEWED GROUSE

Make a red wine marinade in the following way: heat a coffeecupful of olive oil in a small pan; when warmed put in a sliced carrot, an onion, a clove of garlic, a few crushed juniper berries, a sprig of fresh thyme and a bayleaf. Add a large glass of red wine and a little ground black pepper. Simmer altogether for 15 minutes and when cold pour over the bird or birds. Marinate for not less than 4 hours. Take out the bird, put it in a pan with 2 ozs. of chopped bacon and pour over the strained marinade. Add a fresh carrot and onion and herbs and stew very slowly with the lid on for 2 hours. If the juice is going to be needed for stock, add water after the marinade has been poured in.

Grouse Pudding

A pudding made with quite *old unboned* grouse, juicy rump steak and good stock. The pudding to boil rather slowly or it will get dry. The birds are *not meant to be eaten*, merely put in to flavour the steak.

From the *Cookery Book* of Lady Clark
of Tillypronie (Constable, 1909).

Potted Venison

2 lbs. of venison, 8–10 ozs. of fat bacon, garlic, juniper berries, coriander seeds, black pepper, very little salt, red wine.

Cut the venison and the bacon into slices. Put into a deep earthenware pot, add half a dozen each of crushed juniper berries and coriander seeds, a fair amount of ground black pepper and a very little salt. Just cover the meat with coarse red wine, put a lid on the pot and cook in the lowest possible oven for at least 3 hours. When cold, chop the venison and bacon fairly finely, press into small pots, and seal with clarified butter or dripping.

Admirable for sandwiches.

CHAPTER 8

VEGETABLES

THE tender young vegetables of early summer, broad beans, green peas, new potatoes, new turnips, young carrots, are nearly always best quite plainly cooked and eaten with plenty of fresh butter. A little later, when they are more plentiful, cheaper, but less tender, they can be cooked in a variety of enterprising ways, with cream and sauces and stock, with ham and bacon, made into purées, soufflés, soups and salads, and flavoured with fresh herbs.

As well as the classic vegetable dishes such as *petits pois à la française*, glazed carrots and *navets glacés*, I have given in the following chapter a few recipes which may provide new ideas for English kitchens. Most of these are for vegetables to be served as a separate course. The time and trouble necessary to the preparation of fresh vegetables, as well as their delicious fresh flavour, deserve full recognition.

For a summer luncheon what could be better than a cold pâté or terrine, followed by a dish of hot green peas cooked in butter, or peas and carrots mixed, or well-buttered french beans and new potatoes? Small new beetroots, hot, with butter and chives, are good with a grilled pork chop, while baby turnips make one of the nicest accompaniments to braised lamb or mutton. English tomatoes, plentiful from May onwards, are at their best raw, as salads to go with grilled or roast meat and chicken; Florentine fennel, now imported in fairly large quantities, makes the most refreshing of salads. Mediterranean pimentos, aubergines and courgettes (the

Italian zucchine) begin to get reasonable in price by early September, and for people who like Southern food and garlicky smells this is the time for oil flavoured Provençal ratatouilles, and rich Basque Pipérades of eggs, pimentos, and onions served with grilled gammon or coarse country sausages.

ASPARAGUS

Cut the cleaned asparagus all the same length, tie them together in bundles, and put them upright in a deep pan of boiling water, to which a lump of sugar as well as salt has been added. Cook them so that the heads do not come into contact with the water, but are cooked by the steam. Cooking times vary between 15 minutes for small asparagus to 30 minutes for the large ones. Drain them very carefully or they will break.

They are best served with the classic melted butter, Sauce Hollandaise, Sauce Maltaise or the vinaigrette sauce with eggs described on page 168, which goes well with them whether hot or cold. Oil and lemon is good too but asparagus won't stand up to vinegar. The tips of the small green asparagus make delicious omelettes and go well with eggs cooked in cream (see p. 66).

ASPARAGUS WITH PARMESAN CHEESE

One of the Italian ways of eating asparagus is to cut off the entire part of the stalk which is inedible, after they are cooked; then put them in a fireproof dish, sprinkle them lightly with grated Parmesan, then with melted butter, and put them in the oven just long enough for the cheese to melt.

Asparagus with Mayonnaise

Use the large fat asparagus for this dish. Cut the stalks
fairly short and cook the asparagus in the usual way, and
leave them to cool. Serve them with a mayonnaise to
which a beaten white of egg has been added (see Mayonnaise Mousseuse, p. 165).

Broad Beans

Imported broad beans start arriving early in May;
English broad beans are not usually on the market until
early June.

When new, they are best plain boiled and served with
butter. They are also exquisite eaten raw (see p. 22)
when young and tender. When they begin to get large
they can be cooked in sauces with ham or bacon, and in
soups. Delicious purées can be made from very young
broad beans, using the pods (see the soup recipe, p. 46,
and rabbit with broad bean purée, p. 130). Some people
dislike the rather earthy flavour of the skins of broad
beans, but to me this taste is an important part of the
flavour of these lovely vegetables. The French insist that
savory must always flavour broad beans, but for once I
disagree with them; this herb seems to make them bitter.

Fèves à la Crème

2 lbs. of very young broad beans, 1½ ozs. of butter, 2 ozs.
of cream, a teaspoon of flour, salt, sugar, pepper.

Melt the butter, put in the broad beans, and stir until
they have absorbed most of the butter. Sprinkle with the
flour, stir again, and just barely cover the beans with hot
water. Add pepper and sugar, but salt only when the
beans are practically cooked. Simmer steadily for 15

minutes, then stir in the cream previously boiled in another pan.

Enough for four.

FÈVES À LA POULETTE

2 lbs. of broad beans, the yolks of 2 eggs, parsley, ½ oz. butter, 1 teaspoon of flour.

Cook the shelled beans (medium sized ones are best for this dish) in a little salted water. Strain them, keep a little of the water in which they have cooked. Melt the butter, stir in the flour, add a small cupful of the water from the beans; put in the beans and cook for two or three minutes. Stir in the beaten yolks of the eggs, and let them get hot, but the sauce must not boil. Sprinkle with a little cut parsley.

Enough for four.

BROAD BEANS AND BACON

Melt 2 ozs. of diced bacon (or ham, or cold pork) in a little butter. Add 2 lbs. of cooked broad beans, 2 or 3 tablespoons of light béchamel sauce, a little cream, a very little chopped parsley. Simmer together for 5 minutes.

BROAD BEANS AND YOGHOURT

1½ lbs. broad beans, 2 tablespoons of rice, a clove of garlic, 1 egg, a small pot of yoghourt.

Boil the broad beans and the rice separately, strain them and mix them together while hot. Stir the pounded garlic into the yoghourt, season with salt and pepper and add the mixture to the beans and rice. Heat gently, then stir in the beaten egg. As soon as the sauce has thickened slightly, it is ready.

Can be eaten hot or cold. A Middle Eastern dish, called *Fistuqia*.

Broad Beans with Egg and Lemon

Cook the beans in boiling salted water. When they are ready drain them, reserving a teacupful of the water in which they have cooked. Add this to the yolks of 2 eggs and the juice of a lemon. Heat over a very gentle flame, whisking all the time until the sauce is frothy and slightly thickened. Pour over the beans. Serve hot or cold.

Cooked artichoke hearts mixed with the beans are a good combination, and for an hors d'oeuvre add a few prawns or tails of Dublin Bay prawns.

Broad Beans and Pork

½ lb. of belly of pork, 2 lbs. of broad beans, ½ pint of milk, flour, seasoning.

Cut the pork into small strips; put it into a thick pan over a slow fire, and let it cook very gently, with the lid on the pan, for 15 minutes. Season with salt and pepper, sprinkle with flour, stir, and gradually add the warmed milk. Cook gently for another 20 minutes, while the shelled beans are boiled in the usual way. When they are tender, drain them and put them into the pan with the pork. Let them get thoroughly hot before serving.

Purée de Fèves

Cook broad beans exactly as for the broad bean soup 2 on page 46. Strain off all the water and sieve them. Heat up with a little butter. Delicious with bacon, ham, pork chops and duck. A little of the dripping or sauce in which either of these last two has been cooking can be added to the purée before serving. Some cooks remove the inner skin of the beans before sieving them; not only does this take hours but it is quite unnecessary and also lessens the flavour.

BEETROOT WITH HERB BUTTER

Small boiled beetroots, peeled and sliced, heated one minute in a butter worked with chopped chives, a squeeze of lemon juice and a scrap of garlic.

BEETROOT WITH CREAM SAUCE

Boil some small young beetroots. Peel them and put them in a pan with a little butter. When they are thoroughly hot pour over them a tablespoonful of vinegar, and then 2 ozs. (for 1 lb. beetroots) of boiling cream.

PEAS

Shelling peas is certainly a good deal of trouble, but with butter, perhaps a little cream, or ham, or a lettuce heart, they make one of the most perfect summer dishes, not just something to put round the meat, but as a course by themselves.

When obliged to shell the peas some hours before they are to be cooked, wrap them in a damp cloth. In this way they will not lose their moisture. A pound of peas in the pod yields about 6 ozs. when shelled, so that if the peas are to be served as a separate course allow about 3 lbs. for four people.

LES PETITS POIS À L'ANCIENNE MODE

Shell 4 lbs. of new green peas, and wrap them in a damp cloth until it is time to cook them. Open out the leaves

of a good lettuce heart and inside place 2 sprigs of freshly
picked summer savory. Tie the lettuce round with string,
put it in a saucepan and all round put the peas, season
with salt, add half a glass ($\frac{1}{4}$ pint) of water and $\frac{1}{4}$ lb. of
very fresh butter. Cook a quarter of an hour, take
out the lettuce; immediately before serving pour into
the peas three tablespoons of fresh cream beaten together
with the yolk of an egg, a little sugar, and a little
pepper.

Edmond Richardin, who gives this recipe in *L'Art du
Bien Manger* (Paris, 1912) claims that it came from the
monks of the Abbey of Fontevrault, where the remarkable
kitchens can still be seen today.

I do not think anyone need worry unduly about the
savory, a herb which has rather too strong a taste for
delicate green vegetables, but the method of cooking the
peas is excellent.

PETITS POIS À LA FRANÇAISE

2 lbs. of small peas, 3 ozs. butter, 8–12 very small onions,
the heart of a lettuce, seasoning.

Put the shelled peas, $2\frac{1}{2}$ ozs. of butter, the onions
(spring onions are best for this dish, the bulb part only)
and the lettuce heart into a small thick pan or earthenware pot. Season with salt, and a teaspoonful of sugar.
When the butter is bubbling just cover the peas with hot
water. Cover the pan and simmer gently until the peas
are tender. They will take from 30–45 minutes according
to the size of the peas. By the time they are cooked, most
of the liquid will be absorbed. Stir in another $\frac{1}{2}$ oz. of
butter, cut the lettuce into four, and serve.

Peas with Ham

2 lbs. of green peas, 2 ozs. of ham, sugar, salt, 2 ozs. of butter.

Melt the butter in a small thick pan, put in the ham cut into small strips, then the peas. Salt very lightly, add two lumps of sugar, and pour over just enough hot water to come level with the peas. Cover the pan and cook gently for about 30 minutes. If you like, before serving, thicken the sauce with 2 tablespoons of thick cream.

Petits Pois à la Crème

Put small green peas into a pan in which you have melted some good fresh butter; when it is all absorbed, pour over enough boiling cream to cover the peas; season very lightly with salt and a little sugar, cover the pan, and cook very gently until the peas are tender.

Purée of Fresh Peas

To a purée made from 2 lbs. of fresh peas, cooked in salted water and drained, add 1 oz. of butter, a little sugar and pepper, a scrap of fresh mint, and 2 or 3 tablespoons of fresh cream. Heat in a double boiler. Delicious with veal, and a good way of using old peas.

Petits Pois aux Carottes

2 or 3 lbs. (according to their age) of green peas, 1 lb. of new carrots, the heart of a small lettuce, a small onion, 2 ozs. of butter, salt, sugar.

Clean the carrots, cut them in strips, and cook them for about 5 minutes in boiling water.

Put the shelled peas, the shredded lettuce, the whole onion with a little salt and sugar in a pan with the carrots and just cover with boiling water. Cook gently; by the time the vegetables are ready the water should be almost all absorbed; stir in the butter, see that the seasoning is right and serve.

CAROTTES À LA NIVERNAISE

1 lb. carrots, ½ lb. very small onions, stock, sugar, butter.

If the carrots are large cut them into pieces about the size of a cork; if they are very young carrots leave them whole. Blanch them in boiling salted water for 5 minutes. Drain them, put them in a shallow pan with 1½ ozs. of butter, and barely cover them with stock. Cook slowly but steadily until nearly all the stock is absorbed. By this time the carrots should be tender and the remaining sauce of a syrupy consistency. Season with salt, pepper, and sugar, and mix them with the onions which have been first browned in butter, sprinkled with sugar, and simmered in stock in the same way as the carrots, until the sauce is entirely absorbed and the onions brown and shiny.

GLAZED CARROTS WITH MINT

Blanch a pound of small new carrots in boiling salted water for 6 or 7 minutes. Strain, and put them in a heavy pan with 2 ozs. of butter; after 5 minutes' gentle cooking add a tablespoon of sugar; simmer gently. When the carrots are tender season with salt and ground black pepper and stir in a tablespoon of chopped fresh mint.

CAROTTES À LA PAYSANNE

A large onion, 1 lb. small carrots, butter, sugar, salt, cream.

Melt the thinly sliced onion in butter; when it is just turning golden add the carrots, previously blanched for 5 minutes, and cut in half lengthways. Add a very little stock or water, cook slowly with the pan covered. When the carrots are nearly cooked, add a seasoning of salt and sugar and two or three tablespoons of cream. Simmer until the carrots are quite tender.

CARROTS STEWED WITH RICE

(A Turkish Dish)

Clean 1 lb. of young carrots and cut in halves lengthways; cover the bottom of a thick pan with oil; when it has warmed put in the carrots and let them get thoroughly impregnated with the oil; add 2 tablespoons of rice, and stir it round with the carrots; just cover carrots and rice with water, add a little salt. Simmer for about 25 minutes until the carrots and rice are cooked and most of the liquid evaporated; stir in a handful of chopped parsley and mint.

Serve cold, in their liquid, which will be quite thick, with a squeeze of lemon juice.

POTATOES

It is not until June that English new potatoes become reasonably cheap. The early imported new potatoes never seem to be worth their high price, so in the early part of the summer the old potatoes will have to do. For a change, they are good grilled in the way described on page 146. Also a potato purée, with the addition of fresh new vegetables or herbs (see the soup chapter) makes a very good spring soup. The smallest new potatoes are at their best cooked slowly in butter, so that they emerge pale golden outside, melting inside. When they are larger, they make a lovely dish cooked in good stock. Perhaps in this country we eat potatoes so often that very little trouble is taken over their preparation. They repay careful treatment as much as any other vegetable. Because they absorb a good deal of whatever fat they are cooked in, it follows that the fat should always be the best possible; olive oil, butter, pure pork fat, the dripping from a duck, bacon fat, all give their different savours to potatoes. When they are roasted with meat they, as well as the meat, will taste all the better for the flavour of herbs and possibly garlic which has cooked with the meat. If new potatoes are to be boiled they are best put into boiling water.

Although boiled potatoes are one of the first dishes anybody learns to cook, they always remain a nuisance, as the timing must be accurate, and varies with the quality of the potatoes, so for occasions when there are other dishes to be attended to, or when the meal may be late, it is advisable to learn one or two other simple methods of cooking potatoes, by which they will not suffer if kept waiting a few minutes. Two such potato dishes are *pommes de terre à la crème* and *pommes de terre fromagées*.

POMMES DE TERRE AU JUS

Cut medium sized new potatoes into quarters. Just cover them with well flavoured meat or chicken stock. Simmer, uncovered, until the potatoes are tender and the stock nearly all absorbed. Add a good lump of butter and when it has melted serve the potatoes.

POMMES DE TERRE RISSOLÉES

1 lb. of new potatoes, as much as possible all the same size.
2 ozs. of butter.

Choose a small thick pan in which the potatoes will just fit, all in one layer. Melt the butter in this pan, put in the potatoes, whole, cover the pan. Cook very slowly, so that the butter does not burn. Turn the potatoes round several times during the cooking, so that they turn golden all over.

Small potatoes should be cooked in 25 to 40 minutes (according to the size) by which time the butter will all be absorbed by the potatoes. Add salt only when the potatoes are cooked.

POMMES DE TERRE SABLÉES

Cook the potatoes as for pommes de terre rissolées. When they are tender, add a little more butter and throw in a handful of fresh white breadcrumbs and shake the pan so that the breadcrumbs absorb the butter and turn crisp within two or three minutes.

Particularly good with grilled meat.

POMMES DE TERRE À LA CRÈME

Boil some small whole new potatoes, keeping them rather underdone. Make a cream sauce as described on page 167 and heat the potatoes in this, seasoning them with a little nutmeg.

POMMES DE TERRE MESSINE

Make a Sauce Messine (p. 167) and in it heat sliced boiled new potatoes, in a double saucepan, stirring carefully so that the potatoes do not break.

Pommes de Terre Fromagées

Fill a small shallow baking dish with new potatoes, boiled but kept rather undercooked. Pour melted butter over them, then cover them lightly with a mixture of bread-crumbs and grated Gruyère cheese. Cook in a moderate oven, turning the potatoes round from time to time until they are lightly browned.

Grilled Potatoes

Boil medium sized yellow potatoes in their skins. Peel them, cut them in half lengthways, paint with butter and put under the grill until they are golden. Serve with coarse salt, ground black pepper, fresh butter. Delicious. A useful recipe where cooking space is restricted.

Pommes de Terre à la Méridionale

Have some small new potatoes, as much as possible all of the same size. Heat some olive oil in a thick saucepan, put in the potatoes, season with salt and pepper and cook at a moderate heat with the cover on the pan for about 15 minutes. When the potatoes are cooked lift them out on to the serving dish and sprinkle them liberally with a mixture of freshly chopped parsley and garlic; if you like pour over them a little of the oil from the pan, very hot, but most people prefer them dry. The potatoes should be a very light golden colour, and only slightly crisp on the outside.

Navets Glacés

Recipe from *Le Cuisinier Européen*, an old French cookery book of about 1860.

Peel the turnips and trim them all to the same size, roughly in the shape of a pear. Blanch them two or three minutes in boiling water. Drain them, put them in a small thick sauté pan. Cover them with clear bouillon. Sprinkle them with a mixture of salt and pepper, and add 2 or 3 little pieces of whole cinnamon. Cook over a fast flame and remove the cinnamon after 2 or 3 minutes. Let the stock reduce until it is beginning to stick to the bottom of the pan. Take out the turnips and put them on the serving dish. Pour into the pan a little white wine, just enough to detach the remainder of the sauce from the bottom of the pan. Pour this short and thick sauce over the turnips so that they look glazed.

Serve very hot.

NAVETS AU JAMBON

Cut a fairly thick slice of ham into cubes; brown it lightly in butter; add some young turnips, previously blanched in boiling water and also cut into cubes; season with ground black pepper, and very little salt. Cover the pan and cook slowly until the turnips are tender; before serving sprinkle with parsley and a very little chopped garlic.

NAVONI ALL' AGLIATA

(Turnips with garlic sauce)

A Genoese dish. Blanch the peeled turnips in boiling salted water for 5 minutes. Cut them in quarters, and put them to stew gently in a small heavy pan with plenty of olive oil, and season them with salt.

Prepare the *agliata* by pounding two or three cloves of garlic in a mortar, and adding a very little vinegar. When the turnips are cooked, add this mixture to the turnips;

stir well so that the garlic sauce is well amalgamated with
the oil, add a little parsley, and serve.

PURÉE OF SORREL (1)

Wash the sorrel in several waters and pick it over carefully, as for spinach. Cook for about 10 minutes in a little
salted water. Drain as dry as possible, and chop finely.
Put into a pan with a lump of butter. · For a pound of
sorrel add a quarter pint of cream and then two beaten
eggs. When the purée thickens, it is ready.

On a basis of the sorrel purée may be served poached or
hard-boiled eggs, white fish such as fillets of sole or rock
salmon, pork chops or grilled gammon or escalopes of
veal and the purée can also be served cold.

PURÉE OF SORREL (2)

A handful of sorrel leaves, 2 or 3 tablespoons of cream or
béchamel sauce, butter.

Chop the cleaned sorrel and melt it in a little bubbling
butter. Stir it for two or three minutes, season with salt,
and add the cream or béchamel; cook a few more minutes
until the mixture has thickened a little. Serve in the same
way as the preceding purée, as a filling for an omelette,
or the basis of a soup.

SPINACH AND EGGS

Clean 1 lb. of spinach very carefully and drain it well.
Cook it, without water, for about 5 minutes, adding a little
salt. Squeeze the water out of it, put it into a fireproof
dish in which a good lump of butter has been melted; heat
it very gently in the oven. When it is hot, add two or

three tablespoons of boiled cream and 2 sliced hard-boiled eggs and cook another minute or two.

Serve very hot, as a separate vegetable course. 1 lb. of spinach is enough for two people.

French Beans with Egg and Lemon Sauce

1 lb. of french beans, 2 eggs, a lemon, a tablespoon of grated Parmesan cheese, olive oil.

Cook the beans in boiling salted water; drain them, reserving about a cupful of the water in which they have cooked. Keep them hot. Have ready the eggs whisked to a froth with the lemon juice, a tablespoon of olive oil, and the cheese. Add a little of the water from the vegetables and heat this sauce over a low flame, whisking all the time until it has thickened a little. It will only take a minute or two. Pour over the beans and serve at once. Also good cold.

Haricots Verts à l'Italienne

The coarse variety of french beans called scarlet runners are particularly good cooked in this way. Boil the beans in salted water, keeping them rather undercooked. Cover the bottom of a small pan with olive oil, and when it is warm put in the strained beans; add, for 1 lb. of beans, 2 or 3 chopped tomatoes and a little chopped garlic. Cook gently, shaking the pan from time to time for about 10 minutes, until the tomatoes have melted.

French Beans and New Potatoes

Cook equal quantities of small new potatoes and french beans together in boiling salted water, adding the beans 5 minutes after the potatoes. When both are cooked, pile the beans in the middle of a hot dish, put the potatoes round, and pour hot butter over both.

Aubergines

Aubergines, or egg plant, are one of the most useful vegetables as a background for using already cooked meat, particularly mutton, the most difficult of cold joints to utilize to advantage, as it rarely makes an attractive cold dish. The best known of aubergine and meat dishes is moussaká, which is to be found in varying forms all over the Balkans and the Middle East, and several of the recipes which follow are also from the Middle East where mutton is the most plentiful meat. Aubergines are also particularly successful when mixed with tomatoes in some form or other, as in the Provençal Ratatouille (see p. 34) and they also make interesting purées and salads, the kind of little dishes which are served either as an hors d'oeuvre or with meat, like a chutney. Two of these recipes are in the hors d'oeuvre chapter. Aubergines are best cooked in olive oil rather than butter or dripping; they always have a warm Southern look about them, especially when they are cooked with their purple skins on. Most aubergine dishes are as good cold as they are hot, and they can also be heated up without deteriorating in any way, so they are a most versatile vegetable.

Papeton d'Aubergines

The story goes that one of the Avignon Popes complained that Provençal cooking was not as good as that of Rome, and his cook invented this recipe in order to prove that he was wrong. It is also recounted that the first *papeton* was presented to the Pope in the form of a mitre.

Peel 6 aubergines, cut them in thick slices, salt them and leave them to drain. Stew them in olive oil in a covered pan, so that they remain moist; drain them and chop or sieve them. Season and add a chopped clove of garlic, a teacupful of milk and three eggs. Turn in to a lightly oiled mould. Cook 25 minutes in a bain-marie. Turn out and serve covered with a thick fresh tomato sauce flavoured with garlic and fresh basil.

If preferred the *papeton* can be served in the dish in which it has cooked, with the sauce poured on the top.

AUBERGINES À LA PROVENÇALE

3 aubergines, 1 lb. of tomatoes, garlic, parsley, bread-crumbs, olive oil.

Cut the unpeeled aubergines into thick rounds, salt them and leave to drain. Dry them and fry them gently in olive oil, turning them over two or three times, for about 6 minutes. Remove them to a gratin dish; fry the peeled and chopped tomatoes in olive oil, season them with salt, pepper, 2 chopped cloves of garlic, a handful of chopped parsley. Spread the tomato mixture on top of the auber-gines, sprinkle with breadcrumbs and a few drops of olive oil. Cook them in a moderate oven for about ¾ of an hour.

MOUSSAKA

There are a good many different versions of this dish, which is known in Rumania, Yugoslavia, Greece, and all over the near East. Here is a very simple version.

3 aubergines, ¾ lb. minced mutton, 1 onion, 3 large tomatoes, parsley, a clove of garlic, salt, pepper, olive oil, fresh tomato sauce made from 1 lb. tomatoes, peeled and cooked to a pulp in a little olive oil and flavoured with garlic and herbs.

Slice the unpeeled egg plants in rounds about ½ inch thick, salt them, leave to drain for an hour, then dry them

with a cloth and fry in olive oil until they are soft. Chop
the onion, let it turn golden in the oil in which the aubergines were fried, stir in the meat and the garlic, season
with salt and pepper. Simmer two or three minutes.
Arrange the aubergines, the meat, and the sliced peeled
tomatoes in alternate layers in a square cake tin about 2
inches deep. Pour over the sauce and cook for 45 minutes
to 1 hour in a moderate oven. By this time most of the
liquid should have evaporated. Serve in the tin in which
it has cooked, with parsley strewn over the top. Moussaká
can be reheated quite successfully.

AUBERGINES À LA TURQUE

2 large aubergines (the round variety are best for this
dish), 3 large onions, ½ lb. tomatoes, sugar, salt, allspice
(sometimes called ground pimento), garlic.

Cut the unpeeled aubergines into thick round slices.
Salt them and leave them to drain on a colander for an
hour or two. Fry them in oil so that they are browned on
both sides. Take them out of the pan and fry the thinly
sliced onions, not crisply, but just golden yellow, then add
the skinned and chopped tomatoes, and a clove or two of
garlic. Season with salt, a teaspoonful of the allspice, and
a little sugar. Cook until you have a thick sauce. Arrange
the aubergine slices in an oiled baking tin, put a tablespoonful of the sauce on each slice of aubergine, and bake
in a moderate oven for 40–50 minutes. Can be served hot
but best cold.

MARINATED AUBERGINES

Cut unpeeled aubergines in half lengthways; make gashes
in the centre part of the flesh, salt them, and pour over
them some olive oil, black pepper, chopped garlic and

herbs. Leave them to marinate for an hour or two. They should then be grilled, being basted with the marinade, but under a gas or electric grill they cook too fast and get blackened, so it is best to bake them in an uncovered dish in a moderate oven, for about an hour. Cook them, cut side downwards in the pan for all but the last quarter of an hour; then turn them round and baste them with the juices in the pan, and squeeze a little lemon juice over them. Very good as an accompaniment to roast mutton, or grilled chops.

KAZAN KABABI

4 medium sized aubergines, $\frac{1}{2}$ lb. minced mutton, olive oil, salt, garlic, herbs, pine nuts or walnuts.

Cut the stalk end from the aubergines and make long slits almost the whole length of them, about an inch apart, but taking care not to cut right through. Rub them with salt and leave for an hour. Season the minced meat with salt, pepper, chopped garlic and marjoram, mint or basil, add 2 tablespoons of chopped pine nuts or walnuts. Push this stuffing into the slits made in the aubergines. Warm a little olive oil in a pan in which the aubergines will just fit. Lay them side by side in the pan, let them heat in the oil, then add hot water to come half way up. Cover with a plate which fits inside the pan over the aubergines so that they do not move during the cooking. Simmer very slowly for $1\frac{1}{2}$ hours until they are quite soft and only a little of the oil is left in the pan.

MAQLUB OF AUBERGINES
(A Persian dish)

4 medium sized aubergines, $\frac{3}{4}$ lb. of minced mutton, cooked or raw, $\frac{1}{4}$ lb. of rice, 1 onion, 2 cloves of garlic,

2 ozs. almonds, half a teaspoon of ground allspice, ¾ pint of meat stock, herbs.

Cut the unpeeled aubergines in slices about a quarter inch thick, salt them and leave them for an hour. Put the rice to soak in water for an hour. Mix the spice, a little thyme or marjoram and chopped garlic with the meat. Dry the aubergines and fry them lightly in oil, then fry the sliced onion. Put a layer of the fried aubergines in a round fireproof dish; on top put a layer of the meat. Sprinkle with a few sliced blanched almonds and the fried onion. Repeat until all the aubergines and meat are used up, and on top put the drained rice. Pour over half the meat stock, cover the dish and cook over a low flame for about 20 minutes. Add the rest of the stock and cook another 30–40 minutes until the rice is almost cooked.

Put a fireproof serving dish upside down over the pan, turn out the contents and put in the oven for another 10–15 minutes.

The rice will finish cooking and any liquid left will be absorbed. Although this is rather a trouble to make it is one of the best of all aubergine dishes, and the rice, which has absorbed some of the flavour of the meat, is particularly good. A good bowl of yoghourt can be served with it, and a tomato or green salad.

Enough for 6 people. It can be reheated quite successfully, in a covered pan in a gentle oven.

COURGETTES

Courgettes, small marrows, or zucchine, should be prepared for cooking in the same way as aubergines; cut, usually unpeeled, into rounds or longways, salted, and left to drain for an hour or so. They can also be cooked in most of the ways applicable to aubergines, although of course they do not take so long. If liked they can be used instead of aubergines in any of the Provençal or Oriental ways given in this book. They make very excellent fritters, and go well in a ratatouille, or any of the dishes which contain tomatoes and onions.

BEIGNETS DE COURGETTES

Cut small marrows, unpeeled, into thin strips, lengthwise. Salt them and leave for an hour or so. Dry them carefully on a cloth, dip them in frying batter (p. 83) and drop them one by one into a pan of very hot oil, so that they are completely covered. As soon as they are golden (about 2 minutes), take them out and drain them on blotting paper, and serve as soon as they are all cooked.

With some mushrooms or aubergines treated in exactly the same way (the aubergines must be cut very thin, mushrooms rather thick, with the stalk left on) these fritters make a very nice vegetable dish for luncheon.

COURGETTES AU JAMBON

1 lb. small marrows, 3–4 oz. ham, garlic, olive oil.

Cut the unpeeled marrows into four, lengthwise, then into small squares. Salt them, and leave to drain for an hour or two.

Cover the bottom of a thick frying pan with olive oil, put in the courgettes (previously drained and dried in a cloth). Let them sauté gently for 5 minutes, add a little chopped garlic, the ham cut into strips, ground black pepper. Cover the pan, and simmer on a low heat for about 15 minutes, until the courgettes are soft but not mushy. Sprinkle with parsley or other fresh herbs before serving. Can be eaten hot or cold, either as a separate course or with escalopes of veal, roast veal, or pork.

PIMENTOS STUFFED WITH RICE AND HERBS

4 medium sized red pimentos, 1 teacupful of rice, olive oil, lemon juice, fresh parsley and herbs. Boil and drain the rice; season it, and mix with it 2 or 3 tablespoons of chopped fresh herbs (parsley, marjoram, thyme or lemon thyme, or fennel, or simply parsley and a little of the green part of spring onions, or chives). Squeeze in a little lemon juice.

Cut the pimentos in half lengthways, take out the seeds. Put about 2 tablespoons of the rice mixture into each half and pour over a little olive oil. Pour a thin film of oil into a baking dish, put in the pimentos, cover the dish and cook in a gentle oven for about an hour. From time to time baste the pimentos with the oil in the dish, to prevent a hard crust forming on top of the rice.

PEPERONATA

One of the best Italian dishes of pimentos.

4 large red pimentos, 6 large tomatoes, 1 onion, butter and olive oil, garlic.

Cut the pimentos in half, remove the seeds, and cut them into strips; skin and chop the tomatoes. Melt the sliced onion in a mixture of olive oil and butter. Add the pimentos, and simmer, with the cover on the pan, for 15 minutes. Add the tomatoes, salt, and a clove of garlic. Cook until both tomatoes and pimentos are quite soft, and most of the oil absorbed. The mixture should be fairly dry. Peperonata can be eaten either hot or cold, and it can also be reheated without spoiling. When in season add a little fresh basil.

DOLMÁDÉS, OR STUFFED VINE LEAVES

3 dozen vine leaves, 2 teacups of cooked rice, a small onion, a few pine kernels if possible, lemon, stock, olive oil, a little ground allspice.

Fry the chopped onion in olive oil, mix it with the rice and add the pine kernels, salt, pepper, spice and a little olive oil to moisten. If you like a little chopped mutton can be added, or a chicken liver or two, fried and finely chopped.

Blanch the vine leaves and drain them. Spread them flat on a board, the underside of the leaves uppermost. On each leaf lay about a teaspoonful of the rice mixture, roll the leaf up like a sausage, with the ends tucked in, and squeeze each one in the palm of your hand, so that the dolmádés will stay rolled up during the cooking. There is no need to tie them. Arrange them in a pan in which they will just fit, in layers. Pour over them enough stock (or water) to come half way up, cover them with a plate or saucer which fits inside the pan so that the dolmádés do not move during the cooking, and simmer them for about ½ hour. Serve cold with lemon juice squeezed over.

Dolmádés can also be served with yoghourt or with an egg and lemon sauce (about a teacupful of stock with the yolks of 2 eggs and the juice of a lemon whisked over the fire until it is thick and frothy, and poured over the dolmádés when cool).

I have often seen it written that dolmádés are just as good made with cabbage leaves instead of vine leaves, but it is the taste of the vine leaves and the flavour they give to the stuffing which is so delicious, and which gives them their characteristic Oriental flavour.

Mushrooms Cooked in Grouse Stock

Sauté the cleaned mushrooms in butter, adding salt, pepper and a little chopped garlic. When they are almost ready to serve add 2 tablespoons (for ½ lb. mushrooms) of very much reduced stock from a stewed grouse (p. 132) and stir until the sauce is thick.

Mushrooms Cooked in Vine Leaves

I have already published recipes similar to this one, but make no apology for including it again here, as I think many people who have a vine growing in their gardens would be glad to know it.

Blanch about a dozen vine leaves in boiling salted water. Drain them and arrange them in a heavy, shallow baking dish which has a well fitting cover. Pour a film of olive oil over the vine leaves, and fill the pan with cleaned whole flat mushrooms (the great point about this dish is that the vine leaves make cultivated mushrooms taste like field mushrooms). Add a little salt and pepper, 3 or 4 whole cloves of garlic, a little more olive oil, and cover the mushrooms with 2 or 3 vine leaves. Put the cover on the dish and cook in a slow oven for about 35 minutes. Remove the top covering of vine leaves before serving.

CHAPTER 9

SAUCES

BUTTER, cream, eggs, wine, olive oil, fresh herbs; these are the ingredients which make the sauces, whether intricate or primitive, for summer food. After the long years of shortage it is indeed a blessing once more to have these things in abundance. Those who have had few opportunities for experimenting with butter and egg sauces can now learn to make an Hollandaise or a Béarnaise backed up by the confident knowledge that it will not be a disaster if something goes wrong. In fact these sauces are not difficult to make, they require a little patience at first, and experience very soon does the rest, experience of the signs which warn that it is time to take the saucepan from the stove, or that the sauce must be stirred a little longer, or that a few drops of water will bring the mixture back to the right consistency if it has turned out too thick. But however expert one may become at these sauces, they are heavy on expensive materials and often on time, whereas a few fresh herbs and a little butter or olive oil, or an egg and a lemon, or perhaps a cupful of stock and a few pence worth of cream (thin cream is best for all cooked sauces, it has less tendency to curdle than heavy cream) well seasoned and carefully mixed will make little sauces which will turn the salads, vegetables, fish and meat of every day into fresh and original dishes. Make plenty of use of herbs in the summer while they are fresh and green. Fresh butter mixed with chives or parsley or tarragon melting into the juices of a grilled steak is just as delicious in its way as a

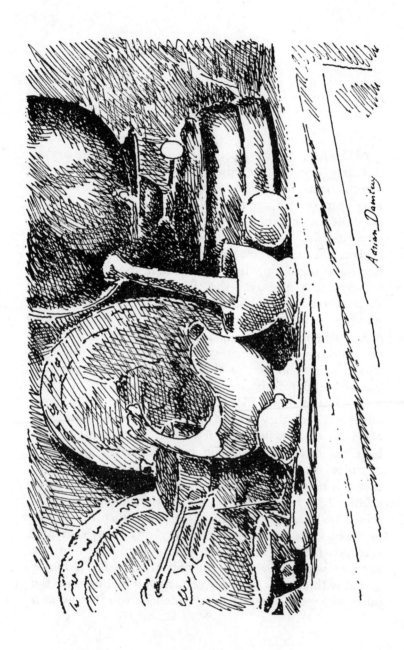

Adrian Damitay

grand sauce of truffles and madeira, and more fitting for the summer time. For grilled lamb or mutton chops use mint instead of parsley. Vinaigrette sauces (oil, lemon, herbs) and mayonnaises give plenty of scope to an inventive cook. For example, for a chicken salad add a little grated horseradish to the mayonnaise, or pounded tunny fish and anchovy in the Italian way; blanched and pounded herbs stirred into a mayonnaise make the *sauce verte* which is so good with salmon trout, a beaten white of egg lightens a mayonnaise to serve with salmon.

One condition essential to the success of any sauce, however simple, is the absolute freshness of the ingredients; use the best quality butter you can afford, unsalted whenever possible, the freshest eggs, and above all the very best olive oil. It is the actual flavour of these ingredients which is important to the sauces, so that although substitutes may give approximately the same consistency and appearance they cannot give the same taste, so why bother with them?

Sauce Béarnaise

The yolks of 3 or 4 eggs, 4–5 ozs. butter, ½ a wineglass of white wine, 2 tablespoons of tarragon vinegar, 2 shallots, black pepper, salt, lemon juice, a few leaves of fresh tarragon.

Put the white wine, vinegar, chopped shallots, and a little ground black pepper in a small pan, and reduce it by fast boiling to about 2 tablespoons. Strain it and add a few drops of cold water. Put in the top half of a double saucepan or in a bowl which will fit into the top of an ordinary saucepan. This underneath saucepan should be half full of warm water and put on to a gentle flame. To the liquid already in the top pan add half the butter, cut into small pieces. Let it melt quickly, then add the rest stirring all the time. Now add the beaten yolks of the eggs and stir very carefully until the sauce thickens. Now add salt (the amounts depends on whether the butter used is salted or unsalted) and a few drops of lemon juice and a few of cold water. Take the sauce from the fire, and stir in the chopped tarragon, and the sauce is ready. At no time should the water underneath the sauce boil and the sauce is not intended to be served hot, but tepid.

Without tarragon, there is no true Béarnaise, but naturally variations can be made by the addition of other herbs. A combination of mint and chives makes a very good sauce for lamb or mutton.

SAUCE HOLLANDAISE

For enough Hollandaise (nobody ever refuses a second helping) for 4 people the ingredients are 4 to 5 ozs. of the best butter, the yolks of 3 or 4 eggs according to how large they are, 1 tablespoon of wine vinegar or 2 of dry white wine, salt, peppercorns, lemon juice, water.

Put the vinegar (on no account use malt vinegar) or white wine in a small pan with 3 tablespoons of water and 3 or 4 peppercorns. Reduce by fairly fast cooking to half its original quantity, then add a pinch of salt (if you are using salt butter be very cautious about the amount of salt added at this stage), remove the peppercorns, transfer to the top half of a double boiler, or to a bowl which will fit into a saucepan without moving about, add a table-spoon of cold water, and while the water in the bottom half of the double boiler is getting warm add the beaten yolks of the eggs, stirring all the time until the mixture looks creamy. Now start adding the butter, which should be soft, not straight off the ice, and divided into small cubes. Add only a little at a time, and whisk continuously. Keep the water underneath hot but not boiling. When all the butter is melted the sauce should already be quite thick, about the consistency of a mayonnaise; now add about 2 more tablespoons of cold water (this gives lightness to the sauce) and a few drops of lemon juice, and taste to see the seasoning is right.

The sauce should now be rather frothy and is ready to serve; it can be kept warm (it is never at any stage more than tepid) over hot water, but not on the fire; but if it is kept waiting long it will lose its characteristic frothiness and more resemble a Béarnaise. It is also possible, with care, to heat the sauce up again, provided it is stirred all the time. If the eggs and butter separate, they can be re-amalgamated by the addition of a few drops of hot water, but if the eggs have curdled there is nothing to be done, for they have scrambled, and cannot be unscrambled.

Hollandaise is one of the most delicious of sauces to serve with fish, asparagus, globe artichokes or any food which has a slightly astringent quality to contrast with the rich smoothness of the eggs and butter in the sauce.

Sauce Maltaise

This is a Sauce Hollandaise to which is added, just before serving, the juice of an orange and a little of the grated peel.

For the quantities given above, a teaspoon of the grated peel and the juice of half an average size orange is sufficient. It is served with the same dishes as Hollandaise, particularly asparagus, and is perhaps even more delicious than the classic Hollandaise.

Sauce Mousseline

To the quantity of Hollandaise given above, add 3 tablespoons of thick whipped cream.

Mayonnaise

The excellence of a mayonnaise depends upon the
quality of the olive oil employed to make it. Use genuine
olive oil, heavy but not too fruity, as a mayonnaise always
accentuates the flavour of the oil. The more yolks of eggs
used the less tricky the mayonnaise is to make, and the
quicker. Lemon juice is better than vinegar to flavour
mayonnaise, but in either case there should be very little,
as the flavour of the oil and the eggs, not the acid of the
lemon or vinegar, should predominate.

In France, a little mustard is usually stirred into the
eggs before adding the oil; in Italy only eggs and olive oil
are used, and sometimes lemon juice.

It is very difficult to give quantities, owing to the
difference in weight of different olive oils, and also because
mayonnaise is one of those sauces of which people will eat
whatever quantity you put before them. For an average
amount for 4 people you need the yolks of 2 eggs, about
one third of a pint of olive oil, the juice of a quarter of a
lemon or a teaspoonful of tarragon or white wine vinegar,
salt.

Break the yolks of the eggs into a mortar or heavy china
bowl; if you have time, do this an hour before making the
mayonnaise; the eggs will be easier to work; stir in a very
little salt, and a teaspoonful of mustard powder if you like
it. Stir the eggs for a minute; they quickly acquire thickness; then start adding the oil, drop by drop, and pouring
if possible from a small jug or bottle with a lip. Stir all
the time, and in a minute or two the mixture will start to
acquire the ointment-like appearance of mayonnaise.
Add the oil a little faster now, and finally in a slow but
steady stream; when half the oil is used up add a squeeze
of lemon juice or a drop of vinegar, and go on adding the

oil until all is used up; then add a little more lemon juice or vinegar. If the mayonnaise has curdled break another yolk of egg into a clean basin, and add the curdled mixture a spoonful at a time. Well made mayonnaise will keep, even in hot weather, for several days. If you make enough for two or three days, and it does separate, start again with another egg yolk, as if it had curdled.

MAYONNAISE FOR POTATO SALAD

Add a little warm water or milk to a mayonnaise made as above, until it is of creamy consistency, easy to mix with the potatoes.

MAYONNAISE MOUSSEUSE

Add a teacupful of whipped cream to a plain mayonnaise, but only immediately before serving.

Another way of making this mayonnaise is to fold the stiffly beaten white of one egg into the mayonnaise, also just before serving. Good for cold salmon, and for asparagus.

HORSERADISH MAYONNAISE

Add 1 or 2 tablespoons of freshly grated horseradish (according to how hot you like the sauce) to a cupful of home made mayonnaise; stir in a little chopped parsley.

Serve with fish and salads.

SAUCE REMOULADE

The yolks of 2 hard-boiled eggs, 1 raw yolk, ¼ pint of olive oil, a teaspoonful of french mustard, salt, pepper, a teaspoonful of vinegar, tarragon, chives, a teaspoonful of capers.

Pound the hard-boiled yolks to a paste, with a few drops of vinegar. Stir in the raw yolk; add the seasonings and oil as for a mayonnaise; stir in the freshly chopped herbs and capers.

The difference between remoulade and mayonnaise is in the consistency as well as in the addition of the herbs. The hard-boiled yolks make a remoulade creamier, not such a solid mass of oil and eggs as a mayonnaise.

SAUCE TARTARE

Tartare sauce can be made either with an ordinary mayonnaise, or with a remoulade as above; the additions are parsley, a little very finely chopped lemon peel and a finely chopped gherkin, with a few capers and if possible a little tarragon. The chopped white of an egg can also be added.

SAUCE VERTE

8 to 10 leaves of spinach, the same number of sprigs of watercress, 3 or 4 branches of tarragon, 3 or 4 sprigs of parsley.

Pick the leaves of the watercress, tarragon and parsley from the stalks. Blanch, with the spinach, in a very little boiling water for 3 minutes. Strain, squeeze quite dry, and pound the herbs in a mortar, then press them through a wire sieve. Stir the resulting purée into a ready prepared mayonnaise. The herb mixture should not only colour but flavour the mayonnaise, and the tarragon is an important element. This quantity will be sufficient for about $\frac{1}{2}$ pint of mayonnaise.

For a hot *sauce verte* add the herb mixture to an Hollandaise sauce.

SAUCE RAVIGOTE

A big bunch of mixed fresh herbs comprising whatever is available among the following: parsley, chervil, chives, cress, watercress, burnet, thyme, lemon thyme, savory, marjoram, wild marjoram, tarragon. A tablespoon of capers and 2 or 3 anchovy fillets, a yolk of egg, olive oil, vinegar.

Chop the herbs, then pound them in a mortar. Add the chopped anchovies and the capers, a little salt and pepper. Stir in the yolk. Gradually add 2 or 3 tablespoons of olive oil, as for a mayonnaise, then a little vinegar.

There are a good many versions of this sauce, hot as well as cold. This one comes from *La Cuisine Messine* by Auricoste de Lazarque, whose sauces are always just a little better than other people's.

SAUCE À LA CRÈME

Heat 2 oz. each of butter and thick fresh cream in a double boiler; stir until thick. Season with salt and ground black pepper. Serve hot. Nice with roast chicken or veal.

SAUCE MESSINE

½ pint of fresh cream, 2 ozs. of unsalted butter, a teaspoon of flour, 2 yolks of eggs, chervil, parsley, tarragon, 2 or 3 shallots, a lemon, a teaspoonful of french mustard.

Chop the herbs and the shallots with a little lemon peel. Work the butter with the flour. Mix all the ingredients together in a bowl, then put them in a double saucepan and heat, stirring all the time. Do not allow to boil. Season with salt and pepper. Squeeze in the juice of the lemon immediately before serving.

This sauce, which is perfectly exquisite, is intended to be served with a poached fish.

Auricoste de Lazarque, who gives the recipe in *La Cuisine Messine*, suggests that with this sauce the fish can be dispensed with; it can; it is perfect poured over hard-boiled eggs, or *oeufs mollets*, either hot or cold.

SAUCE VINAIGRETTE AUX OEUFS

First prepare a vinaigrette, much as you would a salad dressing, with oil, lemon, salt, pepper, chopped parsley, chives and a little shallot or onion. Have ready two soft-boiled eggs (three minutes). Scoop out the yolks and stir them into the sauce, then add the chopped whites. The addition of the yolks while they are liquid, instead of the more usual way of having them hard-boiled, gives a better consistency, as well as a really delicious flavour to the sauce.

This is one of the most useful sauces in existence; it goes well with fish, vegetables, chicken and salads, takes a few minutes to make, and can be varied indefinitely with the addition of fresh herbs, cream, prawns, walnuts, spices, garlic.

SAUCE BERCY

3 or 4 finely chopped shallots, 2 ozs. of white wine, 2 tablespoons of meat glaze or natural gravy from a roast, 1 oz. fresh butter, lemon juice, fresh parsley.

Put the chopped shallots into a small pan with the wine and reduce it by fairly fast boiling to half its original quantity. Stir in the meat glaze or gravy, season, beat in the butter, add a squeeze of lemon juice and a little chopped parsley.

One of the classic French sauces for steak, fish, eggs and

grills. When used for fish, the meat glaze is replaced by *fumet* of fish.

FENNEL SAUCE

Recipes for fennel sauce to serve with fish appear in nearly all old English cookery books. The following, from Richard Dolby's *Cook's Dictionary and Housekeeper's Directory* (1832) is one of the more interesting.

"Pick green fennel, mint and parsley, a little of each; wash them clean, and boil them till tender, drain and press them, chop them fine, add melted butter, and serve up the sauce immediately, for if the herbs are mixed any length of time before it is served up to table they will be discoloured. Parsley becomes equally discoloured from the same cause.

"If approved, there may be added the pulp of green gooseberries rubbed through a hair sieve, and a little sifted sugar."

BEURRE MAÎTRE D'HÔTEL

3 ozs. butter, unsalted if possible, the juice of quarter of a lemon, a large tablespoon of very finely chopped and very fresh parsley, salt, pepper.

Beat the parsley into the butter with a wooden spoon, seasoning lightly with salt and freshly ground pepper; then add the lemon juice, taking care that the whole is well amalgamated. When the butter is to be served with a steak or vegetables or grilled fish, it is not heated but put on a very hot dish and the meat, or whatever it may be, is placed on top of it.

The amounts given will make enough maître d'hôtel butter for about 2 lbs. of steak.

Mint Butter

2 ozs. of butter, 2 large tablespoons of fresh mint leaves, salt, pepper, lemon juice.

Pound the mint in a mortar, add the butter and pound to a smooth ointment; season with salt (very little if salt butter is being used) ground black pepper, a squeeze of lemon juice.

Good with lamb cutlets, grilled sole, carrots, potatoes, green peas.

Tomato Sauce

The nicest way to make a tomato sauce when tomatoes are cheap and good is to cook it only very slightly, so that the flavour is preserved.

Put 1 lb. of skinned and chopped tomatoes into a little heated butter or olive oil, add seasoning and if you like a little chopped garlic, and some fresh parsley, basil or marjoram. Cook until the tomatoes have melted, not more than 5 minutes.

Especially good for grilled fish or fried eggs.

A little port or marsala can be added to the sauce, in which case it should be cooked a little longer.

For a very good tomato sauce in purée form see the recipe in the chapter on Preserves, page 204.

Walnut Sauce

Pour boiling water over 2 ozs. of shelled walnuts; leave a minute or two and then rub off the skins. Soak a thick slice of white bread, without the crust, in water, and then squeeze dry. Pound the walnuts in a mortar with a clove of garlic, a little pepper and salt. Add the bread, a little vinegar, and enough olive oil to form a thick sauce. Press through a sieve, add a little chopped parsley. The sauce should be of the consistency of a thick mayonnaise. Very good with a poached fish, either hot or cold.

Avocado Sauce

Scoop all the flesh from an Avocado pear. Mash or pound it to a purée. Add salt, pepper, lemon or fresh lime juice, and enough olive oil to make the mixture about the consistency of a mayonnaise. Serve with a dry meat such as spiced beef or cold tongue, or with a coarse white fish. One avocado makes a surprising amount of sauce—enough for 4 people. Make it only a short time before it is to be served, or it turns black.

Mint Chutney

A fresh chutney, served in India with curries, but very good also with roast lamb instead of mint sauce, and with grilled fish.

Pound together a large handful of fresh mint leaves, a small onion, 2 ozs. of sugar and a peeled and cored cooking apple. When all the ingredients have turned to a thick paste season with salt and a little cayenne pepper.

In India a green mango is used instead of the apple.

Aspic Jelly

1½ lbs. shin of beef, 2 pig's or calf's feet, 2 carrots, 2 medium sized onions, 2 tomatoes, 2 bayleaves, a sprig of thyme, parsley, black pepper, salt, 3 or 4 bacon rinds, a clove of garlic, a small piece of lemon peel, a small glass of sherry.

Cut the beef into three large pieces, split the pig's feet and wash them. Pack them into a deep pan with the carrots and the onions, unpeeled (the onion skins give a good golden colour to the jelly) add the crushed clove of garlic, bacon rinds, lemon peel, the tomatoes cut in halves, the seasonings (only a little salt). Pour over the sherry, and simmer for 2 or 3 minutes; then add 2 pints of cold water. Bring gently to the boil, cover the pan, and keep barely on the boil for 4 hours. Strain the stock into a basin, leave to set. Next day remove every scrap of fat with a spoon repeatedly dipped in hot water. If the jelly is not clear, put it into a pan, bring it to the boil, beat in two lightly whipped whites of egg and leave barely simmering for 10 minutes. Leave to cool a little and strain through fine muslin. These quantities will make $1\frac{1}{4}$–$1\frac{1}{2}$ pints of good, strong aspic.

Having removed the meat from the pan to make into a salad (see p. 106) put some fresh vegetables in and cover the contents of the pan (the pig's feet etc.) with about 2 pints of water. Two hours slow cooking will yield another $1\frac{3}{4}$ pints of jellied stock, not such a good colour or so meaty tasting as the first, but very adequate as a foundation for soups and certain sauces, or for mixing with chicken creams or *mousses* to make them firm.

To store aspic in a limited space in a refrigerator pour it while still firm into large glass jars, and cover them. If to be kept for any length of time, boil it up every 2 days.

CHAPTER 10

SWEETS

THE sweet course presents no problem in the summer. There is nothing more delicious than fruit and cream, quite plain when strawberries and raspberries first come into season, later when they get cheaper, made into fools, purées, pies; gooseberry fool and gooseberry tart and summer pudding made with raspberries and redcurrants are among the best things of the English table. Water ices made simply from fruit juice and sugar and frozen in the ice tray of a refrigerator make a delicious and refreshing end to a meal. Very simple cream ices, made only with cream and fruit purée, can be varied a good deal. A gooseberry ice cream, for instance, is excellent and unusual. In the early summer, before the berry season starts, lemons are comparatively cheap, and make delicious creams and ices; so do the early imported Spanish apricots which are not ripe enough for dessert. Cream cheeses can be flavoured with liqueurs or candied fruit or simply with sugar; I have given one or two desserts made with whites of egg and chocolate, or honey, which are light and creamy and particularly useful for using the whites of egg which are liable to be left over from the making of sauces and mayonnaises. For July and August, when fruit is plentiful and very varied, there are open fruit pies in the French manner, made with sweetened pastry (p. 175) and filled with apricots, peaches, greengages, cherries, plums.

I do not myself think it necessary to keep a large stock of liqueurs for flavouring fruit compôtes and salads, or to bring them blazing to the table at every meal. Indeed the habit of flambéing everything from prawns to figs has become so prevalent that one can now scarcely dine out in London without for a considerable part of the meal being hemmed in by sheets of flame. An alarming experience in some of those Soho restaurants no larger than a passage. . . .

As far as fruit is concerned only the smallest amounts of liqueurs should be mixed with them. Kirsch certainly helps cherries, and for a change a little port is good with strawberries, but if it is overdone the fruit will be sodden. Miss Eliza Acton's recipe for lemon brandy, quoted on page 207, makes an excellent flavouring for fruit salads. As an all round liqueur, which goes well with almost any fruit, Grand Marnier is perhaps the most useful to keep at hand.

Apricots Baked with Vanilla Sugar

Put fresh apricots in a fireproof dish, with a very little water. Cover them with vanilla sugar (caster sugar kept in a jar with a stick of vanilla). Cook in a very slow oven for about an hour, until the apricots look wrinkled and soft, and coated with sugar.

Serve with fresh unsalted cream cheese (home-made, or Isigny, or Chambourcy). Particularly good for the hard unripe apricots which start arriving from Spain in early June.

Tarte aux Abricots

Halve and stone 1 lb. of apricots, and cook them only a very few minutes in a little sugar and water. Make a pastry as described in the following recipe, then proceed exactly as for the tarte aux pêches (p. 182).

Sweet Pastry for Open Fruit Pies

For a small open fruit pie or tart the quantities are 4 ozs. of flour, 2 ozs. of butter, 2 ozs. of sugar, the yolk of one egg, a very little water.

Rub the butter into the flour, add the sugar, the beaten yolk, and enough water to make a moderately soft dough. Knead very lightly, roll out quickly and lay in a lightly buttered flan tin.

The fruit is packed into the pastry, the edges dusted with sugar, and the pie baked for 25–30 minutes, in the top of a hot oven (Regulo 7 to 8) for the first 10 minutes. Then turn the heat down to Regulo 4 or 5 until the pastry is cooked.

For a large open tart or to fill two 6 inch tins, increase the quantities to 7 ozs. of flour, 3½ each of butter and sugar, 2 egg yolks, and about ½ teacupful of water. Vanilla sugar (caster sugar stored in a jar with a vanilla pod) is an improvement on ordinary sugar for some fruit pies, particularly those made with apricots, peaches or plums. The grated peel of a small lemon can also be added to the dough for the pastry with very good effect.

Apricot Ice Cream

1 lb. fresh apricots, 3 ozs. sugar, ¼ pint of double cream, water.

Halve the apricots and take out the stones. Steam them until soft and sieve them. When cold add a syrup made from the sugar and ¼ pint of water simmered for 10 minutes. Immediately before freezing add the whipped cream. Freeze at maximum freezing point, stirring twice during the process, for 2½ hours.

Walnut Sandwiches

These sandwiches are very good with ices, instead of the usual biscuits or wafers.

Cream together 1½ ozs. butter and 2 tablespoons of shelled and chopped walnuts. Spread on very thin slices of brown bread, with plain buttered bread for the covering.

Strawberries and Cream

When strawberries are good there seems to me to be no necessity to dress them up in any way, but there are different theories even as to how strawberries and cream should be presented. Some like strawberries with their cream; for this you fill a bowl with thick cream and add a few whole strawberries which have already been sugared. Others prefer their strawberries, unhulled, and the cream and sugar separate, so that they can dip each berry into sugar then into cream before tasting it. The ordinary way is to hull the strawberries, sugar them, and serve the cream separately. Some like lemon on their strawberries, others orange juice, or port. I have even seen people put pepper on them.

My own preference is for strawberries accompanied by the little cream cheeses which the French call coeur à la crème and the Italians mascarpone, but of course this needs fresh cream as well, and plenty of sugar to strew over it.

Wild strawberries are, to my way of thinking, infinitely more delicious than any cultivated strawberry, and they don't need any adornment except sugar, although the Italians often put red wine with them, and sometimes orange juice. They make the best ice cream in the world.

Anybody who has the chance of trying can use the recipe for strawberry ice cream on page 178.

FRAISES ROMANOFF

Strawberries macerated with orange juice and curaçao. Arrange in a crystal bowl and cover with crème Chantilly (sweetened whipped cream).

Escoffier's recipe.

ICED STRAWBERRY FOOL

1 lb. of strawberries, 3 ozs. sugar, ¼ pint double cream.

Sieve the hulled strawberries. Stir in the sugar. Add this purée gradually to the whipped cream, so that it is quite smooth. Turn into a shallow crystal or silver dish, and put in the refrigerator for several hours, if possible underneath the ice-trays, so that the fool gets as cold as possible without actually getting frozen. It is important to cover the bowl, or everything else in the refrigerator will smell of strawberries.

STRAWBERRY SOUFFLÉ

½ lb. strawberries, 3 eggs, 1 oz. of dried breadcrumbs, 3 ozs. sugar.

Sieve the strawberries. Cream together the yolks of the eggs and the sugar, add to the strawberry pulp, then add the breadcrumbs. Fold in the stiffly beaten whites of the eggs. Turn into a sugared soufflé dish and steam, uncovered, on top of the stove for about 45 minutes. For the last ten minutes move the dish into a slow oven so that the soufflé turns a pale biscuit colour on the top.

This does not turn out like an ordinary soufflé, but has

a very soft spongy consistency and can be eaten either hot
or cold.

STRAWBERRY WATER ICE

1 pint of strawberry juice (i.e., 2 lbs. fresh strawberries,
sieved) the juice of half a lemon and half an orange, ½ lb.
of sugar and ¼ pint of water.

Make a syrup of the sugar and water by boiling them
together for 5 minutes. When cold add it to the strawberry
pulp. Squeeze in the lemon and orange. Freeze in the
ice trays of the refrigerator at the normal temperature for
making ice. Cover the trays with paper or tinfoil before
freezing.

Enough for 6 or 7.

STRAWBERRY ICE CREAM

Add ¼ pint of whipped cream to a preparation made
exactly as for the water ice above, and freeze for 2½ hours
at the maximum freezing temperature.

SUMMER PUDDING

Although nearly everybody knows this wonderful pudding
one seldom finds a recipe for it in cookery books, so I make
no apology for including it here.

For 4 people stew 1 lb. of raspberries and ¼ lb. of red
currants with about ¼ lb. of sugar. No water. Cook them
only 2 or 3 minutes, and leave to cool. Line a round fairly
deep dish (a soufflé dish does very well) with slices of one
day old white bread with the crust removed. The bread
should be of the thickness usual for sandwiches. The dish
must be completely lined, bottom and sides, with no
space through which the juice can escape. Fill up with the

fruit, but reserve some of the juice. Cover the fruit with a complete layer of bread. On top put a plate which fits exactly inside the dish, and on the plate put a 2 or 3 lbs. weight. Leave overnight in a very cold larder or refrigerator. When ready to serve turn the pudding out on to a dish (not a completely flat one, or the juice will overflow) and pour over it the reserved juice.

Thick fresh cream is usually served with Summer Pudding, but it is almost more delicious without.

RASPBERRY SHORTBREAD

6 ozs. flour, 3½ ozs. moist brown sugar, 2 ozs. butter, ½ teaspoon ground ginger, 1 teaspoon baking powder, 1 lb. raspberries, a little white sugar.

Put the raspberries in a fairly large shallow pie dish, strew them with white sugar. Cut the butter into very small pieces and crumble it with the flour until it is thoroughly blended. Add the sugar, ginger and baking powder. Spread this mixture lightly over the raspberries, and smooth it out evenly, but do not press down. Bake in the centre of a medium oven (Regulo 4 or 5) for 25 minutes. Can be served hot or cold and is most excellent.

RASPBERRY AND RED CURRANT MOUSSE

½ lb. each of red currants and raspberries, 4 to 6 ozs. sugar, 2 whites of egg.

To the sieved raspberry and red currant juce add the sugar and then the stiffly whipped whites of egg. Put into a saucepan over a low flame and whisk continually for about 3 minutes, until the mixture starts to thicken and rise like a soufflé. Pour into wine glasses and serve hot with cream, or into a tall dish in which there is just room for the mousse, and leave to cool. When cold some of the juice will separate and sink to the bottom but can be whipped up again before serving.

A nice sweet for children.

Russian Raspberry Pudding

Put a pound of fresh or bottled raspberries into a small pie dish, and let them stand in the oven till they are quite hot, when they must be taken out. Beat up a teacupful of good thick sour cream with two eggs, one tablespoonful of flour and one spoonful of white moist sugar. When this is all well beaten together, pour it over the raspberries and bake the pudding in a very slow oven till it is firm. It should be of a light brown colour.

The Epicure, February 1894.

Raspberry Ice Cream

Make in the same way as strawberry ice cream (p. 178), with the addition of a few red currants to the raspberries, which intensifies the flavour. Omit the orange juice.

Raspberry Water Ice

1 lb. of raspberries, ¼ lb. red currants, 3 to 4 ozs. sugar, water, lemon juice.

Sieve the raspberries and red currants. Make a syrup by boiling the sugar with ¼ pint of water for a few minutes. When cool, add to the raspberry purée. Freeze in the ice tray, at the normal temperature for making ice, for about 2½ hours. Cover the tray with paper or tinfoil while freezing the ice.

GOOSEBERRY FOOL

Although this is a traditional English sweet it is not often well made, and owing to the lack of cream for so many years a good many people have never made it.

Put 1 lb. of hard green gooseberries in a pan with ¼ lb. sugar (there is no need to top and tail them). Steam them until they are quite soft. Sieve them, and when the purée is cold stir in ¼ pint of thick cream. Add more sugar if the fool is too acid. Serve very cold.

GOOSEBERRY ICE CREAM

Prepare the gooseberries and cream exactly as for gooseberry fool.

Freeze in the ice tray, covered with paper, at the normal temperature of the refrigerator. It will take about 2½ hours. Stir it two or three times during the freezing.

A very good and unusual ice.

TARTE AUX CERISES

Line a tart tin with sweet pastry as described on page 175. Fill with 1 lb. of stoned cherries, arranged closely together, as they shrink so much during the cooking. Sprinkle with sugar. Beat together a teacupful of cream and the yolk of an egg. Pour over the cherries and bake, taking care that the cream remains somewhat liquid.

CHERRY SOUFFLÉ OMELETTE

2 eggs and an extra white, 2 dessertspoons sugar, the grated peel of half a lemon, morello cherry jam.

Spread the bottom of a small oval soufflé dish with a thin layer of bitter cherry jam (or simply stoned, stewed

morello cherries). Grate the lemon peel into the beaten
yolks of egg, add the sugar. Fold in the beaten whites of
the eggs. Pour immediately into the prepared dish so
that it is nine-tenths full; strew sugar over the top, make
a deep incision along the top with a palette knife, put
immediately into a hot oven (Gas 6 or 7) and cook for 9
to 10 minutes.

Enough for 2.

BLACK CURRANT PURÉE

Black currants seem to me best hot, with plenty of very
cold cream, but of course they are very good cold too,
particularly instead of raspberries in Summer Pudding.
To make a hot purée, stew 1 lb. of black currants with ¼ lb.
of sugar (no water). Sieve them, return the purée to the
pan, add a squeeze of lemon juice, and heat up again.

If left to go cold this purée sets almost to a jelly, and is
very good. ¼ pint of thick cream can be added to it to
make a fool, although I think myself it is best with the
cream served separately.

TARTE AUX PÊCHES

Make a pastry as described on page 175. To fill a 6 inch
pie tin, 8 medium sized peaches are needed.

Plunge them into boiling water and leave them a
minute or two. Remove the skins. Stew them in water just
to cover with about 3 ozs. of sugar until they are soft
enough to cut in half, and for the stones to be removed.
Arrange the half peaches in circles on the prepared
pastry. While the pie is cooking thicken the syrup from
the peaches by fast boiling. When the pie is taken from
the oven pour the cooked syrup over the top, then dust
with vanilla sugar. Serve cold.

RUSSIAN FRUIT SALAD

The genuine Russian fruit salad was made with mixed summer fruit covered with a purée of strawberries and raspberries diluted with champagne. Here is a rather simpler and less costly version.

Peaches or apricots, or half of each, strawberries, a little sweet white wine, sugar. Plunge the peaches into boiling water for a minute, and skin them. Cut them in half, take out the stones. If apricots are being used they need not be skinned, but if they are not ripe, steam them for a few minutes so that they become tender without getting mushy. Arrange the fruit in a bowl. Sprinkle it with sugar. Put the strawberries through a sieve, add about 3 ozs. of sugar, and a small glass of sweet white wine or port. Pour the purée over the fruit in the bowl, and serve very cold.

Pears and peaches also make a good mixture, and a purée of red currants and raspberries instead of the strawberries.

MELON STUFFED WITH RASPBERRIES

¾ lb. to 1 lb. of raspberries, a medium sized melon, sugar, kirsch or Grand Marnier.

Strew the raspberries with sugar, pour over them a very small glass of kirsch or Grand Marnier, and leave them for several hours. Cut a slice off the top of the melon, throw away the seeds. Scoop out some of the flesh, cut it into cubes, mix it with the raspberries, and then fill the melon with the mixture.

Wild strawberries are really the ideal filling for a stuffed melon, but raspberries are next best. If using strawberries, then flavour with port instead, but very little, or the fruit will become too sodden. When the small, sweet Cavaillon melons, no larger than a grape fruit, are available, one for each person makes an attractive sweet.

Do not put melons into the refrigerator. Their scent penetrates everything else in it, especially butter.

HOT FRUIT SALAD

This fashion of serving summer fruit has, to me, all the flavour and scent of a warm summer fruit garden. The proportions are important, and the gooseberries must be red ones, not green.

1 lb. of red gooseberries, ½ lb. raspberries, ¼ lb. of red currants, sugar.

Stew the gooseberries, red currants and sugar together for 5 minutes. (No water.) Add the raspberries for 2 minutes only. Serve very hot, with fresh thick cream.

PLUMS

Cold stewed plums must be one of the dullest dishes on earth. Accompanied by custard it is one of the most depressing. English plum tart runs it pretty close.

Hot stewed plums, provided they are a good variety, have been cooked with very little water, and are served with plenty of cream, are much more acceptable than cold plums. But plums don't seem to be what they were. Like all other fruit nowadays they are presumably grown for looks and high yield, not for flavour. The little yellow bullace plums still sometimes to be found in old gardens have a much better flavour than any of the shining purple, red, or golden monsters to be bought in shops. The red fleshed Victorias make a good open plum tart but damsons are best of all for cooking, and greengages (not greengage plums) for dessert. The little yellow plums which the French call mirabelles make lovely jam and

open pies, and purple Pershores are also a good variety
for jams and pies.

The recipe for apricots baked with Vanilla sugar (p.
174) can be very successfully applied to Victorias or other
large and juicy plums.

BLACKBERRY WATER ICE

1 lb. of blackberries, ¼ lb. sugar, ¼ pint of water, if possible
2 or 3 sweet scented geranium leaves.

Make a syrup by boiling the sugar and water together
for 5 or 6 minutes, with 2 sweet scented geranium leaves.
When cool add the syrup to the sieved blackberries, and
put into the freezing tray with a fresh sweet scented geranium leaf on the top. Cover with paper and freeze at the
normal temperature for ice making for 2½ hours. The
sweet scented geranium has an extraordinary affinity with
blackberries and gives them a most attractive flavour.

CREAM CHEESE

Fresh cream cheeses make charming spring and summer
desserts, and can be flavoured in many different ways.
The following few recipes are simply to provide ideas.
Many variations can be made, but these sweets are perhaps
best when they are least complicated.

CREAM CHEESE WITH WINE

Put a pound of fresh cream cheese through the food mill
(it is always advisable to do this for cream cheese sweets
as it makes a smoother mixture). Add ¼ lb. of caster sugar,
and gradually a large glass of white wine and the juice of
a lemon. Serve with it plain biscuits.

CREAM CHEESE WITH ANGELICA

To 1 lb. of cream cheese add 3 ozs. of sugar, the beaten whites of 2 eggs and as much chopped angelica as you like.

Put into a muslin and leave to drain in a cool place for a few hours. Turn out on to a dish and serve with fresh cream.

A cool and fresh looking dessert for the weeks before the fresh fruit comes in.

GERANIUM CREAM

½ pint of fresh cream, 6 small fresh cream cheeses, either Isigny or Chambourcy, sugar, 2 sweet-scented geranium leaves.

Put the cream into a double saucepan, add 4 tablespoons of sugar and two whole sweet-scented geranium leaves. Steam gently, and let the cream get thoroughly hot without boiling. Leave to cool, with the geranium leaves still in the cream. Mix gradually with the cream cheese, until a thick smooth cream results. Leave, in a refrigerator if possible, covered, for 12 hours. Remove the geranium leaves only just before serving.

The cream can be served either by itself or as an accompaniment to fresh blackberries thickly strewn with sugar. The flavour of the geranium leaves is exquisite.

CREAM CHEESE WITH APRICOT BRANDY

Mix ½ lb. cream cheese with 2 oz. sugar, 2 tablespoons apricot brandy, 2 chopped glacé apricots, or 4 fresh apricots when in season.

CRÉMETS D'ANGERS

Whip ½ pint of thick cream until it is absolutely stiff. Fold in the beaten whites of 3 eggs; turn into a clean muslin and place in little heart shaped baskets and leave to drain in a cool place for about 12 hours. Turn out on to a dish and cover with fresh cream. Serve with sugar. The best of all accompaniments for strawberries, raspberries, and apricots.

LEMON ICE CREAM

2 lemons, 3 ozs. icing sugar, ¼ pint double cream.

Put the thinly peeled rind of the lemons with the icing sugar in 4 ozs. of water, and simmer gently for 20 minutes. Leave the syrup to cool, strain and add to it the juice of the lemons. When quite cold, add it gradually to the whipped cream, stirring gently until the whole mixture is smooth.

Pour into the ice tray, cover with paper and freeze at maximum freezing point of the refrigerator for 2½ to 3 hours, taking it out to stir it twice, after the first half hour, and again after another hour.

CHOCOLATE CHINCHILLA

A good recipe for using whites of eggs. ¼ lb. bitter chocolate, grated, a dessertspoonful of very finely ground coffee, the whites of 6 or 7 eggs.

Fold the grated chocolate into the stiffly beaten whites; add the coffee. Turn into a soufflé dish which will just about hold the mixture, and steam, uncovered, for 50 to 60 minutes. Take care that the boiling water does not bubble over into the pudding. When cold turn the pudding out on to a dish and serve with cream. Much less cloying than the usual chocolate puddings.

Honey Chinchilla

¼ lb. honey, 1 oz. shelled walnuts, the whites of 6 or 7 eggs.

Stand the jar of honey in a saucepan of hot water to let it liquefy. Chop the walnuts. Stir the honey into the stiffly beaten whites of egg, add the walnuts. Turn into a buttered soufflé dish and steam for about an hour. Turn out when cold. It is advisable to eat this pudding on the day on which it has been cooked, as the honey tends to separate from the eggs if left standing too long.

Sand Cake

Sand cake came originally from Austria, where it is called Sandtorte. It makes a most excellent cake for luncheon, or to serve with a fruit salad or creamy sweet, or an ice.

This recipe is based on the one given in the 1906 edition of Mrs. Beeton. It is worth recording that the cost in those days worked out at 1/3d.

7 ozs. cornflour, 1 oz. of plain flour, 8 ozs. butter, 6 ozs. caster sugar, 1 oz. shelled almonds, ground or pounded, but not skinned, the whites of 3 eggs, the yolks of 2 eggs, 1 teaspoon of finely grated lemon rind, the juice of half a lemon.

Clarify the butter. This should be done either the day before or in the morning for the afternoon. The butter is heated slowly until it is melted, then poured into a basin through a fine strainer so that all the froth at the top is cleared off—it can also be taken off with a spoon. Leave it to set lightly. When ready to make the cake, add the sugar to the clarified butter and beat until creamy and white. When the proper consistency has been obtained, beat in the yolks of eggs, the ground almonds, the lemon rind and juice, and lastly the flour and cornflour.

Whip the whites of eggs to a very stiff froth, add them as lightly as possible to the rest of the ingredients, and pour the mixture at once into a buttered cake tin. I prefer a square one for sand cake. Bake in a moderate oven for an hour or a little longer. (I always put the cake into the oven, well-heated, at Regulo 6, and after ten minutes turn it down to 5 for the remainder of the cooking time, but this must depend on individual experience.) Test with a skewer, which should come out dry when the cake is done.

When it has cooled a little turn out upside down on to a wire cake rack. Keep until next day before cutting.

CHAPTER 11

JAMS, JELLIES AND OTHER PRESERVES

IT is such a short time since sugar rationing ended that there must be a great number of younger people who have no idea how delicious home-made jams and jellies can be, or how satisfactory is the sight of a larder shelf laden with pots of clear red jellies, thick apricot jam like jars of clouded amber, crimson and purple damson and plum and blackberry, translucent greengage preserves and solid cornelian coloured quince cheese. This is food which is to be a comfort for wintry breakfasts and at tea time, to be eaten with thick white bread toasted in front of the fire, with the curtains drawn and the winds blowing outside. Miss Dorothy Hartley, in her fascinating book *Food in England*,[1] has described how North country housewives, in order to show off the number of different jams in their larders, would make huge jam tarts, criss crossed with pastry, each section filled with a different jam. Sometimes there would be as many as twelve.

Then there are the fruit relishes and chutneys and jellies made in the late summer and autumn to be eaten with game, roast mutton, cold beef and ham; they are worth all the time and trouble that has been spent on them. These things are not cheaper (except for those who grow their own fruit) than bought preserves, but they are much nicer, and it is gratifying simply to fetch a new jar of red currant jelly or raspberry jam from the larder instead of having to go out and buy it from the grocer.

All preserves should be made with the finest ingredients;

[1] Published by Macdonald & Co.

Adrian Daintrey.

the fruit should be ripe but not over ripe, and absolutely dry. Fruit that is at all sodden will not set properly and will not keep. When the jam making season starts lay in a stock of preserving sugar, which is similar to cube sugar, and of the best quality; the jam will have less tendency to stick and burn and the scum will be easier to remove as it rises, giving a fine clear jam.

As well as the usual large preserving pan an asset for jelly making is a 7 lb., or larger, stone jar in which the fruit is packed and left in a very slow oven until the juice flows; a tall narrow earthen casserole serves the same purpose. A large, fine hair or nylon sieve, or a supply of double muslin for straining juice for jellies, clean long handled wooden spoons, and absolutely spotless, dry jars are necessities for jam and jelly making.

There are so many different kinds of jam jar covers now on the market that there need be no bother with cutting out paper and tying with string, but a round of paper dipped in brandy and fitted inside the jar on top of the jam helps to preserve the jam. For pickles and chutneys, brown sugar makes a richer syrup than white, both in taste and colour and wine vinegar or Orleans vinegar is much milder than the savage English malt vinegar; although I have often been told that pickles made with malt vinegar keep better than those made with wine vinegar I have not found this to be the case. English home made jams and jellies are usually delicious, but pickles and chutneys are often far too acid, and I nearly always halve the quantity of vinegar given in any English recipe, however reliable I know the author to be in other respects. Meg Dods whose *Cook's and Housewife's Manual* (1817) is in most ways worthy of all praise gives one of the most gruesome recipes for pickles I have ever seen (a handful each of salt and horseradish, 3 bottles of vinegar, $\frac{1}{2}$ oz. of cayenne and a cupful of mustard seed to pickle 6 lemons). Indeed the English appetite for strong sauces and pickles apparently knows no bounds and I have heard it suggested that if a tax were put on vinegar it would shortly enable the Chancellor to make a substantial reduction in the duty on wine.

For my jam and jelly receipts I have drawn considerably on the work of Miss Eliza Acton (as so many, including Mrs. Beeton, have done before me). Her book, *Modern Cookery*, published about 15 years before that of Mrs. Beeton, is the expression of English country house cookery in the mid-nineteenth century when it must have been very good indeed. It is clear from her directions that she cooked, or supervised the cooking of every dish many times. It is over a hundred years since her book was published, but she writes with such certain knowledge and calm authority that there is scarcely a recipe in her book which could not be followed today with perfect confidence.

Other Victorian works which give splendid recipes for preserves are two manuals of the 'eighties, Cassell's *Dictionary of Cookery* and Spon's *Household Manual*. Two later books of great interest to those who have their own country produce are the *Cookery Book* of Lady Clark of Tillypronie, published in 1909, and *Pot Luck*, a misleading title for a lovely collection of country recipes edited by May Byron and published in 1914, the end of an era when the uninhibited use of the best ingredients, and pride in a well stocked larder were taken for granted.

APRICOT CHEESE

Halve the apricots, stone them, and steam them until soft. Sieve them. Add a pound of sugar to every pint of pulp. Cook, stirring frequently, until the purée starts to candy at the edges. Store in jars.

An excellent and very useful preserve, better than jam

for omelettes and puddings, delicious with unsalted cream cheese, or mixed with whipped cream to make a fool for the winter. The flavour is even better if a few of the stones are cracked and the kernels added to the apricots when sieved. Or a few blanched split almonds can be used instead of the apricot kernels.

APRICOT CHUTNEY

2 lbs. ripe apricots, 10 ozs. brown sugar, 1 onion, $\frac{1}{4}$ lb. sultanas, 1 teaspoon of grated green ginger root or $\frac{1}{2}$ teaspoon of ground ginger, a tablespoon of salt, $\frac{1}{2}$ pint Orleans vinegar, 1 teaspoon of coriander seeds, 2 or 3 cloves of garlic.

Halve the apricots and stone them. Slice the onion and the garlic. Put all the ingredients into a large pan and boil until the apricots are quite soft. Take them out and put into jars. Boil the rest of the liquid rapidly until it turns to a thickish syrup, and pour into the jars. Seal down.

A mild chutney which goes well with cold boiled gammon or tongue.

STRAWBERRY JELLY

Take the small scarlet strawberries, put them in an earthen jar, and stand the jar in a pan of boiling water. Let them steam 3 or 4 hours, the water being always boiling. When they are quite soft pour the strawberries into a sieve, or a cloth, and strain out the juice. Allow 1 lb. of fine white sugar to each pint of juice. Boil it till it stiffens, which it will do in 30 or 40 minutes. The jelly must be made at once, that is to say as soon as the strawberries are strained, as it will not jelly after it has once cooled.

From the *Cookery Book* of Lady Clark of Tillypronie (Constable, 1909).

RASPBERRY JAM, UNBOILED

Equal weights of raspberries and fine white sugar.

Put raspberries and sugar each in a large dish which will go in the oven. Let them get very hot, but not boiling. (This takes 20–30 minutes in a medium oven.)

Turn sugar and fruit in a large bowl and mix them thoroughly together, using a wooden spoon. Turn at once into jars and seal down, putting a round of paper dipped in brandy inside each jar.

This is by far the best raspberry jam I have ever tasted. It preserves almost intact the fresh flavour of the fruit, and will keep for a year.

This jam, and the red currant jelly which follows, are delicious eaten with fresh cream cheese and sugar.

SUPERLATIVE RED CURRANT JELLY
(Norman Receipt)

"Strip carefully from the stems some quite ripe currants of the finest quality and mix with them an equal weight of good sugar reduced to powder; boil these together quickly for exactly eight minutes, keep them stirred all the time, and clean off the scum—which will be very abundant—as it rises; then turn the preserve into a very clean sieve, and put into small jars the jelly which runs through it, and which will be delicious in flavour, and of the brightest colour. It should be carried immediately, when this is practicable, to an extremely cool but not a damp place, and left there until perfectly cold. The currants which remain in the sieve make an excellent jam, particularly if only part of the jelly be taken from them. In Normandy, where the fruit is of richer quality than in England, this preserve is boiled only two minutes, and is both firm and beautifully transparent."

This recipe is from Miss Eliza Acton who adds: "This receipt we are told by some of our correspondents is not generally quite successful in this country, as the jelly, though it keeps well and is of the finest possible flavour, is scarcely firm enough for table. We have ourselves found this to be the case in cold damp seasons; but the preserve even then was valuable for many purposes, and always agreeable eating."

Miss Acton would perhaps have been shocked at the idea, but I find this jelly just as successful if the fruit is put into the pan with the sugar after being washed, but without being stripped from the stalks. The stalks in no way injure either the flavour or colour of the jelly, which as Miss Acton says, does not set very firmly, but is delicious. It is ideal for serving with mutton, venison and hare, and for making Cumberland and other sauces to go with game.

BLACK CURRANT JELLY

¾ lb. sugar to each pound of fruit. Put the black currants, stalks and all, into a large pan with the sugar. Bring to the boil, take off the scum as it rises, and boil fast for 10 minutes. Pour on to a fine sieve placed over a bowl and let the juice run through. Press the fruit lightly with a wooden spoon.

Pour the jelly while still warm into small glass jars and seal. Excellent for making winter desserts.

MORELLO CHERRY PRESERVE

Put 6 ozs. of sugar to every pound of stoned morello cherries. Break a few of the stones and add the kernels to the fruit. Boil, without the addition of water, until the juice is thick.

A very good preserve for sweet omelettes, soufflés, and sauces for puddings.

SWEET SOUR CHERRIES

For 2 lbs. of morello cherries 1½ pints of white wine vinegar, ¾ lb. sugar, 12 cloves.

Leave about ½ an inch of the stalks on the cherries. Put them, unstoned, into wide necked bottling jars. Boil the vinegar, sugar and cloves together for about 10 minutes. While still hot pour over the cherries and seal the bottles. They will be ready in about a month. Good with boiled tongue, and to use for sauces for duck, venison, teal, wild duck and pigeons.

CHERRY BRANDY

Allow 1 lb. of morello cherries to one bottle of brandy, and 3 ozs. of white candy sugar to each pound of fruit.

Leave about ½ an inch of stalk on the cherries, wipe them with a soft cloth, prick them with a needle and half fill fruit bottling jars with them. Add the sugar and fill the bottles with brandy. Seal the bottles. Pour off in 6 months. Use a standard 3 star brandy. Do not, as Cassell's *Dictionary of Cookery* remarks, "make the mistake of supposing that the fruit and sugar will make bad spirit pass for good."

GREEN GOOSEBERRY JELLY

Choose the yellowish green variety of gooseberry, very ripe. They must be well washed, but there is no need to top and tail them. Put them into a pan with about ¼ pint of water to every pound of fruit.

Simmer gently until the fruit is broken and all the juice flowing out. Pour into a hair sieve placed over a large bowl, or into a muslin, and let the juice drip through. The fruit can be gently pressed but not too much. To each pint of juice measure ¾ lb. of sugar. Bring the juice to the boil, add the sugar, and boil in the usual way, until the jelly sets when a drop is poured on to a plate.

GOOSEBERRY AND MINT JELLY

Make green gooseberry jelly as above. During the final boiling add, for every pint of juice used, 4 tablespoons of very finely chopped fresh mint and a tablespoon of wine vinegar.

Delicious instead of mint sauce.

GOOSEBERRY JELLY FLAVOURED WITH ELDERFLOWERS

Make gooseberry jelly the ordinary way, and when it is ready to take off the fire, have ready a bunch of elder flowers tied up in a piece of muslin, which turn round and round in the jelly until it has the desired flavour; it is really like a most delicious grape.

A Lincolnshire recipe given by May Byron
in *Pot Luck*, 1914.

GROSEILLÉE

Cut the tops and stalks from a gallon or more of well-flavoured ripe gooseberries, throw them into a large preserving pan, boil them for ten minutes, and stir them often with a wooden spoon; then pass both the juice and pulp through a fine sieve, and to every three pounds weight of these add half a pint of raspberry juice and boil the whole briskly for three quarters of an hour; draw the pan aside, stir in for the above portion of fruit, two

pounds of sugar, and when it is dissolved renew the
boiling for fifteen minutes longer.

When more convenient a portion of raspberries can be
boiled with the gooseberries at first.

Eliza Acton. Modern Cookery, 1855.

GREENGAGE AND RED GOOSEBERRY PRESERVE

Boil for three quarters of an hour in 2 pints of clear red
gooseberry juice 1 lb. of very ripe greengages, weighed
after they have been stoned and pared; then stir to them
one pound and a half of good sugar, and boil them quickly
again for twenty minutes. If the quantity of preserve be
much increased, the time of boiling it must be so likewise;
this is always better done before the sugar is added.

Eliza Acton's recipe from Modern Cookery, 1855
edition.

PRESERVED PEACHES

Take an equal weight of fruit and sugar; lay the fruit in a
large dish, and sprinkle half the sugar over, in fine powder;
give them a gentle shaking; the next day make a thin
syrup with the remainder of the sugar; and instead of
water, if you have it, allow one pint of red currant juice
to every pound of peaches; simmer them in this till
sufficiently clear.

N.B. Pick them when not dead ripe.

From Pot Luck, edited by May Byron, 1914.

FIG JELLY

Figs are so rare in this country that it is madness to do
anything but just eat them and be thankful. Imported
figs are an absurd price and are rarely good. People who

like figs like them very much and need a large quantity, not one or two wrapped up in cotton wool. However, the small green figs which will not ripen make an excellent preserve.

The following recipe comes from May Byron's *Pot Luck*, 1914, and is very successful.

Take one pound of small cooking figs, remove the stems, and pour over them some very hot, but not boiling water. Leave them for a minute or two, then drain off the water. Then cut each fig in pieces, and to each pound of figs put one pound of sugar, a little grated lemon peel, and the juice of one lemon. Put them into a pan and let them cook very slowly, until the syrup thickens and the figs become clear; stir carefully, and if it gets too thick add a little water. When cold, pour off into jars and cover tightly.

GRAPE PRESERVE

A delicious preserve from unripe grapes can be made in the following way: They should be carefully picked and all that are at all injured should be rejected.

To 1 lb. of grapes add ½ lb. sugar; no water but what hangs about them after they have been washed. Put the grapes into a preserving pan, then a layer of sugar, then a layer of grapes. Boil on a moderate fire, stirring it all the time to prevent its burning, and as the grape stones rise take them out with a spoon, so that by the time the fruit is sufficiently boiled the stones will have all boiled up and been taken out.

Recipe from Spon's *Household Manual*.

PICKLED PLUMS

5 lbs. rather under ripe plums, 5 lbs. sugar, 1½ pints wine vinegar, a stick of cinnamon, cloves.

Prepare a syrup by boiling the sugar and vinegar together, for a few minutes; add the cinnamon and 2 tablespoons of whole cloves. After a few minutes boiling put in the plums which should have been jabbed here and there with a small skewer. Bring to the boil again, remove the scum, and take out the plums at once. Put them in a large bowl. Boil the syrup for another 3 or 4 minutes, pour over the plums. Leave in a cold place for 24 hours, and then repeat the boiling process; i.e. strain off the syrup, bring it to the boil, put in the plums, boil them half a minute, remove them, continue to boil the syrup a minute or two, pour over the plums. Next day the pickle can be put into bottles or jars and sealed. Leave for 6 weeks before opening.

Damson Cheese

To make the best-flavoured damson cheese, the fruit should be placed whole in a stone jar and baked in a very slow oven until it is quite soft. Turn it out into a pan and boil it fairly quickly until it has dried somewhat. By this time the stones should have come to the top and will be easy to remove. Put the fruit through a food mill (moulinette), add a pound of sugar for every 4 lbs. of fruit you have used, and simmer for about ½ hour, until the paste begins to candy round the edges of the pan. Pour into jars. The addition of some of the kernels to the cheese improves the flavour; to do this, boil the stones again when you have removed them from the fruit, then crack them. Add the kernels when you have put the pulp and sugar into the pan. Some people put a little stick of cinnamon into the fruit when it is baking, which gives a rich spicy flavour.

An alternative to putting damson cheese into jars is to pour it into shallow bowls, dry it out in a just warm oven, or the plate drawer of an electric oven, and serve in the winter turned out on to dishes so that it can be cut into slices for dessert.

To Pickle Damsons

3 quarts fresh damsons, rub dry with cloth, prick them. Dissolve 1 lb. lump sugar in 1 pint best distilled vinegar; when boiling pour over damsons in deep jar, and cover close. Next day pour off the liquor, reboil and pour over again; the same the third day. Let stand one day longer, and then scald altogether, pour into jars and keep from the air.

The amount of sugar and vinegar seems very small in proportion to the fruit, but in fact a good deal of juice comes from the damsons and the quantities are exactly right. A quart of damsons is approximately 2 lbs.

Rowanberry Jelly

Rowanberries, the fruit of the mountain ash, are to be had for the picking in many parts of England, Scotland and Wales and are common in suburban gardens. Their beautiful red berries have a most attractive sour-sweet flavour and make lovely jelly for eating with game, particularly hare. Sometimes the rowanberries are mixed with apples to make the jelly, as rowanberries do not jelly very easily, but with the right amount of boiling (approximately 20 minutes, using the following recipe) they will.

Here is a recipe given by Lady Clark of Tillypronie.

"For game, venison, or roe deer.

"Gather the rowanberries when *quite ripe, quite sound, quite dry*. Pick them from the stalks and put them in a deep pan. Cover them completely with water and boil until they seem soft, which will be in 5 to 15 minutes. Mash them slightly and strain through a flannel bag, giving the bag a squeeze so as to have part of the pulp. Boil this either directly after straining or next day.

"Allow 1 lb. of sugar to 1 pint of juice and skim very carefully. Before putting the jelly into pots, see that it *will* jelly; sometimes it will not become firm under ¾ of an hour boiling; sometimes it gets firm much quicker. When ready pot it. It mellows and improves when 1 or even 2 years old. Miss Lamont, of Pitmurchie, gave this recipe to Mrs. Innes, of Learney."

THICK BLACKBERRY JELLY

Stew some blackberries in a very little water until they are quite soft. Put them through a sieve so that you get all the pulp, but no pips. To each pint of pulp put a pound of sugar and boil till the mixture jellies.

If possible, add 1 or 2 sweet-scented geranium leaves to the blackberries while they are stewing; these will give them a delicious flavour.

MULBERRY JAM

Put equal quantities of mulberries and preserving sugar together in a large bowl and leave overnight. Next day put them in a pan, without water, and bring slowly to the boil; continue boiling for 15 to 20 minutes, until the juice sets when a little is dropped on to a plate.

MULBERRY JELLY

Put the fruit into a stone jar, cover it and put in a very low oven until the juice flows.

Strain through a muslin or fine hair sieve, and allow 1 lb. of sugar to each pint of juice. Boil gently for 15 to

25 minutes, according to whether you have a small or large quantity of fruit.

A few blanched split almonds, added while the jelly is boiling, are an improvement.

TOMATO SAUCE TO STORE

Italian tomato paste in tins is so cheap to buy and so good that it is hardly worth while making it at home, but people who grow their own tomatoes may be interested in this Italian recipe.

A dozen onions, 4 carrots, a head of celery, 1 lb. of butter, ⅛ pint of olive oil, 16–18 lbs. of tomatoes, salt.

Put the oil and butter in a preserving pan, and when it is warmed put in the sliced onions, carrots and celery; when they have turned yellow add the tomatoes cut into quarters and a tablespoon of salt to every 3 lbs. Cook until the whole is reduced to a thick mass and almost sticking to the pan. Sieve. Pour the purée either into bottles or preserving jars. If bottles they must be corked and the corks tied down with string; preserving jars should be screwed down. Leave a couple of inches space at the top of the bottles or an inch for the jars. Put the bottles or jars into a large pan of water (they should not touch each other and can be wrapped in several sheets of newspaper which will prevent their doing so) and steam for about 3 hours. Leave them to cool in the water, and store in a cool dry place.

The same recipe, in smaller quantities, makes an excellent sauce for pasta, or any dish for which a fresh tomato purée is wanted. For these dishes, use it when it has been sieved, adding fresh herbs, garlic, a little port or marsala, and possibly a little sugar.

VINE LEAVES

So many English gardens have a vine growing on a wall that it may be interesting to note how vine leaves can be used in cookery. They have a pungent lemony flavour, and the stuffed vine leaves of Greece, Turkey and the Balkans are fairly well known. In France all sorts of small game birds, quails, ortolans, becfigues, and partridges are wrapped in vine leaves and braised; one of the best mushroom dishes is the Italian one of funghi stewed in oil on a bed of vine leaves (see p. 158) for vine leaves possess the property of both preserving and enhancing the flavour of whatever is cooked with them. Spon's *Household Manual*, published in the 'eighties, says that vine leaves placed on top of pickles will preserve the vinegar sharp and clear and impart a nice flavour. In old English cookery layers of vine leaves were placed between greengages which were to be preserved in syrup, in order to give the greengages a good colour. Tinned vine leaves from Greece and Turkey can be bought in Soho shops, but they are very salt and need prolonged steeping in cold water before they can be used. Fresh vine leaves can be preserved in oil in the following manner.

VINE LEAVES PRESERVED IN OIL

Pick a large bunch of vine leaves. Blanch them one minute in boiling salted water. Leave them to drain until they are quite dry. Pack them flat into wide shallow jars and cover with olive oil to the depth of a good half inch above the top layer. Seal the jars. They can be used during the winter for making excellent dishes out of ordinary cultivated mushrooms, or for wrapping round partridges or other small birds to be cooked in the oven, but are too soft to be used for *dolmádes*.

Candied Angelica

Fresh angelica has a most powerful and sweet scent, which it does not however communicate to other foods, although it will cling to your hands for hours after you have handled it. It also has very little taste in its fresh state and is rather stringy, but when candied is I think one of the most exquisite of all sweet-meats. It grows successfully in English gardens, and here is an old recipe for candying it, from Henderson's *Housekeepers Instructor or Universal Family Cook*, 1809.

Cut your angelica in lengths when young, cover it close, and boil till it is tender. Then peel it, put it in again, and let it simmer and boil till it is green. Then take it up, dry it with a cloth, and to every pound of stalks put a pound of sugar. Put your stalks into an earthen pan, beat your sugar, strew it over them, and let them stand two days. Then boil it till it is clean and green and put it in a colander to drain. Beat another pound of sugar to powder, and strew it over the angelica; then lay it on plates, and let it stand in a slack oven till it is thoroughly dry.

Basil Vinegar or Wine

Fill a wide mouthed bottle with fresh green leaves of Basil, and cover them with vinegar or wine, and let them steep for 10 days; if you wish a very strong essence, strain the liquor, put it on some fresh leaves, and let it steep fourteen days longer.

From Richard Dolby's *Cook's Dictionary
and Housekeeper's Directory*, 1832.

If the basil is steeped in dry white wine, the resulting concoction makes a good flavouring for winter soups, sauces, and meat stews.

Meg Dods (*The Cook's and Housewife's Manual* 1829) says of basil vinegar "the French add cloves and lemon rind: we admire this addition".

LEMON BRANDY

(For flavouring sweet dishes)

Fill any sized wide-necked bottle tightly with the very thin rinds of fresh lemons, and cover them with good brandy; let them remain for a fortnight or three weeks only, then strain off the spirit and keep it well corked for use; a few apricot kernels blanched and imposed with the lemon-rind will give it an agreeable flavour.

Eliza Acton. *Modern Cookery*, 1861 edition.

CHAPTER 12

BUFFET FOOD

A VERY understandable mistake often made at buffet luncheons and suppers is the over complication of the food and the diversity of dishes offered. Several fine dishes of attractively prepared food look hospitable and tempting, but it is bewildering to be faced with too many choices, especially if some are hot and some cold. The taste of the food is lost when you find four or five different things all messed up on your plate at the same time; so have as the most important dish something rather simple which everyone will like, and provide variety with two or three salads, so long as they are easy ones to eat.

An excellent centrepiece for a party of this kind, particularly for those who haven't time for cooking but do not want to resort to a professional caterer, would be one of the smoked turkeys which an enterprising firm have recently perfected (it is the first time that smoked turkeys, well-known in America, have been put on the market in this country).[1] Smoked turkey is not of course cheap, but all you have to do is unwrap the bird and put it on a dish; with its dark golden skin it makes a handsome appearance, carves easily into thin slices, there is no waste, and the brown and white meat are equally delicious. The salads to go with it should be rather mild as any strong flavour will conflict with that of the turkey; the classic potato salad with a mayonnaise made with lemon juice instead of vinegar, raw sliced mushrooms with an oil and lemon dressing, cucumbers with a cream dressing, or cubes of crisp cold melon go well with smoked turkey.

If something soft and creamy, such as a chicken or ham mousse, is to be the main dish, have as a contrast crisp raw salad vegetables, cucumber, radishes, or fennel cooled in bowls of salted iced water and perhaps some hard-boiled eggs stuffed with a green or red mayonnaise; these are easy to eat and always popular.

For a less conventional supper party a *roulade* of beef or veal with a colourful stuffing of eggs and parsley and ham,[2] or a loin of cold roast pork well spiked with garlic and herbs[3] make fine dishes. The main thing is for the hostess not to wear herself out for days beforehand, fussing about with aspic, making patterns with mayonnaise and sticking little things on sticks. If time is limited, buy good quality ham, plenty of it, and make it interesting by serving something unusual with it, such as a bowl of the

---

[1] See page 31 for the address.
[2] See the recipe for Farso Magro, page 104.
[3] See page 107.

beautiful Italian fruits in mustard syrup (to be bought in Soho shops) or pickled peaches, plums or cherries,[1] or Cumberland sauce, or Avocado sauce.[2]

Start with a hot soup which can be served in cups (a walnut soup, or a white fish soup)[3] accompanied by hot biscuits. (Romary's celery or cheese sticks heated in the oven.) As dessert, an iced, thick fruit fool[4] which can be served in bowls is better than a fruit salad which has to be chased all over a plate balanced on your knees.

The presentation of party dishes, and of course of all food, is an important point. Cold food should certainly have a lavish and colourful appearance, but to varnish it with gummy gelatine or smother it with whirls of mayonnaise seems to me a misconception of what makes for an appetizing appearance. The effect needed is not of food tormented into idiotic shapes but of fresh ingredients freshly cooked and not overhandled. The most elementary hors d'oeuvre such as a plate of red radishes with a few of their green leaves, a dish of green and black olives and another of halved hard-boiled eggs (not overcooked), with butter and bread on the table is ten times more tempting than the same ingredients got up in a pattern all on one dish and garnished with strips of this and dabs of that. You are, after all, preparing a meal, not decorating the village hall.

As for hot food, if it has not acquired an appetizing look during the cooking, a few blobs of cream or a border of mashed potatoes will do little to improve matters. There are of course ways of making good food look especially beautiful. The colour, size and shape of the serving dish is obviously important; food should never be crammed

[1] See chapter on Preserves.
[2] See page 171.
[3] See pages 50 and 53.
[4] See chapter on Sweets.

into too small a dish; serve rice and pilaffs on large shallow platters, not pressed into a deep glass casserole; for the serving of fish and of grilled chicken, which should be spread out rather than piled up, a long narrow dish is best.

See that the dishes are appropriate to the food. Peasant and country stews of beans or lentils, deep brown *daubes* of meat and game, onion and oil flavoured ragoûts of pimentos or purple-skinned aubergines lose some of their particular charm (and also get cold) if transferred from the earthen pots in which they have cooked to a smart silver entrée dish, and all the delicious brown bits on the bottom and sides of the dish are lost. Dark glowing blue china, the dark brown glaze of slip ware pottery and plain white always make good backgrounds for food; it would be an admirable thing if contemporary porcelain and pottery designers would pay a little more attention to these matters; does it ever occur to them that faded greens or greys, pale blues and washy yellows do nothing to enhance the food which is to be served and eaten off their plates and dishes?

Boeuf à la Mode

Boeuf à la Mode can be eaten hot, but is at its best cold, when the stock has turned to a clear soft jelly, and the meat, which can be cut with a spoon when hot, is a little firmer and will carve into good slices. It is a dish typical of the best French household cooking, combining the flavours of meat, vegetables, wine and garlic, and as it must be simmered for a long time it is not worth making with a small quantity of meat. It makes a most admirable cold dish for a summer luncheon or supper party. In detail the recipes for Boeuf à la Mode vary from region to region, but the essentials of the dish are always the same —beef, carrots, calf's feet, garlic, wine, herbs.

The following recipe makes an excellent Boeuf à la Mode: 4 lbs. of lean round of beef in one piece, 4 rashers of bacon, 4 to 6 cloves of garlic, 2 onions, 2 lbs. of carrots, thyme, 2 bayleaves, 2 calf's feet, ½ pint of white or red wine, a small wineglass of brandy, meat stock or water, dripping, herbs, salt and pepper, and a large, deep dish in which to serve the meat.

Lard the meat from side to side with strips of bacon and the garlic cut into spikes. Rub a little salt and ground black pepper all over the meat.

Brown the sliced onions in dripping, then put in the meat and let it sizzle, turning it over so that it is well browned all over. Now pour over the warmed brandy and set light to it. When it has stopped burning, pour in the wine. Let this bubble for two or three minutes. Add 2 carrots, the herbs, and the cut up calf's feet. (Pig's feet will do instead.) Cover with stock or water, and put the lid on the pan. Leave it to simmer as gently as possible for four to five hours, either on top of the stove or in the oven. An hour before it is cooked the rest of the carrots can be added, or they can be boiled separately and put into the serving dish when the meat is cooked. This last is the better method to my mind, as they are apt to give rather too strong a flavour of carrots to the jelly.

When the beef is tender, take it out, put it in the serving dish. Arrange the carrots round it. Test the stock for seasoning, and pour it through a strainer on to the meat. Next day, when the jelly has set, remove the fat from the top with the aid of a spoon dipped continually in hot water. The few remaining particles can be removed with a cloth dipped in warm water.

The jelly should be firm and clear, the meat soft, and when cut will reveal the pink circles of bacon and the white chips of garlic. Remember that although the meat may seem overcooked when hot, it will be firmer when cold.

GALANTINE OF TURKEY

Young turkeys are obtainable during the early summer and make a very good dish for a supper party.

To make a galantine, which is really worth the trouble, get the poulterer to bone an 8 lb. bird. The other ingredients are 1 lb. of lean veal or pork or ½ lb. of each, ½ lb. of bacon, ¼ lb. of tongue, carrots, onions, seasonings, herbs and spices, 2 calf's or pig's feet, if possible a small tin of truffles and a few pistachio nuts.

Cut the breast meat of the boned turkey into fillets. Also cut off the meat from the legs and chop it. Chop or mince the veal or pork, the bacon and tongue and mix with the chopped turkey meat. Season with salt, pepper, nutmeg, marjoram and thyme or lemon thyme. Add the sliced truffles and the pistachio nuts. Lay the turkey on a board, and stuff it with the meat mixture, interlarded with the fillets from the breast. Close it by pulling the skin together, so that it is in the shape of a fat sausage. Sew up the skin. Wrap it in a cloth, tie the ends securely, and put 3 or 4 circles of string round the galantine itself. Put it in a long deep pan with carrots, onions, the pig's or calf's feet, the bones of the turkey, a piece of pork rind, bay-leaves, salt and pepper and just cover with water (or stock if available). Simmer gently for about 2 hours. Take out the galantine and continue cooking the stock very gently for another hour. As soon as the galantine has cooked sufficiently, untie it, wrap it up again in a clean cloth, and put a light weight on it. Next day, unwrap it, brush it over with meat glaze if possible. Put it on a long dish surrounded by squares of the jelly, which has been strained, the fat removed and clarified if necessary. (See p. 172.)

Chicken Mousse

A boiling chicken weighing 3½–4 lbs., a calf's foot or 2 pig's feet, a carrot, an onion, garlic, lemon peel, a few bacon rinds, parsley, ½ pint thick cream, the whites of 2 eggs, herbs, 2 tablespoons of brandy.

Simmer the chicken for 2 hours or so with the calf's or pig's feet, the carrot, the bacon rinds, onion, garlic, a piece of lemon peel, a little salt, ground black pepper, a bay leaf, thyme, and the giblets of the bird (except the liver) all just covered with water. Take out the chicken when it is cooked and leave the rest to simmer another 1½–2 hours.

Skin the chicken, remove all the flesh from the bones. Chop the flesh, then pound it in a mortar with a clove of garlic, a little extra salt and pepper, and a sprig or two of parsley. Cook the liver of the chicken a minute or two in butter, add the brandy, set light to it. When the flames have gone out add both liver and juice to the chicken, pounding until it is amalgamated with the chicken meat. Stir in a ¼ pint of the strained stock, then the whipped cream.

Leave for an hour or so and then stir in the stiffly beaten whites of egg.

Next day, when the stock has turned to jelly, remove the fat, cut the jelly into squares and put it round the mousse, which looks best piled up in a fairly shallow dish in which there is just room for the jelly around it.

With it serve a thick mayonnaise into which have been incorporated some strips of raw celery or fennel.

Terrine of Duck

Duck makes one of the best of all terrines, for it needs little of the extra fat in the form of bacon and pork which has to be provided for hare, rabbit, pigeons or pheasant, and the full flavour of the duck can therefore be appreciated.

Before making the terrine prepare an aspic by simmering a calf's foot or 2 pig's feet with an onion, carrot, bacon rinds, herbs, lemon peel, garlic, salt and pepper for four hours, well covered with water. Strain and remove fat when set.

To make the terrine you need, besides a 3 to 4 lb. duck, $\frac{1}{4}$ lb. bacon, a 3 or 4 oz. tin of good chicken or goose liver pâté, 2 cloves of garlic, thyme, bayleaf, mace, ground black pepper, 2 tablespoons each of brandy and port.

Partly roast the duck. Remove all flesh from the bones. Keep aside the breast and chop all the rest with the bacon and garlic. Add the pâté, herbs, seasonings and port and brandy. Arrange the mixture in layers in a fairly deep earthenware terrine or pie dish, alternating with layers of the breast cut into small fillets. Fill up with some of the melted aspic. Cover with greaseproof paper and the lid of the dish. Stand in a pan containing water and cook in a medium oven for $1\frac{1}{2}$ to 2 hours. Cover with a piece of paper and leave with a 2 or 3 lb. weight on it for several hours. Fill up and cover with the rest of the prepared aspic, just melted. Leave to set, and seal with pork fat.

If the whole duck will not be needed at once cook in two or three small dishes. If properly sealed these terrines should keep for three or four weeks in a cool larder.

SMOKED TONGUE

A smoked tongue should be soaked in cold water for 12 hours, and simmered with carrots, onions, peppercorns and bayleaves, with water just to cover for $2\frac{1}{2}$–3 hours according to size. If to be eaten cold let it cool a little in the stock, then take it out, peel off the outer skin, and remove the gristly part. A hot boiled tongue can be eaten with boiled vegetables, and whether hot or cold needs to be accompanied by some kind of sweet-sour sauce or mild chutney.

When it is necessary to provide a variety of cold foods for a number of people, cook a boiling chicken, a piece of gammon and possibly a piece of shin of beef in the pan with the tongue, and serve them all cold with the vinaigrette and egg sauce described on page 168 as well as a salad and pickled fruit. One of the best pickles for this type of cold meat is the Italian *mostarda di Cremona*. The stock from the boiled meats makes excellent soup.

WHITE WINE CUP

The directions for wine cups are usually of so complicated a nature, calling for several different liqueurs and spirits and a variety of fruit, that most people are bewildered by them. In fact the simpler these drinks are the better. Sodden fruit floating about in a glass is thoroughly unattractive, and there is no necessity for a variety of flavourings. Two flavourings to avoid are mint and pineapple; they swamp everything else.

Here is a very easy white wine cup, which I have found very successful. The wine I always use is a Muscadet from the Loire, which has a delightful fresh flavour, but this is a matter of individual taste.

Put a piece of cucumber peel, a piece of orange peel, a sprig of borage and 2 lumps of sugar into a jug; pour over it about 1½ fluid ozs. (a small glass) of brandy. Leave to macerate 20 minutes. Add a bottle of dry white wine, 2 cubes of ice, and a wineglass of soda water.

ICED COFFEE

Make some fairly strong black coffee in the following way: put 12 ozs. of finely ground coffee and 6 ozs. of sugar into an earthenware jug, pour over it 4 pints of boiling water. Put the jug in a saucepan of hot water and leave it over a very low flame for ½ hour. Leave to cool, and strain through a fine muslin.

Pour into the ice trays of the refrigerator and freeze at the normal temperature for making ice, for 2½–3 hours. When it is to be served, turn out into glasses or cups and stir about 2 tablespoons of cream into each one (about ½ pint altogether for the above quantity of coffee which is sufficient for 10 to 12 glasses).

Café Liégois

Make the coffee as for iced coffee, add ½ pint of whipped cream and freeze in the ice trays, with the refrigerator turned to maximum freezing point for 2 hours. The mixture must be stirred from time to time and the trays should be covered with paper.

Serve in glasses, with a tablespoon of whipped cream on top of each.

CHAPTER 13

IMPROVISED COOKING FOR HOLIDAYS AND WEEKENDS

THE kitchens of holiday houses, whether cramped and larderless, or vast, bare, with a day's march between sink and stove, usually have a stony bleakness in common. However adequate the beds or satisfactory the view, the kitchen equipment will probably consist of a tin frying pan, a chipped enamel saucepan, one pyrex casserole without a lid, and a rusty knife with a loose handle.

Some extra organization before setting off, a basket packed with a small supply of kitchen comforts, does much to alleviate the irritation of coping with a capricious and unfamiliar stove and the vagaries of the food supply in the country or at the seaside. A good kitchen knife and a bread knife are essential pieces of equipment (cutting sandwiches with a blunt instrument may be part of holiday routine, but is very exasperating). A food mill for making purées and mashed potatoes saves hours of time, a sieve for sauces is never to be found except in one's own kitchen; some muslin squares for draining cream cheese made from the milk which inevitably goes sour, a large thermos jar in which to store the ice which has to be begged from the local pub or fishmonger, your own potato peeler, a pepper mill—these things may be a nuisance to pack, but they will prove worth the trouble. Assuming that there will be either no oven or that if there is you will only find out how it works on the last day of your stay it is advisable to take a heavy pan for pot roasting or slow simmering, and an

asbestos mat over which it may be left on a low flame while unattended.

As well as being simple, holiday food ought to provide a change from all the year round dishes; it is nice to do away with the routine roast, but without having to rely on tins. One hopes to find garden vegetables, and perhaps butter, eggs and cream; possibly there will be wild rabbits, and river fish, there might even be fish from the sea (the best lobsters and crabs I have ever eaten were bought from fishermen during seaside holidays, carried home with their angry claws tied up in a handkerchief, and dropped thankfully into a pot or bucket filled with boiling water, and eaten with butter and salt).

Village shops however will not provide imported cheeses or sausages; so it is worth while taking a small supply of Parmesan or Gruyère cheese, some tins of Frankfurter sausages, wine for cooking (cheap wine is generally only to be found in large towns). Olive oil is another essential supply, or you will have to buy it at considerable expense in medicine bottles from the local chemist. Some good pasta or rice will provide substantial dishes for hungry walkers and swimmers, and since people on holiday usually demand large breakfasts see that there is a good pan for fried eggs and bacon and potatoes. Cheap pans which blacken and burn make for hard work and bad temper.

Marketing and preparing for three or four meals at a time is an obvious necessity at holiday time, and the following few recipes may provide ideas for people who like to provide their family and friends with nice food even though it has to be improvised, but who obviously don't want to spend all day grappling with an inadequate stove, cold washing up water, and dented saucepans in which the food sticks in the middle while it remains quite uncooked round the edges.

Rabbit in White Wine

Three dishes can be made from one large rabbit or two smaller ones with very little work.

Keeping the hind legs separate, cut the rest of the rabbit into 6 or 8 pieces. Season them well with salt, pepper, lemon juice and plenty of thyme. Into a casserole, with a little dripping put a quarter pound of bacon cut into squares; let it melt a little; add the pieces of rabbit and let them brown on each side. In another saucepan bring half a tumbler of white wine to the boil, set light to it, and when it has finished burning pour it over the rabbit. This process reduces the wine and will give body and flavour to the sauce. (If you happen to be in the cider country use draught cider instead of white wine; in which case simply heat it up before pouring it over the rabbit.) Add hot water to come just level with the pieces of rabbit, cover the pan and let it simmer about an hour. Have ready in a bowl the liver of the rabbit pounded with a clove of garlic, a handful of chopped parsley and one of breadcrumbs. At the last minute add this mixture to the sauce, stirring over the lowest possible flame for a minute or two. The sauce will thicken, but if it boils again the liver will separate into tiny particles, which will not affect the taste of the dish but will take away from its appearance. Should mushrooms be available add half a pound of them, sliced, to the dish ten minutes before finishing the sauce. Tomatoes, fried, grilled or à la Provençale (stuffed with parsley and garlic) go well with rabbit, and sauté potatoes.

Rabbit Pâté

Put the two legs of the rabbit which you have kept aside into a pan with a tumbler of white wine or cider. Cook them for 20 minutes and when it has cooled take the meat from the bones; (the orthodox way of preparing pâté is to take the meat off the bones before it is cooked, a method which makes a good deal of hard work). Cut a few of the best pieces into small fillets and put the rest through a mincer, or chop it finely. Add 4 or 5 rashers of bacon, also chopped, and the contents of a small tin of liver or pork pâté; season the mixture rather highly with ground black pepper, a little grated lemon peel, thyme, garlic and a scraping of nutmeg; arrange the minced mixture and the little fillets in layers in any small receptacle which can be used for steaming—a pudding basin will do if there is no earthenware terrine, or one of those aluminium tins with a close covering lid which are sold in camping equipment shops; moisten the pâté with some of the liquid in which the legs of the rabbit were originally cooked, preferably reduced by 10 minutes fast boiling. Cover the pâté with greaseproof paper and steam for ½ an hour. (Pâtés are usually steamed in the oven, but the top of the stove is quite satisfactory.) When it has cooled pour over it a layer of melted dripping, which will seal it, so that it can be kept for several days; it will be excellent with toast, taken as it is on a picnic, or made into sandwiches.

RABBIT AND LEMON SOUP

Out of the bones of the rabbit and the usual soup vegetables, herbs and seasonings make a stock; it will not be very strong, but it doesn't matter. Add any of the sauce which happens to be left over from the original rabbit dish. Strain the stock and in it boil 2 tablespoons of rice; have ready in a bowl 2 eggs beaten up with the juice of a lemon. Pour some of the soup over this, stirring hard, then return the mixture to the pan, letting it reheat a minute or two without boiling. This soup, although it

has not such a fine flavour, is similar to the Greek
Avgolèmono which is made with chicken stock.

BOEUF EN DAUBE

This is another way of making three dishes with one batch
of ingredients. 3½ to 4 lbs. of stewing beef in one piece, 1
lb. of carrots, garlic, onions and a calf's or pig's foot and
red or white wine are the necessities. Make a few holes in
the beef with a small knife and in these put some half
cloves of garlic. Rub the beef all over with salt, pepper and
fresh thyme. Brown the meat on both sides in a little
dripping; pour over a tumbler of wine and when it
bubbles set light to it. Keep it boiling until the flames die
down. Remove the meat and wine to a capacious
casserole; add a sliced onion, the calf's foot cut up, and
the carrots, plus a couple of bayleaves and another branch
of thyme. Cover the meat with hot water, set the pan on a
very low flame and cook it until the meat is absolutely
tender; it may take anything from four to six hours,
according to the toughness or otherwise of the meat. This
part of the cooking can be done regardless of the time
you are going to dine; the daube can be strained, left
to cool, the fat skimmed off, and reheated gently, or
it can be served as soon as it is cooked. In any case
put the hot beef on to a serving dish with the carrots
and only a small portion of the gravy. With it serve
either a bowl of well-buttered *pasta* or mashed potatoes, to
soak up the juice of the meat. For the next day's meal put
what is left of the beef into a bowl; over it pour the
liquid which you have reserved, which will set to a jelly.
With a small spoon dipped in a bowl of hot water skim
off the fat, and your dish is ready to serve. Potatoes,
baked or boiled in their jackets, a fresh garden lettuce, a
salad of finely sliced raw cabbage, a rice and tomato

salad, almost anything except brussels sprouts, will go with it.

In the meantime, with the calf's or pig's foot which you have kept aside make a second lot of stock; add some more onions, carrots and herbs and 2 pints of hot water; simmer it for about an hour, and strain it. With this any number of soups can be devised but one of the most successful is an improvised onion soup.

Onion Soup

For 4 people slice 6 large onions very thinly; on this depends the success of the soup. In your casserole melt two tablespoons of beef dripping; cook the onions in this, stirring fairly often so that they turn gently brown without getting crisp, and finally form an almost amalgamated mass; season with salt and pepper, and pour over the heated stock, adding water if there is not quite enough. Cook for another 10 to 15 minutes; always supposing there is no oven or grill with which to *gratiner* the soup, prepare a thick slice of toast for each person, lightly buttered and spread with grated cheese. Place each one in a soup plate and ladle the onion soup over it.

Shell Fish Risotto

Not quite the orthodox risotto but excellent, and simple. For four people you will need a small lobster or two crawfish (langouste) tails, or 2 dozen prawns, which should have been cooked in a court-bouillon of white wine, water, an onion, and herbs. Leave them to cool in the liquid, and then take them out of their shells. If lobster or crawfish cut them into dice; if prawns cut each in half.

In a fireproof shallow casserole or braising pan melt 2 ozs. of butter. In this fry a sliced onion until it is golden.

Put in the rice (two teacupsful) and stir round until the butter is all absorbed; pour over boiling water to cover the rice; you will have to stir it from time to time, but not continuously. When the first lot of water is absorbed add more until the rice is all but cooked; now add about a breakfast cup of the stock in which the fish was cooked; three minutes before serving stir in the shell fish, two tablespoons of grated Parmesan and a good lump of butter. Serve more cheese separately.

The risotto will take approximately 40 minutes to cook, and for the last 10 minutes it must be stirred constantly.

CHAFING DISH LOBSTER

Olive oil, spring onions, tomatoes, sherry, marsala or white wine or vermouth, lemon, salt and papper, a cooked lobster.

Warm 3 tablespoons of olive oil in a chafing dish or sauté pan. Put in the bulbous part of 6 to 8 spring onions, whole. Let them melt a minute, add two quartered tomatoes (skinned if possible), salt and pepper, let them cook 2 minutes; pour over a small glass of the sherry, marsala, white wine or vermouth (white wine or vermouth are best). Let it bubble. Add the lobster meat cut into squares and let it heat through gently.

Squeeze a little lemon juice over, and sprinkle with a little of the green part of the spring onions.

PRAWNS ON THE GRASS

1 lb. of spinach, 2 hard-boiled eggs, 4 ozs. of peeled prawns, 3 to 4 ozs. cream, salt, pepper, nutmeg, butter.

Cook the cleaned spinach, drain, squeeze dry in your hands and chop it, not too finely. Melt a little butter (about 1 oz.) in a chafing dish or sauté pan, heat the spinach, season it with salt, pepper and nutmeg. Put the prawns on top and pour the cream over. Cover the pan and simmer gently for 3 to 4 minutes.

MOULES AU GRATIN

Mussels are not generally obtainable in England during the summer months, but for those people who may find themselves in perhaps a holiday house in France or the Mediterranean, where mussels are eaten all the year round, I include this one recipe, which is one of the best of mussel dishes.

Open the mussels over the fire in a heavy pan, in their own liquid. When they have cooled shell them, and put two mussels into the half-shells. Arrange them in a fire-proof dish, and pour melted butter or olive oil over them, then a light sprinkling of breadcrumbs mixed with an equal quantity of Parmesan cheese, a little chopped parsley and garlic, and pepper. Pour over a little of the strained juice from the mussels and put into a moderate oven sufficiently long for them to get hot. Serve quickly, with lemon.

When mussels are to be opened over the fire, shelled, and then reheated in a sauce, take great care not to over-cook them in the first place or they will be shrivelled and tough.

COLD OMELETTE

Make a plain omelette with three or four eggs; instead of folding it slide it out flat on to a plate. When it is cold garnish it with a purée made from cold chicken and ham or with the rabbit pâté already described, in fact with any cold meat mixture as long as it is not too liquid. Roll the omelette as you would a pancake.

Mushrooms

I have no advice to offer as to the safety or otherwise of eating unfamiliar fungi. My own knowledge of the subject is limited to personal experiment, from which I have so far emerged unscathed; I have only two or three recipes to give for those people who are sure enough of their knowledge or judgment to cook and eat those fungi which they find in the woods or fields. There are only three deadly fungi, and one of these, the Amanita Printania, superficially resembles the common field mushroom. This may account for the fact that in Italy, where all kinds of fungi which would terrify English people are constantly eaten, the ordinary field mushroom is very rarely picked.

On the west coast of Scotland I have, to the horror and disgust of the inhabitants, cooked and eaten several different fungi. The best of these were the apricot coloured, trumpet shaped cantharellus. They need plenty of washing and if they are large they should be cut into strips (the small ones are the best). They should be stewed gently in oil, for 15 or 20 minutes (longer if they are large ones) with the addition at the last minute of a little garlic, parsley and breadcrumbs (to absorb the oil), salt and pepper. Strips of ham or bacon can be added, and they can be used as a filling for omelettes, or piled on top of scrambled eggs; in France and Italy they are fairly commonly eaten, either as a separate dish or an accompaniment to chicken, or in a risotto.

Boletus

Boletus edulis, the cèpes of France, are quite common in English woods and forests. They are delicious when absolutely fresh, but very quickly go sodden and rotten.

The stalks are tough and should be chopped finely; Boletus are best stewed in oil, for about 40 minutes, with the addition of chopped shallots, garlic and parsley. There is also an excellent way of stuffing and baking them; prepare a finely chopped mixture of ham or bacon, garlic, breadcrumbs, a very little Parmesan cheese, and the chopped stalks. Put a tablespoon of the stuffing in each cèpe, fill them up with oil and bake them in a slow oven, in a covered dish, for about an hour. From time to time add a little more oil.

FIELD MUSHROOMS

To grill field mushrooms wash them, remove the stalks and marinade them for an hour in olive oil flavoured with salt and pepper and a little fresh thyme. Put them under the grill with a little of the oil, and cook them fairly fast, turning them over and over so they do not dry up. The large flat field mushrooms are also delicious fried, preferably I think in bacon or pork fat, rather than butter. Don't let the fat get too hot before putting in the mushrooms, and when they appear to have absorbed it all, turn the heat down, and in a minute or two the mushrooms start to yield their juice. Continue cooking them gently, sprinkling them with salt and pepper. They should be cooked skin side down and need not be turned over. Eat them with fried bread.

MUSHROOMS COOKED IN CREAM

To make a really good dish of mushrooms in cream very fresh little button mushrooms from the field are needed.

Clean them (say ½ lb.) with a damp cloth and do not peel them. Bring a coffeecupful of water to the boil and squeeze in a little lemon juice and a pinch of salt. Put in the mushrooms and let them cook about 2 minutes. Strain them.

The sauce is prepared by stirring 2 or 3 teaspoons of flour into ¼ pint of cream. Bring to the boil and when the sauce has thickened put in the strained mushrooms and cook another 5 minutes, adding ground black pepper and more salt if necessary.

POTATOES AND MUSHROOMS

When you have picked only a few mushrooms, not enough to make a whole dish of them, try this mixture of mushrooms and potatoes.

1 lb. of potatoes, ½ lb. of mushrooms, 1 oz. of butter, a clove of garlic, a small onion, olive oil, the juice of half a lemon, parsley.

Cut the peeled potatoes into thin slices. Heat the oil and butter in an earthenware pan and sauté the chopped onion. Add the garlic, then the potatoes. Simmer for 10 minutes then put in the cleaned and sliced mushrooms, and barely cover with water. Season with salt and pepper, cover the pan, and cook on a moderate flame until the potatoes are tender. Add a little chopped parsley and the lemon juice, and serve in the pan in which it has cooked.

Two or three fillets of anchovies can be added at the same time as the mushrooms.

PIGEONS STEWED WITH LETTUCES

Pigeons are often tough little birds, but in the country there are often a great many to be disposed of. A pigeon gives an excellent flavour if cooked with the meat and vegetables for a broth; with three pigeons a very nice little terrine or pâté, enough for about 8 people, can be made. Baby pigeons are very good split in half and grilled.

Older birds make a good country dish cooked in the following way with lettuces.

For each pigeon you need 2 cos lettuces, a cupful of meat or chicken stock, a rasher of bacon and some parsley, shallots, herbs and the usual seasonings. First blanch the pigeons in boiling water for 5 minutes and cut them in half. Then blanch the lettuces. Cut the lettuces down the middle, without separating the two halves; spread them with a mixture of chopped shallots, parsley, herbs, salt and pepper. Put half a pigeon in the middle, tie them up, and place them in a pan lined with the bacon rashers; pour the stock over them and simmer gently for about an hour and a half; put them in the serving dish, thicken the sauce with a yolk of egg, squeeze in a little lemon juice and pour over the pigeons.

ROASTED CHEESE

This is not a particularly summery dish, but is so quick and easy to make, and provides such a good meal in a hurry, and for people who live alone, that it is worth knowing. The best cheeses to use for it are cheddar, Gruyère, Emmenthal, or Bel Paese.

Cut 6 or 7 slices from a French loaf, each about $\frac{1}{4}$ inch thick. Cut the same number of slices of cheese, a little thinner. Cover each slice of bread with a slice of cheese and arrange them in a long fireproof dish (or baking tin if you are making a quantity) and put them in the top of a very hot oven (Regulo 8). In 8 to 10 minutes the dish will be ready, the cheese melting and the bread just getting crisp. Sprinkle them plentifully with freshly-ground black pepper before eating them, or if you like with a tomato sauce made as follows:

For the amount given, melt two chopped ripe tomatoes in butter, add salt, pepper, a scrap of garlic, and a little chopped parsley, or any other herb you like. Cook for about 3 minutes only. Pour over the cheese as soon as the dish is taken out of the oven.

HERB CHEESE

Into ½ lb. of home made milk cheese stir about half a teacupful of chopped fresh lemon thyme and sweet marjoram, in equal quantities, with the addition of a chopped fresh bayleaf. Season with salt and ground black pepper, pile the cheese up in a dish, and leave it several hours before serving, to give the flavour of the herbs time to penetrate the cheese. This cheese has a lovely fresh flavour, eaten simply with brown bread, or with the addition of 2 or 3 tablespoons of grated Parmesan, can be stirred into a dish of hot spaghetti or noodles.

Instead of lemon thyme and marjoram, chopped borage leaves give a very delicate and unexpected flavour of cucumber to a cream cheese.

CHAPTER 14

PICNICS

PICNIC addicts seem to be roughly divided between those who frankly make elaborate preparations and leave nothing to chance, and those others whose organization is no less complicated but who are more deceitful and pretend that everything will be obtained on the spot and cooked over a woodcutter's fire, conveniently to hand; there are even those, according to Richard Jefferies, who wisely take the precaution of visiting the site of their intended picnic some days beforehand and there burying the champagne.

Not long before the war I was staying with friends in Marseille. One Saturday night a picnic was arranged for the next day with some American acquaintances; it was agreed that the two parties should proceed in their own cars to a little bay outside Marseille, and that we should each bring our own provisions. On Sunday morning I and my friends indulged in a delicious hour of shopping in the wonderful market of the rue de Rome, buying olives, anchovies, salame sausages, pâtés, yards of bread, smoked fish, fruit and cheese. With a provision of cheap red wine we bundled the food into the car and set off, stopping now and again for a drink; so that we arrived at our rendezvous well disposed to appreciate the sun, the sea and the scent of wild herbs and Mediterranean pines. Presently our friends drove up and started to unload their car. One of the first things to come out was a hatchet, with which they efficiently proceeded to chop down olive branches, and in no time at all there was a blazing fire.

Out of their baskets came cutlets, potatoes, bacon, skewers, frying-pans, jars of ice, butter, tablecloths, all the trappings of a minor barbecue. Our reactions as we watched these proceedings were those of astonishment, admiration, and finally, as realization of the inadequacy of our own catering dawned, dismay. How wilted they seemed, those little packets wrapped up in rather oily paper; the olives which had glowed with colour in the market stalls of the rue de Rome looked shabby now; the salame seemed dried up and the anchovies a squalid mess. Miserably, like poor relations, we sat with our shameful bundles spread out on the grass and politely offered them to our friends. They were kind, but obviously preferred their own grilled cutlets and fried potatoes, and we were too embarrassed to accept their proffered hospitality. Presently they produced ice cream out of a thermos, but by now we were past caring, and finally it was their turn for surprise when they found we hadn't even provided ourselves with the means of making a cup of coffee.

Then there was the hospitable family I remember in my childhood; they owned a beautiful house and an elegant garden and were much given to out of door entertainments, pageants and picnics. On picnic days a large party of children and grown-ups would be assembled in the hall. Led by our host and hostess we proceeded through the exquisite formal Dutch garden, across the lane and over a fence into a coppice. Close on our heels followed the butler, the chauffeur and the footman, bearing fine china plates, the silver and tablecloths, and a number of vast dishes containing cold chickens, jellies and trifles. Arrived at the end of our journey, five minutes from the house, our host set about making a fire, with sticks which I suspect had been strategically placed by the gardener, over which we grilled quantities of sausages and bacon, which were devoured amidst the customary jokes and hilarity. The picnickers' honour thus satisfied, we took our places for an orderly meal, handed round by the footman, and in composition resembling that of an Edwardian wedding breakfast.

Since those days I have had a good many opportunities of evolving a picnic technique on the lines laid down by Henry James, "not so good as to fail of an amusing disorder, nor yet so bad as to defeat the proper function of repasts."

Before deciding upon the food, its packing and transport must be planned. (I am assuming for the moment a car-transported picnic.) Those who are lucky enough to possess an Edwardian picnic hamper, fitted with spirit lamp and kettle, sandwich tins and a variety of boxes and bottles, need look no further. These hampers may be cumbersome, but they are capacious and solid; an aura of lavish gallivantings and ancient Rolls Royces hangs about them, and they are infinitely superior to the modern kind in which the use of every inch of space has been planned for you in advance. (At the Lord Roberts work-shop in the Brompton Road there are deep square baskets of very solid construction, large enough to hold a good deal of food as well as several bottles, which cost only about 12s. 6d. This establishment is full of happy ideas for all addicts of eating out of doors, for they sell large hampers, unfitted, so that you can pack whatever you please, baskets with divisions for bottles, baskets for thermos jars, and the most comfortable garden chairs in existence.)

As to plates and glasses, if I am going to have them at all I will have china plates and glass glasses. Admirable though plastic may be for some purposes, I do not care for the look of food on it, and any kind of drink, tea, coffee, wine, beer or fruit juice, is spoilt for me if I am forced to drink it out of a brightly coloured composition mug.

A spirit lamp and kettle plus a tin of Nescafé provide a hotter and fresher cup of coffee than any which ever came out of a vacuum flask. Iced coffee on the other hand can be transported in thermos jugs, and a large thermos jar filled with ice is a blessing for those who don't care for warm drinks, or who like to put ice into coarse red picnic wine.

As for the food, preparing it always seems to me half the fun. The possibilities are almost without limit, and fantasies can be indulged. On the whole though I think that such elegant foods as foie gras and lobster in aspic should be excluded as they seem to lose their fine lustre when eaten out of doors, whereas the simpler charms of salame sausage, fresh cheese, black olives and crusty French bread are enhanced when they are eaten on the hillside or the seashore. Sandwiches I rather like (George Saintsbury considered that venison makes the best sandwiches and I think he is right) but many people do not, so there must always be alternatives; thin slices of ham rolled round Frankfurter sausages, or Frankfurter sausages split in half enclosing a slice of Gruyère cheese are good ones. Remember that such delicious foods as home made terrines of duck and so on aren't really ideal for long journeys on a hot day because the jelly (if it has been made as it should be) will melt en route; mayonnaise also has a dismaying habit of turning into a rather unappetizing looking oily mass when the weather is hot. A cold chicken with a cream sauce is a better bid than a chicken mayonnaise. Cold steak and kidney pudding is fine picnic food, so is cold spiced beef, which cuts into nice slices. Cold escalopes of veal, fried in egg and bread-crumbs, make excellent picnic food provided they are very thin and very well drained after frying. Hard-boiled eggs are time honoured picnic food, so I always take a few, but they are not everybody's taste. Cheese seems to me essential for an out of doors meal; next to the salty little Mediterranean goat and sheep's milk cheeses

English Cheddar or Cheshire, or Gruyère are perhaps the easiest picnic cheeses. Some people like a rich moist fruit cake for a picnic, but I prefer a slab of the dryest, bitterest chocolate available (Terry's make a good one but the best is the Belgian Côte d'Or) to be eaten in alternative mouthfuls with a Marie biscuit. Apples and figs and apricots, because they are easy to eat and transport as well as being good in the open air, are perhaps the best fruit for a picnic.

The nicest drinks for picnics are the obvious ones. A stout red wine such as a Macon or a Chianti, which cannot be unduly harmed by the journey in the car; vin rosé (particularly delicious by the sea); cider, lager, shandy, black velvet; iced sherry and bitters. For a very hot day Pimm's No. 1 couldn't be bettered but involves some organization in the matter of cucumber, lemonade, oranges, mint, borage, and all the paraphernalia, and a thermos jar of ice is essential.

For soft drinks the most refreshing are tinned grapefuit, orange or pineapple juice, and tomato juice. (In this case include the tin opener.) Delicate china tea, iced, with slices of lemon and mint leaves is admirably reviving. An early edition of Mrs. Beeton asserts that "Water can usually be obtained so it is useless to take it". For the walker's picnic perhaps the perfect meal has been described by Sir Osbert Sitwell "the fruits of the month, cheese with the goaty taste of mountains upon it, and if possible bilberries, apples, raw celery, a meal unsophisticated and pastoral . . ."

SMOKED COD'S ROE SANDWICHES IN BROWN BREAD

Make a paste of ¼ lb. of smoked cod's roe, as described on page 25. Spread it on buttered Hovis bread.

SMOKED TROUT OR SMOKED MACKEREL SANDWICHES

Fillet the trout or mackerel (smoked mackerel, although not so well known, are cheaper than smoked trout, and excellent), spread buttered rye bread with a layer of horseradish cream and place the fillets of fish on top.

BACON AND LETTUCE SANDWICHES

One cos lettuce; one large rasher of bacon for each round of sandwiches; a mustardy French dressing. Shred the lettuce fairly fine and toss it in the dressing without letting it get sodden. Cut each rasher of bacon in half and fry very lightly. Put a layer of lettuce on the buttered bread and the bacon on top.

PAN BAGNA

A Provençal sandwich which makes delicious out of door food. See the recipes on pages 27 and 28.

SHOOTER'S SANDWICH

"The wise, 'at least among the children of this world,' to use one of Walter Pater's careful qualifying phrases, travel with a flask of whisky-and-water and what I call a 'Shooter's Sandwich'. This last is made thus: Take a large, thick, excellent rump steak. Do not season it, for that would cause the juice to run out, and in grilling it keep it markedly underdone. Have ready a sandwich loaf one end of which has been cut off and an adequate portion of the contents of which has been removed. Put the steak, hot from the grill, and—but only then—somewhat highly seasoned, into the loaf; add a few grilled mushrooms; replace the deleted end of the loaf; wrap the loaf in a double sheet of clean white blotting-paper, tie with twine both ways, superimpose a sheet of grease-proof paper, and more twine. Place a moderate weight on top, and after a while add other weights. Let the thing endure pressure for at least six hours. Do not carve it until and as each slice is required.

"With this 'sandwich' a man may travel from Land's End to Quaker Oats, and snap his fingers at both."

T. Earle Welby, *The Dinner Knell*, Methuen, 1932.

I have also tried keeping this sandwich in the ice box when packing, moving house, and other times when, although too busy to cook, everyone needs good nourishing food. It is excellent for this purpose. E. D.

French Garlic Loaves

Heat a couple of French loaves a few minutes in the oven. While they are still hot, split them lengthwise and spread each side with butter into which you have pounded one clove of garlic, some chopped parsley and a little salt. Put the two halves together, and when you get to the picnic cut them into slices in the ordinary way.

Prawns with Watercress Dressing

For a seaside picnic it is nice to have some fish; you won't probably find it there, so take it with you. Buy the ready peeled prawns, put them into a suitable jar, season with salt and pepper, and take in a separate bottle a generous quantity of French dressing made with lemon juice instead of vinegar, into which you mix a good handful of very finely chopped watercress.

Cold Spiced Beef

Soak a piece of salted silverside in warm water for half an hour. Make about a dozen incisions all round the beef into which you insert half cloves of garlic rolled in chopped fresh herbs; rub it all over with ground cloves and ground black pepper and put it into a pan with half a glass of red wine, enough water to cover, and thyme, bay-leaves, marjoram, rosemary and an onion. Bring it to the boil, then cover it closely and put it in a low oven until it is tender—about 1 hour and 20 minutes for two pounds of beef: but as the quality of salt beef varies considerably it is advisable to try it from time to time, for if it is over-cooked it will crumble to pieces when cut. When it is done, take it out of the pan and put it on a board, cover it with a piece of greaseproof paper and put a weight on it. Next day it can be cut into fine slices.

Figs and Cream Cheese

Dried figs are delicious for a picnic; agreeable to bite on at the end of a meal. Have with them a home-made sour milk cheese, very slightly salted, or little French cream cheeses.

Oriental Picnics

I

"When I was going through the course of Garrison instruction, and accustomed to long days out surveying, I was partial to a galantine made of a small fowl, boned and rolled, with a block of tongue and some forcemeat introduced into the centre of it. A home-made brawn of tongue, a part of an ox-head, and sheep's trotters, well seasoned, and slightly spiced, was another spécialité.

"A nice piece of the brisket of beef salted and spiced, boiled, placed under a weight, and then trimmed into a neat shape is a very handy thing for the tiffin basket; and a much respected patron of mine recommends for travelling, a really good cold plum pudding in which a glass of brandy has been included."

2

"The traveller's luncheon basket, and that of the sportsman are analogous. A friend of mine with whom I used to walk the paddy fields adopted the plan of taking out a digester pot, previously filled with stewed steak and oysters, or some equally toothsome stew. This he trusted to his syce, who lit a fire somewhere or other, in the marvellous way the natives of this country do, and, as sure as there are fish in the sea, had the contents of the pot steaming hot, at the exact spot, and at the very moment we required it."

Culinary Jottings for Madras,
"Wyvern", (Col. Kenney Herbert, 1885).

3

Charles Baskerville, the American painter, has described an Indian picnic given by the Maharajah of Jaipur, in 1937.

"Yesterday we spent the whole day picnicking . . . a lorry with lunch and bottles followed our car . . . one thing I particularly like about these outdoor luncheons is the cold fried fish. Besides the European food there are always some spicy Indian dishes . . . cold curry of boars' head (without the eyes) or peppery leaves of spinach fried in batter . . . of course a hamper of whisky, beer, gimlets, cider, and water is always taken along."

4

My own experience of Indian picnics wasn't always quite
so satisfactory. There was one in particular, a moonlight
picnic near the Kutub Minar, the leaning tower near
Delhi. There was nothing wrong with the transport, the
food, or the moonlight; we had merely reckoned without
the hordes of half wild dogs which are a familiar feature of
Indian outdoor life. Scarcely had we time to draw the
cork of a bottle of the Rhinegold Australian hock which
we were lucky to get in war time India than we were
surrounded by nearly every dog in the province; literally
surrounded. They did not apparently want food, or at any
rate not our food; they simply formed a circle round us at
a respectful distance and stared and howled.

First we pretended not to notice, then we shoo-ed them
away several times, but they returned immediately, with
reinforcements, re-formed their dreadful circle, and howled
and stared and sniffed again, until they forced us to get
into our cars and return to the city, leaving them in posses-
sion of their ruin.

5

In Egypt the picnic season starts sometime in March, with
Shem el Nessim, the "smelling of the Zephyrs", a day which
is kept as a public holiday, when the whole population
goes out to eat in the open air and greet the first day of
Spring.

An agreeable form of picnic in Cairo was the felucca
party; on board a hired Nile sailing boat Arab servants
would carry the food; there were copper trays of pimentos,
small marrows and vine leaves stuffed with rice, large,
round shallow metal dishes filled with meat and spiced
pilaff, bowls of grapes and peaches and figs and melons

cooled with lumps of ice, mounds of flat Arab loaves stuffed with a salad of tomatoes, onions and mint; there would be music and the wailing of Arab songs as the boat swung rather wildly about, the crew made Turkish coffee, and we drank the odd, slightly salty red Egyptian wine from the Mariut, one of the oldest wine producing regions in the world.

A Provençal Picnic

Ford Madox Ford has described (in *Provence*, Allen and Unwin, 1938) a Provençal picnic of heroic proportions; the scene was one of the beautiful *calanques* along the coast from Marseille, a beach accessible only in boats; the whole banquet was cooked on the spot, in huge cauldrons, beneath the umbrella pines. Sixty-one bottles of wine were consumed by sixteen adults and a shoal of children; half a hundred weight of bouillabaisse, twelve cocks stewed in wine with innumerable savoury herbs, a salad in a dish as large as a cartwheel, sweet cream cheese with a sauce made of *marc* and sweet herbs, a pile, large enough to bury a man in, of apples, peaches, figs, grapes . . .

A Breakfast Picnic

"He (William Hickey's father) engaged one of the Nunnerys, as they are called, for which he paid fifty guineas . . . Provisions, consisting of cold fowls, ham, tongues, different meat pies, wines and liquors of various sorts, were sent to the apartment the day before, and the two servants were allowed to attend. . . . It was half past seven in the morning before we reached the Abbey. . . . We found a hot and comfortable breakfast, which I enjoyed, and which proved highly refreshing to us all; after which some of our party determined to take a nap in their chairs. . . . Their Majesties being crowned, the Archbishop of Canter-

bury mounted the pulpit to deliver his sermon, and as
many thousands were out of the possibility of hearing a
single syllable, they took that opportunity to eat their
meal, when the general clattering of knives, forks, plates,
and glasses that ensued produced a most ridiculous effect,
and a universal burst of laughter followed."[1]

Bill of Fare for a Picnic for Forty Persons

"A joint of cold roast beef, a joint of cold boiled beef, two
ribs of lamb, two shoulders of lamb, four roast fowls, two
roast ducks, one ham, one tongue, two veal-and-ham pies,
two pigeon pies, six medium-sized lobsters, one piece of
collared calf's head, eighteen lettuces, six baskets of salad,
six cucumbers.

"Stewed fruit well sweetened, and put into glass bottles
well corked; three or four dozen plain pastry biscuits to
eat with the stewed fruit, two dozen fruit turnovers, four
dozen cheesecakes, two cold Cabinet puddings in moulds,
a few jam puffs, one large cold Christmas plum-pudding
(this must be good), a few baskets of fresh fruit, three
dozen plain biscuits, a piece of cheese, six pounds of
butter (this, of course, includes the butter for tea), four
quartern loaves of household bread, three dozen rolls, six
loaves of tin bread (for tea), two plain plum cakes, two
pound cakes, two sponge cakes, a tin of mixed biscuits, half
a pound of tea. Coffee is not suitable for a picnic, being
difficult to make."

From an early edition of Mrs. Beeton.

The Ideal

"Bright shone the morning, and as I waited (They had
promised to call for me in their motor) I made for myself

[1] William Hickey's Diaries.

an enchanting picture of the day before me, our drive to that forest beyond the dove-blue hills, the ideal beings I should meet there, feasting with them, exquisitely, in the shade of immemorial trees.

"And when, in the rainy twilight, I was deposited, soaked, and half-dead with fatigue, out of that open motor, was there nothing inside me but chill and disillusion? If I had dreamed a dream incompatible with the climate and social conditions of these Islands, had I not, out of that very dream and disenchantment, created, like the Platonic Lover, a Platonic and imperishable vision—the ideal Picnic, the Picnic as it might be—the wonderful windless weather, the Watteauish landscape, where a group of mortals talk and feast as they talked and feasted in the Golden Age?"

Logan Pearsall Smith, *All Trivia*,
Constable & Co.

Liquid measures conversion chart

fluid ounces	British measures	U.S. measures	milli-litres	convenient metric measures
	1 tsp	1 tsp	5	
¼	1 dessert-spoon	2 tsp	7	
½	1 tbs	1 tbs	15	
1	2 tbs	2 tbs	28	¼ dl
2	4 tbs	¼ cup	56	½ dl
4		½ cup or ¼ pint	110	1 dl
5	¼ pint or 1 gill		140	1½ dl
6		¾ cup	170	1¾ dl
8		1 cup or ½ pint	225	2¼ dl
9			250	¼ litre
10	½ pint	1¼ cups	280	2¾ dl
12		1½ cups or ¾ pint	340	3½ dl
15	¾ pint		420	4¼ dl
16		2 cups or 1 pint	450	4½ dl
18		2¼ cups	500	½ litre
20	1 pint	2½ cups	560	5½ dl
24		3 cups or 1½ pints	675	1½ pints
25	1¼ pints		700	7 dl
27		3½ cups	750	¾ litre
30	1½ pints	3¾ cups	840	8½ dl
32		4 cups or 2 pints or 1 quart	900	9 dl
35	1¾ pints		980	
36		4½ cups	1000	1 litre
40	2 pints or 1 quart	5 cups or 2½ pints	1120	
48		6 cups or 3 pints	1350	
50	2½ pints		1400	
60	3 pints	7½ cups	1680	
64		8 cups or 4 pints or 2 quarts	1800	
72		9 cups	2000	2 litres
80	4 pints	10 cups or 5 pints	2250	2¼ litres
96		12 cups or 3 quarts	2700	
100	5 pints		2800	

Solid measures conversion chart

British measures		metric measures	
ounces	pounds	grams	kilos
1		28	
2		56	
3½		100	
4	¼	112	
5		140	
6		168	
8	½	225	
9		250	¼
12	¾	340	
16	1	450	
18		500	½
20	1¼	560	
24	1½	675	
27		750	¾
28	1¾	780	
32	2	900	
36	2¼	1000	1
40	2½	1100	
48	3	1350	
54		1500	1½
64	4	1800	
72	4½	2000	2
80	5	2250	2¼
90		2500	2½
100	6	2800	2¾

Temperature equivalents
for oven thermostat markings

Fahrenheit (°F)	Gas mark	Centigrade (°C)	Heat of oven
225	¼	110	very cool
250	½	120-130	very cool
275	1	140	cool
300	2	150	cool
325	3	160-170	moderate
350	4	180	moderate
375	5	190	fairly hot
400	6	200	fairly hot
425	7	220	hot
450	8	230	very hot
475	9	240	very hot

CUMULATIVE INDEX

page references are preceded by
M for Mediterranean Food
F for French Country Cooking
S for Summer Cooking

SOME DIFFERENCES IN USAGE BETWEEN
BRITISH AND AMERICAN TERMINOLOGY

aubergines = eggplants

courgettes = small zucchini

cos lettuce = Romaine lettuce

haricot beans = dry white beans

marrows = large, overgrown zucchini

spring onions = scallions

brawn = head cheese

tunny fish = tuna fish

prawns = like jumbo shrimp

castor sugar = superfine sugar

icing sugar = confectioners' sugar

pig's trotters = pig's feet

minced = ground

stoned = pitted

grilled = broiled

rashers = strips

single cream = light cream

double cream = heavy whipping cream

SOME OVEN TEMPERATURE EQUIVALENTS

Fahrenheit (F°)	Gas Mark	Centigrade (C°)	Oven Heat
250	½	120	very slow (very cool)
300	2	150	slow (cool)
325	3	165	moderately slow (moderately cool)
350	4	180	moderate
375	5	190	moderately hot
400	6	205	hot
450–500	8–10	230–260	very hot

OVEN TEMPERATURE DEFINITIONS

180°F (85°C) = simmering point of water

212°F (100°C) = boiling point of water

220°F (108°C) = jellying point for jams and jellies

234–240°F (115°C) = soft-ball stage for syrups

255°F (119°C) = hard-crack stage for syrups

320°F (160°C) = caramel stage for syrups